How Do We Fix This Mess?

The Economic Price of Having It All
and the Route to Lasting Prosperity

ROBERT PESTON

and LAURENCE KNIGHT

How Do We Fix This Mess?

The Economic Price of Having It All
and the Route to Lasting Prosperity

HODDER &
STOUGHTON

First published in Great Britain in 2012 by Hodder & Stoughton
An Hachette UK company

2

Copyright © Robert Peston 2012

The right of Robert Peston to be identified as the Author of the Work has been
asserted by him in accordance with the Copyright, Designs and Patents Act 1988.

A CIP catalogue record for this title is available from the British Library

Hardback ISBN 978 1 444 75709 5
Trade Paperback ISBN 978 1 444 75710 1
Ebook ISBN 978 1 444 75711 8

Typeset by Hewer Text UK Ltd, Edinburgh
Printed and bound in the UK by Clays Ltd, St Ives plc

Hodder & Stoughton policy is to use papers that are natural, renewable
and recyclable products and made from wood grown in sustainable forests.
The logging and manufacturing processes are expected to conform
to the environmental regulations of the country of origin.

Hodder & Stoughton Ltd
338 Euston Road
London NW1 3BH

www.hodder.co.uk

To Max, Simon and Siân,
without whom nothing would be possible

CONTENTS

INTRODUCTION

I SAT JUST BEHIND THE DRIVING SEAT AS WE HEADED FOR THE SWAMP

How do we fix this mess? I don't know. But don't stop reading now. Perhaps if we have a clearer understanding of what went wrong, we'll have a better idea of what needs to be done. This book is a map, of sorts. It tries to explain how years of steady and rising prosperity became a dangerous boom, and how that boom became the worst bust we have experienced since at least the 1930s. Sometimes we will fly to 40,000 feet so that we can make out the shape of the bigger fault lines in the global economy. And on other occasions we will be right in the middle of the jungle, observing how bankers, regulators, politicians – and, oh yes, most of us – were by turns greedy, gullible, lazy and short-sighted, and how we wilfully refused to see how our improving living standards were not being earned in a sustainable way.

You may fear the narrative will be gloomy. But I hope you will be proved wrong, because our plight is far from hopeless. You may become furious – with those you trusted to prevent our big banks from taking reckless risks, and with yourself, for your own collusion in the mother of all borrowing binges. The basic story is a simple one. For years, maybe as many as thirty years, we in most of the rich West failed to respond properly to the challenge of globalisation, to the increasing competition from the emerging economies of China, India and Brazil, among others. We did not work harder and smarter. Instead we borrowed – from the likes of China, even though Chinese people are still much poorer than us – to finance the lifestyles we thought we deserved. And now, as a nation, as a group of nations, we have to pay back much of the debt, which inevitably makes us feel poorer, and will continue to do so for years to come.

Quite how we became so indebted is not such a simple tale. It involves a series of crackpot ideas that were held as almost divine truths by those we mistakenly trusted to run the global economy. It was taken on trust that:

1) A world in which some countries were permanently borrowing and others were always generating surpluses would naturally return to equilibrium and balance without a crisis;

2) It was at best pointless or at worst damaging to economic prosperity for regulators or governments to intervene in markets to prevent fast rises in lending (to households, or businesses, or banks) or sharp increases in asset prices (such as house prices);

3) Bankers would follow the spirit of highly complicated global rules designed in a staid, provincial Swiss town in order to strengthen their respective banks, rather than ruthlessly manipulating these rules to hide the risks they were taking;

4) New financial products, which almost no one under-stood, must be making the global economy safer rather than threatening to blow it up;

5) Allowing the highly remunerated salesmen and traders of investments banks and the managers of retail banks to live and work together in giant conglomerates would not create a dangerous, bonus-obsessed gambling culture in banks that are essential to our financial wellbeing.

That said, if you are looking for a slick manifesto of sure-fire reforms that will put us back on the path to unimaginable riches, then you should probably stop reading now. It is not in my nature to be quite so prescriptive and didactic. Sorry. What I am going to give you, I hope, is an analysis of the flaws in the running of the worldwide financial system and the global economy, which may suggest to you the sort of mend-ing that needs to be done. The clean-up will take years. And there is no quick fix, so you need to brace yourself for perhaps a decade of economic stagnation. As it happens, I don't think that is reason to weep. We are a very rich country. And we can be a perfectly happy country if we learn how to make the most of what we have got rather than obsessing about how to have more and more.

This epic has the alternative title 'Globalisation gone Wonky'. Its stars – accident-prone, benighted antiheroes in many cases – include the bankers, the central bankers, the financial regulators, the finance ministers and the Chinese (all 1.3bn of them). There is a main plot – of Britain, America and much of the rich West living beyond its means till the credit-worthiness of their economies was undermined. And then there is a subplot, of much of the eurozone living beyond its means till the credit-worthiness of many of its economies was undermined. Perhaps that sounds repetitive, but I don't think it will be. Because although the plight of Greece and Spain and the other weaker eurozone economies has much in common with the plight of the UK and the US – banks that lent far too much and hid the risks they were taking; property prices that spiralled out of control; governments that failed to spot when tax revenues would be ephemeral because they stemmed from a bubble – it is the crisis in the eurozone that has the potential to wreak maximum havoc.

The journey of the past twenty years and the next ten, through changing terrain, is simply hair-raising. We have allowed others, our governments and the so-called authorities, to take us from boom to bust. So perhaps it is time for us to stop being passengers and become drivers – or at least to try to influence the drivers. But to determine the direction of travel requires a more detailed understanding of how we arrived here, in this place that few of us like. My claim to be your cartographer is simply that, for more than six years at the BBC and over twenty years before that on national newspapers, I have had the privilege of sitting close to the driving seat, where I provided live commentary on where we were heading. And I confess, during much of the journey, I had little idea we had taken such a wrong turning. That said, at the moment that we were heading straight for the swamp, I succeeded in spotting the looming disaster and shouted out a warning: I was largely ignored and was even asked to shut up. Now I have written this book, partly to help myself understand how and why I failed to identify the scale of the looming calamity till we were careering down the mountain with lousy brakes and an unresponsive steering wheel.

In trying to capture the peaks, troughs, plains and bogs of the financial and economic landscape, I have had invaluable help from Laurence Knight, a former investment banker (and no, I have never asked him whether he has repented) and BBC colleague. He has been the best kind of collaborator: resourceful, imaginative and challenging. But for the avoidance of doubt, if you hate the analysis or spot howling errors, they are all my fault. I would also like to thank the BBC just for being the BBC: more than ever, it is a privilege to work for a news organisation which is sincerely and wholly committed to trying to understand and explain the world in an unbiased way.

This book explains my sense of how we have got to where we are. It will chart the economic and business landscape we currently inhabit. And it will attempt to plot the paths we might take from here: those that would lead to maintained or even perhaps modestly improved prosperity and a better life; and those that could lead us to penury and social strife. However, as you have probably guessed, I am not going to pretend that there is a road to Shangri-La, where we will suddenly all find ourselves becoming richer and richer again. We tried that road in the late 1990s and early years of this century, and it was the road to ruin. What we have to recognise in Britain, much of Western Europe and the US is that we are already very wealthy societies, and our capacity to become relatively wealthier – when we face such competition from the vibrant economies of the developing world – is limited. Our mission, should we choose to accept it, is to work more intelligently and industriously to preserve what we've got, and find ways to build a happier society by sharing the spoils in a manner perceived to be fairer. It is pragmatism, not socialism, to worry that vast and widening gaps between rich and poor are unsustainable when most people are struggling to maintain their living standards.

For what it is worth, I am reasonably confident that we will eventually arrive in a place where we run our economies in a more sustainable way – for a while. That said, the lesson of history is that at precisely the moment when we believe we've solved the mystery of how to manage our economies safely, the next financial crisis will rise up in front of us and biff us on the noggin. Boom and bust will be with us forever. It was our foolish conviction that the smooth road to sunny uplands would go on forever which got us into such trouble. A more realistic ambition to set ourselves would be to steer the economy in a way that tempers the extremes of bonanza and recession.

But before we can do that, we need to revisit the quite astonishing mess that has been made of Western economies, in part by the lethal flaws in global finance. If there is a simple message of this book it is that we all need to acquire knowledge of the workings of the financial system that underpins our prosperity – and then we have to use that knowledge by telling our governments what we want from that system. Lazily trusting a financial priesthood – the bankers, the central bankers, the regulators – to manage it all for us has been the route to penury.

CHAPTER 1
BANKERS GAMBLED WITH OUR MONEY: THEY WON, WE LOST

If I know anything much about the nitty-gritty of banking and finance, that is as much down to luck as design. Like more young people than we probably care to acknowledge, I had absolutely no idea what I wanted to do when I finished university in 1982. A failure of imagination led me first to Brussels, to study what was then called the European Economic Community for a few months, and then into the City. My knowledge of political and administrative French was poor, so for weeks I attended lectures where I thought I was learning about the Haddock Committees, until someone explained the concept of 'ad hoc' to me. And initially I was at least as bemused by the language of the stockbrokers I subsequently joined (backwardations, contangos, and so on). But as it turned out, both my brief undistinguished spell at l'Université libre de Bruxelles and a year at Williams de Broë Hill Chaplin, as apprentice to the benevolent, harrumphing Major Diggle, turned out to be pretty useful – though I did both largely because I thought I ought to be doing something, anything.

Major Diggle was a good person, bemused – I always assumed – by the comprehensive-school educated young person he had hired to sell stocks and shares to continental investors. For him, stockbroking appeared to be about travelling to Paris, staying in the majestic George V Hotel, drinking champagne cocktails fairly early in the day, and speaking French with an impeccable English accent to assorted French bankers and insurers who could apparently be persuaded to deal with the firm. Those were the days when banking and broking were much more about who you knew rather than what you knew. It was the end of the era of the amateur gentleman stockbroker, who was about to be made history by the lethal professionalism of the invading hordes of American bankers from the Goldman Sachses and Morgan Stanleys.

But some things never change. And I suppose the most important lesson I learned from working in the City – albeit briefly – is that when money is the sole stock in trade, and making money is the be all and end all, a big part of the day job involves getting around the rules that limit the amount of money you can make. To be clear, I am not talking about criminality here. But I did witness systematic breaches of the spirit of regulations, even if the letter was followed. I saw this in the way that brokers used special trading desks to effectively charge clients twice for a single transaction. I also witnessed a blind eye being systematically turned towards anonymous clients dealing through Swiss bank accounts who seemed to be profiting from inside information (these mysterious clients would buy or sell shares the day before announcements were made that would affect the price of those shares). Insider trading had only recently become illegal. But back then the practice of profiting from confidential information was ingrained in parts of the City and – sad to say – among an older generation of journalists too. As it happens, Swiss banking secrecy made it impossible to be sure who was behind the questionable trading I noted at the time. But I knew of one stockbroking firm where after the always shrewd share-trading orders came in from Switzerland, the partners placed their own copycat orders: they profited from someone else's alleged illegality. Rather than asking the Swiss bank to take its ethically challenged business elsewhere, this broking firm joined the party. Which is why I emerged from my stint as a broker not wholly convinced by the City's fervent claim that minimal regulation and self-regulation was best for the British economy. Simply trusting those rewarded with bonuses and shares of their firm's profits to only do what is right and proper looked naïve to me.

That said, I didn't storm out of the City in high dudgeon, repelled by its moral ambivalence. I just became bored, very quickly. Having sold a pile of grotesquely over-valued shares, about which I knew very little at all, to a young Frenchman with bad skin at a huge insurance company ('*Pardonnez-moi, cher monsieur!*'), I felt a little embarrassed and nonplussed. If that was the job, I couldn't imagine doing it for years and years, however remunerative it would be. There had been more satisfaction as a fourteen-year-old selling cauliflowers and avocados to what would now be called North London MILFs when I worked at Edmonds the Greengrocer in Park Road, Crouch End. It was time to escape.

At last came my lucky break. A friend of a friend from university, Lucy Kellaway, was working on a weekly financial paper called the *Investors Chronicle*, which was owned by the same big company, Pearson, which owned the *Financial Times*. Today Lucy Kellaway is a sort of Alexander Pope of modern British business mores, cruelly funny about the pretensions and self-regard of corporate leaders. Back then she wrote two-hundred-word analyses of whether ICI shares were going up or down – and had just been recruited by the *FT*. There was a job going, Lucy said. And peculiarly, the then Editor, Gillian O'Connor, was persuaded that my time at Williams de Broë was relevant experience. This was the eureka moment for me. I'd found my vocation (although it almost killed me until the heavy-drinking culture of journalism and the City was supplanted by the abstinence of the invading American bankers and financiers).

At the *IC*, I had two responsibilities: retailing and banking. Both industries were to define the UK in the subsequent thirty years, but I regarded retailing as a fun beat and banking as an awful chore. Little did I know how fortunate I was that O'Connor had made me the banking reporter. This was the moment I acquired the expertise (what little I have) that differentiated me from most business and other journalists and helped me to generate a whole string of scoops in subsequent years. Memo to budding journalists: when you're given what seems like the job from hell, it may turn out to be the making of you.

A related piece of good fortune was that I became the understudy and bag carrier for the doyenne of banking journalists, the late Margaret Reid, the *IC*'s banking editor. This redoubtable woman – who had written the definitive account of the crisis of the UK's smaller banks in the early to mid 1970s, what's known as the Secondary Banking Crisis – forced me to learn how banks work. I had studied a bit of economics at Oxford, but that told me precisely nothing about the financial system that underpins wealth creation. So it was only in this, my first journalism job, that I became aware of why banks need capital to protect themselves against losses, the meaning and importance of concepts like liquidity, and the devastating things that can happen when banks lose the confidence of their creditors. It felt like learning a dead language, a load of arcane, technical stuff far removed from our everyday lives. It was misery. But in fact it was a code-breaker or key to understanding stuff that really does matter to all of us: without this education I would have been unable to see the dangerous risks that banks were taking in 2005, 2006 and 2007, why the closure of a series of financial markets in August 2007 would be so devastating to our livelihoods, and why it was inevitable that the government would bail out some of our biggest banks in 2008.

Most business journalists spend their entire careers focussing their attentions primarily on stock markets, and the big companies whose shares are traded on those stock markets. Newspapers have historically been about who is up and who is down on the famous FTSE 100 index and what Tony Benn is fond of calling Mr Dow Jones. That reflects the prejudices of newspaper editors, who in the past rarely knew much about business and the economy and couldn't have cared less (these days at least they know they're supposed to think that business matters). There was almost nothing in newspapers about bond markets, markets in complicated financial products called derivatives, foreign exchange markets, commodity markets and the assorted other markets which had grown to be bigger than stock markets and probably more important to our prosperity. Also, few journalists took an interest in debt markets and the way that banks operate. For years all this borrowing and lending was thought of as the equivalent of a sewage system or an electricity grid – necessary, but dull. It was much more exciting and fun to tell the story of which famous companies were expanding, which were enjoying growth in profits, which were in serious schtuck. And nor was it just the media that was ill-equipped to keep a watchful eye on the largest part of the financial economy, the part hidden below the waterline. You would have been hard-pressed to find an MP or minister taking a proper interest in all this. We were collectively complacent, leaving it to the financial priesthood, the class of regulators and central bankers, to keep an eye on the lethal hazards lurking in the financial ocean and to steer our ships away from the icebergs. But if journalists and politicians were ignorant, the regulators were, as we shall see, naïve and complacent. Thanks to Ms Reid, I at least had one functioning financial eye in my head, and so went on to become banking correspondent at the *Independent* in 1987 and banking editor of the *Financial Times* in 1992.

That said, over the succeeding years, the financial industry grew and mutated at breakneck speed. All sorts of abstruse and impenetrable new products and markets developed, where transactions worth trillions of dollars in aggregate took place. So even after working for a decade on what's probably the world's leading business and finance newspaper, the *Financial Times*, I didn't understand enough about the riskiness of much of what was happening on markets till the die was cast. The scales probably fell from my eyes in the spring of 2007, when I was on a mission for the BBC's *Today* programme, to shine a light for its four million listeners on some of the darkling corners of finance. I was shoving a microphone into the faces of bankers, asking them to explain collateralised debt obligations (CDOs) and credit derivatives, otherwise known as credit default swaps (CDSs). A sort of financial sausage, CDOs are tradable debt fabricated out of lots of other bits of tradable debt. They are investments manufactured out of the offcuts and offal of other investments, which when minced together are supposedly non-toxic. CDSs are a bit easier to explain: they are insurance against the risk that a loan to a business or a government will go bad, insurance against a default by the borrower (and, sorry to say, they could also be insurance against a CDO going bad).

I bowled up to the Canary Wharf trading floor of one of the world's biggest investment banks, Morgan Stanley. This was where it conducted its business in what it called 'leveraged credit'. Now 'leverage' means debt. And 'credit' means 'debt'. So 'leveraged credit' means debt that has become even more indebted – a concept that would have stretched the paradox-manufacturing powers of Lewis Carroll. It was the place where debt was traded in its most reconstituted and remanufactured form, as CDOs, CDSs and other investment artifices, such as Collateralised Loan Obligations, which are made out of the debt of highly leveraged or indebted companies; Collateralised Mortgage Obligations, made out of you-know-what; and so on. There were electronic screens, hundreds of them, for as far as the eye could see. The vast open-plan space, with its serried rows of desks and twinkling computers, was like the flight deck of the Death Star, thronged by brilliant young people whose purpose was to make and flog this leveraged credit stuff. Now the first thing that stunned me was the revelation that – at the time – this trading floor was generating more revenue for Morgan Stanley than its traditional and historic business trading in shares. That was extraordinary: if you had asked most people back then who had heard anything at all about Morgan Stanley (a small subset of the population in any case) how they thought Morgan Stanley made its money, they would have said from selling shares and perhaps bonds to investors. Most would not have said that Morgan Stanley – or Goldman Sachs, or Lehman, or Barclays Capital, or Merrill Lynch – generated billions of dollars of revenues from creating and trading collateralised debt obligations and credit default swaps.

There was a second revelatory moment for me on the Morgan Stanley trading floor. I asked the chap with the title of 'Head of Leveraged Credit Trading' to explain to me in language his grandma or grandpa could understand exactly what he did for a living, and what a CDS and CDO actually are. Ten minutes later, the face of his public relations minder had become ashen, and it became clear that his grandparents would have had no problem understanding what their grand-child did for a living – so long as they happened to be in charge of a huge hedge fund. But if like me they just had a passable working knowledge of business and finance, they might as well have been listening to someone speaking Ancient Sumerian or pure gobbledegook. I only had the faintest idea what he had just said. And it occurred to me that if I didn't understand what was actually happening on this trading floor, what risks were being created, it was highly likely that the directors on the board of Morgan Stanley didn't understand the risks their firm was taking. I don't say that because Morgan Stanley's board was filled with ignorant or stupid individuals. In fact, Morgan Stanley had more genuine financial experts on its board than was the case at Royal Bank of Scotland, for example. It's just that those who tended to be on the boards of these big global banks were either financial specialists who were too old ever to have worked at the coalface in the huge, young leveraged credit industries or were the great and the good of the business world, whose practical experience was a million miles from

CDOs and CDSs. Too many of those on bank boards were like me: excessively trusting that their general knowledge of business and finance would allow them to get a proper handle on what their firms were doing. These banks had acquired huge exposure, in various ways, to leveraged credit, without those at the top understanding what this meant. They had stocked up – innocently in most cases – on products that in the wrong hands and in the wrong quantities could and would turn out to be lethal. I didn't know the scale of the gamble they had taken, but this was for me a 'Houston, we have a problem' moment: it was when I began to fear that the banks had been taking big uncalculated risks.

False optimism

If I didn't properly understand CDOs and CDSs till it was too late – till they had infected more or less every part of the financial system – I was in a better position than most journalists, having had a privileged ringside seat on a revolution in banking and markets that started in the mid 1980s.

When I first became a banking journalist, our banks were run by solid unflashy men (all men) who had left school at sixteen or eighteen, joined the banks as trainees and acquired knowledge, experience and qualifications when working. Banking, like accountancy, engineering or even journalism, was to a large extent a craft skill. You learned on the job and there was no great advantage in being a graduate. In part, that was because much of banking was simpler in those days: it was much more domestic than today and about knowing customers well enough to prevent too much being lent to those who would struggle to repay it. Of course, banks still made big mistakes. For example, Lloyds was almost bankrupted in the 1980s by losses on its huge loans in Latin America. The late Sir Brian Pitman, the long-serving chief executive of Lloyds, once told me that his bank would have gone bust if it had been forced to tell shareholders and creditors how much of its lending in the region it would never get back – which would have been the case under the disclosure rules that now apply. And it is widely thought that National Westminster Bank was in dire straits in the mid 1970s, due to its exposure to the so-called secondary or smaller banks. Both banks were kept alive by a culture back then of institutionalised secrecy, actively promoted by the Bank of England. As for Barclays, it suffered horrendous losses on commercial property loans in the early 1990s. Another of the pillars of British banking, Midland, came close to being destroyed by the reckless takeover of an American bank, Crocker, in the 1980s – and was eventually swallowed up by HSBC (which was a Hong Kong bank run by Scots).

What's striking about all these banking crises and accidents is that – although they were serious – no one argued at the time that their demise would bankrupt the British economy. And yet in 2008, the UK was looking at economic Armageddon when HBOS and Royal Bank of Scotland both went to the brink of collapse and had to be rescued by taxpayers. What happened between the late 1980s and 2008 to make the life or death of the bigger banks the life or death of the economy?

There were a series of important and unhealthy changes:

1) Banks became much bigger and took much greater risks relative to their capital, which is the reserves they hold as a buffer to absorb losses and protect depositors from those losses;

2) Banks reduced the amount of cash and liquid assets (assets that can easily be sold and turned into cash) they held – which is another kind of buffer for their business – in this case one that allows them to repay creditors as and when creditors panic and want their money back;

3) Banks became much more connected to each other and dependent on each other, by lending to each other much more – which meant if one bank became sick, there would be contagion to many banks;

4) Banks became more complicated and more international as businesses, making it much harder for directors, shareholders, creditors and regulators to understand the risks they were really taking – which meant, first, that those stewards, owners, lenders and referees didn't stop the banks from taking dangerous risks; and second, they panicked when things went wrong because they couldn't assess the scale of the problem;

5) Banks copied each other, by making very similar investments and loans – so when those investments and loans went bad, there was an epidemic of big banks becoming sick.

Now banks and bankers behaved in this reckless way, not because of some terrible conspiracy to bankrupt us all, but because – perhaps wilfully, perhaps innocently – they did not believe they were behaving recklessly. They believed technological and financial innovation was making their world safer. Sophisticated IT programmes were written that in theory made it easier for all organisations to keep tabs on operations all over the world and supposedly allowed banks to have a better grasp of the risks they were running. Bankers were convinced that they could lend and invest much more, at much lower risk, than in the past, because they thought (wrongly) that a revolution in computing power and financial analysis gave them a better understanding of their activities than their predecessors.

And it was not just the bankers who believed there had been some kind of evolutionary leap to create the all-seeing super-banker. Regulators, central bankers, investors, and politicians were also convinced that progress had created a safer financial system.

Here, for example, is what the IMF said in 2007, which most would say is after the financial crisis had actually begun, about the health of Wall Street:

> Core commercial and investment banks are in a sound financial position, and systemic risks appear low. Profitability and capital adequacy of the banking system are high by international standards ... Despite a recent uptick following subprime difficulties, market measures of default risk have remained benign.

The UK's regulatory authority, the Financial Services Authority, shared this complacency. In June 2007, its director of wholesale firms, Thomas Huertas, said this to me in a BBC interview (to be clear, Mr Huertas' view was that of the FSA as a whole):

> The major institutions are very well capitalised. They show very very strong earnings. Anywhere short of a major depression, the firms are much much better placed than

they have been to withstand economic shocks. We do encourage the firms and the firms are responding to do stress testing to prepare for the worst. So in our view firms are in fact taking steps to prepare for the proverbial rainy day.

Another statement by the IMF, made in 2007, best captures why the experts paid to protect us from the excesses of the financial sector were so misguided:

Although complacency would be misplaced, it would appear that innovation has supported financial system soundness. New risk transfer markets have facilitated the dispersion of credit risk from a core where moral hazard is concentrated to a periphery where market discipline is the chief restraint on risk-taking. The conduit mechanism, in turn, has facilitated broader credit extension, with the important qualitative nuance that much of the recent credit growth has reflected lending to new, previously excluded borrowers, as opposed to 'more money thrown at the same people'. Although cycles of excess and panic have not disappeared, the subprime boom-bust being but the latest example, markets have shown that they can and do self-correct.

It is worth translating this, because more or less everything that went wrong is captured here. The IMF was saying that innovation meant debt was being traded much more and risks were being dispersed: the risks weren't concentrated in the banking system as much as they had previously been; they were shared with all sorts of other investors. What's more, this innovation had created all sorts of new credit, much of it going to individuals and businesses which hitherto had either been unable to borrow or could only borrow at prohibitive cost. So banking innovation was socially progressive – it was giving poor people the opportunity to buy homes and accumulate assets, for example. And at the core of the IMF view was an ideological conviction that markets had stopped and would stop too much being lent in a reckless way; markets 'can and do self-correct', as the IMF put it.

Arguably it was this blind faith in the rationality of markets that was at the heart of all our subsequent economic troubles. That is not to say that a market-based system, as opposed to a communist system, hasn't turned out over the past fifty odd years to be the least-worst system for organising an economy. The triumph of capitalism in China, if not the triumph of democracy there, tells you that markets have much going for them. So what follows should not be seen as some kind of rallying cry for the nationalisation of everything and for all important economic decisions to be taken by civil servants and politicians. It wasn't an accident that the Soviet Bloc fell apart and market-based capitalism spread like wildfire from East Germany to Eastern Siberia. The command economy of the old USSR crumbled in large part because the gap between the living standards of the West and the East was becoming too large for Soviet citizens to tolerate. But if a market-based economy is generally preferable to a system in which all decisions on production and wages are taken by a central bureaucracy, that does not mean leaving markets unchecked and unregulated will inevitably generate sustainable improvements in prosperity and spoils distributed in the fairest way.

To be clear, the flaws in markets are not the great discovery of our age. The Wall Street Crash and the Great Depression of the 1930s were examples of boom and bust caused by wild euphoria on markets. So too was the Dutch tulip mania of the 1630s or the British railway bust of the 1840s. Markets are no more than collections of people buying and selling; they are social constructions. And people, as we all know, are prone to bouts of herd-like and manic behaviour, to euphoria and self-delusion. We're all prone to believe, after a period of stability and prosperity, that stability and prosperity are the norm. So in the 1990s and early parts of the new millennium, as the UK, US and much of Europe seemed to become richer year after year without any major accidents, we perhaps began to think that an economic life without significant setbacks, a recession-free economy, would be with us forever. Think about your own case or that of your parents. If they had seen house prices going up without a pause for a decade, it was rational to believe, surely, that they would continue going up for another decade or longer. Which is why many people in the UK, the US, Spain and Ireland borrowed far too much in the years before the crash of 2007–8 in order to get on the housing ladder or move up the housing ladder.

And there was an identical process going on in the banking industry. Banks were taking bigger and bigger risks, lending more, investing more, because assets had been rising in value for years, and fewer and fewer borrowers were reneging on their debts. If Gordon Brown believed it was the end of boom and bust, he wasn't alone. And for banks there was a second source of false corroboration for the seductive notion that they were no longer prone to normal downturns. They were all using new complicated financial models – run by computers – called Value at Risk models, to assess how much they could lose at any instant if there were a sudden fall in markets (or indeed a sudden rise – because banks are constantly and continuously placing bets that some asset prices will rise and some will fall). But the problem is that the information fed into these models was of recent vintage. The data captured movements in markets that had taken place in the previous ten years or so, when things had been pretty stable. But the data did not include the equivalent of a 1929 crash or the infamous drop from £20,000 (in today's money) to a penny in the price of a tulip almost four centuries ago. The banks' computer models for minimising risk were built on the assumption that the very worst that had happened in the past would not and could not happen again. That made these early-warning and protective systems quite close to useless – because the banks were not guarding themselves against the extreme risks that had transpired in the past and did indeed happen again. Worse than that, every year that passed with comparatively little bad stuff happening in markets, the more data was fed into these models showing that big swings in prices were unlikely to happen. That had the perverse consequence of encouraging bankers to double up on their bets just as the cycle in rising asset prices was reaching its inflated peak. In other words, a system designed to limit risk-taking had the effect of encouraging dangerous risk-taking.

For me, the fatuousness of these models was best shown by remarks made to the *Financial Times* on 13 August 2007 by David Viniar, the chief financial officer of the world's most powerful investment bank, Goldman Sachs, a few days after what most people see as the start of the credit crunch – the moment a whole series of important financial markets, used by banks to raise hundreds of billions of dollars, simply stopped functioning properly. Mr Viniar said: 'We are seeing things that were 25-standard deviation moves, several days in a row.' What he was saying, in impenetrable banker-speak, is that what had been happening in wholesale markets was unexpected. The world was not behaving in the way it was supposed to, as per the assumptions and data fed into the banks' Value at Risk models. On the basis of Goldman's risk assessment, precisely how unlikely was the market malfunction that had just happened? Andrew Haldane, the director in charge of financial stability at the Bank of England, tried to translate Mr Viniar's jargon into language we can understand:

> To provide some context, assuming a normal distribution, a 7.26-sigma daily loss would be expected to occur once every 13.7 billion or so years. That is roughly the estimated age of the universe. A 25-sigma event would be expected to occur once every 6 times 10 to the power of 124 lives of the universe. That is quite a lot of human histories. When I tried to calculate the probability of a 25-sigma event occurring on several successive days, the lights visibly dimmed over London and, in a scene reminiscent of that *Little Britain* sketch, the computer said: 'No.' Suffice to say, time is very unlikely to tell whether Mr Viniar's empirical observation proves correct.
>
> (Andy Haldane, 'Why Banks Failed
> the Stress Test', 13 February 2009)

To put it another way, Goldman's risk model assumed that the closure of asset-backed commercial paper and asset-backed bond markets – which *had* taken place – could not have taken place in the lifetime of the universe, or indeed many many lifetimes of the universe. Which shows not that something unbelievably improbable had transpired, but that bankers had been putting too low a probability on market shocks that had happened before and would happen again. Before we move on, for those of you who like jargon, the bankers – and regulators, which sanctioned investment banks' use of these flawed systems for controlling risks – were ignoring what statisticians call a fat-tail in the distribution of possible outcomes and managing risks on the basis that outcomes would be normal.

That said, and this is an important point, many bankers knowingly took risks that were dangerous – although as individuals they never thought these risks could collectively bring the financial system close to collapse. The huge pay incentives to gamble were described to me by an investment banker:

> Some clients wanted to invest in developing countries like Russia and Brazil. We lent them additional money to increase the size of their bets. This put us at risk: if the market collapsed, wiping out all the clients' money, we could also stand to make a loss on what we'd lent them. Market collapses were not uncommon in Russia and Brazil; we were very conscious of this risk – more so than our clients. Yet my trader still argued with the banks' internal accountants that the risks involved were small. That's because his bonus depended on how much profit the accountants were willing to recognise. Of course, in 2008 every one of those trades blew up. Yet nobody blamed him for failing to foresee such a massive market meltdown. And even if they had, he had cashed in his bonuses long before.
>
> (Interview with the author, August 2012)

The big point, I think, is this one. Calamities in markets, that wreck or come close to wrecking entire economies, happen periodically. Depending on what you classify as such a trauma, you would probably argue that over the past hundred years there have been two or three massive financial crises in the UK (a near collapse of the UK banking system just before the First World War, the Secondary Banking Crisis of the 1970s and the 2007–8 debacle) plus two or three other lesser ones (including the popping of the dot-com bubble in 2000 and Black Monday on stock markets in 1987). You will notice that the more serious events are those where banks are at the heart of the problem, and the reason for that will soon become clear. But what is striking is the human propensity to forget about previous crises and to assume that a new crisis-free era has arrived. Here is the central paradox of financial history: we know that there will be harmful banking crises every fifty years or so, and lesser market shocks every twenty or thirty years; but we also know that as years go by without such a shock bankers and investors will become unshakeably convinced that there won't be a crisis in their lifetimes, and will begin to take ever more dangerous risks. The challenge for regulators and politicians, in trying to reduce the incidence and severity of future crises, is somehow or other to ground the optimism of those who make important decisions on markets in a more realistic view of history and the future.

Perhaps the most shocking indictment of regulators' and bankers' article of faith that markets will self-correct is what happened to the price of credit derivatives on the debt of big banks and financial firms in the run-up to the 2007 market meltdown. The price of insuring the debt of banks like Royal Bank of Scotland and Lehman Brothers against the possibility of default – against the likelihood they wouldn't repay their debts – became cheaper and cheaper just as these banks were taking bigger and bigger risks. It is worth thinking about this for a second: the more that the banks lent, the more that they recklessly provided credit, the cheaper it was for their creditors to insure against the risk that it would all go horribly wrong. Markets did not self-correct; they self-harmed.

Credit where credit's (not) due

Here is the rotten heart of the iteration of global financial capitalism that has evolved: banks' over-confident creation of masses of new credit was reinforced by the export of vast capital surpluses being generated by the producing countries of China, Japan, the oil-rich Gulf states and Germany (see chapter 4). Bankers and investors became more and more irrationally exuberant (to steal Alan Greenspan's resonant phrase) and certain that a new golden age of ever-rising prosperity had arrived. They magnified the indebtedness of the consuming countries, like the UK and US, by lending more and more to households, to businesses and to governments. It is important to point out that these trends – the credit creation by banks and flood of cash from the producing nations – were lethally interconnected: they mutually reinforced each other.

On the one hand, all that money sloshing from China into loans to the US government, for example, meant that what the US government had to pay to borrow was kept low. And when the cost of borrowing for the US government fell, so too did the cost of borrowing for US banks (a fall in interest rates paid by the debtor perceived as most likely to always pay its debts, the government, cuts the cost of borrowing for most other debtors, including banks; lenders and investors who want to earn a higher rate of interest, a higher yield, than what the government pays are forced to lend to riskier borrowers, such as banks). Or to put it another way, the massive flow of funds from the producing nations to the consuming nations meant that interest rates in the consuming nations were suppressed. And with banks able to borrow cheaply, they were prepared to charge lower interest rates to households and businesses. In fact it was so hard for banks to get a decent return from lending to households and businesses with strong finances, they started to look more kindly on borrowers who would have been seen traditionally as too risky, such as people on very low incomes, or even without jobs, looking to buy a home, or businesses bought by private-equity funds with massive amounts of debt.

For better or worse – probably worse – this was also a golden age of financial innovation. Some of this innovation and new 'financial technology' persuaded banks that there had been a meaningful reduction in the risks of making so-called subprime loans to house buyers and of extending credit to companies that were borrowing mind-boggling sums (companies that were labelled as 'highly leveraged'). The innovations included the notorious collateralised debt obligations and collateralised loan obligations. There was also the growth of what is known as shadow banking, the creation of new institutions called conduits and structured investment vehicles (SIVs), that did a lot of lending outside the conventional banking system (although still connected to the banking system) in a manner that turned out to be insidious. There was a great global credit-creating loop, where money poured in from the likes of China to the US (for example) and was then turned into even more money by Western banks, which fuelled spending and investing within the US on Chinese-made products, which further amplified the flow of money from China to America. And as the surge of money from the producing countries to the consuming ones became broader and deeper, so there became a shortage of safe places to invest that money – which provided an incentive for investors to take greater risks and for bankers to hide and disguise the true risks of the financial products (such as CDOs) that they were selling to investors. In this cheap money world, anyone prepared to pay a slightly higher interest rate – such as poor people desperate to own a home in the US, or property developers in Ireland and Spain, or the Greek government – found they could borrow undreamed-of sums.

One way to see all this is as China, Germany, Japan and the oil-rich Gulf states providing the fuel or stimulants for a lending binge by the banks. Think of it perhaps as an enormous global party. China, Germany, Japan and Saudi Arabia brought the booze to the party, though they consumed very little of it themselves. Some of the booze was drunk by Western banks. But then the Western banks found a clever way to adulterate and increase the quantity of the booze without reducing its potency. For a while they thought they were manufacturing vats of finest quality claret, when in fact it was the kind of toxic stuff that makes you go blind. Everyone – the bankers, consumers, businesses and governments, in the US, the UK, Greece, Ireland, Spain, Portugal and so on – got legless. So they failed to notice that they were beginning to dance dangerously close to a wide-open window on the fiftieth floor of a massive tower block. What made the party all the more dangerous is that the putative grown-ups, the central bankers and regulators, convinced themselves it was all good clean fun. For example, when the chairman of America's Federal Reserve, Alan Greenspan, cut interest rates after the dot-com crash and after 9/11 in the early years of the new century, he spurred lenders and investors to take even greater and crazier risks in the quest for profits, or what has become character-ised as 'the search for yield'. By cutting interest rates too much as the party was getting started, Greenspan and other central banks encouraged investors and creditors to lend more and more to those who would find it impossible to repay what they owe.

A lending hand

One of the most important points to understand here is that when banks are in a mood to lend, they can create almost unlimited amounts of money – and can really give a boost to economic activity. And the corollary is also true – that when banks are feeling anxious and worried about whether house-holds and businesses are financially overstretched, they can suck money out of the economy and force it into recession. Think of it like this: when a bank lends to a company or household, the company or household will put the cash into another bank, which then has the cash available to lend to someone else, who then deposits the money into another bank, which can then make another loan, and so on. Now the authorities – or rather central banks which sit at the heart of national banking systems – have some modest ability to increase or decrease the ability of commercial banks to create loans and money in this way. A central bank can insist that commercial banks only lend out a proportion of their depos-its, that they always keep some percentage of their deposits as reserves at the central bank. The Chinese central bank, the People's Bank of China, for example, tries to retain control over lending by Chinese banks by varying the reserves they are obliged to hold. By contrast, the Bank of England aban-doned the use of these reserve requirements, because it did not believe they were very effective – and it now influences money creation in other ways. What matters is that in today's global almost-borderless financial system, banks have enormous power to increase or shrink the amount of credit and money in an economy.

That said, because banks are lending other people's money, not their own, and are not supposed to take crazy risks with that money, there are what is known as prudential constraints on how much banks can lend. And these prudential constraints – the amount of capital and liquidity (or cash) that banks have to hold – do have a powerful impact on banks' capacity to create credit. Before we explore this interplay between the regulation of banks and how much they lend, it is important to consider why banks matter so much to all of us. Now in all the barrage of negative publicity about banks in recent years, it is easy to forget that they are really important institutions fulfilling a number of vital social and economic functions. In fact, given that it is hard to find commercial entities which perform quite such a useful role, banks have had to work very hard to become quite as unpopular as they have recently become (in spite of the stigma attached to usury or money-lending throughout history, in twentieth century Britain the bank manager was usually a pillar of the community). Perhaps their most valuable role is that they take the surplus cash that many of us have at various times and they then lend it to those who lack the savings for the things they wish to buy, such as a house, or a pair of shoes, or a new production line. A world without banks would be a world in which it would be much harder for businesses to invest and create jobs, and those born poor would have to save for decades before they could even think about buying a home. Banks, when managed sensibly and carefully, make us richer by helping employment-creating businesses expand, and can promote social mobility by providing opportunities to borrow for those who aren't born wealthy.

There are limits to the social utility of banks. For example, because banks are never supposed to put our savings at risk in a serious way, they have a powerful incentive not to lend to those least likely to pay it back, even though these are often businesses and individuals who most need the money. Or to put it more crudely, banks typically don't lend to really poor households. And they rarely lend to young entrepreneurial businesses, since these are the businesses that most often go bust quite quickly, even if a few of them turn into a Google or Facebook. In spite of these shortcomings, it is pretty hard to argue that we would be better off if there were no banks. If we can't live with banks, as some would say, we probably can't live without them.

Now the primary requirement of banks, which is to keep our savings safe, is not as easy as it may sound. Because when banks lend our money, even to borrowers who seem as sound as a pound, there is scope for all sorts of accidents that can prevent those borrowers from repaying what they owe – to the detriment of the banks and their depositors. For example, a couple in seemingly good jobs who have borrowed to buy a house can suddenly find that one or both of them have lost their jobs, making it difficult for them to keep up payments on a bank loan. Or a solid profitable business can lose a couple of big regular orders that would undermine its ability to make interest payments. So the lesson of history, which many banks forgot, is that it is reckless not to keep a big pot of rainy day money, which is there to protect depositors from losses when debtors do not repay all they owe. This rainy day money is called capital.

Here is the thing: because banks are entrusted with our precious savings, not any old business can be a bank; only institutions that have been vetted and approved by an official regulator, in the UK's case the Financial Services Authority – which at the time of writing is due to be broken up into two new regulatory bodies – are licensed to take deposits, and all senior bankers are also vetted and approved by regulators. These regulators also determine how much capital and liquidity banks have to hold, to minimise the danger of losses made by the banks impairing the value of our savings.

I am going to get pedagogic on you now – because part of why the banks and our economy got into such a mess in 2007–8 was the design and implementation of rules about how much capital banks have to hold. What I need to explain is how there is a tension between the interests of depositors and those of top bankers when it comes to setting the quantity of capital held by banks. Or to put it another way, you and I as savers would want our banks to hold loads of capital; but those running banks have a strong personal financial incentive to minimise how much capital is in their banks.

Regulators set capital adequacy requirements for banks – a ratio of how much capital they have to hold in relation to the loans and investments they make, which are collectively known as banks' assets. If, for example, banks are forced by regulators to hold capital equal to 10% of their assets, then a bank with £1m of capital can make £10m of loans. But if this minimum capital ratio is set much lower, at 2%, then the bank with £1m of capital would be allowed to make £50m of loans. Now I have been talking blithely about 'capital' without saying what it is or where it comes from. Well it is money provided by the owners of the bank, the shareholders. And although it can be lost, if debtors don't repay what they owe, it can also be increased, when the bank makes profits.

Let's go back to our example of the bank with £1m of capital making £10m of loans and investments, which we'll call Pesto Bank. To finance its £10m of lending and investing, Pesto Bank has borrowed £10m from depositors and other creditors. Now let's assume Pesto Bank is paying 2% on average to borrow, and is charging 7% on average to its debtors. The spread or difference between its cost of funds and what it receives in interest is 5%. That means it is generating a gross profit of 5% on its £10m of loans, or £500,000. As it happens, Pesto Bank is a New Age bank, where its employees don't receive massive bonuses. The total cost of running the bank, in wages, electricity, and so on, is just £350,000. That means there is £150,000 left over for the owners, the shareholders, the providers of that £1m of capital. They'll take out £75,000 as their reward in a dividend, and £75,000 will be left in the bank. Here is the important thing: that £75,000 reinvested in the bank's reserves would allow the bank to borrow a further £750,000 to lend a further £750,000 (remember that the bank has to retain a capital adequacy ratio of 10%, in this example). And if you're wondering why those shareholders deserve to receive that £75,000 dividend, remember it only takes one of Pesto Bank's customers to go bust, and to be unable to repay a £1m loan, for the shareholders to lose every penny of the £1m of capital they have put into the bank.

Now let us take a look at what would happen to Pesto Bank if it were allowed to lend £50m for every £1m of its capital – that is if its minimum capital ratio were reduced from 10% to 2%. If Pesto Bank is still borrowing at 2% and lending at 7%, Pesto Bank would make a gross profit of £2.5m – or five times greater than it was making with a capital ratio of 10%. In order to make those extra loans and manage the additional deposits it has taken in, Pesto Bank has had to hire a few more people. So its overheads have also gone up five-fold to £1.75m. And because the bank has done so well, I as the chief executive have demanded that I receive a bonus of £250,000. But even after all those extra costs and my bonus, there is still £500,000 left over for the owners, or more than three times what was earned for them when the bank was forced to hold much more capital relative to its loans and investments. Their dividend this time will be a handsome £200,000, representing a 20% return on their investment, compared with 7.5% in the previous example. And £300,000 will be retained in the bank – which can then underpin a further £15m of borrowing and lending by Pesto Bank.

What I hope you will have noticed is that the bank with a smaller amount of capital relative to loans and investments generates massively bigger profits, which allows it to pay vastly bigger bonuses to its senior executives and directors, and to distribute much bigger dividends to shareholders. Surely therefore we would want banks to have lower capital ratios. That is certainly what many bankers would argue. But think for a second about the relative risks for depositors. When Pesto Bank lends fifty times its capital, only 2% of its loans have to go bad for all that capital to be wiped out, whereas when the bank lends ten times its capital, a full 10% of loans would have to be lost for shareholders to lose everything. So there is a much greater danger that depositors will not be able to get all their money back, when a bank has a 2% capital ratio and lends fifty times its capital than when a bank has a 10% capital ratio and lends ten times its capital.

To put it another way, you would probably want to be a top

executive and shareholder in Pesto Bank Mark 2, because the bonuses and dividends would be bigger, for as long as Pesto Bank Mark 2 doesn't go bust. But you would probably want to be a depositor in Pesto Bank Mark 1, because your money would be safer. As I am sure you have gathered by now, banks with less capital relative to their loans and investments are much more prone to falling over, everything else being equal.

The process of a bank borrowing and lending more relative to its capital is called 'increasing its leverage' or 'leveraging up'. And the reverse process, of cutting the volume of loans made relative to capital, is called deleveraging. Typically banks took on much more leverage in the years before the 2007–8 crash and have deleveraged since. For the rest of us, leveraging up is normally associated, while it's happening, with fairly lively economic activity, pretty strong growth in GDP or output, whereas deleveraging is frequently the cause of a slump or recession. The reason should be obvious: when banks are increasing their leverage, they are lending more and more, so there is much more money available to finance investment by businesses and spending by households. Since the crash, we have lived through a period of sustained deleveraging. The Credit Crunch of 2007–8, which precipitated the recession of 2008–9, was a period of sharp deleveraging. And since then, banks have continued to deleverage, though at a slower pace, which is one important reason why the economy remains so weak.

Now, as we have seen, when a bank increases leverage, the risk of that bank becoming insolvent increases: the bank would have less capital relative to its loans to absorb losses if the loans were to go bad; and when a bank's capital has been wiped out by losses, the bank would be bust, because the bank would be unable to repay its depositors and would therefore have failed in its primary responsibility (to keep depositors' money safe). So it is important that banks have sufficiently large stocks of capital to absorb any losses that may be coming their way. But sound banks need more than just adequate reserves of capital to cope with whatever accidents may befall their debtors. They also need to retain large stocks of what are known as liquid assets – assets that are cash or can easily be turned into cash – just in case there is a sudden surge in depositors asking for their money back.

The flip side of banks' social utility, their ability to turn savings into loans to business and households, is that they are inherently unstable. The way to think of it is like this: there is no bank in the world that could repay all its depositors at once, if they all asked for their money back at precisely the same moment. The reason, in the jargon, is that banks borrow short and lend long. Or to put that into English, banks borrow from individuals, businesses and assorted institutions that can normally ask for their money back at a moment's notice; but they lend this money out for a few months, a few years or even a few decades. What is known as banks' 'maturity-transformation' function is an inescapable flaw in their design. So it would be a very foolish and reckless bank that lent out every single penny of the money it took in from depositors. Every bank keeps some money in cash or in the form of tradable assets, such as bonds that can easily be sold for cash, so that when a depositor asks for his or her money, the bank can provide the money.

Imagine what would happen if a few depositors went to a bank and were told that they couldn't get their money back. The rumour would spread like wildfire that the bank had run out of cash – and every depositor in that bank would start to fear that their respective savings were not safe. They would all clamour to be repaid. At that juncture, it would be curtains for the bank, even if its balance sheet was still showing that it had reserves, so that in a technical sense it was still solvent. With depositors screaming for cash, the bank would be forced to sell all its assets to raise the needed funds. And in any fire sale of this sort, assets would be sold for a knockdown price, or for less than their official value in a bank's books. For example, if a bank had provided a billion pounds of mortgages with depositors' cash, it might well in those emergency circumstances sell those mortgages to another bank for £800m, to raise cash. But in selling for £800m, the bank would be incurring losses of £200m – which could well wipe out its capital, and turn it from a solvent bank into an insolvent bank. When there is a run on a bank, when a bank suffers a liquidity crisis, there is a very big danger that it will soon become insolvent.

In other words, a well-run bank will make sure it holds enough cash and liquid assets to meet not only the requirements for cash of its depositors on a normal day, but also quite a bit more – just in case there is a surge of withdrawals. As you will have gathered, the perception that a bank is not safe is as imperilling to its survival as the reality. And once a bank proves itself unable to return the savings of its depositors, the game is up: all depositors will scream for their money, and the bank will collapse. But just as with capital, those who run banks have a powerful incentive to minimise the amount of cash they hold: cash is dead money; it is not earning interest, so the more cash held by a bank, the smaller its profits, and the smaller the bonuses and dividends it pays. That is why regulators are supposed to force banks to hold a minimum amount of cash and liquid resources – although, as we will soon find out, this is something that regulators completely forgot to do in the boom years.

The new banking

In later chapters we will look at how Northern Rock, Royal Bank of Scotland and HBOS were all taken to the brink of collapse by reckless lending and a failure to maintain adequate capital and liquidity – and you might feel you will be able to make a judgement about whether it was profit-hungry executives and shareholders who were more at fault, or complacent and naïve regulators. For now, let us look at the big trends for all British, European and US banks. The first thing to note is that the leverage of banks has been rising steadily for more than 100 years. In the United States, for example, banks would typically hold capital equivalent to around half of their loans and investments in the 1840s. Later, in 1880, a typical US bank had capital equivalent to around a quarter of all its loans and investments, whereas the equivalent ratio for British banks was not far off 20%. But more than a century on, by mid 2008, Royal Bank of Scotland held capital capable of absorbing losses around a tenth of that, or only 2.2% of gross loans and investments, while Northern Rock's capital-to-assets ratio in 2007 was just 1.7%. To put this another way, a century ago a bank would go bust if a quarter of its loans went bad; in the latest financial crisis, one of the biggest banks in the world, RBS, was no longer viable if it could not get back 2% of what it was owed; and in the case of Northern Rock, if it lost just one in every £60 of its loans, it was kaput. On average, by the time of the 2008 banking crisis, British banks had capital equivalent to less than 3% of their loans and investments, a fall of more than three-quarters through the course of the twentieth century, and US banks held only a bit more capital. And the particularly sharp nosedive in the amount of capital held by banks, in their capital ratios, occurred in the decade before the crash, after drifting down in a more gentle way over the previous ninety years.

For a better understanding of why this matters, let us take a look at what happened in the late 1920s and 1930s, when the British economy contracted a little more deeply than in the recession we've just endured (although in that earlier malaise the recovery came earlier and was much stronger). What is striking is that back then, lots of small banks were going bust all over the US, but not a single bank of any significance collapsed in Britain. Now in some ways the British banking industry in the 1930s looked remarkably similar to how it looks today, with just a handful of big deposit-takers dominating the industry. So why were British banks more robust in the 1930s than in 2008, when two giant banks, RBS and HBOS, two medium-sized banks, Northern Rock and Bradford & Bingley, and a host of tiddling building societies and British offshoots of Icelandic banks had to be rescued and broken up – at enormous cost to taxpayers and all our wealth?

In 1930 the British banking industry was dominated by five big banks. These were Barclays, Lloyds, Midland, National Provincial and Westminster. In 1970, National Provincial and Westminster merged to form NatWest, which was itself acquired by Royal Bank of Scotland in 2000. Midland was bought by HSBC in 1992 and trades as HSBC today. So the Big Four banks today – HSBC, Lloyds, Royal Bank of Scotland and Barclays – are more or less equivalent to the Big Five in 1930. That said, in 2008 in the UK there was also HBOS, to take the number of serious players to five; and a recent acquisition spree by Spain's Santander in the UK means there is still a Big Five, even after the controversial takeover of HBOS by Lloyds. There seems to be something about the size and structure of the British economy that gives sustenance to a quintet of very large banks, but no more than that (although

Nationwide and the soon-to-be enlarged Co-operative Bank are trying to test the theory that five is the only number when it comes to big players in British banking). Anyway the important point is that in some ways the structure of the British banking industry has been remarkably unchanging over many decades. That said, look beneath the bonnets of the banks and we get a different view. In the case of Midland Bank in June 1930, for example, it had £28m of capital and reserves backing £315m of loans and investments, so its gross ratio of capital to assets was 9%. Midland back then was holding four times the capital relative to the risks it was running of, for example, Royal Bank of Scotland, before the acute phase of RBS's crisis. Midland and its peers were also much stronger than modern banks in a number of other ways. Back in 1930, Midland had made loans of £214m, which means it had lent out just 56% of the £379m it had taken in from depositors and its other creditors. In contrast, modern big banks like RBS and HBOS, at the height of the boom, actually lent out more than they had taken from ordinary customers in the form of dependable deposits. RBS, HBOS and Northern Rock had become dangerously reliant on raising money from the kind of investors and banks which would stop lending to them or would demand their money back at any whisper of trouble ahead (and we will look at quite why that was such a lethal error later in our story). What is more, Midland held cash equivalent to 10% of its current-account and deposit liabilities, and a further 9.4% in very liquid form. In total, it had 'cash items' equivalent to 21% of deposits. Or to put it another way, it was much better placed to cope with a panicky withdrawal of funds by customers than today's banks – many of which barely had any cash at all.

Other figures – from the Bank of England – show how

vulnerable our banks became. From 1968 to 2008, banks' holdings of sterling cash, plus British government bonds, plus money they could call in at any time, plus their balances at the Bank of England, plus other high quality tradable bills, fell from 30% of their loans and investments to about 0.5%. Or to put it another way, over forty years they went from having enough pounds to be able to withstand the mother of all bank runs to a position where a request from just a few of their bigger creditors for their money back – such as those who manage billions of pounds of investors' cash in Boston, Massachusetts or Singapore or Geneva – could force them to seek emergency loans from the Bank of England. Here is another way of seeing how British banks became much less stable. In 2000, bank loans provided by British banks were all financed by regular deposits from customers. This was a good thing because savers like you and me only once in a blue moon decide en masse to move our money (the run in 2007 at Northern Rock was pretty close to being unique). So British banks that financed their loans with their customers' deposits were not massively at risk of running out of cash in a hurry. But that source of strength vanished very fast. By 2006, a quarter of all the loans and investments made by British banks were financed by selling bonds to big investors and borrowing from financial institutions. By 2008, there was a £900bn gap between the money lent by British banks and the money they had taken in from depositors. That £900bn was all obtained on wholesale markets, from financial institutions – including other banks – and big investors. Which was a desperate mistake because much of that £900bn could have been – and was – demanded back in 2007 and 2008, as fears increased that a number of big banks all over the world were facing losses and might not be able to pay their debts. This funding gap was the reason why Royal Bank of Scotland and HBOS went from being walking wounded in the summer of 2008 to being almost at death's door in the autumn: their creditors had the right to demand to be repaid in a hurry, and they exercised that right.

There is another relevant lesson from early twentieth century history. In 1930, the big banks published monthly balance sheets: they provided important information about their financial health more regularly than banks do today. However, they kept an element of mystique about how strong they really were. All the banks had 'hidden' reserves – contingency funds and property that was deliberated undervalued – which they shrouded in mystery. This created the useful and true perception that the banks were stronger than could be seen from the accounts they put into the public domain. Now we live in an age where we demand transparency from all our important institutions. Governments and regulators have forced almost all banks everywhere in the world to abandon the use of hidden reserves, and Britain's big commercial banks put all their capital on display from 1970 onwards. But there is a great paradox here: transparency has not delivered greater confidence in the robustness of banks. Today there is more mistrust of banks' balance sheets: a fear that banks are hiding their liabilities and losses; a concern that banks are covering up toxic waste. There are lots of reasons for this mistrust: the greater complexity of financial products, whose underlying value few really understand; the huge global spread of banks' operations; and horribly complicated regulations that allow banks to set aside much less capital as loss-absorbing protection for some kinds of loans that are deemed to be less risky, and which offer the potential for abuse and for obscuring real risks (these are the complicated Basel Rules, which are going to play a big role in our story). This incapacity of banks' creditors to confidently evaluate banks' health and strength was a major cause of why, in 2007, they stopped lending to banks – and why the global financial system seized up in a devastating way.

We did not learn anything new in the banking crisis of 2007 and 2008 about how to keep banks strong and depositors' money safe. The basics of sound banking are broadly unchanging. But bankers, investors and regulators for years forgot the basics. And to recap, these are the basics:

1) Banks need enough capital to absorb possible losses;

2) They must retain sufficient cash to meet whatever requests for money they may face from depositors;

3) They should not lend more than the funds they have borrowed from reliable or dependable sources, which in normal circumstances means they should not lend much more than the deposits they take from customers;

4) If they are borrowing substantial sums from professional investors for a fixed term or maturity, they should not lend that money for longer than the relevant fixed term or maturity (to avoid the danger that they won't be able to repay those investors when the loans fall due);

5) They should avoid, where possible, becoming such complicated businesses that no human can possibly understand the risks they are running.

Our biggest banks ignored these cardinal rules in the years before the great crash. And our regulators failed to enforce these rules properly. You may be asking yourself why on earth bankers took such foolhardy risks. Well you can probably work out the answer from my discussion of what happened at Pesto Bank when it lent far more relative to its capital: in the good years, before it all went horribly wrong, throwing caution and prudence to the wind generated massive profits and dividends for shareholders and enormous bonuses for banking executives. You may recall that when Pesto Bank became more leveraged, it made far bigger profits, and was therefore able to deliver fabulous rewards to its top bankers. And when Britain's banks borrowed and lent vastly more relative to their capital resources, there was a sharp rise in their profits in relation to their capital, or what is known as return on equity. The Bank of England has estimated that this return on equity went from an average of between 5% and 10%, which is where it had been for more than forty years until the 1960s, to 12.5% in the 1980s, to 23% in the decade before the 2008 disaster. And the Bank of England's analysis shows that most of that recent increase in the return on equity, the profitability of banks, did not come from banks becoming smarter or more efficient in a sustainable way. Banks had not transformed their productivity by designing massively better current accounts or stupendously clever services of various sorts. All they had done was what Pesto Bank did in our example: they lent massively more relative to their capital. They had increased their leverage and they were taking much greater risks (although they succeeded for a while in hiding how much extra risk they were taking, by 'gaming' or exploiting those rules set by regulators, the Basel Rules on capital adequacy).

Risk and remuneration

For a good number of years, there were wonderful rewards for bank bosses from all this extra risk their organisations were taking. Here is how Andy Haldane of the Bank of England puts it:

> In 1989, the CEOs of the seven largest banks in the United States earned on average $2.8 million. That was almost 100 times the median US household income. By 2007, at the height of the boom, CEO compensation among the largest US banks had risen almost tenfold to $26 million. That was over 500 times the median US household income. Those are high returns by any measure.
>
> (Wincott Annual Memorial Lecture,
> Westminster, London, 24 October 2011)

As for Britain, let us look at the pay of two individuals who – in the 1990s and in the past decade – were probably regarded as the stars of their industry: the late Sir Brian Pitman of Lloyds and the once knighted and now de-knighted Fred Goodwin of Royal Bank of Scotland (for a period after RBS's takeover of NatWest in 2000, Goodwin was feted as the star manager of his industry, reputedly doing to RBS what Sir Terry Leahy had done to Tesco). In 1995, Sir Brian attracted a bit of media attention because his remuneration – that's salary plus a performance-related element – increased an unusually sharp 28% to £571,383. This was considered high compared to what the bosses of the UK's biggest banks had been receiving in the years from 1990, which tended to be in the range of £250,000 to £400,000 (in 1991, the boss of NatWest, Tom Frost, received between £250,000 and £295,000). Over ten years later, in 2006, Sir

Fred received just under £4m in pay. And in Sir Fred's case, that would have been a frustrating year for him: he could have earned considerably more if the bank had hit its target for growing earnings per share (profits divided by the number of shares in issue). Over at Barclays in the same year, the then Chief Executive, John Varley, earned £2.5m, whereas Bob Diamond – who succeeded Varley at the top of Barclays and at the time ran Barclays Capital, the investment banking arm of the group – made £10.7m. At both Barclays and Royal Bank, some hundreds of bankers below board level earned as much or more than either Sir Fred or Mr Varley (with the number of these highly paid bankers being greater at Barclays, because of the size of its investment bank).

The pay of the top bankers went up between ten- and twenty-fold from 1990 to 2006. By way of comparison, average gross pay for an employee in the UK went from £13,760 in 1990 to £24,134 in 2006 (equivalent to $^1/_{166}$ of what Sir Fred took home); average gross pay did not even double. In the 2007–8 tax year, financial services were responsible for 45% of all bonuses paid in the country, a total of £19bn or around 1.4% of GDP, even though the sector only accounted for 3.7% of Britain's workforce. In fact, the official data understates City rewards at the top end, because the vast majority of people classified as working in financial services – those who sit behind tills or in call centres – are not paid large bonuses. The big money is distributed to a few thousand traders, analysts, managers and sales people at the investment banks, while the biggest money went to hedge fund and private-equity superstars. At the height of the credit boom, even a relatively junior employee of an investment bank could be earning hundreds of thousands of pounds. Of course, bonuses have shrunk since the financial crisis, but the fall has been in a slow ratchet: in 2009 – the year of the global recession – they still stood at roughly the same level they had been in 2006. By 2011, according to research by the Centre for Economics and Business Research, the aggregate of bonuses paid in the City – the total bonus pool – was £4.4bn, compared with £11.6bn at the 2007 peak. Meaningful numbers of individual bankers still earn £10m each or more, and thousands earn six-figure sums.

Were the bankers worth the massive inflation in their rewards? Well, at the time, the increase in their profits seemed to justify their soaring remuneration. But we now know that these rises in profits were not only unsustainable but were being made in a highly dangerous way, as the banks lent more and more relative to their protective capital. And even though the profitability of almost all big banks has shrivelled since 2008, the rewards for those who run those banks remain very large. Last year, the package of the boss of Royal Bank of Scotland, Stephen Hester, was worth up to £7.1m, including long-term incentives – although following a public outcry in January 2012 he waived an entitlement to a bonus of just under £1m (and we will not know till 2014 how much he will actually receive from those longer-term incentives). And in 2012, Hester's total remuneration package, again including long-term incentives, had a maximum value of £8.2m. To be clear, Hester was not responsible for the disaster at RBS. He was brought in to fix it. But some have argued that his pay is outrageous given that Royal Bank of Scotland is more than 80% owned by taxpayers: RBS is in effect part of the public sector (and is viewed by the Office of National Statistics as formally part of the public sector), and rewards on that scale would be enough to pay the wages bill of two or three large schools. Meanwhile at Barclays, the 'realisable' remuneration of the then Chief Executive, Bob Diamond – that is his pay, bonuses, contribution to his pension pot and shares that have become his from past incentive schemes – was £21m in 2011 (according to the consultants Manifest and MM&K; when Diamond quit Barclays, he gave up his entitlement to most of this). That package is somewhat greater than what was ever awarded to his predecessor, John Varley, even though the profits Barclays earns on its capital have fallen sharply in the past few years and its share price is a quarter of where it was five years ago. And at the so-called universal banks, such as Barclays, Royal Bank of Scotland and HSBC, some investment bankers – both traders and senior managers – still earn many millions of pounds each, more than their ultimate bosses, the banks' chief executives. In early 2011, the Chairman of Royal Bank of Scotland, Sir Philip Hampton, conceded to me that a significant proportion of investment bankers are overpaid:

There is, if I can use the expression, a sort of gangmaster cultural phenomenon in this, that you recruit top people who really do make a difference, who really do move markets and get business and are really high achievers. But they do tend to associate themselves with people who aren't such stars, but they want them around and they trust them, sometimes they move with them and there is a team associated with it. And the disparities [in pay] between the top stars in the team and some of the journeymen players, if you like, is probably not as marked as it should be.

(*Britain's Banks: Too Big to Save?*,
BBC1, 18 January 2011)

There is another point about the rewards for executives at Barclays and at other big banks. Whether or not they are state owned – and Barclays has not been semi-nationalised like RBS and Lloyds – when mega banks get into difficulties, they are always bailed out and rescued by taxpayers, because the dangers to the British economy of letting such banks collapse are simply too great. No prime minister or Chancellor of the Exchequer would ever allow Barclays to go bust in a chaotic way, because the economy would seize up (the process of moving money around would be thrown into confusion, the flow of credit to businesses would be disrupted, households' savings would be jeopardised, and so on). And because banks receive a degree of protection from taxpayers and the state that is not available to other businesses, there is a powerful argument that bankers such as Mr Diamond should not be rewarded on the same scale as those who run businesses that can go bust. Now if a way could ever be found that would allow Barclays and its ilk to go bust and not be rescued by the state – and the Treasury is implementing reforms that go some way in this direction – then perhaps there would be no legitimate public interest in how and how much Mr Diamond is paid. But if taxpayers are at risk of picking up the tab when bank bosses mismanage their institutions, there is a question as to why they are paid on the same scale as successful entre-preneurs, who receive no protection from the state and who put their livelihoods on the line for their businesses.

In 2008 when it all went wrong for banks and for the econo-mies of Britain and America, bank bosses and traders lost some of their accumulated wealth, if it was held in bank shares. And their pay fell a bit, although not remotely in proportion to what happened to the value of their banks. Nor did they hand back the vast bonuses and rewards they had pocketed in previous years, even though we now know those bonuses came from profits generated in a way that came close to bankrupting us all. As for the allegedly sophisticated institutions that lent to banks, they weren't forced to endure write-offs of their loans to banks. That said, the share prices of banks collapsed, heaping big losses on pension funds, hedge funds, individual investors and other shareholders. But these shareholders had their losses capped at whatever price they paid for the shares. So those mainly responsible for the banking crisis suffered limited pain – in stark contrast to the impact on the rest of us. In Britain, taxpayers, the state, came to the rescue with unprecedented financial support for banks, in the form of loans, investment and guarantees, worth £1.2 trillion at the peak or 83% of the value of annual economic output. We don't yet know how much of that £1.2 trillion will be permanently lost, but it will certainly run to tens of billions of pounds. And even this massive bailout was unable to prevent pretty much every British citizen paying a further price, during an economic contraction worse even than that of the 1930s, as pay for most employees stagnated, hundreds of thousands of people lost their jobs, and many more feared for their employment. There is also the cost for all of us in the income we are still losing and will lose for many years to come as the British economy performs well below its potential.

Today our economies in the West remain in the doldrums and banks are perceived to be providing too little support to our economic rehabilitation: having lent too much before the crash, they are now criticised for lending too little. Also the banks continue to benefit from precious state help, especially taxpayers' promises to all big banks that they will never be allowed to die. What has happened to bankers' remuneration, their pay? Well it has been reformed, so that bonuses are no longer paid in single enormous lumps but are broken up into smaller amounts given in stages over several years – in the hope that if the deals that generated the bonuses go bad, some of the bonuses can be clawed back. Even so, bankers can still earn more in a year than most people earn in several lifetimes.

CHAPTER 2

WHAT HAS GLOBALISATION EVER DONE FOR US?

It was not till 4 March 2009 that I understood the power and meaning of globalisation, in spite of it having been one of those concepts that littered my journalism for years. I am not the most relaxed of flyers, so it was slightly unusual for me to look out of the aeroplane window as we circled Shenzhen Bao'an airport in Guangdong province, Southern China. What I saw below was completely outside my previous experience: mile upon mile of factories and roads, all built in just a few short years; a completely man-made industrial landscape all the way to the horizon; and, perhaps most shocking, almost nothing that seemed to be green or growing. Over a decade or so, the economy of this coastal strip had increased its output, its GDP, four-fold, and fifty-fold over thirty years. Its production, of everything from clothes to toys and electronics, filled the shelves of Wal-Mart in the US and Tesco in Britain. Guangdong made the goods that we hoovered up in the longest and strongest consumer spending binge that Britain and America have ever known. And in the process its economy grew to the size of Sweden's, generating a total income approaching $600bn a year (and today its GDP is $860bn, a little larger than that of the Netherlands). But there was a big difference between the economies of Sweden and Guangdong. Sweden had a population of about 9m and its income per head was well over $50,000. Guangdong's income was shared between 79m permanent residents and an estimated 31m migrants, or 110m in total: their annual income per head was well under $5,000, and many of Guangdong's less skilled workers were earning just a few dollars a day, or less than $1,000 a year, for toiling in airless factories from dawn to dusk and from dusk to dawn. Even so, Guangdong represented an escape from grinding poverty for countless numbers of dirt-poor peasants. Many, including the local Chinese (if they had time to muse between factory shifts and sleep), would have said that Guangdong represented the positive, transformative effects of globalisation.

My landing in Guangdong now seems a world away. The particular model of globalisation that made China rich and the West richer is creaking. In the UK, US and much of Western Europe we are learning that borrowing to buy the stuff made by China is a massive and painful bill deferred, not a bill avoided. China itself is struggling to further modernise its economy, as it faces sharp competitive pressures from other Asian economies that can manufacture even more cheaply than it can, and as it recognises that the hugely indebted West may never again be the buoyant market it once was. On my most recent visit to China, at the end of 2011, what struck me was the scale of the change in attitudes, rather than the economic change: almost every Chinese person to whom I spoke said in a matter-of-fact way that the dictatorship of the Communist party was unsustainable; though no one seemed to have an idea of how a more open and democratic society could be created or whether that could happen without hideous violence and chaos. China, arguably, has too little democracy and is too reliant on exports and investment. We in the West, arguably, are too obsessed with material wellbeing, are too desperate for jam today, and are too indebted. China and the West are embarking on a period of profound change. No one can be certain where it will end.

But before we explore the long, hard road that lies ahead, let us look at some of the good things delivered by globalisation in the boom years. It would be bonkers to say that although we're in a pickle now because of the flaws in financial aspects of globalisation – or global financial capitalism – that everything about globalisation was bad. By the end of this chapter, I hope you will see that globalisation is the name for a process that has improved the lives of more people by a greater amount than at any time in history. The faults of globalisation are big and ugly. But it has delivered some good things: a more efficient economy; faster and socially useful innovation; rapid catch up with the developed world of living standards in China, much of Asia, a good deal of South America and parts of Africa. You can think of this section as an explanation of why dumping globalisation – even if that were possible – may not be the best idea. And I am going to get my apology in early. This chapter is a bit of a jamboree bag (if you are old enough to know what that is) of only loosely connected ideas (the equivalent of the toffee, the plastic toy, and the comic all in the one exciting mystery package). We will take a first look at why globalisation and the rise of China are so inextricably linked, how the creation of a worldwide market has increased the available resources for the development of new products, and why English is the linguistic currency of a connected world.

The good in globalisation

What does 'globalisation' mean? For most of us it is the idea of the world becoming smaller: holidays in Thailand, mange tout from Kenya, the *New York Times* on-line, that sort of thing. This is the fabric of our lives; it feels mundane. Which is why it is worth remembering that much of it is relatively new, the stuff of futuristic fiction when I was growing up in the 1960s and 1970s. There are of course other people for whom globalisation is not about vast numbers of small additions to what they can buy, where they can go, their sources of knowledge and so on. For them, globalisation has been a worldwide conspiracy of Western business leaders and investors to rape the rest of the world's cheap labour and natural resources. Until recently, globalisation was the explicit target for protesters across the planet (or at least, across the richer Western parts of the planet) – and today's Occupy protests, more narrowly focussed on the role of bankers, are the inheritors of some of their angst. Remember the riots in Seattle at the 1999 meeting of the World Trade Organisation? For the protesters – many of them middle-class Westerners – globalisation was about big companies trampling on the poor and the environment. The anti-globalisation movement of the late 1990s could be summed up by the image of a child in Bangladesh working night and day to stitch together shoes that end up on the feet of overweight white middle-class children in America or Europe. It was the idea that was used in a 2008 video by the band Radiohead to support MTV's EXIT campaign for global human rights. You would have to be hard-hearted not to be moved by the contrast.

But while many in the West might agree that anti-globalisation protesters had a point, that point resonated less clearly with many of the exploited workers in developing countries.

Because, for many of the world's poorest, the exploitation of globalisation is better than what went before: better than being a bad harvest away from starvation. The United Nations calculates that average incomes worldwide, even after adjusting for the rising cost of living, have risen by 70% since 1980, reaching just over $10,000 per person in 2011. In some developing countries the growth has been spectacular. Nowhere more so than in China, where income per capita has shot up fourteen-fold to reach $7,500 in 2011 (compared with around $33,000 in the UK). The UN data is based on what is called 'purchasing power parity': the figures are adjusted to reflect differences in the cost of living, such as the fact that haircuts and bus journeys in a place like China, where wages are so low, are much cheaper than in the US and UK. In respect of living standards, China has pulled away from the other huge developing nation, India, where average incomes almost quadrupled over the same period to about $3,500. These two gigantic nations – with populations of 1.3 billion and 1.2 billion respectively – together represent well over a third of the world's population. And even with India lagging behind China, there has been an unprecedented improvement in living standards for extraordinary numbers of people in the space of a generation.

The experience of other smaller developing nations has been varied. In descending order of population, Indonesia's per-head income has risen just under three-fold to $3,700, Brazil's rose by a more modest 40% to just over $10,000, Pakistan's doubled to $2,500, Nigeria's increased just 30% to $2,000, and Bangladesh's rose two and a half times to $1,500. In Russia – following its post-Soviet economic implosion in the 1990s – per-capita income has more than recovered to a respectable $14,500, which is about 10% higher than it was in the late 1980s (for Russia, reliable data is not available as far back as 1980). Although some developing economies have performed better than others, the direction almost everywhere has been onward and upward.

As for the rich developed world, the economic performance before the 2007–8 financial crash was respectable: we became even richer. Again with 1980 as the start date, average per-head incomes have risen 49% in the European Union, 69% in the US and 84% in Japan. And the boom in developed countries from the early 1990s up until 2007 was the longest and most stable since the 1960s. Thanks largely to imports of cheaper and cheaper goods from China and similar low-cost manufacturing economies in Asia, inflation in the UK, EU and US fell from the double-digit rates of the 1970s and 1980s and stayed down. Interest rates were kept by central banks at relatively low levels. Unemployment fell, living standards rose. Businesses were confident that the good times were here to stay and invested more. The extremes of the economic cycle seemed to have been banished, and the era was labelled by economists as the 'Great Moderation'. In retrospect, it would have been better to style this period as the 'Grand Illusion' – because too much of the growth in incomes in the developed economies stemmed from consumers, businesses and governments borrowing far more than was healthy or sustainable, to finance excessive consumption. But at the time we enjoyed the party and did not worry about the morning after.

But even with incomes in the West artificially boosted, what is most striking about the last thirty years is the way in which developing countries – particularly those in East Asia, and especially China – have been catching up. Till recently, the one exception to this story of economic progress was Africa south of the Sahara Desert. In this one region, incomes have shrunk slightly over the last thirty years, to just below $2,000, according to the UN data. But even here there has been growth in the past decade or so. And the picture in Africa is not uniform: some countries – such as Ghana, Uganda and Angola – have enjoyed rapid growth in the last five years, whereas Zimbabwe, war-torn Somalia and Ivory Coast have been trapped in penury.

The star of the globalisation epic has – of course – been China. But some believe that in the next thirty years India could rival China for top billing, although it has hit something of a roadblock at the time of writing, with its economy slowing down sharply. Here is one way of seeing the magnitude of what globalisation is doing for them: the population of the European Union is 500 million people, or about a fifth of India's and China's combined population. The number of people in the US is barely over 300 million. So if the living standards of these Asian giants, and those of other developing countries, continue to converge with those of the West, and if Western populations continue to stagnate, economic power – and perhaps political power too – will shift more profoundly than at any time for a hundred years, or since the US emerged as the world's pre-eminent economic and political force. It is an open question how India and China will translate their growing economic muscle into political influence on the world stage. But it is not seriously in doubt that they will have huge muscle to exercise. The point is that by 2042, according to UN projections, the most populous part of the world by quite a margin will be the Subcontinent – that is India plus Pakistan, Bangladesh and a few others, with 2.2 billion people, or about a quarter of the world's population. And a further 2.5 billion people would be split between Asia's other two main population zones: East Asia (China plus Japan and Korea) with some 1.6 billion people, and South-East Asia (the Indochinese Peninsula plus the East Indies and Australia) with 800 million. So long as living standards in these regions continue to improve, the UK, and even the US, could look like puny economies – the seven-stone weaklings of geo-politics.

Of course, it is one thing to note that *average* incomes in developing countries are catching up with the West. That does not necessarily tell you how the very poorest are faring. But the news here is also encouraging. Three decades ago, 84% of the population of China lived on less than the equivalent of $1.25 a day (in 2005 money), according to calculations by the World Bank. By 2005, that had dropped to 16%. Or to put it another way, 900 million people – more than the population of Europe – were lifted out of what the World Bank considers extreme poverty. Even so, the World Bank estimates that China today contains 170m people still living on less than $2 a day, along with well over a million millionaires. Other Asian countries, particularly in the Far East, have seen a similar reduction in poverty. Indonesia, the world's fourth most populous country with 240 million people, has seen its extreme poverty rate fall from 63% of its population in 1984 to 19% by 2009. India saw a quarter of its population lifted above the $1.25 threshold between 1978 and 2005, although 42% still remained below that misery line. Other regions have made more limited progress. Latin America and the Middle East, both starting from much lower levels of poverty, have seen a further 5% of their people climb off the very bottom rung over the last thirty years. But in Eastern Europe severe poverty has worsened on the World Bank's measure. And in Sub-Saharan Africa about half the population is stuck in extreme poverty, a proportion that has hardly budged since 1981.

How to interpret these statistics? Well the first thing to note is that the World Bank's data is far from perfect. The data is gathered from governments, which calculate the numbers in different ways and which may choose to distort them. Also it is moot whether earning more than $1.25 represents a serious escape from deprivation – after all, it is massively less than what a beggar can gather on a typical British high street. Also it matters that the world's population has been rising. So, although the *proportion* of people worldwide below the $1.25 poverty line fell from 52% to 25% between 1981 and 2005, the drop in the total numbers of people living in destitution has been less impressive, from 1.9 billion to 1.4 billion. The battle against poverty has been taking place against very strong headwinds. In Southern Asia – which, along with Africa, has the highest population growth in the world – the number in poverty has not really budged from around 600 million. And in Sub-Saharan Africa the number has increased, from 210 million to 390 million. That we remain perhaps an age away from ending deprivation was underlined by a 2011 report from the charity Save the Children, which estimated that 2.6 million children die every year from malnutrition. Almost half the children in India lack adequate nutrition and so suffer from stunted growth. And in Nigeria the number of children with stunted growth due to malnutrition is on the rise.

That said, in the case of some individuals and even whole cities, the social and economic advances are almost beyond belief. Shanghai, with a population of well over 20 million, is today one of the most prosperous cities in the world, with widely admired schools and universities and a futuristic skyline that is perhaps the most potent symbol of globalisation. It is also home to some of the wealthiest entrepreneurs in the world, whose parents were scratching a living as dirt-poor peasant farmers. If there is a cost here it is in the comprehension gulf between toiling, grafting parents and children who have it all and want more. This is how one of China's new billionaires, Guo Guangchang – the founder and chairman of China's biggest private conglomerate, Fosun – put it to me:

> I was born in the countryside, my parents were farmers. They don't quite understand what I am doing now. They are not living an extravagant affluent life, but a normal middle-class life. I bought a house and a car for them and my sister is looking after them . . . For people in my parents' generation, they care about more normal life, enough food to eat and enough clothes to wear. But for people in the younger generation, they are more modernised, and have similar life expectations to their counterparts in America.
>
> (Interview with the author, December 2011)

On the same trip to China, I also visited a farmer who lived just a few miles outside Shanghai and was living in conditions similar to those you would have expected to see in rural Britain in the early nineteenth century: he lived in two rooms; his clothes did not look as though they had ever been washed; and there was no hot water and no lavatory. And yet even he spoke of a transformation for the better in the quality of his life. In China as a whole, life expectancy has risen to seventy-five years from sixty-three in 1970, and mortalities for under-fives has fallen from 11% to below 2%. About 81% of Chinese children go to secondary school, up from half just thirty years ago, and 94% of the population is literate.

The marketplace of the world

In China, the liberation from poverty of unprecedented numbers in the space of a generation has, to a large extent, been the product of global trade – whose resonant symbol is the corrugated-steel containers carried across the world in special container ships. Today, the largest container ships in the world can transport over 7,000 of those forty-foot metal boxes in one go. To put it in perspective, that's roughly equivalent to 100 million packets of cornflakes. It was the advent of container ships that killed off the old docks of London: the enormous deep-sea vessels were too big to navigate the Thames as far upstream as the East End. New port facilities were opened in 1970 further down the river at Tilbury to handle them. But over the years, even Tilbury proved unable to deal with the ballooning number and size of container ships wanting to dock at the UK's shores, so the coastal ports of Felixstowe and Southampton took up the slack. Tilbury's erstwhile owner, the Dubai-based port operator DP World, is now building a new mega-port even further down the Thames. But for the time being, Felixstowe – which is owned by Hong-Kong-based Hutchison Whampoa – is the UK's biggest port. In 2010 it handled the equivalent of over 1.6 million 40-foot containers. That's 21 billion boxes of cereal. But by international standards, Felixstowe is a tiddler: it is not even in the top twenty global ports by volume of handled cargo. China, of course, has the world's biggest container port, in Shanghai, and six in total of the world's ten largest ports are there. Shanghai handled nine times more freight than Felixstowe in 2010. If you want to visualise the volume of goods processed in Shanghai, it would be equivalent to almost 200 billion corn-flakes packets or around a thousand Empire State Buildings every year.

The proliferation of container ships has been caused by and has also facilitated almost uninterrupted growth in global trade since the end of the Second World War. The total volume of goods exports has increased at an average annual rate of 6% since 1950, which means that it has doubled every twelve years. But, and this may surprise you, the rate of growth has slowed over the decades: the value of goods being shipped across seas and driven across borders increased six-fold between 1960 and 1980; from 1980 to 2010 the rise was three-fold. In the recent period, most of the growth has been in manufactured goods. Just after the Second World War, fuels, minerals and agricultural products – the basic inputs of production – were around half of international trade. But since then cars, clothes, chemicals and computers – either in finished form or as components for assembly – have come to represent about 70% of goods exports. But even the rate of growth of manufacturing exports has dropped, from 10% per annum in the thirty years after the War, to around 6% since.

Which does not mean that trade has become quiet and uneventful. It has, for example, become more global, touching many more countries. A generation ago, trade was dominated by Europe, North America and Japan. Since the mid 1980s, the rest of East Asia – and particularly China – has come into its own: the share of the West plus Japan in the total trade in goods has fallen from about three-quarters to a little more than half today. Also, trade is no longer just about moving physical objects around the globe. With the help of modern telecommunications, trade in services – finance, law, software, telesales, tourism, construction expertise – has really taken off. Worldwide trade in services quadrupled between 1980 and 2010, and accounts for about 20% of total trade these days. Excluding travel and transport services – which involve moving people or objects around the planet – trade in services has increased six times. And although trade in services is an area where countries such as the UK still have a competitive edge, there is increasingly serious competition from the likes of India. No longer is any aspect of trade the preserve of the rich countries.

Note that trade has continued to grow a lot more quickly than the global economy, which implies that our lifestyles increasingly depend on imports and exports. Today, trade accounts for about 60% of the value of everything produced on the planet. That's up from about 24% in 1960. There is double-counting here: a computer circuit board, for example, is counted once when it is shipped from Japan to China, and once more when the completed computer is shipped from China to the US. But a world without trade would be a world of much poorer people. Economists at the giant US bank Citigroup forecast that the percentage of global GDP represented by trade will reach a maximum of 76% by 2030 – with much of the future increase delivered by India and (perhaps) Africa. They point out that today most trade in East Asia and Latin America is bilateral with the rich West. But that is changing. Chinese goods imports from the rest of Asia have increased from 2% to 4% of global trade in the last ten years. And China has overtaken the US to become the main trade partner of Brazil and Chile (as just two examples).

Some of the increase in trade stems from better transport and communications. But for the past sixty years the big cause has been trade liberalisation, the progressive and steady removal of tariffs and other restrictions on the movement of goods and services across borders. The virtues of free trade have been rediscovered: prior to the First World War, selling goods and services across borders was just as important a part of the world's economy as it was again to become thirty years ago. The nineteenth century was a heyday for free trade and free markets, promoted for much of the Victorian age by the world's most powerful economic bloc: Britain and its empire. But after the Wall Street Crash of 1929 and the ensuing economic crisis, governments adopted protectionist policies, in a futile and self-defeating attempt to shelter indigenous industries. The erection of barriers to trade ossified the global economy – whose dynamism was gradually restored after 1945 with the gradual dismantling of protectionism.

The journey towards more open and global trade happened piecemeal, first between the US, Europe and Japan, then more ambitiously within Europe with the creation of the Common Market. There were also attempts at the United Nations to put together genuinely global trade agreements, which culminated in 1986 with what was known as the Uruguay Round of negotiations. That was when large parts of the developing world decided to join a trading system dominated by the West and Japan. The paradigm of what could be achieved was Japan. A country devastated by war in 1945, with virtually no natural resources, Japan had grown to become the world's second biggest economy and its third biggest exporter by the 1980s, thanks above all to its access to Western markets. The Uruguay Round talks took eight years to complete, but eventually in 1994 resulted in 123 countries creating the World Trade Organisation (WTO). WTO members agreed to initiate international competition in manufactured goods, as well as in services and intellectual property (although agriculture remained heavily protected). They agreed that the WTO would police the agreement, which provided important reassurance to businesses that governments could be deterred from sneakily reintroducing trade barriers by the back door.

The thinking behind these trade agreements is that the world can produce the stuff that we need more efficiently through a single, integrated global economy, than would be the case if each individual nation had to produce everything its population needed by itself. It is the idea, still best expressed by the English nineteenth-century economist David Ricardo, that we are all enriched if countries concentrate on producing the goods and services where they have a comparative advantage. The implication is that removing barriers to trade makes all countries better off in the long term. What it does not mean is that some countries should make all the things and services where they can do so more cheaply than other countries. Ricardo's insight was that 'comparative' advantage is what matters. To take a real-world example, Korea has a comparative advantage in making consumer electronics and the UK has a comparative advantage in pharmaceuticals. So Koreans and British people are better off if they – in effect – swap TVs for medicines, rather than each trying to be self-sufficient in both. But that is true only at a particular instant. In a dynamic competitive world, there will be entrepreneurial Koreans trying to gain a global advantage for Korean-made pharmaceuticals. And what is perhaps shocking is that if Korea were to succeed, there would not be a lot of point in trying to protect Britain's pharmaceutical industry from external competition by imposing high taxes on imports. Shutting out external competition would only end up making British people poorer – it would protect some jobs at the price of forcing everyone to pay over the odds for medicines. More sensible would be to try to regain competitive advantage, by reorganising the indigenous drugs industry to make it more productive and innovative, and also to help workers and capital flow into other industries where the UK's comparative advantage may now lie.

To state the obvious, comparative advantage depends in part on a country's climate and geology. But it is much more than that. Intangibles such as the education system, the transport network, work ethic, language, the legal system and so on are also important. Think of London's financial services sector. It has specially constructed buildings, with vast open-plan trading floors. London has international transport and communications links, such as a big hub airport at Heathrow that makes it relatively easy to fly to see customers or colleagues based overseas – although the business community has increasingly been saying Heathrow is operating uncomfortably close to capacity and has put pressure on the government to review a populist decision to oppose the construction of a third runway. The UK has a reliable and robust legal system, used for writing and settling contracts all over the world. London has an enormous pool of expert bankers, lawyers, accountants and consultants – many of them not British nationals. It has an indigenous workforce that speaks the international language of business, English; who can and do fill the less well-paid administrative jobs at the big international banks. And, until comparatively recently, British governments rarely had anything but a positive word to say about the City of London and the financial services sector: Margaret Thatcher gave huge personal support for the development of Canary Wharf, the vast financial centre just down the river from the City of London; Gordon Brown slashed capital gains tax, which gave a super-boost to the take-home pay of the super-rich, superstars of hedge funds and private equity; successive Chancellors of the Exchequer, Brown and George Osborne in particular, have gone in to bat for the interests of the City when the European Union has wanted to impose new rules perceived to be damaging. Since Mrs Thatcher's Big Bang deregulation in the 1980s, the City has grown and grown to become the biggest international financial centre in the world, overtaking New York on many measures.

What the City represents is the self-reinforcing success of similar businesses that are clustered together. The success of industrial clusters of all sorts can be seen all over the world. Cities, regions, or even entire countries, often become global specialists in a particular business line. That's because it frequently makes commercial sense for companies to be grouped near their bitterest rivals. The most basic and everyday manifestation of this is when you go down to the high street and notice that a whole load of antique shops or restaurants are all next to each other. Why on earth would an antique dealer actually choose to be located next to a competitor who is trying to put them out of business? Well, it is because of the advantages for customers of knowing that if they want to buy an antique, there is only one place they need to go for a selection of what's on offer. The benefit for clients of knowing where to go for antiques in general generates incremental business from which all the antique dealers benefit. A version of that has also happened on an enormous scale in Silicon Valley, which is now *the* place to go if you are setting up an on-line or technological business and are looking for investment. And there are plenty of other huge benefits for those businesses that form the cluster. Each business has easy access to a vast pool of highly skilled people. They can reduce costs by sharing expensive necessary infrastructure, IT and transport networks, for example, and support services. And without giving away precious proprietary knowledge, they can discuss common problems and share expertise. What industry clusters like the City of London or Hollywood, the Swiss watch industry and the IT industry in Bangalore have in common is that they sell to customers in every corner of the planet; they serve a global economy. And the more connected the world becomes, the more these clusters will grow and proliferate. Strikingly, these clusters are pretty robust: once an industry is established in a particular location, it is hard to shift. For example, France's Rhone valley is home to a pharmaceutical industry in Lyon that traces its history back to the silk manufacturing industry of the sixteenth century. As the years passed, silk became dyeing, which then became chemicals, which then became pharmaceuticals, which latterly has evolved into virology. Today, Lyon hosts multinational drug companies and a cluster of leading specialist research facilities, including one of only four laboratories in the world equipped to study the most dangerous diseases such as Ebola.

The innate comparative advantage of strong clusters makes it hard for other countries to make inroads into the same industry. But it is not impossible, especially when an important new resource becomes available. Thus the textile clusters of Britain were smashed by the cheap labour that became available in China and the Far East. For more or less the same reason, Korea became the world's biggest shipbuilder in 2000, overtaking Japan, which had in turn crushed the British shipbuilding industry, a world leader until the Second World War. And latterly it is Korea's turn to be usurped by China. Together Korea, Japan and China produce 90% of the world's big ships.

The European share of this market – which includes the UK – is a paltry 2%, while the US builds almost no such vessels. The success of Asian industrial strategy shows that, in contrast to the UK's dismal experience of the 1960s and 1970s, it is possible for governments to 'pick winners' – to promote sustainable indigenous businesses – if there is a big underlying advantage to be exploited. In Asia the biggest underlying advantage has been an abundant supply of cheap, diligent labour.

Clusters are generally brilliant for host countries and terrible for those that lack them, but there is a nuance here. There are risks for any country of putting too many of its eggs into one industrial basket – because if that industry is jeopardised, so too is the prosperity of the country. Also, clusters can become over-mighty, so big and successful that they distort the economies in which they are based, and can skew economic policy-making in a way that is not healthy. For instance, there is evidence that the City outgrew its optimal size for the UK (and this is a point to which we will return). The rewards offered by the City sucked in the UK's best brains, who were not then available to manufacturers or other industries. In the boom years, it forced up the value of sterling, in a way that made life very tough for British exporters. And its international banks sucked in vast amounts of flighty, unreliable capital – which could and was withdrawn at the click of an execute command on a computer, bringing banks and the entire British economy to the brink of Armageddon in the autumn of 2008. But for the world as a whole, there are benefits from the development of optimally sized clusters – because it means that goods and services are produced cheaper and better than would otherwise be the case, and our money goes further.

Globalisation and innovation

Globalisation has also led to more innovation. When the market is the world, there is an incentive to invest more in research and development, because the rewards of finding the right product to sell to a global population are that much greater. There is also a spur to greater collaboration between research centres and companies in different countries. Think of the global health-care industry. Between 1990 and 2003, eighteen countries came together to sponsor a joint project by academics to read the entire DNA sequence of a human being – the Human Genome Project. Their success has spawned a vast research industry: businesses have invested enormous sums to commercialise this knowledge. It may not be long before we are routinely genetically decoded by our local GP. The ethical challenges here may now be as important as the practical ones: a process that originally took dozens of scientists thirteen years to complete can now be performed by a machine in a day. The cost still runs into several thousand dollars. But the price is falling, and the process is speeding up, thanks to research by companies such as Illumina. We could be informed of our genetic predisposition to suffer heart disease or a stroke, which could encourage us to take evasive action in the way we live our lives. And we could be given advance notice that we have genetic disorders and hereditary diseases, such as the brain-degenerating disorder Huntington's – although plainly there are arguments against being given too much personal knowledge of the horrors that may lie ahead for us, if there is not a great deal we can do to ward them off. That said, there will be breakthroughs. Specialist research companies and giant pharmaceutical firms continue to work on drugs that treat, or even cure, hereditary diseases. Spinal muscular atrophy – a painful and untreatable disease that causes the progressive wasting away of muscles – may now become curable thanks to drugs being developed by global companies based in Switzerland, Novartis and Roche, and by Biogen of the US.

In an integrated global economy there is more money than there has ever been to develop useful new products and services, sometimes life-saving products and services. There is, of course, a question as to whether the products and services with the greatest commercial potential are necessarily those that in other ways we would regard as most important. Some diseases may not be common enough in general, or prevalent enough in richer societies, to attract the biggest research budgets. And that is why not all decisions on research, or indeed the allocation of resources for other purposes, can be left to the market alone. But without a global market, and protection of ownership of global products with global patents, there would be less money for life-enhancing innovations – and the incentives to do the expensive research would be fewer.

Nor are the benefits of globalisation restricted to health care. The logic applies in any product or service where demand is global – from electronics to soap powder. Unilever, the multinational maker of food stuffs, detergents and personal care products, with brands such as Dove Soap, Lynx, and Sure, spends more than €900m on research and development every year and employs more than 6,000 people in research facilities in the Netherlands, the US, China, India and the UK. You may sniff at whether €900m on new deodorants, ice cream and detergents is money well spent. But jobs in the stagnating economy of Britain are supported by the propensity of many millions of people in China, Indonesia and India to spend a disproportionate amount of their growing income on personal hygiene and appearance (spending on personal care rises much faster than spending on food when incomes reach a certain level).

Open markets, closed borders

If globalisation has in large part been about greater flows of goods and services across borders, you would think the same rules would apply to people. And of course they do in terms of travel, for both business and leisure. But, popular prejudice to the contrary, globalisation has not been associated with a dramatic commensurate rise in emigration. In 2010 there were 214 million migrants throughout the world, compared with 75 million in 1965. This may sound like a significant increase, and it is in absolute terms. But as a share of the world's population, the number of migrants has risen from 2.3% to 3.1%, which is not dramatic. Although restrictions on the flow of goods, services and money have all been progressively eased since the war, the same has not applied to people. Most countries still maintain strict immigration controls – indeed, some Western countries have tightened them in recent years.

A number of leading cities have received a disproportionate share of immigrants and have become much more international – so they almost transcend their respective host nations. In the US, some 36% of New Yorkers and 40% of Angelinos were born outside the country, according to the 2010 census; a significant rise from 18% and 15% respectively in 1970. In London, the proportion is 35%, up from 5% in 1951. In Paris, it is 21%. In Amsterdam it is 50%. These figures only cover legal residents. Once you add in illegal immigrants and temporary residents, the foreign-born population in many of these urban communities could well be in the majority. Asia too has its share of multinational cities. In Singapore, for example, 27% of the five-million-strong population are non-resident foreigners and a further 10% are foreign residents. Many of the rest are Chinese and Malays who arrived in the fast-growing Chinese–Malay city-state over the last two generations. Tokyo, meanwhile, plays host to nearly half a million foreigners, a fraction of its 13 million population, but up from the 118,000 (mostly Korean) foreign residents registered in 1981. As you may have spotted, the cities attracting the big cross-border influxes are among the world's wealthiest. Which is what you would expect, because they offer the best job opportunities. And the lure of employment is a magnet over thousands of miles: in London, for example, about a quarter of immigrants come from Southern Asia, a quarter from Europe and a quarter from Africa.

But since wealthy Western countries – and, increasingly, the wealthy Asian countries as well – are so attractive to immigrant workers, their governments are becoming pickier about who they let in. Workers with the most sought-after skills and talents enjoy the greatest freedom to settle where they like. And governments tend to make it relatively easy for big multinational businesses to relocate their top people from one country to another, because they don't wish to alienate these companies and risk seeing their job-creating investments go elsewhere. In the US, the number of L visas – used by large international corporations to transfer executives and their families from abroad – increased five-fold from 1988 to reach 155,000 in 2007, before the recession hit. Meanwhile, the number of H1-B visas – used by US companies to bring in highly skilled foreign workers, particularly from India – rose three-fold from their introduction in 1991 to reach 160,000 in 2001, since which time the number issued has been held down by a cap. Some countries – Australia, New Zealand and Canada – employ a formalised points-based system for most immigration, awarding places on the basis of skills seen to be most valuable. The UK is moving in that direction too. From 1990, the US placed a 140,000 quota on the number of permanent residency rights – Green Cards – issued each year to immigrants coming to the US for employment, and has explicitly prioritised highly qualified workers. Virtually all other legal immigration to the US is limited to the families of existing citizens and residents. If you have money or economically desirable skills (or preferably both), you can more or less live where you like: for what's called high-quality human capital, there are few barriers to movement across borders. For most of the rest of the world, the barriers at borders remain in place, and are becoming harder to traverse.

Today's flows of people are reinforcing the competitive advantage of the so-called global cities such as London, New York, Dubai, Shanghai and the privileges of an elite element in the workforce. Much of the immigration of a generation ago was characterised by places such as Bradford in Britain, or Kreuzberg in Berlin, or the vast US farms that employ migrant crop-pickers: a large influx of workers would arrive – from Pakistan or Turkey or Mexico – to fill a sizeable hole in the indigenous supply of low-skilled labour. These days there is a movement of people at various speeds, depending on their qualifications and resources, across a network of large, rich cities in all the continents. These cities suck in the most talented people from diverse backgrounds, people with the expertise and knowledge to sell products and services anywhere. All of which is great for London, New York and Singapore. But their gain may well be at the expense of places that have lost much of their talent. In some Sub-Saharan

African countries, for example, the brain drain from emigration is yet another hurdle to economic development, notwithstanding the cheques regularly sent home by expat family members. Moreover, even if this pattern of migration spreads eventually to the cities of developing countries – as may be happening in East Asia – what emerges for the world may not be totally healthy. Since every country wants to attract this mobile upper class that has all the skills and money, its voice is loudest in shaping government policies in important areas, including taxation and welfare. In Britain in 2012, for example, the Chancellor George Osborne announced he would cut the top rate of income tax from 50p in the pound to 45p, even though opinion polls demonstrated that the vast majority of British people were opposed to a reduction that would benefit no more than 250,000 people on highest incomes. But Osborne made the unpopular cut because he was repeatedly warned by business leaders that their ability to recruit and retain talent was being undermined by a tax rate which was a bit more than in other comparable economies. In other words, the world's population is splitting between a small, itinerant über-class which has a growing and disproportionate share of money and political clout, and the rest of us.

Only connect

This bifurcation of citizens is one of the great trends of our age. But there are countervailing forces. Technology, for example, may be giving the opportunity to more people everywhere to acquire knowledge, make more of themselves and – perhaps – join the class of global patricians. These days even in the slums of Rio de Janeiro, for example, almost everyone has a mobile phone (although often they are shared by families and many aren't entirely legal). A decade ago, Rio's slum dwellers had no telecommunications. The take-up of mobile phones in developing countries over the last decade has been phenomenal. In China, the number of subscribers has risen from less than 5% of the population in 1999 to 73% in 2011. In India it has gone from virtually zero to 72% over the same period. Latin America has seen the biggest rise: in Brazil the proportion has hit 123% of the population, due to the number of people with more than one mobile. Even Sub-Saharan Africa, normally the laggard, has almost kept pace. In Nigeria, mobile subscribers have gone from nothing to 59% of the population in the twelve years to 2011. And the impact on these regions has been even greater than the figures may suggest. Before the advent of the mobile phone, most people did not have access to a private phone at all. Old-fashioned fixed-line telephone networks were much more expensive to build than mobile networks. In developing countries they tended to be limited to big towns and cities. Rural dwellers were cut off. Even in the cities, only the wealthy could afford to pay for a private connection.

Adding up the total number of all phones, mobile and traditional fixed-line, telecommunications ownership in the rich world rose from 93% of the population in 1999 to 155% in 2010 (or more phones than people), according to the World Bank. In the West, the mobile phone has been a great convenience; it has improved our productivity, and arguably – with the proliferation of the smartphone – it is now having a profound impact on how we engage with other people and how we undertake research. But in the developing world the mobile phone has been revolutionary. Back in 1999, when I went to China with a bunch of journalists on a trip with the then Prime Minister, Tony Blair, the erstwhile political editor of the *Sun* newspaper, Trevor Kavanagh, got himself on to the front page of his tabloid newspaper by ordering a Chinese takeaway from his local in England via his mobile while standing on one of the more touristy parts of the Great Wall of China. It may have been a cheesy and perhaps slightly patronising story, but it illustrated how small the world was becoming. When you go to China today, you take it for granted there will be a strong 3G mobile signal more or less everywhere, even in fairly remote rural areas – and phone penetration (mobile and fixed-line) has increased from 12% of the population in 1999 to about 94% in 2011. In Brazil, total access to phones has risen from 23% of people to about 145%. As for India and Sub-Saharan Africa, they hardly had fixed-line networks at all, and today mobiles are commonplace. In other words, in the space of ten years, the mobile phone has gone a long way to close the telecommunications gap between the rich and poor parts of the planet.

Mobile technology is no longer just about being able to call people. In Africa, it is about branchless banking, transferring money electronically and paying for goods and services, through the M-Pesa mobile service used by millions of people in Kenya and elsewhere – in a development that has leap-frogged much of Europe and North America. It's also about getting access to the Internet, although mobile broadband and the smartphone are only just beginning to hit the developing world. In China and in Latin America, Internet access has gone from almost nothing in 1999 to about a third of the population in 2010. In the rich world, about three-quarters of the population have the Internet. India and much of Africa have barely got off the starting blocks in respect of mobile Internet or fixed-line Internet access, because so much of their populations are still in rural areas yet to be properly networked. In India, Internet access stood at an estimated 8%

in 2010. But for relatively urbanised Nigeria, the government claimed that the Web had reached 30% of the population by 2011. The expectation in India, and throughout the developing world, is that wireless technology will have exactly the same impact on people's access to the Internet over the coming years as it has already had on their access to a voice line. Third-generation mobile broadband was only launched in India in 2011, and so far only about 3% of mobile users own smartphones. But if mobile access to the Web takes off in the most remote and poorest parts of the developing world, the cultural and educational impact could be quite extraordinary. Remember these are places often without libraries, museums or even access to reliable global news. The arrival of the mobile Internet would open up a world of information and knowledge on a scale that is difficult for us in the West to comprehend: it would be like opening a door to hundreds of years of accumulated knowledge in the space of a few short years.

What does the free flow of information around the world mean for economies? Well, it should narrow the gap between the richer and poorer regions. We can learn from each other, about how to improve crop yields, or manage cash, or lobby government for subsidies. And vital services, such as banking, saving, and health consultations, can be delivered virtually, obviating the need for the development of expensive physical infrastructures. Here in the West, one consequence is the demolition of protection against competition from abroad: call centres, administration centres and software houses can be located wherever there is an educated workforce and decent broadband connections. In this respect, India seems to be gaining more than China. India's share of the rapidly expanding global trade in services has jumped six-fold in the last fifteen years to about 3.5%. Combined with India's high levels of education, it is the proliferation of English speaking that has spurred its service sector growth.

Lingua franca

In terms of levelling the global economic playing field, the proliferation of telecommunications and the English language has been very powerful – which is one reason why India has done well. According to its 2001 census (whose details were not published until many years later), 86 million Indians said English was their second language and 39 million described it as their third language. As defined by a proper facility with the language, vastly more Indians than Chinese speak this leading international language of business (which many would see as a benign legacy of the British Raj). The country's powerful IT industry is largely clustered in one city, Bangalore. What is now the country's biggest single industrial cluster got started in the 1970s thanks to a concentration of public-sector employees with technical training. That allowed the first IT firms to set up there, poaching the workers they needed. Over time, purpose-built industrial parks with satellite and fibre-optic cable connections were established, helping Bangalore become the place to be for Indians in the IT industry: the Indian Silicon Valley.

But India may have to work harder to remain a global winner, because one of its competitive advantages, the number of its English speakers, is no longer the point of difference it was. On current global trends, by the latter half of this century virtually everyone of working age on this planet will speak English fluently. Consider Europe. In 2006, a study carried out by the European Commission found that about 43% of people from non-English speaking EU countries could already speak the language to conversational level, while 89% said they thought their children should learn the language. By 2008, 95% of upper-secondary-school children were doing exactly that, according to Eurostat, as were 82% of primary school and lower-secondary-school children. The language is even more dominant in universities; most research in Europe is published in English, as are most doctoral theses. The teaching language at many European universities is becoming English. In May 2012, one of Italy's leading universities, the Politecnico di Milano, announced that most of its courses would be taught and assessed entirely in English from 2014. 'Universities are in a more competitive world. If you want to stay with the other global universities, you have no other choice,' Professor Giovanni Azzone, the rector of the institution, told the BBC. The education world is simply responding to the demands of global commerce. When companies from different parts of the world work with each other, they do so in English. European companies with global reach – such as Siemens and Deutsche Bank of Germany, or Alcatel, Aventis and Vivendi in France – have made English their language for internal communications. Even in the European Commission, an institution originally designed by the French to advance the Europeanisation of French foreign policy, English has supplanted French as the principal working language. So complete is the Gallic capitulation that in 2011 the French government announced that children should be taught English at nurseries from the age of three.

In India, English is already one of the country's two official languages. This is partly because the country – rather like Europe – has no universally spoken language of its own. Hindi, the other official language, is only spoken by 54% of the country. English is the language of the urban elite, of business, administration and national newspapers in India. But it won't be an elite language for much longer. Just as in Europe, school children in most of India are now taught English from the age of six. In 2005, the Indian government concluded in its new national curriculum framework that, considering the popular demand to learn the language, the academic debate over whether to introduce it at such an early stage had become irrelevant.

In Africa, English is an official language in more than half the continent, used in government and administration. As in India, what had been a legacy of the British Empire has provided much needed glue in countries that have many indigenous languages and dialects. In Nigeria, which is by far the most populous country in Africa, with 160 million people – more than Russia – pidgin English is spoken by half of the country. Just as standard English is used to cross linguistic divides globally, pidgin is used for communication between the Yoruba, Igbo and others. Local variants of English are likewise used across much of Malaysia and the Philippines: the number of English-speaking Filipinos exceeds the population of Britain. In South-East Asia, alongside Chinese, English has dominated commerce for decades, due to the influence of the Anglo–Chinese trading enclaves of Singapore and Hong Kong. And its use is spreading there too: in Indonesia, a former Dutch colony with few historical connections to the UK, it has become a matter of pride for middle-class families to stump up the money to send their children to private English-language schools, where many of the teachers are drawn from neighbouring Australia.

The point is that English is the linguistic equivalent of Facebook, or Microsoft Office. If you want to reach the maximum number of people on the planet, you have to use it. For which those of us who grow up in countries where it is the first language should probably be grateful. It is the language of international business, trade, research, science, law and government. And its role is now being reinforced by the Internet. Of course, English is not the only language on the Web. Indeed, other major languages – notably Mandarin and Spanish – have claimed a growing share of what in the 1990s had been an almost exclusively English-language technology. But truly global websites are in English. Perhaps the best example of this is Facebook itself. Just over half of its 800 million user pages are in English, even though less than 30% of its users come from English-speaking countries. If you want the world to hear you, you speak in English.

Because speaking English seems to be one of the tickets out of poverty, there are imaginative schemes for obtaining this ticket. In India, the academic and entrepreneur Sugata Mitra is trying to solve the English teaching problem with what he calls a 'granny cloud'. In a pilot scheme, he assembled 200 volunteers in the UK – many of them retired schoolmistresses – to speak to children in remote parts of India for an hour a week via Skype. For most of the children, it is the only opportunity they have ever had to interact with a genuine English speaker. And in an earlier experiment, Mr Mitra put a 'computer-in-a-wall' – just like a cash point – in some Indian villages. He found that the children very rapidly taught themselves how to work the computers without any formal training. As access to mobile broadband devices and to the English language expands, more children and young people around the world should be able to acquire more of the skills they need to participate in the global economy.

This combination of a universal language, English, and on-line social networks – Facebook, Twitter and the rest – are already transforming global politics. The Arab Spring, the rebellions against autocratic governments that spread across North Africa and the Middle East, was the Twitter Revolution. Many of the protesters were young and middle class, with liberal attitudes and access to technology. Their use of social media and the Internet helped them organise their protests, circumventing official restrictions, and send video reports to the wider world about what was happening. The Internet was their window on a world of possibilities: it showed them that there were alternatives to living in fear of demagogues, that the revealed will of the people is hard to resist. These changes to the global status quo have caught most of the supposed experts of the West totally off guard. In January 2011, at the World Economic Forum in Davos, I attended a private briefing by one of the world's most distinguished security experts, organised by a powerful global investment bank. He told us all that the recent outbreaks of protests in Tunisia and Egypt would be put down relatively quickly. Within days, protests had begun to explode all over the Middle East and President Hosni Mubarak stood down after thirty years in power. In the succeeding months, the distribution of power within the region had been transformed, with regime changes in Tunisia, Egypt and Libya. And the transformation continues.

An English Internet is the warp and the weft of global commerce. You might think that because English is the native language of Britain and America, and because the Internet and social media owe so much to the enterprise and imagination of US companies (and one or two British visionaries, notably Sir Tim Berners-Lee), that we in the developed West must therefore emerge as economic winners in a world where the playing field for global business is the web in our mother tongue. But the thing about level playing fields (or in this case, what the journalist Tom Friedman would call a 'flat world') is that they expose the innate strengths and weaknesses of the players. To extend the metaphor, it is noticeable that America remains world champion in two sports, American football and baseball, that it invented and almost nobody else plays. As for the UK, we invented three sports played by vast numbers of countries – association football, rugby and cricket – and in modern times have been among the best in the world only sporadically. The painful truth about globalisation is that it has exposed the economic frailties of Britain and America – but rather than responding by becoming fitter, leaner and meaner (a strategy that seemed to work well for British cyclists and rowers at the 2012 London Olympics), we took a perform-ance-enhancing drug. We borrowed more and more, to boost domestic consumption and our lifestyles. Eventually we became dangerously addicted; poisoned. The story of the rest of this book is what went wrong with globalisation, for us, and how we can try to fix it.

CHAPTER 3

FINANCE GOES GLOBAL AND THE CASINO RULES OUR LIVES

If global trade has been the machine that has enriched much of the world, then global finance should have been the oil that lubricated the machine. But financial globalisation has been rather more than lubrication for wealth creation. As fast as trade has grown in the past thirty years, as fast as the global economy has grown, the growth of financial markets has been a huge multiple of that. As just one example, from 1977 to the crash of 2007–8, the value of foreign exchange trading, or trading in currencies, increased by 234 times, whereas the monetary value of everything the world produces every year (what is known as nominal GDP) rose just seven times (according to data from the IMF and the Bank for International Settlements). Also, as noted by Lord Turner, the Chairman of the Financial Services Authority, the value of foreign exchange trading has increased from eleven times the value of global trade in 1980 to seventy-three times in 2010.★ In other words,

---

★ Lord Turner, 'Future of Finance', LSE, 2010.

mind-boggling quantities of currencies are being traded for reasons that have almost nothing to do with the needs of most businesses and households. Financial globalisation seems to have become disconnected from what we might see as 'real business' globalisation. The amount of foreign exchange bought and sold every day in the currency markets is $4 trillion. That's about one quadrillion dollars a year, or sixteen times the value of everything produced in the world annually, world GDP, and far more than the amount of currency transactions needed to pay for all of the world's trade in goods and services, and all of the overseas expansion by companies, and all of the foreign currency loans made by banks and all of the long-term foreign currency investments made by pension funds and the like (if this is the first time you have encountered a 'quadrillion', it is – in this book's usage – a 'thousand trillion'). Why would there have to be transactions changing euros for dollars, or yen for euros and so on equivalent to seventy-three times all the trade in the world, if foreign exchange was being used primarily to support imports and exports, with a bit on top for what we need when we go on holiday? What on earth is going on?

Foreign exchange growth has been driven by an explosion of high-stakes betting on markets; it is the result of an exponential rise in financial speculation, or what the Governor of the Bank of England, Sir Mervyn King, has styled the 'casino' activities of banks and financial institutions. There are plenty of other statistics that show that financial activity has become detached from the needs of the real world – although not, as we will see in later chapters, detached from any impact on the real world and all our lives. The toxic paradox of financial globalisation is that much of the massive incremental growth in speculation and lending has benefited a small minority, but the costs of cleaning up the excesses have fallen on all of us.

Let us begin with a relatively modest instance of how the rules of *Alice in Wonderland* have been applied to global financial markets. In the mid to late 1990s, a whole new market was created, in what are called credit derivatives or credit default swaps. They are a form of insurance contract against a borrower defaulting or being unable to pay their debts. The original idea was a decent one – just like many financial innovations, it started out by responding to a legitimate need. Credit derivatives allowed an institution, such as a bank or investor, that had lent money to a company or government to be doubly certain it would get its money back. In that sense they sound like a good thing: surely it is just old-fashioned prudence to pay an annual premium to a financial firm, which was often an insurance company, to protect you from the risk that your creditors will be unable to pay you back. But here is what happened after credit derivatives were invented: the value of these contracts grew from nothing, less than twenty years ago, to more than the value of global GDP, more than $60 trillion, in 2007. Or to put it another way, the value of the insurance contracts increased to massively more than the value of the underlying loans that were insured. The same loans were insured many times over, all at the same time. How on earth could this be? How could the value of insurance be greater than the value of what was being insured? Well, what happened was that credit default swaps in the debt of specific companies or governments were often bought for pure speculation, by hedge funds – for example – that had not lent to the relevant companies or governments. In that sense, trading in credit default swaps became a sort of Wild West market. The market price of a company's credit default swap, for instance, would rise and fall in line with what happened to the company's share price. This is only natural, because if investors' confidence in a company rises and they buy its shares, that is a signal that the company is becoming stronger and therefore better able to repay what it owes. But the thing about this market in credit derivatives is that for some years it grew and grew away from the prying eyes of regulators and watchdogs. There was also a bit of fog around the market, so investors found it hard to see what their rivals were doing in it. What that meant was that any speculator who wanted to take a bet on a company's performance in a more clandestine way could do so by buying and selling credit derivatives – and you can muse about why some investors would want some kind of veil pulled around their betting, and whether that is an altogether healthy practice. Some traders have told me that it was possible to deal in this market with the benefit of insider information (which is illegal) and no regulator would ever have noticed – though naturally they add that they have no evidence to prove that ever actually happened.

Frankenstein's monsters

But there was also something else going on that led to the explosive growth of financial derivatives – which gives an important insight into how financial innovation can create not just a Frankenstein's monster but an army of such monsters. Because the thing about financial innovation is that it creates a demand for more financial innovation, to deal with the effects of the first lot of innovation (stay with me, please!), or it can create the supply of a whole new breed of financial product. Now in this case, the invention of credit derivatives also helped the development of a new form of investment, with the hideous name of 'collateralised debt obligations' or CDOs. I wish I could say of a 'collateralised debt obligation' that it 'does what it says on the tin'. But you would probably assault me on Twitter if I did that. Now rest assured that later in the book we are going to get into CDOs in more detail. The thing to know about them at this stage is that they are bonds, or tradable debts, made out of particularly risky debts. Credit derivatives were therefore very useful to the manufacturers of these CDOs, because they could attach them to some of the CDOs and then sell these bonds as though they were very safe or (in the jargon) AAA-rated. If you are already lost, just remember that a credit derivative is an insurance contract against the risk of a debt going bad. So a CDO that has been insured in this way is surely a rock-solid investment. Think of credit default swaps and collateralised debt obligations as a kind of new financial technology that allowed risky loans – especially subprime loans to poor Americans wishing to buy a home – to be reprocessed into bonds or collateralised debt obligations that were then billed as being as sound as a pound. It was technology to turn tainted meat into gourmet sausages, or ordure into gold. Credit derivatives begat collateralised debt obligations – and demand for collateralised debt obligations created incremental demand for credit derivatives.

Now the really smart investors – notably the rocket scientists at hedge funds – worked out that credit derivatives offered a way to make an absolute fortune out of the overweening exuberance of the most naïve or optimistic investors and the fecklessness of financially over-stretched banks and governments. Or to put it another way, they could get very rich by betting on the impending penury of others. They would buy credit default swaps as a pure punt that subprime loans would go bad, or that Lehman Brothers would go belly up, or that the Greek government would be unable to honour its debts, without owning any of the relevant underlying debt. For example, when Lehman Brothers filed for Chapter 11 protection under US bankruptcy laws, there was what is known as a credit event. Which meant that all those investors who had bet on its demise by taking out insurance to cover the risk of its collapse, by buying credit derivatives, made a killing. As the former fund manager David Pitt-Watson once said to me, think of it as you taking out life insurance on your neighbour, and then making out like a bandit when he or she dies. One fabulous example of the shrewdness or ruthlessness with which hedge funds exploited this market was the bet made by Paulson & Co on the CDO market going bad in 2007. Described by the reporter Gregory Zuckerman as 'the greatest trade ever', Paulson & Co is said to have earned $15bn, and its eponymous founder, John Paulson, to have personally pocketed $4bn.

Of course, none of this would matter terribly much if no one got hurt – unless you take the view, which some do, that the ability for individuals to make fortunes beyond anyone's wildest dreams unbelievably quickly is not good for the happiness and solidarity of the places where we live. But for every winner of these bets, there were losers. Huge banks and insurers – blinded by their greed – were on the wrong end of these bets, and had to be bailed out by taxpayers on an unprecedented scale, because their collapse would have hurt us all. The most conspicuous example was the US insurer AIG, nationalised by the US government in 2008 after it was forced to pay out extraordinary sums on the credit derivative insurance it had provided to others. AIG received a record $182bn of support from American taxpayers, equivalent to $600 for every US citizen. AIG was just the most extreme example of the pain inflicted on a series of financial institutions whose health is vital to the functioning of the global economy. Most, on reflection, would probably say that it is hard to criticise Paulson or other hedge funds for seeing an opportunity to exploit credit derivatives for enormous gain. But the kind of financial innovation typified by credit derivatives, and the growth of the market, has been neither beneficial nor harmless. As they say of firearms, maybe it is not the product but their use that is the problem. Because the deployment of these financial products has the potential to wreak such havoc, it is fair to ask whether the permissive attitude to them taken by regulators and governments has been a disaster.

There are three reasons to be anxious about both the astonishing growth in financial trading and the increasing complexity of the products traded. First, there can be a significant influence on the price that households and businesses pay for important goods and services that is unrelated to the proper or underlying supply and demand for those services. One example would be the way that bets on commodity and energy prices influence the price of bread and petrol. For oil, the value of transactions in futures (or bets on the future price of oil) has risen from a fifth of the world's annual production of oil in 1980 to ten times the value of that production (says the New York Mercantile Exchange or NYMEX), with much of that increase stemming from a decision by professional investors to acquire exposure to this market. That raises the question whether the price you pay to fill up your tank with petrol is being set by real demand and real supply, which is what most of us would probably say is how it should be, or by frenetic speculation by assorted investors, hedge funds, specialist commodities traders and banks on whether the oil price will rise or fall. The evidence suggests that in the long-term, real demand and real supply is still the dominant force. But speculation can have a big impact on the price in the short term. And the short term can last for days, weeks, months or even years – which means it can have an impact on what you and I pay for the essentials of life.

Second, financial innovation – even financial innovation initially motivated by the best of intentions – can frequently succeed in gulling or ripping off investors; even investors such as banks or pension funds that are supposed to be clever and capable of looking after themselves. It is very hard to escape the conclusion, for example, that a collateralised debt obligation that was manufactured out of other collateralised debt obligations that was made out of thousands of poor quality loans was simply a ruse to persuade investors to pay the price of gold for something that was in fact gold-painted lead or worse. You might not think that matters much, especially if those investors are big boys with deep pockets with no connection to you. But as it turns out, some of the investors were banks looking after your savings. And the fear that loads of these banks were going bust, partly because of such reckless investing, sparked the credit crunch and banking crisis. So perhaps we should revisit the idea that it is fine and dandy for investors to be ripped off, that *caveat emptor* should apply, so long as the investors are big, putatively sophisticated institutions. Maybe we should be worried by financial innovation that institutionalises what economists would call rent extraction.

Third, and I am not going to labour this point now because we are going to come back to it time and again, much of the financial innovation did precisely the opposite of what its proponents claimed for it. The claim for the new financial products was that they would help individual investors manage and reduce their risks. But their cumulative impact was to make the financial system as a whole much riskier. The sheer complexity of many of the new products hid the underlying risks. And the creation of one set of new products engendered a motivation for yet another round of innovation, to develop products that would hedge or insure the supposed risks of the first set of products. The result was a global financial system as mysterious, complex, turbulent and difficult to forecast with precision as the weather. And, to extend the analogy, whether or not you believe that increased CO^2 emissions have boosted the risk of catastrophic floods and storms, the evidence is inescapable that the massive increase in the lending and speculating of giant global banks made the financial system much more vulnerable to calamitous meltdown.

Bird's-eye view

Not everything about financial globalisation has been disastrous. Let us return to our view from 40,000 feet over the great oceans of finance, and look at how the currents have been building and shifting. Here are a few more of those market statistics that can induce vertigo:

- The total cumulative worldwide amount of all foreign direct investment by companies – or investment that crosses national borders in factories, shops, and assorted productive assets – stood at $19 trillion in 2010, according to the United Nations. That's equal to 30% of global GDP; almost a third of the value of everything produced on the planet in that year. It's up from 6% of GDP in 1980. What this means is that many more of the wealth-generating businesses in all our countries are ultimately owned by companies and their respective owners from foreign nations.
- The outstanding stock of cross-border loans made by

banks – or what the Bank for International Settlements calls banks' 'total foreign claims' – stood at $30 trillion at the end of 2011, equivalent to 43% of world GDP or output. That's up from 12% in 1980, and reached a peak of $36 trillion in March 2008.

- There is another $29 trillion in international bonds and other debt securities. These are loans or IOUs that can be freely bought and sold between investors around the world, much like stocks and shares. That's international debt equivalent to another 43% of GDP. In 1987 the figure was just 6%.

- Here comes the big one. The total notional amount of derivatives contracts (including those credit derivatives we have just discussed, but also lots of other bets on other products and markets) was more than $700 trillion in 2011. That's more than ten times world GDP, up from about 10% of GDP in 1987. In other words, the derivatives market has grown over a hundred times more quickly than the global economy has in the last twenty or so years. But although all our fortunes are now inextricably linked to these massive derivative markets, the high-rolling parts of the casino identified by Sir Mervyn King, even senior and influential politicians were barely aware of their existence till recently, and most would still be hard-pressed to explain them.

- Then there is the part of the financial markets that most people would associate with financial globalisation, the stock markets – such as the London Stock Exchange (which these days exists in cyberspace), the New York Stock Exchange (still operating on a famous trading floor filled with rambunctious traders), the Tokyo Stock Exchange, and so on. Here is what may surprise you:

the value of all the shares listed on all the stock markets in the world is substantial, about $50 trillion at the time of writing, or a sixth smaller than global GDP; but it is a tiny fraction of the aggregate value of all the outstanding debt and derivatives in the world.

So the first thing to notice is that the global economy is powered more by debt than by equity; by loans rather than by investments – shares – that confer ownership. As our story builds, I hope you will understand why this matters, and why it makes for a less stable economy and society. At this stage, let us look at what is underneath some of the individual numbers.

Foreign investments

First, foreign direct investment (or FDI), which is all the money committed by businesses to international ventures – be it the construction of new factories in China, the purchase of a new corporate headquarters in London, or the international mergers and acquisitions that in the boom years were never off the front page of the *Financial Times* but are now fewer and further between. Although the total amount of outstanding FDI in the world has reached almost a third of GDP, that figure adds up to many years worth of investments. The actual rate of investment has averaged 2.5% of world GDP per year over the last decade, well over double the rate of the 1980s and early 1990s. To put it another way, around one fortieth of everything that everyone earns on the planet ends up going to finance the expansion of businesses overseas.

Now you might think most of the money would go to where the returns are fastest and the need greatest – in the developing economies. But, in fact, between a half and two-thirds of the world's FDI goes to the rich industrialised nations. The UK has been a particularly large recipient, because for thirty years its right and soft-left governments have had fewer scruples than other countries about selling more or less any asset to anyone. The British attitude, for better or worse, is that everything is in the shop window. And if a foreign company wants to buy a British company or invest directly in a new manufacturing facility (for example), that is great – so long as the investor pays the going rate. In that sense, Britain is one of the world's open economies, as a matter of public policy. The idea is that foreigners bring in valuable job-creating cash and – just as important – expertise. But other developed countries, notably America and Germany, are not quite so relaxed about everything being available to sell to the highest bidder. Their governments are more concerned about handing control of all, or any, assets to overseas interests whose ambitions in the long term may not completely dovetail with those of Germany and America. For example, in 2005 China's CNOOC withdrew an $18.5bn takeover offer for a relatively modestly sized US oil company, Unocal, because of vocal opposition from Washington politicians. By contrast, in June 2012, a strategically important part of the City of London's infrastructure, the London Metal Exchange – the market which handles 80% of all futures trading on industrial metals (bets on the future price of metals) – was sold for £1.4bn to Hong Kong Exchanges and Clearing, which hosts the stock market of China's offshore financial centre. There was barely a peep of protest from British MPs at the transfer into Chinese ownership of the 135-year-old market.

All that said, a growing share of the money for foreign direct investment is flowing in what we might think of as the natural direction, downhill to where it can be most efficiently deployed.

An increasing proportion is going to developing economies, particularly the fast-growing ones in Asia. China is an important destination, receiving about 7% of all FDI over the last decade. India has also started attracting serious amounts of money since it started to make foreign companies feel more welcome in the last ten years, although it still gets less than half what mainland China does. And although different countries have varying degrees of trust or mistrust of the ambitions of the overseas investors, many would see FDI as a good thing. In the UK, for example, the British motor manufacturing industry was brought to its knees in the 1970s, wrecked by – inter alia – lousy indigenous management, truculent trade unions and lamentable government interventions. Today it is a smaller industry, but it is among the most efficient in the world – thanks, in large measure, to the comprehensive transfer of ownership to new Japanese, German and (latterly) Indian owners. In the first three months of 2012, the UK enjoyed a trade surplus in motorcars for the first time since 1976 – a quite remarkable improvement in fortunes. That said, the scale and diversity of the businesses that the UK has sold to foreigners is remarkable. Our biggest airports and leading domestic mobile phone brand are owned by Spanish interests, Ferrovial and Telefonica respectively. Our nuclear power stations are owned by EdF of France. Much of civil aviation is in the Franco–German hands of EADS. And many of the City's biggest businesses are foreign-owned. Is the UK right to be so relaxed? Does the nationality of ownership of assets not matter, in any material sense? Well, some would fear that when the economic going gets tough, companies feel more nationalistic. If a business feels under pressure to cut costs and make savings, it will tend to cut jobs in the countries furthest from its headquarters, other things being equal. It may protect jobs in the country it calls home. That is in part human nature; patriotic sentiment is a real thing. It is also realpolitik: the government and media of its home country can do it more damage than those of its overseas territories. So with the UK economy disproportionately dominated by overseas multinationals, it is arguably more susceptible to rises in unemployment and the closure of important plants, as and when there are substantial economic shocks. If UK MPs are a little more alive to the risks of selling everything to the highest bidder, it is due to the takeover of Cadbury by the giant US food and snacks conglomerate Kraft in 2010, because Kraft went back on its promise to keep open a factory employing 400 people at Somerdale in Bristol. But the important point about inward investment is that it brings in skills as well as money, and the money does not tend to be withdrawn in a panic; it is sticky.

Banks and bonds

Closer to home, there's another class of stickyish investors and providers of finance, the banks – though banks are certainly much flightier than they once were. It was once the case that banks would only lend when they knew the borrower well, and having done so they would stick with the loan and borrower through fire and rain. It doesn't quite work like that any more, as we will see as our story becomes gorier. Banks sell loans to each other and to outside investors much more freely these days. But what matters at this juncture is that banks lend much more across borders than they once did. The international loans business has steadily grown and grown over the last thirty years – partly as a corollary to the growth of FDI. For example, in 2008 a $55 billion loan had been lined up for the giant mining company BHP Billiton, to help it acquire Rio Tinto, another giant mining company. In the end the takeover did not happen. But it would have been the biggest international loan ever arranged. Both BHP and Rio are huge Anglo–Australian multinationals, with mines and smelters everywhere that minerals are to be found. And that single loan would have been equivalent to about 5% of the size of Australia's economy. No one bank could have lent it. So the plan was to break it up into lots of chunks, provided by many banks. There were seven of the world's biggest banks, from the US and Europe, appointed to put the loan together. They in turn brought in dozens of other lenders from all over the planet.

They shared out the loan in this way because banks – like most investors – practise what is known as 'portfolio theory'. This is the financial equivalent of not putting all eggs in a single basket, underpinned by some mathematical analysis. What the maths says is that it is possible to control the risk of investing for a preferred level of reward or return by dividing a pool of money between different kinds of investments. Which sounds perfectly simple to do. Except, as it turns out, finding investments whose performances are not correlated with each other is harder than you might think. Or to put it another way, you may have put each of your eggs in what looked like separate and distinct baskets, but if they are all then loaded on to the same lorry which then drives into a ditch, every egg on board will be smashed. In a way, the great banking crash of 2008 was the equivalent of the world's biggest lorry, filled with all the banks' loans and investments, careering into a trench the size of the Atlantic. Now, the most widely that any investor can spread his or her investments is across the entire planet. And this idea has turned our banks into curious and complex hybrid beasts. They borrow from all over the world. And they lend to all over the world. Sometimes, like Spain's Santander or Britain's HSBC, they will buy entire retail banks outside of their domestic market. But even when they don't do that, they have investment and wholesale operations that operate in a global marketplace. Banks lend and invest well beyond the customers in their home countries about whom they may have direct and detailed knowledge. And if you feel uneasy about that, you are right to do so: in the pursuit of maximising their mathematically optimised return on investment, banks tended to forget that having a relationship with customers counted for something. As we will explore, banks put too much trust in investment theory and mathematical models, to their and our ruin.

It is not just the banks that have been expanding their business and investments overseas. Other big institutional investors who look after large pots of money – pension funds, hedge funds, private-equity funds, insurance companies, money managers, sovereign wealth funds (the funds that manage the money of governments or royal families) and the investment managers who look after the investments of the super-wealthy – also followed the logic of portfolio optimisation, and spread their money across the planet. Unlike banks, these investors rarely make direct loans (although that too is changing). They tend to buy shares and bonds. The international bond market has multiplied in size even more rapidly than the international loans market. Whereas it took the international loans business thirty years to grow from 12% of world GDP to 30%, the international bonds market – whose origins go back to borrowing by governments and railway companies in the 1820s – has grown from 6% to 43% in just twenty-five years.

Bonds are pieces of loans that are easy to buy and sell. A

company or a government – Tesco or the Italian Republic, for example – might want to borrow $1bn for twenty years. But rather than getting the loan directly from a bank or a group of banks, it may ask a financial adviser – normally an investment banker – to cut up the loan into a million bits, each worth $1,000. Then it will sell those bits, each of them an individual bond, to investors. Now from the point of view of the purchasers of these bonds, such as a pension fund, they are a simple and efficient way of getting a steady, reliable flow of income, which is the interest rate or so-called 'coupon' paid by the borrower. One advantage of buying a bond rather than lending more directly is that if the pension fund starts to worry that Italy will struggle to repay its debts (which may sound familiar), the pension fund can sell the Italian government bonds to other investors through the market: selling a plain vanilla bank loan is much harder, although not impossible. Also the pension fund can lend as little as it likes, perhaps just $1m rather than the $250m it might have to lend if Tesco was taking out a conventional loan. Another point is that the pension fund can delegate the research on the credit-worthiness of the borrower to the leading credit-rating agencies or analysts at investment banks; it does not have to get to know the borrower, say Tesco or Italy, in a personal sense. Finally, and most importantly, the pension fund can mix the Tesco or Italian bonds with its holdings of lots of other bonds, which means that if it makes losses on its holding of Tesco or Italian bonds, the chances are these will be offset by profits on other investments.

As for the borrower, the great thing about the existence of the bond market is that it provides a huge source of money – the aggregate resources of pension funds, hedge funds, insurance companies and so on – separate from the banks. And the more money there is available at any moment to borrow, the cheaper it should be to tap into that money – so the lower the interest rate that Italy or Tesco should in theory pay. Or to put it another way, if the only source of loans was conventional loans from banks, borrowers would probably have to pay a higher interest rate. Also a big company can often borrow for a longer period when issuing a bond than would be the case with a bank loan – because pension funds and insurance companies like to buy investments that match the long-term nature of their liabilities (a pension fund will typically have to pay pensions to its savers for the thirty years they may stay alive after retiring, so it makes sense to buy bonds that will pay interest for thirty years).

The growth in the international bond market is one indicator of how rapidly financial markets have become interlinked over the last three decades. An 'international' bond is a debt whose contractual terms have been written under internationally recognised (often English) law, and then marketed to a global audience of investors. But the international markets are only half the story of the explosive growth of debt. There are also enormous domestic bond markets, which have been big for much longer. The world's largest domestic bond market is that for US Treasuries, or the bonds issued by the American government to meet virtually all of its borrowing needs. The value of all the domestic bond markets in the world was $70 trillion in 2011, or around 100% of global GDP, up from 72% of GDP in 1989 – and equivalent to more than twice the size of the international markets. So the growth of domestic bond markets is yet another proxy for how much extra borrowing there has been in recent years. It is striking that these markets are not very 'domestic' as you and I would recognise the word: more and more overseas investors have been buying these debts. Take the market for US Treasuries: 41% of US government bonds are foreign-owned these days, compared with just 15% in 1985. As for the market in UK gilts, which is the name for British government bonds and is the main source of borrowing by HM Treasury, 31% of gilts are owned by foreigners. According to the UK Debt Management Office, the agency that borrows on behalf of the British government, those overseas holdings are up from 11% when records began in 1987. America has so many foreign creditors in part because the dollar is the world's most important and most traded currency. As we'll see in the next chapter, China, Japan and various oil-producing countries have earned hundreds of billions of dollars a year from exports and have chosen to retain much of it in the form of dollar investments. Where those dollars are under the control of a government, such as China's, in official reserves, the preference has been to avoid risk – and US Treasuries have traditionally been viewed as the safest of the world's investments (though that perception may be changing), apart from gold. The US government estimates that around $3.7 trillion of its tradable debt – US Treasury bonds and bills – are owned by overseas governments: China is the biggest owner, with 13% of the entire market, followed by Japan. Or to put it another way, it is quite hard for some lenders to the American government, such as the Chinese authorities, to put their money anywhere else. If they were to repatriate the money into the Chinese currency, the renminbi or RMB, for example, the RMB would rise in value – and that would damage Chinese exports and exporters, which China has conspicuously wished not to do. But according to the International Monetary Fund, 49% of all lending to the Italian government comes from abroad. And that is pretty dangerous for Italy, more so than for the US, for two reasons: Italy's government debts, at around 120% of Italian GDP or output, are regarded as unsustainably large; and very few overseas investors have a compulsion to lend to Italy, in the way that the Chinese are compelled to lend to America.

Welcome to the casino

Now most of what I have described so far – trading in shares, bonds and commodities – are usually called cash markets, or markets where a payment is made for a financial or physical asset and delivery is immediate (or almost immediate). But connected to these cash markets are vast futures, options and other derivatives markets: the futures markets are where you can bet on the future price of a currency, or bond, or commodity; the options markets are where you can buy an 'option' to buy or sell some kind of asset at a future date and at a specified price (you have the option or right to buy or sell at the time you choose – it is not obligatory to buy and sell then); and the derivatives markets are the generic name for any kind of fancy market that in some sense 'derives' from the conventional markets (usually known as 'cash' markets). To be clear, derivatives markets include futures and options markets, but are not limited to them.

There is another important distinction in derivatives. Their markets can be centralised and systematised, operating through recognised exchanges such as the Chicago Mercantile Exchange in the US or NYSE Liffe and the London Metal Exchange in London. Or they can be what is known as over-the-counter markets, where private deals are done between banks and other financial institutions, away from a regulated exchange. The volume of outstanding deals at any time in the private over-the-counter market is a huge multiple of those on the more regulated exchanges. Now although derivatives are often denigrated as being mainly about betting and naked speculation, or about gulling innocent investors, like most financial innovations many of them were invented to fill real needs of real businesses – and some are almost as old as commerce itself. Take, for example, futures markets in grain or oil. For the farmer or the oil producer, managing the business is less risky and more predictable if some or all of the harvest due in six months or the oil to be pumped out of the ground next year can be sold today at a specified price for future delivery. If a business can be confident of the revenues it will be receiving in a few months' time, it can organise its spending in line with the money that will be coming in. For the industrial-scale baker or the power generator, there are corresponding advantages in fixing costs a few months ahead by setting the price today for those future deliveries. Few, I think, would describe that kind of management of future expenses and revenues – taking some of the risk out of the business, or what is known as 'hedging' – as wild and irresponsible gambling. The problem is that once a market of this sort has been established, it tends to attract the great global herd of professional gamblers: banks' dealing desks, hedge funds, wealthy individual speculators and so on. And even if you regard concerns about the extent to which derivatives markets are dominated these days by financial players and assorted speculators as Luddite prejudice, there is surely an issue about how these markets have, again, often done the opposite of what they were supposed to do. The markets were developed to allow businesses to manage and reduce risk. In practice, their topsy-turvy growth, the erratic and opaque distribution of ownership, and the sheer complexity of many of the individual derivative products has made it harder to identify the size and location of risks. The proliferation of derivatives in the five years before the crash of 2007–8 magnified the riskiness of the financial economy and ultimately led to an enormous bill for taxpayers.

One way of thinking of many derivative contracts, especially in the over-the-counter or OTC market, is as a private side-bet by two financial firms on the future direction of a cash market. Here is an example. Let's say a pension fund reckoned that the price of Greek government bonds was set to rise. It could have bought the bonds in Greece, in which case it would have been the genuine legal owner of Greek debt, and the Greek government would have been making interest and principal payments directly to the pension fund. But there was another way of making this investment. It could have asked one of the global investment banks – Deutsche Bank or Barclays or my own bank, Pesto Bank, for example – to make a bet. If the value of Greek bonds were to go up, Pesto Bank would pay the pension fund money; and if Greek bonds were to fall, Pesto Bank would be quids in from the pension fund. Now stop and think about what this means. If a regulator wants to know who is exposed to Greek bonds and how much they are exposed, it is not sufficient for it to count the number of bonds actually legally owned by investors. The British pension fund and Pesto Bank would have an economic exposure to the performance of Greek bonds that would not show up anywhere in official bond statistics. All of which makes it difficult to work out who makes the profits and who the losses when Greek bonds rise and fall. This should help elucidate why, in practice, regulators have found it so immensely difficult to quantify potential losses from Greece defaulting on its debts or leaving the eurozone. To be clear, our Greek bond example is a relatively simple form of derivatives deal, which by no means represents the greatest risk-management challenge for regulators or the banks themselves. Later we will encounter much more complicated mechanisms for transferring and disguising risk, whose impact on the fragility of the financial system or global economy would challenge all but a god-like intelligence.

Thanks to the data-gathering efforts of the Bank for International Settlements – the unique bank that works for national central banks – we have a view from the stratosphere of the derivatives market. And what the BIS data tells us is that it has grown at a dizzying speed since the 1980s to become the biggest generic category in all financial trading. To recap, the outstanding notional amount of all these derivative bets is ten times world GDP or more than $100,000 per person on the planet. Before you start complaining that no one asked you whether you wanted to take that $100,000 bet, the underlying risk is not quite as great: there is an enormous amount of double-counting in the data. In our example, Pesto Bank might have called a hedge fund that it knew to be pessimistic about Greek bonds, and suggested that it place the other side of the bet. In which case Pesto Bank now has two derivatives: the pension fund's bet that the bonds will go up, and the hedge fund's bet that they will go down. In the middle sits Pesto Bank, in theory taking no risk at all and scooping fees from both the pension fund and the hedge fund. Lovely jubbly, you might say; double bonuses all round! Except that there is a risk for Pesto Bank. It is called counterparty risk – or the risk that when it came to the crunch, either the pension fund or the hedge fund would not be able to honour its debts. And if the debtor in this case were not to pay up, there would be a big loss for Pesto Bank and its shareholders. Which raises an interesting question: should we view the two matching bets as a zero risk for the financial system – because the bets net out against each other – or as a double risk, because Pesto Bank is potentially exposed to the risk of non-payment by customers whether Greek bonds rise sharply or fall sharply. The BIS includes both deals in its statistics, thus enlarging the perceived size of the derivatives market, although we at Pesto Bank are tempted to argue (wrongly, probably) that the two deals actually cancel each other out.

Also the 'notional amount' of each derivative, which is what the BIS adds up in its data, is often a bigger number than the money really at risk in each individual bet. According to the BIS data, over three-quarters of the market is made up of various forms of interest rate and foreign currency swaps. An interest rate swap, for example, could be a deal where you would swap your commitment to pay variable interest rates on a loan you have taken out for a fixed rate – or you might swap your right to receive a fixed rate on your savings for variable payments linked to the official Bank of England rate. Now the notional value of the derivative would be the debt or savings underlying the deal, which could be real debt and savings or imputed debt and savings – depending on whether the swap deal you have done is sensible risk management or naked gambling. But even if you speculate wrongly on the direction of interest rates, which can be very painful – if, for example, you end up receiving a fixed rate of 3% at a time when the variable rate in the market is 6% – your savings should still be intact: you will take a hit on the interest you receive but not on the real or notional underlying savings. In other words, the whole of the notional value of the swap is not normally at grave risk of being lost. That said, losses can turn out to be even greater than the BIS data would imply when a real business (say a shop or property developer) makes a bad bet on the direction of interest rates via an interest swap. If that business' borrowing costs were to rise at a time of general economic difficulties, that business could find itself unable to repay its business creditors and could go bust – and in this instance the aggregate losses could end up being much bigger than the notional value of the swap, as connected suppliers and creditors might also go bust.

Other types of derivatives can be seen as more volatile and risky. For example, there are almost $9 trillion worth of bets on company shares and stock market indexes like the FTSE 100. That's about a fifth of the value of all the world's stock markets (including some double-counting from the point of view of net risk, since some of the bets are on share prices to rise, and some on share prices to fall). Then there's the credit derivatives market, which I mentioned at the start of this chapter. Since the crash of 2007–8, the value of this market has fallen, to 'only' $29 trillion, up from nothing in 1993, and roughly equal to the entire international bond market. Such is the creativity of bankers and hedge fund managers – or maybe such is their addiction to gambling – that it is possible to buy or sell a derivative representing a bet on almost anything. All that matters is that there is a bank or investor prepared to take the other side of the bet. More esoteric derivatives allow investors to take a punt on the weather in the Caribbean, the unemployment rate in Japan, the UK housing market, the risk of political unrest in China, the US presidential election results, inter alia. They contribute to a remarkable $43 trillion of derivatives that are described as 'unallocated' by the BIS: bets equivalent in value to 61% of global GDP are so wacky or complex or obscure that the world's central bankers cannot put them into a general category. What is more, valuing most derivatives, and not just the more obscure ones, is difficult:

there is no generally accepted price on a recognised market for many of them; instead they are valued according to complex calculations by the banks themselves, which introduces all sorts of doubts about whether this 'fair value' shown in banks' accounts is a true value. In order to work out the value, the banks that write the derivatives have to make judgements about things that are arguably impossible to know in any precise or scientific way, such as how many other companies would go bust this year if one or two big ones were to do so, or what would be the probability of the oil price going to $150 per barrel if it makes it as far as $120.

To repeat, the big thing to take away from all this is that a market designed to help minimise and manage risk has made it impossible for anyone to determine the size and location of the big risks in the global financial economy.

Speculation and the City

Now let's look at how the riskiness of all financial trading can be magnified by using what is known as leverage, which is the euphemism for trading with borrowed money. When a hedge fund or other speculator buys a derivative, he – and it is typically a he, often pumped up on testosterone – usually only has to put up a fraction of the money needed. Nearly all derivatives are designed so that the bank is in effect lending the money that the investor needs to make his bet. Of course the banks are not totally feckless. Every day they will look at the market, and if the bet is going against the speculator, then the banks will demand more cash from him to cover the loss: there will be what is known as a demand for more margin – a margin call. Betting on margin, betting with borrowed money, means speculators can put on more and bigger bets with limited resources. Which means that the winnings are bigger if all goes well, and the losses can be horrendous. Paradoxically (and we will return to this) it was the banks – which were supposed to be the equivalent of the risk-averse bookmakers – which turned out to be the most leveraged and the biggest risk takers in the turmoil of 2007–8. Many hedge funds actually managed themselves in a more prudent way.

Speculators typically make money when they are right. And if they are right, then arguably it is a good thing if they are putting on bets that help bring the market to its senses – whether that means prices have to rise or fall. So perhaps we should say 'hooray' for hedge funds. But there are two different senses to being right. An investor can be right about the underlying value of a company or market. Or the investor can be right in a less profound sense: the investor can simply make a good guess about which way prices are heading, irrespective of the fundamentals of the matter. So a pure speculator, trading on gut instinct and little else, can be right about the direction of markets and assets and wrong about the fundamental value of those markets and assets. Or to put it another way, investors who attempt in a rigorous way to assess what a business or asset is really worth – whether a company is cutting corners when generating profits, for example – are few and far between. Much more common are the investors whose approach is simply to guess whether investors in general are likely to feel bullish or bearish in the coming seconds, minutes, days and months. Which is why many would say I am being too kind to hedge funds and other speculators, because many of them trade on what is known as 'momentum'. They work out where the herd of investors is galloping and then gallop in that direction even faster. So when in the late 1990s they spotted that investors were going crazy for technology shares, they doubled up their bets that technology shares would rise, regardless of whether the growth prospects of the relevant technology companies justified the investors' confidence (and there has been a similar outbreak of mania for shares in social media companies in recent months – until the flop of Facebook's share sale sent momentum in a downward direction). Actually this humanisation of what goes on is not quite right, because vast amounts of the trading are actually carried out by machines, algorithmic computer programmes, which scour the markets for price anomalies, automatically buying and selling securities and other liquid assets to correct those anomalies, and buying and selling in great size when trends develop. This computerised 'high-frequency' trading, alongside the great mob of living and breathing momentum investors, can massively increase the volatility in markets, which is in itself pernicious, because it becomes much harder for real businesses to assess what returns they have to generate to satisfy their owners. At times, the volatility is dangerously extreme – as was the case with the Flash Crash of 6 May 2010, when the US stock market, as measured by the Dow Jones Industrial Average, plunged around 9% at 2.45 p.m., only to recover within minutes (an unexpected fall as fast and as great as that, if sustained, could have bankrupted many investors). There was another bout of wild swings in US shares on 1 August 2012, because of malfunctions in the electronic systems of a firm specialising in high-frequency automated trading, Knight Capital, which led to losses for that firm of $440m.

Momentum trading or herd investing has the damaging effect on all our wealth and prosperity of making the booms boomier and the busts even more devastating. In good years, the herd of investors becomes manically euphoric, urging the companies in which they invest to take bigger and more dangerous risks. And in periods of recession or low economic growth, they can become irrationally depressed, forcing up the cost of vital investment capital for real businesses and excessively reinforcing the instinct of wealth creators in those real businesses to be too risk-averse. In that sense, momentum investors can exacerbate the extremes of the highs and lows in markets, the highs and lows of asset prices, which in turn can have a very damaging impact on our prosperity – which the Japanese found after a crazy property boom turned to bust in the early 1990s, precipitating more than a decade of economic stagnation. We are learning the same painful lesson today with an economy suffering from chronic anaemia after the excesses in markets of the first years of the millennium.

In practice, the level of speculation in financial markets goes way beyond what's needed to correct obvious pricing mistakes. It has instead become a source of some of the market's most egregious errors. For now it is important to note that when share prices or property prices or oil prices are too high or too low, that matters to all of us. These prices are ultimately paid by everyone and affect everyone. They dictate whether and how companies choose to invest, how much governments borrow and spend, whether we as individuals feel confident about taking a mortgage to buy a house, whether the price of filling up our cars is painful, and so on.

The British dilemma

Household budgets aside, you could say that Britain and its people have something of a conflict of interest when reflecting on the extraordinary growth of financial services over the past couple of years – what the Chancellor George Osborne has styled 'the British dilemma' – because British-based firms have profited enormously from the expansion of international finance. No urban centre has ridden the rise and rise of the global financial services industry quite like London. The City of London's long history as a financial centre, the English language and a political and regulatory environment perceived as a benign and 'light touch' – which in the boom years was seen as a great merit – helped London trump Frankfurt and Paris as the financial centre for Europe. But London has also enjoyed a stroke of luck that contributed to the way it has usurped New York, the world's other leading financial locus – it is in the best time zone for global finance. The big international banks divide the world into three huge longitudinal blocs: the Americas are typically run out of New York, Asia from Singapore, Hong Kong and Tokyo, and 'EMEA' – or Europe, the Middle East and Africa – from London. But, geographically speaking, the world also has a fourth big time zone: the Pacific Ocean. Not a lot of business happens in the Pacific. Which is why the global financial markets have increasingly gravitated towards London, on the opposite side of the world, as their centre of trading operations. London's mornings overlap with Asia's afternoons, and its afternoons overlap with America's mornings. When it is afternoon in New York, however, traders are sleeping in Beijing and Hong Kong and going out for the evening in London. After lunch, trading in New York is pretty much about what is going in America – still the biggest economy in the world, so pretty important – rather than what is happening in the rest of the world.

Take the currency market. It consists of a clique of big banks that offer to buy and sell foreign exchange in tens of millions of dollars at a time, to investors, companies and governments alike. They operate twenty-four hours a day, via overlapping shifts in Asia, London and New York, and only close at weekends (and at times of crisis, which have been uncomfortably frequent in recent years, they open even then). London's trading desks accounted for 37% of the market in 2010, according to the Bank for International Settlements, well ahead of the US at 18%. Moreover, London's share has risen steadily from 26% in 1989 – and that is despite the disappearance of a dozen of the currencies on London's door-step into the euro since 1999. Also London appeared to rein-force its position as the place for trading currencies when in early 2012 the British Chancellor of the Exchequer, George Osborne, reached agreement with the Hong Kong Monetary Authority to establish the City as the main offshore centre for trading the Chinese currency, the renminbi or RMB. In one sense that represented a huge coup for the UK, because unless there is some kind of economic catastrophe in China, one day trade in the RMB may well rival trading in the US dollar – given that the Chinese economy is already the second biggest in the world and still growing fast.

What's more, it is not just the currency markets. London is the dominant player in the assorted 'over-the-counter' markets that are operated informally by the banks, instead of being organised on a national exchange like the London Stock Exchange. London has a staggering 70% share in the trading of international bonds and 47% of trading in interest-rate derivatives (that means a turnover of $1.4 trillion in London every day). The UK economy has become more and more dependent on the financial services industry. Depending on how you measure it, financial services contribute between 9% and 15% of British GDP, having roughly doubled in size since the turn of the millennium and having shrunk a bit since 2008–9. To an extent the growth of the City offset a 30% shrinkage of manufacturing in Britain as a share of GDP to 10% over the same period, to which (arguably) it contributed.

We will return in later chapters to the question of whether the City is boon or burden for Britain, but one thing is clear: the UK has been hooked on banking and financial services. In the years leading up to the crash of 2007–8, approximately a third of all UK economic growth was contributed directly or indirectly by financial services. The sector is bigger, relative to the size of the economy, than in any other large rich developed country (though of course it is bigger in specialist offshore financial centres such as Singapore and Luxembourg). It consistently contributed the largest trade surplus of any British industry (many of which were consistently in deficit). And a large proportion of taxes were paid by banks or came from the massive volume of transactions in shares and property. At the peak in 2007–8, financial services were responsible for almost 14% of all British tax receipts.

The social impact of the City has also been huge. Some regard its enrichment of thousands of people as a good thing. Others bemoan its impact on widening the gap between the super-rich and the poor, its exacerbation of inequality in Britain. The impact on the capital of the UK has been the most pronounced. Because of the fortunes earned by British-based bankers and hedge-fund managers, and a favourable tax climate, London became the home-from-home of choice for the world's super-rich. A recent survey by Citigroup's private bank of 4,000 individuals worth more than $100m each or more showed that the wealthy of Asia, Russia, Continental Europe, the Middle East and Africa all identified London as their preferred location for a second home. They wish to live next-door to their money, or where their fortunes are managed for them. And they like a town filled with restaurants and hotels whose prices are beyond what any public servant – from head teachers, to senior doctors, to politicians – can afford to pay.

As for London itself, it became a wealthier city in absolute terms and it became a faster-growing city. The main lobbying group for the British financial services industry, TheCityUK, estimates that financial services in London employed 641,000 people in 2010, 15% of all employment in the region, and contributed £70bn of what is known as gross value added (an important measure of the value of goods and services produced), a quarter of all the income generated there. Banking was by far the biggest earner, making more than £23bn of gross value added – more than twice the contribution of insurance. With the remorseless rise of the City, London became semi-detached from the UK, and much more prosperous than anywhere else: typical incomes in the South-East and the capital were around a quarter higher than in the North-East of England and Wales, for example*. London also became a much more divided city, with ghettos of the very rich and of the very poor. One illustration of this bifurcation is that one of my richer friends recently moaned to me that if he didn't move out of his Kensington home for a couple of years to allow an underground swimming pool to be constructed beneath his basement and garden, his home would be unsellable in a few years' time (or at least not sellable for the £20m or more he would expect to receive for it). Meanwhile, a few miles across town in Tower Hamlets, just to the east of where all the money is made in the City of London, there is the highest concentration in the UK of children and older people living in income deprivation, as defined by their dependence on means-tested benefits from the state.[†]

---

* 'Poverty and Inequality in the UK 2011', Institute for Fiscal Studies.
† 'English Indices of Deprivation, 2010, A London Perspective', Greater London Authority.

If Britain is the place where the plutocracy chooses to work and play, it is also the place where banks provide the finance for their global businesses. TheCityUK says 41% of all international banking conducted in Europe is done out of London. At the heart of the British dilemma about the City – whether we should love it or hate it – are the banks. British-based banks are bigger relative to the size of our economy than the banks of any other sizeable economy, with the exception of Switzerland. Their loans and investments are collectively equivalent to more than five times the size of UK GDP, and on that measure they are proportionately six times bigger than those of America. London has always been a bigger centre for international lending than New York. And after the internationalisation and expansion of UK-based banks was encouraged by Margaret Thatcher's deregulation of the City, London pulled way ahead of New York as a centre for cross-border lending. By the mid 1990s, the total volume of international loans and investments of banks located in the UK – many of them, it should be noted, foreign banks with huge operations in London, such as Deutsche Bank, JP Morgan, BNP Paribas or UBS – was more than double the international loans of all banks located anywhere in the US. London reinforced its position as the pre-eminent international lending and borrowing centre while the overall market quadrupled in size, all the way to the financial crisis of 2007–8. Our own banks also became among the biggest borrowers in these international markets – and pumped themselves up to become among the biggest in the world. Even the smaller banks, such as HBOS and Northern Rock, expanded more rapidly than at any time in their history and became increasingly dependent on raising money from the fast-growing international bond markets and from foreign banks.

Was this a great British success, proof that the UK could be a world leader and world beater in a thoroughly modern industry that provided the financial fuel for globalisation? Well it looked that way for a while. But Northern Rock, Royal Bank of Scotland and HBOS, among others, forgot one of the cardinal rules of banking, which is not to become dependent on finance that is neither steady nor reliable: living as they did at the centre of the world's fastest growing and most international financial centre, they borrowed and they borrowed from other financial institutions to fund a reckless lending binge. When suddenly the supply of money to them was switched off in the summer of 2007, and was not switched on again as the seasons rolled by, there came a terrible moment of truth for them and all of us. In the autumn of 2008, Britain's banks faced total collapse unless they were refinanced and rescued by the state – by taxpayers. The amount of money they needed came close to bankrupting Britain – and it has impoverished all of us. We have paid quite a price for our boast that we have the biggest and most international financial centre in the world.

CHAPTER 4
A SURREAL ECONOMIC SYSTEM: THE POOR LEND TO THE RICH

We were told we were living through a golden economic age. From 1986 to 2008, the output of the world (global GDP) grew at 3.6% a year on average, accelerating to 3.8% after 1994. And although there have been times when world GDP growth was faster, in the 1960s for example, this time the prosperity was more fairly shared out. It wasn't just rich Europe and the US becoming even richer – the fastest growth was in developing countries, especially in Asia. Living standards in the so-called emerging economies were rising at unprecedentedly fast rates. It was surely the end of economic history; prosperity for all was now assured.

Globalisation, technology and the creativity of bankers were apparently bringing rewards to everyone. In the UK, from 1992 to 2008, the average annual growth in GDP or economic output was 3%. There was not even a single three-month period of contraction, let alone a proper recession (which is defined as six months or two consecutive quarters of economic contraction). This was the longest period of unbroken rapid growth in the UK since at least the Second World War (or to put it another way, since reliable statistics first became available). After years of being the sick economic man of Europe, the UK was showing even the mighty German economy how to do it. Having lagged behind Germany for much of the postwar era, in productivity growth and improvements to living standards, Britain was catching up and even overtaking Germany in some respects. In these latter years, growth in the US and much of continental Europe was slower than in the three decades after the Second World War. But growth there seemed to be steadier, less volatile. And remember that by the 1990s Germany and the US were very rich countries.

Markets had triumphed over Communism. The British and American way of doing business, unfettered by meddling governments and irksome regulation, had proved itself the best of all possible wealth-creation systems. We had never had it so good; not because of luck, but because we had finally found the optimal way of running the economy, or, more properly, of 'not running it'. To a great extent, politicians and regulators were taken out of decisions about how banks and businesses do their wealth-creation thing. The brilliant bankers and entrepreneurs were liberated to do their stuff.

Markets can do it all – or almost everything – was the prevailing view, held by those right at the top of governments, powerful international organisations and banks, in the two or three years before it all went spectacularly wrong in the great crash of 2007–8. It was the religion of those on the right of the political spectrum who privatised and liberalised in the 1980s: Margaret Thatcher in the UK and Ronald Reagan in the US. And it was taken as an empirically proven truth by their centre and centre-left successors, Bill Clinton in America, and Tony Blair and Gordon Brown in Britain. In 2003, the most intellectual of this troika, Gordon Brown, gave voice to the putative historic failure of the left to recognise the vital role played by markets in a modern economy: 'the left has too often failed to admit not just that, in order to promote productivity, we need markets, but also that we should normally tackle market failure not by abolishing markets but by strengthening markets and enabling them to work better'.* Or to put it another way, the role of even a left-of-centre government was not to supplant markets but to help markets be everything they could be. It was no coincidence therefore that he and Tony Blair failed to curb the unprecedented expansion and internationalisation of British banks: they saw this as entrepreneurial ambition in the service of the nation, not the reckless pursuit of bonuses that many would later claim it to be. A policy of standing back from the City of London, in the belief that this was the way to maximise the harvest of golden eggs, was made explicit in December 2005, when Gordon Brown praised the regulator he had created, the Financial Services Authority, for its 'risk-based approach of financial regulation that is both a light touch and a limited touch'.†

As for the great referee and policeman of the global economic game, the International Monetary Fund, its public statements in the few years before it all went wrong encapsulate the woefully blinkered optimism of those whose job it is to keep governments and big banks on the economic straight and narrow. The IMF's World Economic Outlook (WEO) of April 2004 described economic conditions and prospects as 'among the rosiest' for ten years. A couple of years later, the IMF repeated that we were all living through an 'extraordinary purple patch'. As late as April 2007, just four months

---

* Gordon Brown, 'A Modern Agenda for Prosperity and Social Reform', 3 February 2003.
† Gordon Brown at the Advancing Enterprise Conference in London, 2 December 2005.

before the great markets meltdown that pitched the global economy into the worst slowdown since the 1930s, the official forecast from the IMF was that 'world growth will continue to be strong' and actually (and amazingly) said that economic risks had lessened since September 2006.

Senior IMF officials were saying in August 2007 that the outlook was 'very favourable', even though a financial earthquake – the shutting down of a raft of securities markets on which banks were dependent for raising trillions of dollars – was already underway. What's perhaps most shocking is that just days before the collapse of Lehman Brothers, when the entire financial system was in jeopardy, the message from the IMF was that 'the worst news is behind us' and that the US would avoid a serious recession. The global economy was being managed on the basis of faith-based denial. Pretty much all world leaders shared the complacency. The final statement that came out on 7 June 2007 from the G8 summit of world leaders under the German presidency nodded at a big potential source of instability in 'global imbalances' (more on this soon) but the government heads thumbed their noses at the oncoming storm:

> We note that the world economy is in good condition and economic developments are now more conducive to an adjustment than in the past, not least because we have made progress in implementing our joint strategy.
>
> (G8 Summit Declaration, 7 June 2007)

The experts paid by all of us, through the tax system, to know what's going on in the global economy and prevent crises, were clueless or hubristic about the looming challenges, even as they stood on the tracks and watched the lights of the express train of financial apocalypse drive full speed towards them (and us).

The British government was probably just as myopic about the accumulating risks as any – perhaps more so. In the relevant period, the individual with greatest personal responsibility for the stewardship of the British economy was Gordon Brown, who was Chancellor of the Exchequer from 1997 to 2007, or for most of the dangerous boom years. His tenure as Chancellor was longer than anyone for 190 years, or since Nicholas Vansittart slogged to reduce Britain's substantial national debt between 1812 and 1823 (sound familiar?) Perhaps more importantly, as my book *Brown's Britain* elucidates, he was the most powerful Chancellor of modern times. It was a point of honour for Brown that he was in charge of all financial and economic decision-making: the prime minister at the time, Tony Blair, was informed of the contents of budgets or other of Brown's important decisions, but rarely consulted about them. Gordon Brown got some big things right: reducing the public-sector deficit in his early years, handing the fight against inflation to the Bank of England and – perhaps most important of all – keeping the UK out of the euro. He also got a couple of big things seriously wrong. His apparent confidence that he had permanently flattened the extremes of the business cycle, his repeated references to policies that he thought had delivered economic stability and stifled the dreaded Mr Boom and Mr Bust, now look misplaced. Also his trust in the City was arguably too great.

That said, some of Gordon Brown's reforms have left us better-placed to cope with a malaise that can be partly laid at his door. If he hadn't in 1997 handed control over interest rates and monetary policy to an autonomous Bank of England and also transferred management of the national debt to a new agency at arm's length from the Treasury, the Debt Management Office, the UK might well by now have been boycotted by international investors. That would have led to a collapse in sterling in the foreign exchange markets, and an inability to borrow to finance the UK's huge deficit, the massive and unsustainable gap that opened in 2008–9 between what the government was spending and what it was borrowing. Or to put it another way, Mr Brown may have failed to force us or warn us to take our collective feet off the economic accelerator. He may have done nothing to curb the reckless accumulation of debt by banks and households. But he strengthened the vehicle we drive, so that we were not all killed in the subsequent crash. That said, one of Mr Brown's close colleagues told me that Brown was not especially aware of the significance of the creation of the Debt Management Office at the time it was being set up – and it is only in retrospect that we can see how sensible the DMO (after consultation with the Treasury) has been in paying higher interest rates to borrow for longer periods, resisting the temptation to become hooked on short-term cheap borrowing (one of the reasons that the Italian government has been teetering on the brink of financial crisis is that it has to persuade investors to lend it extraordinary sums every year in order to refinance the massive bulk of its debts that have relatively short maturities). Just maybe it was these structural changes on Mr Brown's watch that helped the UK dodge the indignity of following Ireland, Greece and Portugal in holding out the begging bowl to the International Monetary Fund (which was, of course, the humiliating fate of the 1976 Labour government).

That said, when Brown finally left office in 2010, serving three years as prime minister after his long stint as Chancellor, the British economy was weaker than at any time since the

1930s, and certainly weaker than when he first took office in 1997. If he is to be forgiven, it would be because the man he described in February 2005 as 'the world's greatest economist', Alan Greenspan – the long-serving former chairman of the US Federal Reserve and probably the most powerful central banker of all time – was the great promoter of the idea that the triumph of markets had massively reduced the risk of financial catastrophe. These two, Brown and Greenspan, had something of a mutual love-in. At the end of 2005, Greenspan said of Brown that he 'has achieved an exemplary record as steward of the economy of the United Kingdom and, indeed, is without peer among the world's economic policymakers' (Alan Greenspan, when accepting an honorary degree with Gordon Brown, from New York University, 14 December 2005).

Brown and Greenspan's particular blind spot was for the growing risks being taken by big banks as they lent and borrowed more and more relative to the tiny amounts of capital they possessed; capital that was supposed to absorb the losses if the loans went bad. They also failed to slow households' borrowing binges. Of all his many speeches, Gordon Brown probably today most regrets saying, at the annual Mansion House dinner on 20 June 2007, that we were witnessing 'an era that history will record as the beginning of a new golden age for the City of London'. The financial catastrophe would hit just eight weeks later.

Bipolar globalisation

That said, Gordon Brown was not totally blind to the underlying driver of so much of this crazy lending and borrowing: the deficits of some economies and surpluses of others, or what are known as 'global imbalances' – although it is inconceivable that he grasped the magnitude of what was going wrong. Had he known where it was all heading – Hades in a turbo-charged handcart – he would not have been shy in warning, in his declamatory pulpit style, that the end of the world was nigh. These 'global imbalances' underlie much of what's gone wrong. This is a dreadful, technocratic, euphemistic phrase to describe a simple but extraordinary characteristic of the way that globalisation has operated in practice. Broadly, the global economy has divided between two groups of countries: the thrifty hard-grafting, high-producing countries and the spendthrift, consumer countries. In the first category were most of the fast-growing manufacturing economies of East Asia, especially China, and also Japan and Germany. With them were the big oil-exporting countries, led by Saudi Arabia and Russia. What all these countries had in common was that collectively they produced far more than they consumed, which meant they generated vast surpluses or savings from their exports.

The UK was in the less distinguished second group, which consisted of the great consumers, or all those countries that bought – and continue to buy – vast quantities of Chinese, Japanese and German exports, and fossil fuels from the Middle East, but were not able to sell enough to the rest of the world to pay for them. This is the group of the consuming or deficit countries, which includes the UK, the US and a big chunk of the eurozone.

To give a bit more specific detail on these imbalances, in 2011 Britain bought £32bn of goods and services (mostly goods) from China, but sold a mere £9bn to China. This would not matter if we ran enormous surpluses with other countries – and, as it happens, we do sell much more to the world's biggest economy, the US, than we buy from it. In fact, our surplus with the US offsets about half of our deficit with China. But the UK also runs substantial deficits with Germany, Japan and Norway (for gas). So overall in 2010, the UK had a deficit on its current account of £37bn, and £29bn in 2011 – which was worryingly large after a weakening in the value of the pound that cut the cost of what we sell abroad and should have helped our exporters. More significantly, since 1983 the UK has not once achieved a surplus on its annual current account (although in 1997 the deficit was tiny) – which means that for almost thirty years we have not been paying our way in the world: we have bought more from the rest of the world than we sold abroad. We have been consistent net debtors. And from 1999, the average net deficit on our trade in goods and services was equivalent to 2.2% of everything we produce, our GDP. Inevitably, therefore, there was an increase in the total indebtedness of the UK (that is all categories of debt, or household debt, business debt, financial debt and public-sector debt all lumped together).

The US's deficit in goods and services trade is even bigger, in proportionate terms: 3.7% of GDP in 2011, up from 3.4% in 2010. The absolute size of the gap between US exports and imports is mind-bendingly large, $560bn last year, of which the goods deficit with China was a striking $296bn (up from $273bn in 2010). These deficits mean that the US and UK – and much of Western Europe – were borrowing from the rest of the world to finance the lifestyles of their citizens. In other words, we weren't selling enough stuff to pay for all the things we wanted to buy.

For years, that did not seem to be a problem: we could still have all those cars, and smartphones and laptops, because we could buy them all on credit. In total, the big consuming countries have collectively been running deficits of around a trillion dollars a year on average since 1998, according to data from the IMF and Bank of England. And the corollary of this is that the big producing countries were running surpluses of the same magnitude. To repeat, Germany, China, Japan and the energy exporters were lending the US, the UK and parts of Western Europe around a trillion dollars per year, equivalent to $2,000 to each of us, so that we could buy all those things we believed we deserved to have – and many of which were produced in the workshops of Germany, China and Japan.

They've done the working; we've enjoyed cosseted lifestyles. When you visit Chinese factories, you meet individuals who work twelve, fourteen or sixteen hours a day, usually for as little as a few dollars a day, and who frequently sleep in dormitories above the production line. And often they will manage to save around half of what they earn. It's all about working for a better life tomorrow, or next year or in ten years. When you ask the Chinese why they save, they say it is to accumulate enough money to return to the village where they grew up to start a business, or to pay for their children's university education, or to make provision for retirement. Much of their saving is a necessity, stemming from the absence of social provision, of a welfare state providing a proper safety net. And there is also great job insecurity. A Western businessman who makes prams in Southern China tells me he can dismiss any worker who isn't pulling his or her weight without any consultation or lengthy discussion – although he says it is getting harder to hire and fire, partly because of a growing shortage of labour. Recently I asked a young Chinese production-line worker, who sat by a conveyor belt for ten hours a day pressing fuses into circuit boards, whether she had a long-term plan to escape the tedium of her job. She said she was scrimping on all the basics to accumulate enough cash to set up her own company back in the remote rural district from which she had migrated. This story, of working all hours in menial jobs and saving everything to start a business, I've also heard from the Chinese children of peasants who twenty years ago set up companies and are now billionaires.

By contrast, in the boom years British people in aggregate saved very little, around 3% of earnings on average. Many of us saved nothing at all and went deeply into debt. Credit cards, store cards, personal loans were being thrown at us. We didn't even need a job to enjoy the trappings of the good life – the branded clothes, the electronics, made by the Chinese factory worker but which that worker could not aspire to own.

So who would you rather be, the British or American person financing an improving standard of living on credit or a Chinese worker sitting on a monotonous production line for all daylight hours? Is it surprising that we opted to borrow to support our lifestyles rather than working harder? Probably not. For each of us as individuals, it seemed rational to buy everything with debt. When the moment came to repay what we owed, we could just take out a new loan. And here's what made our unsustainable lifestyle even more seductive. Not only did the Chinese and Germans and Japanese do all the work and then lend us all that money to acquire the fruits of their labour; the money they lent us became more valuable, it bought more and more each year, because the price of the stuff they were making fell. We imported deflation from China. The Chinese became more and more productive, which meant that the stuff they sold to us became cheaper and cheaper. We got more bang for our buck, thanks to China's improving productivity, not our own. With the benefit of hindsight, this global bifurcation between producing/saving countries and consuming/borrowing countries looks bonkers. But since the Germans, Japanese and Chinese were prepared to lend us all that money so that we didn't actually have to work any harder or smarter to maintain or improve living standards, is it any wonder that we persuaded ourselves we were worth it and paid homage to the economic miracle?

There was a blindingly obvious lethal flaw in this Dali-esque version of global capitalism, where poor countries lent to rich countries to sustain the illusion that the rich countries were becoming richer – and the terrifying thing is that we were blind to it, till it was too late to do anything about it. There would inevitably come a moment when the consuming countries – which as you'll remember were borrowing collectively at an annual average rate of around a trillion dollars a year, and rather more than that in 2006–7 – would have borrowed more than they could afford to repay. There would come a moment when the creditors of the US and the UK, for example, might notice that the debts in those economies had become too large. At that moment, this bipolar form of globalisation would no longer work quite so smoothly; it would become harder and more expensive for many creditors in the rich countries to obtain the finance they need. Unfortunately, the surreal system of poor financing rich could not be dismantled and replaced overnight; it would limp along for many years, with big costs to both the debtor nations and creditor nations. To be clear, it is not that there was a chilling realisation one morning for China's ruling Politburo Standing Committee that they had taken a bit too much of a punt on America's credit-worthiness and asked for all their money back. That said (and at the risk of name-dropping) in the summer of 2011 I did ask the Chinese premier, Wen Jiabao – in a BBC interview in the old Rover factory now owned by

Shanghai Automotive Industry Corporation at Longbridge in the British Midlands – whether he recognised that in the long-term it was unsustainable for China to accumulate these vast surpluses every year. He agreed it was, but didn't offer much of a prescription for how China planned to become less of a creditor to the rich West on any specific timetable. But what did happen was that the banks and investors who collectively funnel the savings of China, Germany, Japan and the other surplus countries to the households and businesses of Britain, America, Spain, Ireland, Greece and the other great consuming nations did begin to notice from 2007 onwards that their debtors – such as poor home owners in the US or over-stretched banks in Ireland – were struggling to repay what they owed. Later, these investors became alarmed that even governments of developed economies, such as Greece, Italy and Spain, had borrowed more than they could probably afford. For me, the best way of seeing the great crash of 2007–8, the subsequent economic recession and malaise, and today's eurozone crisis, is as the historic moment of failure of our model of global financial capitalism – because it is the moment the great creditors started to ask for their money back. The great financial flows from East to West, from producer to consumer, from them to us, are globalisation's fault line – and we are now enduring the serious aftershocks of the earthquake they caused.

Creditor nations

We remember 2007–9 as a terrifying time of bank collapses and the sharpest, deepest, most widespread recession since the 1930s. These were symptoms of the underlying malaise rather than the disease itself. Far better to see the global financial and economic crisis as the very painful moment when we had to contemplate repaying our debts, and to start thinking about how we might actually earn our way in the world.

How was it that underneath the bonnet of globalisation there was such an unstable and dangerous engine? What was it that turned Germany, Japan and China into such fearsome exporters not only of goods but of money? Well, some of the explanation is cultural. In Germany, for example, where saving as a proportion of disposable income has for years been between 10% and 18%, there is an ingrained habit of long-term investment and thrift. At the end of the boom years in 2007, the savings ratio in Germany was almost 17%, which meant that a typical German was saving just over a sixth of their after-tax earnings, five times as much as a typical British person.

That German savings habit, and the country's resulting tendency to produce much more than it consumes, has some institutional causes. Low and stable inflation in the postwar era, for example, delivered by an independent central bank, the Bundesbank, made it easier for businesses to plan for the long term and reassured ordinary people that their savings would be safe. Germany's banking system is designed to collect those savings from communities and channel them into finance for family-owned businesses – the famous *Mittelstand* – which have a legendary propensity to invest for the long term. Year after year of public investment in infrastructure – not least the massive investment in the former East Germany after reunification in 1990 – helped make the German economy the most competitive in Europe. A national system of annual wage agreements between industries and their unions, with unions represented on the boards of companies, has held down pay and given German workers a huge competitive advantage over other countries within the euro.

The country was also seemingly immune to the housing bubbles that were pumped up in the US, UK, Spain and Ireland, and drove up consumer spending in those countries as home owners banked on their new wealth in overvalued houses. Due to a large stock of social housing and the strong legal rights enjoyed by tenants, Germany has one of the lowest rates of home ownership in Europe, at about 41% of households, compared with over 71% in the UK. Moreover, the few Germans who do take out mortgages typically borrow at rates that are fixed for years into the future, meaning their finances – and hence their propensity to change their spending – do not yo-yo depending on whether interest rates are going up or down. And then there are the great historical events that have a profound effect on a nation's psychology, such as the 1923 hyperinflation that preceded the Great Depression and the rise of Hitler. This shocking and traumatic history persuaded the Germans that a stable economy and steadily rising prosperity are the sine qua nons of a healthy democracy.

So thrifty hardworking Germans have built an economy in which exports of goods and services represent 45% of their country's GDP or national output compared with 29% in the UK (and 26% in France). As for Germany's current account balance, that has consistently been in surplus to the tune of 5% of its GDP since 2004. In fact, Germany has recorded a current account surplus pretty much every year since 1951. There were two episodes of substantial deficits: in 1979–81 when the oil price soared; and in the 1990s, due to the cost of unifying West and East Germany.

Germany is the world's fourth largest manufacturer and third biggest exporter. It even sells $87bn of goods to China, running a deficit with that country which – as a proportion of GDP – is 30% of the US deficit with China and 40% of

Britain's deficit with China. Another measure of Germany's export success is that its exports to China per German citizen are $1,050, compared to US exports of $330 per US citizen and just $230 for each British person. Why does Germany perform so much better than Britain and America in trade with China? Well, it makes what the Chinese need and want. Around 40% of its exports there are the machines and kit desired by China's manufacturers. In that sense, Chinese and German exporters have a symbiotic relationship. And 17% of German exports to China are luxury cars sought by the rapidly enlarging Chinese middle class. When most of the world was struggling to grow in 2010, Germany sold $12bn of motor vehicles to China, up from $1.3bn in 2005. Around a tenth of the output of German car manufacturers goes to China. When you go to Beijing and Shanghai, parts of which feel like the most prosperous places on the planet, it is quite hard not to be run down by the latest Mercedes or BMW.

As for another of the great creditor nations, Japan, its story since the Second World War has much in common with that of Germany. The other big loser from the war, Japan needed to be rebuilt. Humiliated, Japan turned to industry to help restore national pride. Occupation by the US under General MacArthur enlarged trade corridors to the West. Japan – already the most industrialised economy in the region – was the first East Asian country to discover the export-led development model that in later years would be so successfully imitated by the so-called Tiger economies, Korea, Taiwan, Singapore and Hong Kong, and more recently on a huge scale by China. The Japanese model was based on massive saving and investment – and the mutual support of businesses linked through networks or *keiretsu*.

Japan's central bank bought increasing amounts of dollars,

keeping the yen weak, which helped its exporters. The country ran huge persistent surpluses with the rest of the world. And by the 1980s there were worldwide fears, particularly acute in the US, that it was impossible for any economy to compete with Japan. The rise and rise of Japan was discussed in much the same apocalyptic way as many today discuss the growth of the Chinese economy. But the seeds of Japan's undoing were being sown. The rise in the dollar's value – partly due to Japan's currency interventions – seemed to be out of control. Between 1978 and 1985 the dollar had appreciated by about a third against the yen. As a result, the US deficit with the rest of the world had grown to about 3% of GDP – which was puny compared to the 6% deficits seen later under George W Bush, but was a big concern to the US during the economically conservative Reagan years. In 1985, the central banks of five countries – including Japan and the US – came together in Paris to announce the 'Plaza Accord', a joint agreement to bring the dollar's value down to a more sustainable level. And over the subsequent three years the dollar did exactly that, halving in value against the yen.

For Japan, this was bad news. Its export success was to an extent built on the weakness of the yen and the strength of the dollar, although the growing quality of its products, especially in cars and electronics, was also very important. In order to counter the dampening impact of a strengthening currency, Japan's central bank cut interest rates, sparking an investment boom. The problem was that after the regeneration of the previous decades, Japan already had plenty of modern factories and first-rate infrastructure. So the cheap money leaked into the property and stock markets, pumping up an asset price bubble as extreme as any seen in any country in modern times. For a while, between late 1989 and early 1990, the total value of the Japanese stock market was considerably greater than the value of the stock market of the far bigger US economy. And the prices paid for commercial property and – that particular Japanese obsession – golf clubs were so high as to be redolent of seventeenth-century tulip mania. In 1987 alone, Tokyo residential prices rose by almost 70%. It all came to a juddering halt in 1990. Property and share prices collapsed – and have never regained previous highs. As of July 2012, the Nikkei Index that shows the general market value of Japanese companies was still 77% below its 1989 peak. What did most economic damage was the fact that Japan's banks had lent far too much to property developers and businesses. As the economist Richard Koo has persuasively explained, it was the collective decision of Japanese companies with big debts to systematically repay their debts over many years that kept Japan's economy mired in recession or close to recession for two decades after the bust. Japan's economic growth rate, which had averaged about 10% in the 1960s, and 4% to 5% in the 1970s and 1980s, has dropped to a measly 0.9% in the twenty years since the great bust.

But even though British and American economists frequently cite the Japanese experience of the past twenty years as an example of extreme economic failure, a closer examination of the numbers shows that perhaps we should be so lucky to experience that kind of failure. Japan is still the world's third biggest manufacturer and a huge exporter. However, after the devastating earthquake and tsunami of 2011, which led to the shutdown of Japan's nuclear generators, the country became much more dependent on imported energy. So for more than a year its trade balance went into substantial deficit and the surplus on its current account – the broadest measure of what Japan earns from abroad – almost halved in the first six months of 2012. Also, the relative stag-nation of Japan's population means that per capita GDP growth during its supposedly dismal decades lagged only slightly behind the US, even on the official figures (annual GDP growth per capita of 1% since 1989, versus 1.4% in the US). Although the official statistics appear to show that the income of the country, per head of population, is significantly lower than in the US, this fails to adjust for the greater extremes of income in the US or the superior quality of infrastructure or publicly shared resources in Japan. The Irish journalist Eamonn Fingleton has persuasively argued that the typical Japanese citizen is at least as well off, if not better off, than the typical American. The big simple point is that for most people it's the income they actually enjoy and the quality of life they lead, rather than the aggregate GDP of the economy, which matters. And on that basis Japan does not look like such a flop.

Of course, not everything in the Japanese garden has been coming up roses. As the stagnating population becomes older, problems may arise: there will be fewer active workers paying the taxes that support the welfare and health costs of an expanding retired population, albeit a retired population with levels of personal savings well in excess of what's characteris-tic for the UK. But the Japanese experience should at the very least lead us to re-examine our basic presumption that low-aggregate GDP growth is necessarily a bad thing. What matters at least as much as the rate of increase in GDP is how that GDP is shared. And there is not a great deal of evidence that the US and UK, with their greater extremes of income, are somehow better or happier societies than places like Japan and Scandinavia where there is less of a gap between top earners and the rest. In fact, the evidence of opinion polls and surveys shows that the reverse is the case: communities with narrower gaps between rich and poor seem to be more contented communities. The Japanese experience also poses interesting questions for the liberal presumption of a place like Britain that relatively unfettered immigration and population growth benefits everyone through accelerating GDP growth. Other factors also matter, such as whether the incremental income generated by migrants stays in the country and what happens to the stability, cohesion and quality of life of communities that experience substantial influxes of people who don't want to put down roots.

Then of course there is China, the economy which transformed global trade and has been bankrolling an American economy which has been losing its competitive edge – for all that the US still boasts some of the most formidable businesses the world has ever seen. It may be a cliché but it is still true that China turned itself into the workshop of the world: exports have soared fifty-three-fold in real terms between 1980 and 2010, compared with an almost three-fold increase in exports by the rest of the world. For the past six years, China has been running an annual trade surplus with the rest of the world of between $150bn and $400bn. In 2011 it exported goods worth $1.9 trillion, equivalent to almost $1,400 of merchandise sold overseas for every man, woman and child in the country.

China's surplus with the US is huge and politically contentious (well, in the US at least). Even in 2011, when the US economy was relatively sluggish, China sold $295bn more goods to America than it bought from America. And since 2002, the US trade deficit with China has consistently been well over $100bn a year. Inevitably, China has accumulated vast stocks of American dollars, the consequence of all those overseas sales. And its dollar holdings have been magnified by the deliberate policy of the Chinese central bank, the People's Bank of China, to buy vast quantities of the American currency to hold down the value of China's renminbi and maintain the international competitiveness of Chinese goods. China and Hong Kong today have direct ownership of $2 trillion of US government bonds, other forms of US tradable debt and US shares – and, in fact, the Chinese holding could be much higher, since some of its investment in dollar assets is held in other overseas centres such as the City of London. This means the Chinese people have lent at least $2 trillion to the citizens of America, thus holding down the cost of money (the interest rate) for millions of Americans and in effect financing comparatively lavish lifestyles in a country perceived for years as an enemy.

It is always moot, when there is such a big debt, whether it is the borrower or the lender that has the upper hand. Certainly it would be very embarrassing for the US if China decided at a stroke to stop financing the US government's substantial deficit – the gap between what it spends and tax revenues. But the ensuing collapse in the value of China's US investments would also be pretty embarrassing and painful for the Chinese government. There is an uneasy balance of power between China as creditor and the US as debtor.

But why has China entered into this co-dependent financial relationship with the world's biggest economy? Well it was because China – like many East Asian countries – had decided that for all the risks of lending too much, those risks were preferable to the ones associated with borrowing too much. In a one-party state, where citizens do not have the ability to choose the government most likely to fulfil their perceived needs, it is vital to the ruling Communists that they deliver more jobs and rising earnings to the vast Chinese population.

This is thought, by the government, to require GDP growth of at least 8% a year, without massive shocks. And one important way of avoiding serious shocks is to avoid becoming dependent on credit provided from overseas.

Crisis in Asia

This was a lesson learned in 1997 and 1998, when a number of other fast-growing Asian countries ran into serious financial difficulties, because foreigners who had lent vast sums to them demanded their money back. That episode was the first warning that the religious-like faith among Western political leaders in the virtue of untrammelled global financial markets – a faith reinforced by the collapse of Communism – may have been misplaced. Initially, of course, it made great economic sense for investors from slow-growing developed economies to invest in the faster-growing developing economies of Asia. Everybody was a winner: the Western investors earned rewards greater than what was available in their own backyards; Asian businesses and governments secured more and cheaper finance than could be obtained locally. Asian economies were encouraged to open up to foreign investors, and money flowed the way that economic theory said it should: downhill, from countries with more money than opportunities, to countries with more opportunities than capital.

What followed was that Asian economies ran big deficits – averaging 6% of GDP in Malaysia and Thailand during 1990–97 – as they borrowed money from overseas. The money was supposed to help those countries buy equipment from the rest of the world to build their businesses and economies, so that eventually they would become more than capable of repaying the debts. But a lot of the borrowed money was not put to productive purposes, and went to politically well-connected but inept businessmen, or was wasted on white elephants, or was siphoned off by corrupt politicians. The investors should have known better than to expect the great flood of cash all to be invested wisely. While times were good, it was far too easy for the Asians to borrow, particularly in dollars. Foreign money flowed into Asian bank accounts and government bonds and stock markets. And too much of the credit was 'hot' money that could be pulled out quickly in a panic. These flighty dollars had only a casual short-term relationship with Asia, and lacked the roots that are put down, for example, when a multinational corporation decides to build a factory or buy up a whole company.

The rot started in the spring of 1997 when investors began to pull their money out of Thailand – and the Thai currency, the baht, was then devalued. There was then a chain reaction of speculative attacks on the currencies of Malaysia, the Philippines, Singapore, Indonesia and South Korea. The Thai baht, Korean won and Malaysian ringgit all lost half their value against the dollar in the space of a few months, while the Indonesian Rupiah dropped a massive 85%. Some countries – including Thailand, Indonesia and South Korea – were unable to repay their debts and requested emergency help from the International Monetary Fund. It was a humiliating moment for them. Foreigners incurred huge losses, on the devalued currencies or on dollar loans that couldn't be repaid.

And the damage did not stop in Asia. The contagion spread around the world. The following year it hit Russia. Just like the Asians, Russia had also borrowed a lot of money from the West, although the scale of its dependence on foreign loans did not show up in a current account deficit, because the country's oligarchs earned so much money from oil exports.

But the oligarchs moved their earnings offshore. When foreigners lost their nerve, the supply of finance was cut off and the country's opaque banking system collapsed: Boris Yeltsin's government was forced into the humiliation of halting payments on the country's domestic debts.

A year later, the crisis hit Brazil. The country had kept its currency pegged against the dollar. But unlike China and the Asian countries today, Brazil kept the value of the real too strong, not too weak. The currency peg was supposed to help the Brazilians bring down inflation: the country had suffered from bouts of hyperinflation in the late 1980s and early 1990s, with the inflation rate varying between 1,000% and 7,000%. Wages continued to rise in Brazil, and the country's economy could not compete in global trade. Brazil became a deficit country: it borrowed more and more money from the West to pay for imports the country could not afford. Strikingly, Brazil's – and later Argentina's – experience has to an extent been repeated by the Southern European countries since the euro was created in 1999. Brazil's currency peg collapsed in spectacular fashion when investors lost confidence and ran.

The West was not immune to the 1997 Asia crisis. With Russia's woes and great volatility in markets came huge losses for an enormous US hedge fund, Long-Term Capital Management (LTCM). It only had $4bn of capital to absorb the losses, so those banks and financial institutions that had lent it more than $100bn and had further exposure to it of almost a trillion dollars faced the possibility of not getting their debt repaid. There was fear of damage to banks and other creditors if LTCM was forced into a fire sale of investments and loans. For a time LTCM's crisis looked as though it would hobble Wall Street in the way that the collapse of Lehman Brothers did in 2008. So the New York Federal

Reserve organised emergency finance from a so-called 'lifeboat' of fourteen banks and large financial institutions, to allow LTCM to be wound up in an orderly way.

The 1997 crisis had lessons for everyone. It was an early warning of what happens if countries run deficits for too long, and pay for them by borrowing money from the rest of the world. It showed the risks of rigidly fixing your exchange rate for too long – something the architects of the euro would perhaps have done well to consider. And LTCM should have shown the West that the risk of financial meltdown was not unique to the developing economies.

However, the lessons appear to have been learned almost exclusively in Asia and Latin America. The country that came out of the crisis best, considering how big a financial hole it was staring into at the time, was Malaysia. Its government blocked foreigners from taking their money out of the country. And despite claims in the West that such anti-market practices would blow up in the Malaysian government's face, they worked. A dire situation was stopped from becoming even worse, and – once the panic had subsided – business recovered. And for all East Asian countries, an important lesson had been learned. They vowed that never again would they expose their livelihoods to the whim of foreign creditors; they would no longer mortgage their economies to overseas lenders. They decided that as far as possible their economies would be self-financing. They made a big push to generate surpluses from trade, in part by holding down the value of their currencies at levels that would make their exports cheap.

There was an extraordinary consequence. The global financial economy was redesigned as if by Salvador Dali. Because after the 1997 crisis, the great rivers of global capital started flowing uphill. What do I mean by that? Well, investment should gravitate to young growing economies like those of East Asia where the prospects for profits are best. But instead these economies, their central banks and their giant sovereign wealth funds – such as Singapore's Government Investment Corporation and Temasek – put their spare cash into low-yielding dollars.

The 1997–8 Asian crisis encouraged the growing, producing economies of Asia, especially China, to accumulate vast surpluses year after year, which were lent to the consuming economies of the West, keeping interest rates in those consuming economies lower than they would otherwise have been, and encouraging a borrowing binge in those economies. In other words, there is a causal link between the collapse of the Thai baht all those years ago and economic stagnation in today's Britain, as British householders struggle under the burden of debts built up in the boom years when it was so cheap and easy to borrow.

On top of the surpluses generated by the great manufacturing nations of East Asia and Germany, we must add the enormous collective surplus of the world's oil exporters. Since 2005 the oil exporters have collectively accounted for 28% of the world's current account surpluses, thanks to a soaring oil price. The seemingly unstoppable rise of Chinese demand for oil has outstripped the readily available supply, and pushed the oil price up to a level where it became economic for a country like Canada to start extracting the stuff from tar sands. In a way, the oil producers' surpluses can be thought of as a by-product of the Chinese Communist Party's policy of promoting breakneck speed economic growth.

As Germany, the great oil-producing countries of the Middle East and much of Asia started to lend more and more to the developed and rich Western economies, the debts of those consuming economies were increased by the way that banks captured all that money swirling around the world and magnified it – using techniques that we'll explore later. So before you conclude that I have taken leave of my senses, I am not arguing that banks and bankers are blameless for the mess we're in. Far from it. That said, Stephen Hester – the chief executive of Royal Bank of Scotland – has argued that banks' ill-advised inflation of their lending and borrowing was in a sense a mechanistic and automatic response to huge global flows of money. He is not completely wrong. Bankers cannot be absolved of personal responsibility for the terrible loans and investments they made. They lent and invested recklessly, and enriched themselves in the process. Which is why those who blame bankers for our predicament have a good case. That said, the bankers were not exclusively at fault.

Going for broke

Taking the actions of the banks as transmitters and amplifiers of all that debt as read, where does that leave the British economy? The UK is more indebted, in aggregate, than at any time in its history. According to the consultants McKinsey in 1987, the total debt of British households, businesses, financial institutions (including banks) and the government was equivalent to 189% of GDP, or less than twice the value of everything we produce per annum.* Back then, government debt was 48% of GDP, companies' debt was 43%, household debt was 51% and financial debt (those are loans between financial institutions and banks) was 47%. All of those debts have risen steadily since then, but really exploded in the past decade,

---

* See 'Debt and Deleveraging', McKinsey Global Institute, 1987.

increasing a staggering 197 percentage points since 2000. By the middle of 2011, the aggregate indebtedness of the UK had soared to 507% of GDP, five times the value of our annual economic output – with government debt at 81% (actually not massively high compared to similar economies), business debt at 109%, household borrowings around 100% of GDP and financial debt at a staggering 219% of GDP.

On McKinsey's figures the UK is the second most indebted big economy on earth, just a tiny bit less indebted than Japan. But the structure of UK and Japanese debt is very different – because it is Japanese government debt that is so enormous, equivalent to 226% of its GDP in the middle of 2011. And here's a paradox: if Britain's big debts are due in part to the propensity of British people to save too little, it is only because Japanese individuals save so much, and lend their savings to the government, that the Japanese government avoids going bust. As for smaller economies, Ireland is more indebted than the UK, with aggregate debts of 663% of GDP – but that's hardly reassuring given that if Ireland had not been bailed out by the eurozone and IMF, it would have defaulted. As for arguably the economy with the least sustainable debt burden on the planet right now, Greece, its aggregate debts are only 267% of GDP – a fraction of Britain's. Which only goes to show that it is not just the headline numbers for debt burdens that matter: it is whether that debt is sitting on an economy with the capacity to generate the income to pay the interest and principal.

Greece is widely seen as bust, whereas the UK has kept its badge of supreme credit-worthiness, a top AAA rating from the trio of influential rating agencies for its government debt. How so? Well, there are a number of vital structural differences between the UK and Greece. The UK has a bigger, more vibrant private sector able to generate reliable tax revenues. The UK's tax revenues are less vulnerable to economic shocks than those of many other countries (according to an analysis by the IMF, which – before you snigger – has worked hard since the crisis of 2008 to see the Western economies in a less rose-tinted way). And, as I have mentioned, the Debt Management Office has borrowed on behalf of the British government for very long periods at low fixed-interest rates, which means that the overall interest bill paid by the government will not rise rapidly, as and when interest rates in general rise. In a little noticed but important analysis by the IMF of which governments were most at risk of a financial crisis if economic growth slowed down or interest rates suddenly rose sharply, the UK emerged as the strongest of the lot: even Germany and the US were more vulnerable than Britain. Which, some would say, contradicts the coalition government's repeated claims that at the time of the 2010 general election, and before the austerity programme launched by the Chancellor George Osborne, Britain was minutes away from going bust. It is true that UK government debt was rising at a rate that almost everyone agreed was unsustainably fast, adding about 10% of GDP to the debt mountain every year. But the IMF analysis suggests there was greater leeway for a more gradual reduction in this deficit than the Tories and Lib Dems thought.

Right now, there seems little likelihood that the UK government will be boycotted by investors and will either be unable to borrow or will be forced to pay lethal and penal interest rates. The UK is neither bust nor is likely to go bust (and even if investors in general decided they didn't wish to lend to Her Majesty's Treasury, there's always the Bank of England as lender of last resort). But if the UK is not on the way to the financial knackers' yard, which is where poor Greece has arrived, and if it's not facing the kind of creditors' strike that has taken Italy and Spain to the brink of disaster, there is still a price to pay for all that debt pressing down on the UK. Interest costs for the government would probably increase if – as could well happen – it were eventually to lose its cherished AAA credit-rating.

Also, our golden age of growth from 1992 to 2008 was based to a large extent on unsustainable consumption financed by unsustainable borrowing. This was particularly true of retail spending. We became hooked on buying and borrowing. Instead of working more industriously and more cleverly to meet the challenge of China, India and the other emerging economies, instead of saving to finance consumption by households and by governments, we borrowed so that we could have all those goods and services we thought we deserved. We flunked the challenge of taking on China and India at their own game. We could have worked harder at becoming more productive. We could have invested more in the equipment and know-how that would have allowed us to sell much more overseas. We could have invested much more in developing our skills and brain power. But we didn't do enough of any of those things. Instead, we borrowed to buy the property and trinkets essential to our view of the good life.

The future's overdrawn

Whether we own up to it or not, we can't go on forever living on China's credit. What became clear in 2008 is that we will have to find a way of paying much of that debt back. That will take at least a decade and perhaps longer – given that in the round we haven't begun to pay any of it back (households have repaid some of what they owe, but government debt is still on an inexorably rising trend). And when we repay debt, we're spending less and investing less. Which means economic activity slows down, growth grinds to a halt. The recovery will take many years – perhaps as long as the fifteen years of the great boom. In the meantime, millions of British people feel poorer and are poorer, as incomes stagnate and prices rise.

How much of the 1992–2008 increase in our incomes will disappear? That is hard to say. But it is reasonable to assume that the 3% growth we enjoyed in the boom years may be as little as a third of that, or 1%, in the coming ten years. Actually right now that 1%, if we could count on it, wouldn't look so bad, after a contraction in output during the 2008–9 recession of 6.3%. And with the UK economy shrinking again at the time of writing and recovery so lacklustre, it looks as though it will be 2015 or even 2016 before our economic output is as great as it was at the last peak, during the first three months of 2008. As the economist Jonathan Portes has pointed out, that means the current depression will be considerably longer even than that of the Great Depression of 1930 to 1934 (and for those unfamiliar with economists' jargon, a depression in this case is defined as the period before the real level of GDP regains its previous high, as opposed to a recession, which is a period of at least six months during which GDP contracts).

To be clear, this is a slump that has hurt and will hurt millions of people over many years. There is a paradox that during the official recession, 2008–9, the disposable incomes of British people actually rose a bit, even though output collapsed 6.3%: as the Institute for Fiscal Studies has shown, millions of people received a sharp increase in tax credits and benefit payments, or transfers from governments. That boost to personal payments by government to individuals and families was partly an accident: benefits and tax credits were automatically increased at the onset of recession by an RPI inflation rate that happened to be high at that vital moment and then fell.

Transfers from the government protected most households' real incomes. For millions of people in work during the recession, it was a case of 'Crisis? What crisis?' They were richer, thanks to falling inflation and rising payments from the state. But of course there was a big cost: it led to a surge in the British government's deficit in 2009 to a tenth of GDP, which could not be maintained forever. So this protection of living standards could only be temporary. Cuts in public spending, including in benefits and tax credits, were almost certainly inevitable and have indeed followed.

The spending power of hugely indebted British households has been protected to an extent by the decision of the Bank of England to reduce Bank Rate to 0.5% on 5 March 2009 and to keep the official interest rate lower than it has ever been. The Bank of England has calculated that if its Bank Rate returned to normal levels, of say 5% (not high by modern standards), interest payments for British households would be crippling, on a par with what tipped the UK into a pretty bad recession twenty years ago.

Or to put it another way, what keeps the Chancellor up at night is the fear that one day the Bank of England would have to raise interest rates again. Because if it were to do so, millions of indebted families would suddenly feel a lot poorer – and the risk is they would really slash spending, tipping more shops and retail businesses into bankruptcy. But even without an interest rate rise, living standards have already come under remorseless pressure. Since 2009, there has been a big increase in energy prices and food prices, and an end to the years and years of goods made in China becoming cheaper and cheaper. VAT is up significantly. Wages have been flat or even falling. Benefits and tax credits have been squeezed by a cost-conscious Treasury. Households' living standards are massively under pressure. And that's happening as serious cuts in public spending are only now beginning to sting. Which is why British people may be experiencing the longest sustained attack on their living standards ever. The Institute for Fiscal Studies estimates that median or typical real net household income is falling 7.4% from the end of the official recession in 2009–10 to 2012–13 – which is more or less the same as the largest fall since records began in 1961. And the respected forecasters predict that in 2015–16 typical household income will still be lower than in 2002–3, which would certainly be the longest recorded period of no growth. If there were longer periods of stagnation in personal prosperity before reliable data was compiled, there can't have been many.

In other words, the official recession of 2008–9 was not when most people felt poorer. For them it was recession only in name. The bill for living for many years beyond our means arrived in 2009 and is still being paid. And what enrages many is that the financial pain is sharpest for those with little personal culpability for the mess we're in, and that the pain is arguably least for the bankers and speculators who pocketed their vast bonuses and share-trading windfalls and are more responsible for the mess we're in.

Here's what should really concern us. Although the main driver of these collapsing living standards is the necessary switch from an economy driven by debt-fuelled spending to an economy trying to find a more sustainable source of growth, we are really struggling to get our debt down. Since 2008, the UK's aggregate debt has been shuffled, not repaid.

As households and companies have become a bit more thrifty and have repaid some of their debts, government debt has risen sharply. The government kept spending to prevent recession turning into an extreme slump while tax revenues were shrinking. And when essential public services start to be financed through borrowing rather than tax, it is immensely difficult to cut the borrowing: if prices are rising, as they have been, cutting public spending can mean savagely reducing the quality and availability of vital public services.

As for perhaps the most important part of the UK's debt burden, that borne by households, the consultants McKinsey make the striking claim that the ratio of these debts to disposable income won't return to the 'pre-bubble trend for up to a decade'. McKinsey argues that the UK is still at a very early stage in reducing debts sufficiently to allow a significant rebound in economic growth (to repeat, growth tends to remain insipid or worse while households and the public sector repay what they owe – either by choice or by necessity – because they invest less and spend less). But if it is any comfort, we are not alone in struggling to repay our debts. Looking at the ten largest developed economies, McKinsey says only three of them have seen a fall in indebtedness or 'leverage' since the crash and recession of 2008. To give more of a clue as to how and when our economy will recover, McKinsey looked at the experience of two Scandinavian countries, Sweden and Finland, that experienced credit and housing booms (rather like us) in the 1980s and suffered an economic and financial bust in 1990. Both Sweden and Finland returned to fairly robust growth in a matter of a few years, on the back of specific phases of recovery. McKinsey looked at what it calls these 'markers' of recovery to assess how early or late in the rehabilitation process the UK and the US may be – and it also examined Spain, as a eurozone economy with huge corporate debts and biggish household debts. It concluded that the US was returning to health faster than the UK and Spain.

McKinsey argues that the US is furthest ahead in the deleveraging or debt-reduction process, with its ratio of aggregate debt to GDP having fallen 16 percentage points to 279% since 2008. What's most striking in the US is that a fall in private sector indebtedness has significantly exceeded an increase in government borrowing – with household debt actually falling in absolute terms, in large part because of write-offs of housing debt. Today the US economy is recovering faster than Britain's, which is good news for most Americans, even those who may have lost their homes in the financial crash. What is interesting is that the US advantage may reside, to an extent, in the way that householders peremptorily walked away from their unaffordable mortgages and handed back the keys to their respective properties or were evicted from their homes by banks – forcing the banks and other lenders to incur big losses. Banks and citizens took substantial early losses and then moved fast to restore their finances. From the outside, it may all have seemed brutal. But arguably these mortgage write-offs and home repossessions have facilitated an earlier restoration of the confidence of banks and consumers than in the more paternalistic UK and eurozone, where there is a tradition of easing the adjustment pain for households.

In the UK, banks behaved in what would be seen by many as a more socially responsible manner than US banks: they allowed many home owners with unaffordable mortgages to suspend payments for a period, or move to paying interest only, or enjoy some other relaxation of the normal lending conditions; banks exercised what's known as 'forbearance'.

Between 5% and 8% of all British mortgages are in forbearance, with the terms of the mortgages temporarily eased to help struggling borrowers, according to an analysis by the Financial Services Authority. At least one in twenty of all those with mortgages is in some financial distress, but bank and borrower have conspired to anaesthetise the distress. This manifestation of a British or even European social conscience came at a price. The problem with easing the pain for those with big housing debts in this way is that neither bank nor borrower recovers properly: banks don't fully recognise the losses they are likely to one day incur on the mortgage; home owners still have their excessive debts round their necks, even if the burden of servicing those debts has been temporarily reduced. McKinsey contrasts the 14% of British mortgages either in forbearance or explicitly delinquent with a very similar proportion in the US that have been cancelled – or 'written off' in the jargon – or are in the process of being written off.

In Britain, the pain for banks and home owners of dealing with big and unsustainable debts may simply have been stretched out and postponed, rather than eliminated. Perhaps we in the UK are now starring in a financial remake of the film *Sean of the Dead*: are we a country of zombie banks and zombie home owners? There is evidence that banks are unable to lend as much as the economy needs, because they have not yet written off all their bad loans, and households are unable to spend and invest what the economy needs, because they remain shackled and fettered by their excessive debts. The tragedy of economies stifled and suffocated by having borrowed too much, now struggling just to refinance past financial obligations, is that the costs of the malaise are greatest for the blameless young – who are deprived of job opportunities and hope. Which is why, arguably, the zombies must die; or at least be quarantined.

Many would say that it is obvious what the UK has to do in the long term to preserve and enhance prosperity, to put us in a position to genuinely earn the standard of living and public services to which we have become accustomed. We have to save more, invest more, work harder, work smarter and close that deficit on our trade in goods and services; we have to end our addiction to borrowing from the great producing economies. But transforming our economy into a scrimping, grafting, making and trading economy will be the labour of many years – a heroic project that will demand financial sacrifices by the vast majority of us. That begs two important questions. What can be done to protect the poorest and most vulnerable in the long period of transition? And are there any initiatives – conventional or radical – that could speed or ease the reconstruction of our economy?

Holding back the recovery are the unwillingness and incapacity of consumers and government to spend as they once did, and the inability of banks to lend what businesses and the economy need. We should probably cheer that banks are not lending as recklessly and intemperately as they were. But it is not cause for celebration that a lending feast has been followed by famine. Fixing finance – mending the banking system – is probably the single most important thing we need to do to rehabilitate our economy.

CHAPTER 5

DID I BREAK THE ROCK – AND DOES THE BANK OF ENGLAND HAVE A LONG LEASE ON THE PRECIOUS PROPERTY CALLED THE MORAL HIGH GROUND?

One of the strangest periods of my journalistic career ran from the summer of 2007 to the beginning of 2009, when I was routinely accused of trying to bring the British economy to its knees. In the autumn of 2008, the Chief Executive of the British Bankers Association, Angela Knight, wrote to MPs, saying of my disclosures on the BBC about the banking crisis that 'the market turbulence caused is extraordinarily substantial and has been particularly damaging both for the institutions involved, for the sector, its customers and now the UK economy.' She implied, in a letter to the Chairman of the House of Commons Culture, Media and Sport Select Committee, John Whittingdale, that I should be made to shut up:

It occurred to me that as the BBC is a publicly funded broadcaster that your Committee may have a view on its role and responsibility should information of this type be passed to it – it is after all not essential to broadcast in advance of an announcement, information which is price sensitive and has the effect of damaging or even preventing sensible action being taken.

(Letter from Angela Knight to
John Whittingdale MP, October 2008)

Her view appeared to be that even though I knew that HBOS was in such dire straits that it needed to be bought by Lloyds, and that Royal Bank of Scotland was on the verge of collapse and needed to be bailed out by taxpayers, this was not information that needed to be communicated to the BBC's viewers, listeners and readers. At the same time, the former Tory leader, Michael Howard, wrote to the Financial Services Authority asking the City watchdog to investigate where the leaks to me were coming from. And Greg Hands, a Tory MP who is now a government whip, wrote to the chairman of the Serious Fraud Office, Richard Alderman, asking the SFO to investigate 'allegations of fraudulent behaviour' at the heart of government, in relation to disclosures made to me about how ministers were dealing with the banking crisis.

It was all a bit odd. To my mind, it showed quite how shocked we all were by the spectacle of the financial foundations of the British economy crumbling before our eyes. In practice, it was not difficult to deal with this kind of pressure. Few would argue that it was not in the public interest (in the proper sense) for the BBC to broadcast and publish stories about the parlous condition of the banks on which we all rely.

It was much harder for me a year earlier, when I faced widespread and sustained criticism that in some way I was 'talking down' the UK's economic prospects. That was a charge levelled at me after I disclosed that Northern Rock had requested an emergency rescue loan, 'Emergency Liquidity Assistance', from the Bank of England, 'the lender of last resort', when many accused me of having caused a run on the bank. Actually there were two charges: first, that the collapse of Northern Rock was my fault; second, that in some sense it was my public duty not to report bad financial and economic news, and that I was wrong to claim that the crisis afflicting financial markets which began in August 2007 would have a negative impact on all our prosperity.

If those critics had made a different point – namely that journalists in general had failed to shine a bright enough light in the preceding few years on the great bubble in lending and property – that, I think, would have been harder to answer. In my own case, I did write and broadcast in 2006 and early 2007 that there were dangerous speculative excesses in markets, but I certainly didn't shout loudly enough. I wince when I recall a meeting I had some time at the end of 2006 with the then head of the BBC's Newsroom in which I said, in a blasé way, that there was going to be a great bust one of these days because of the ludicrous way the banks were throwing cheap money at risky borrowers, whether it was private-equity purchasers of companies or indigent US citizens buying their first homes. 'So when would the great bust come?' I was asked. 'Goodness only knows,' I said. And because we could not put a time on it, there was no urgency to get it on the *Ten O'Clock News*. That was a mistake.

More broadly, the media was too infected with the popular enthusiasm for borrowing as much as you could to buy a house. Property sections in newspapers and series on television about creating your dream home helped to reinforce the idea that only the insane would fail to mortgage themselves to the hilt to buy a property. In newspapers, where I worked for many years, vast amounts of the advertising was connected to the property industry, placed by mortgage lenders, estate agents, financial advisers and so on. The property supplements weren't really proper journalism: they were quite close to what we called 'advertorial', cheerleading for all those businesses that profited from the house-buying frenzy. And the personal finance pages gave us comfort that bingeing on debt and property was almost a public duty. Our homes became more than our homes: they were our personal pension funds. So the media did not exactly put a dampener on the trebling of house prices and the 50% rise in personal indebtedness (relative to GDP) in the decade before the crash. The best that can be said for the media's failure to play a sceptical watchdog role during the bubble years is that those whose primary paid responsibility was to prevent financial and economic instability – the Financial Services Authority, the Bank of England and the Treasury – were arguably even more hopelessly inadequate.

If I had been uncomfortable and sceptical when the party was getting out of control, on an oppressively hot summer day, 9 August 2007, I became a loud, truculent killjoy. I was on leave, and was sitting in a cafe in central London. In the compulsive way that so annoys my family, I was going through emails on my BlackBerry, when I came across an intriguing one from the giant French bank, BNP Paribas. This is what it said:

BNP Paribas Investment Partners temporaly (sic) suspends the calculation of the Net Asset Value of the following funds:

Parvest Dynamic ABS, BNP Paribas ABS EURIBOR and BNP Paribas ABS EONIA.

Truth be told, I had never heard of Parvest Dynamic or the other funds, so was nonplussed. It was the bit that followed that was momentous (or at least it was for me):

> The complete evaporation of liquidity in certain market segments of the US securitisation market has made it impossible to value certain assets fairly regardless of their quality or credit-rating. The situation is such that it is no longer possible to value fairly the underlying US ABS assets in the three above-mentioned funds. We are therefore unable to calculate a reliable net asset value ('NAV') for the funds.
>
> In order to protect the interests and ensure the equal treatment of our investors, during these exceptional times, BNP Paribas Investment Partners has decided to temporarily suspend the calculation of the net asset value as well as subscriptions/redemptions, in strict compliance with regulations, for the following funds: Parvest Dynamic ABS effective 7 August 2007, 3 p.m. (Luxembourg time); BNP Paribas ABS Euribor and BNP Paribas ABS Eonia effective 7 August 2007, 1 p.m. (Paris time).

Odd as it may seem, this was a life-changing moment. The best explanation why is given in the column I wrote at that moment on my BlackBerry, in that cafe, for my BBC blog, Peston's Picks. Here is that column:

> I am a long way from a properly functioning computer screen. But thanks to the miracle of mobile telephony, I

have been able to read BNP Paribas's explanation for prohibiting investors from cashing in more than a billion pounds of funds linked to the US subprime market. BNP's statement is scary, to put it mildly. The giant French bank says that it cannot value the assets in these funds due to the 'complete evaporation of liquidity in certain market segments of the US securitization market.'

The terrifying bit is not BNP's citing of the disappearance of two-way trade in bonds and derivatives linked to poor quality US home loans, or what it calls the 'evaporation of liquidity'. That's just a statement of the obvious – bad news we've known about for some weeks. No. What gives the game away is that BNP, the pride of France and one of Europe's biggest banks, doesn't dare take the long view and offer to buy these illiquid investments from investors who want to sell.

In theory, BNP should be able to ascribe an economic value to the assets in the funds, independent of their market price. And as a well-capitalised bank, it ought to be able to buy these assets at this fair value from investors and hold them to maturity or until normal conditions return to credit markets. So why won't BNP do this? Could it be that it fears that the assets in the fund are toxic garbage that defy rational valuation?

Is there reason to believe that many of the securities manufactured out of subprime loans are worse than ordure? I'm afraid so. Here are just three reasons:

1) As the *FT* pointed out this morning, many of the underlying subprime loans were taken out by fraudsters who lied about their incomes on mortgage application forms, and will therefore never be repaid in full.

2) When repackaged as mortgage-backed bonds, they were given ratings by the credit-rating agencies based on delinquency experience during the benign conditions of the past few years – which almost certainly means that the ratings flattered their innate (poor) quality. Or to put it another way, investors have bought the financial equivalent of poisoned mutton dressed as prime lamb.

3) Hundreds of billions of dollars of these mortgage-backed bonds have been re-engineered as collateralised debt obligations. These CDOs are customised bonds of varying quality and varying yields. There is nothing intrinsically noxious about them. However there are CDOs made out of other CDOs, called CDOs squared, which are marketed as high-quality investments – and they've been bought by the 'one-born-every-minute' brigade. What's more, there's accumulating evidence that even the simpler CDOs have been bought by naïve investors, who had no idea what they were buying.

It is wonderfully ironic that a disproportionate share of losses from America's dodgy mortgages should be borne by financial institutions in France and Germany – and that the European Central Bank is pumping cash into the banking system to avert a possible crisis. The incongruity is that the Anglo–American model of financial markets is despised in many European capitals; it is droll that their banks were seduced by Wall Street. But although I allow myself a chuckle, it is a hollow one. I fear there'll be plenty more damage to come from America's exports of subprime poison. (Peston's Picks, 18:00 UK time, 9 August 2007).

As the column said, 9 August was an extraordinary day on financial markets, when a vital source of funds for banks and financial institutions simply disappeared. And because this caused huge problems for eurozone banks, the European Central Bank provided an unprecedented €95bn of emergency overnight loans to them. Putting all this together – the seizing up of important financial markets, the provision of record rescue loans by the European Central Bank, the refusal of BNP Paribas to put a value on asset-backed securities – represented the big one for me, or potentially the biggest story of my twenty-five-year career. It felt like the bursting of a huge bubble, which could have painful implications for all our wealth. I decided to immerse myself in what was going on, to the exclusion of everything else.

Brewing storms

This financial crisis had been building for several years. During the latter phase, the evidence of something seriously awry was that it became increasingly difficult for banks to raise money by issuing what are known as asset-backed securities. As we discussed earlier, banks can only lend if they can borrow. Actually that is not quite right. They can also lend if they can raise money by selling to investors and other banks the loans they've already made. And one of the ways they sold these loans was in the form of asset-backed securities. The buyers of these asset-backed securities were acquiring an interest in the mortgages and property loans made by the banks. Here is how to think of it: a bank mashed together lots of mortgages and loans, probably 5,000 mortgages for a typical 'securitisation' (which is what the process of creating one of these bonds is called); the buyer of the asset-backed bonds or securities was buying a slice of all these mortgages and loans. So the buyers of these securities would be paid interest and eventually get all their money back if those 5,000 people who had taken out the relevant mortgages paid what they owed; and of course if investors did not want to hold these bonds till maturity, they could always sell them on the market (until the relevant markets seized up in the summer of 2007). The value and price of an asset-backed bond depended on the perception of the financial health of the 5,000 home owners whose mortgages were backing the bond.

There are several categories of asset-backed securities. There are those, called asset-backed commercial paper, that are in effect a form of short-term debt, with a maturity of just a few weeks or months. Then there are asset-backed bonds, which are mortgage-backed debt with a maturity of years. Finally, there is another important distinction, between relatively straightforward asset-backed bonds – of the sort sold, for example, by Northern Rock – and collateralised debt obligations, the securities that caused enormous losses for the likes of UBS, Merrill Lynch, and other giant global banks. Now, as I have said, in a securitisation of mortgages, around 5,000 mortgages worth around a hundred million pounds are stuck together with financial glue and then sliced up into individual asset-backed bonds. Each of these bonds is an IOU, which has a claim on a bit of those 5,000 mortgages – which means a claim on the interest and repayments of the borrowers who took out the mortgages and (in a worst-case scenario) the underlying mortgaged properties. Even with these simplest and most vanilla of bonds, there is a hierarchy of claims on the mortgages. There are senior and junior bonds: the investors in the senior bonds have the right to be paid back what they are owed before holders of the junior bonds.

This hierarchy of interests becomes much more sophisticated and complicated with collateralised debt obligations or

CDOs. A CDO is a structure that takes a pool of mortgages, or a pool of loans, often with some insurance added, and then creates a great variety of new bonds out of that pool of debt. Some of those bonds will be classed as low risk; they will be given an AAA credit-rating by the credit-rating agencies. Some of them will be classified as much higher risk, say BBB. And their riskiness depends on where they stand in the queue for the mortgage and principal payments from the bonds and loans that are in the great pool of debt. If you own a CDO bond that has an AAA rating, that means you get paid interest from bonds and loans in the debt pool before anyone else gets that interest. In theory, the only way you would not be paid what you are owed would be if very large numbers of home-owners standing behind the mortgages in the CDO debt pool defaulted on what they owe – which was seen as very unlikely to happen. So the idea behind CDOs is that for any pool of mortgages or bonds, whether good-quality mortgages or subprime mortgages provided to people with poor economic prospects, there will always be some money repaid. And there-fore through this process of putting bonds and mortgages into a vast pool and then creating 'tranches' of bonds with greater or lesser claims on the interest paid by those bonds and mortgages, it should always be possible to manufacture good-quality investments out of poor-quality loans and bonds.

For a period, this CDO innovation had significant social consequences, because it meant that much more money was made available for lending to very poor people in America, people who in the past would never have been able to borrow to buy a home. Subprime loans to individuals who might not even have a job could now be sliced and diced into bonds, some of which had an AAA rating and could therefore be sold to investors all over the world. Surely this showed the good

that Wall Street could do, because suddenly a class of the
financially excluded could for the very first time borrow to
buy their own homes?

To make the CDOs supposedly even safer, subprime loans
from many different parts of the US were mixed together in
the debt pool. The reason was that in the history of the US
housing market there had never been a housing slump affecting every part of the giant US economy at exactly the same
time. The thought was that if the CDOs mixed California
subprime loans with New York home loans with Florida loans
and so on, as and when Florida borrowers had difficulty keeping up the payments, the New York borrowers would still be
paying on time. Even if there was a terrible housing recession
in California, those who held the AAA tranche of the CDO
could still be certain their bonds were worth 100 cents in
the dollar, because New York home owners, for example,
should not be experiencing serious difficulty paying their
mortgages.

And there was another great CDO wheeze, which was to
create yet more CDOs – what were known as CDOs squared
– by mixing together the lower quality tranches of different
CDOs into a new debt pool. If you combined various
BBB-rated or low quality CDO bonds in this pool, you could
in theory create new top quality AAA-rated CDO bonds out
of them, by repeating the process of creating tranches of
bonds with varying claims on the interest paid into the pool
by the BBB bonds. New AAA bonds would have first claim on
the interest paid by the BBB bonds into the pool. And you
could increase the quality of these AAA bonds made out of
BBB bonds by persuading a big insurer, such as the notorious
AIG, to insure the new AAA bonds against the risk of default
via a credit default swap. If you have stuck with me through

this tortuous explanation you will have noted that the investment bankers of Wall Street and the City of London appeared
to have uncovered the secret of alchemy. They were creating
AAA-rated investments, thought of the world over as the
equivalent of solid gold, out of the financial equivalent of lead.
A world renowned senior banker explained the miracle to me
like this: 'If you were in charge of risk at an investment institution or bank and you saw that your colleagues were loading up
your organisation with AAA investments, you didn't check
what the investments were, you didn't think twice, because if
they were badged as AAA you knew they would be fine.'

Now for me, it is not the basic idea behind securitisation in
general, or even the refinement in the form of collateralised
debt obligations, that is flawed. Why should the amount of
mortgages and the price of mortgages available to home
buyers be dependent purely on what banks can borrow in
conventional ways? What is wrong with innovation that has
the effect of getting pension funds, insurance companies and
other investors to provide money to the housing market via
investments in asset-backed bonds and CDOs – whose consequence is to significantly increase the volume of mortgages
available and cut the price of those mortgages? Surely for
millions of us wanting to buy a home, all of that sounds good.
And there are apparent benefits in respect of the stability and
strength of banks, because the risks of lending to the housing
market are no longer just sitting on their balance sheets; those
risks are shared with lots of other investors too, which means
that in a recession the pain would be distributed more widely,
and presumably felt less acutely by individual banks.

When seen in that way, and without the knowledge we now
have of what went wrong, it is easy to understand why the
world's regulators and central bankers generally thought that

securitisation was beneficial and to be encouraged. The optimism of Alan Greenspan about how the financial world was becoming safer and the rest of us were becoming richer as a result of banks' creativity does not look quite so ludicrous. Except for a couple of things.

The first flaw in all this innovation is that it ignored a basic rule of finance, which is that it is harder to control credit quality if you don't know your customer. And the problem with the securitisation model, especially the CDO refinement, is that it introduced an enormous distance between the providers of the funds – Dutch people saving for their retirement in a Netherlands pension fund, for example – and the ultimate borrower, which could be a one-parent family in Arkansas. One way of seeing the length of gap between lender and borrower was given by the Bank of England.* If you assume there are 150 mortgage-backed bonds in every CDO, 125 CDO bonds in a CDO squared, 200 pages in every bond prospectus, and 300 pages in every CDO prospectus, then to read all the relevant documentation related to an investment in a CDO squared, you would have to read 3,787,800 pages – which, even if you were a speed reader, would take you seven years. And for completeness in your research, if you also wanted to read the paperwork for the 5,000 mortgages going into each mortgage-backed bond that was in the various debt pools making up your CDO squared, you would probably have a reasonable grasp of the investment you had made after 1,789.7 years of continuous reading, with no comfort breaks. Suffice to say, faced with a due diligence challenge of that magnitude, many investors simply looked at the official AAA ratings of assorted CDOs

---

* See Andy Haldane, 'Rethinking the Financial Network', April 2009.

and CDO-squareds, and assumed that was all they needed to know.

The pension funds and other investors providing the cash channelled to home owners via securitisation could never have controlled the quality of the mortgages. They relied on mortgage brokers operating all over the US. But the brokers had little incentive to make sure the borrowers could repay the mortgages, because they earned commission based on the volume of mortgages they provided – and they did not under-write any of the mortgages themselves, so as and when the loans went bad, they did not suffer. As for the banks that were providing the money for the mortgages put into the market by the brokers, they too had little incentive to control the credit quality, because they were parcelling the loans up for sale to investors in the form of mortgage-backed bonds and CDOs. So no one in the system of providing the subprime mortgages took formal and personal or institutional responsibility for making sure the money only went to home buyers who stood some chance of being able to repay what they owed. And it probably won't surprise you to learn therefore that hundreds of billions of dollars were lent to individuals and families who could only afford to keep up the payments on their mortgages for a brief period when interest rates were artificially low.

If this flaw in the system was ignored for years, it is because banks and investors placed too much faith in data and experts. The data said that a severe housing crash affecting every part of the US simultaneously had never happened, which meant – surely – that if you held a CDO composed of mortgages from all over the US, you couldn't lose all your money. The data also said that default rates even on subprime mortgages were relatively low. And the experts, the credit-rating agencies – such as Moody's and Standard & Poor's – used that data to conclude that many of the bonds created out of these subprime loans could be given an AAA rating. But the experts ignored the fact that when you have financial innovation that channels vast amounts of extra money into a market such as the subprime mortgage market, the historic data becomes irrelevant. What use is default data gathered from the tiny subprime home loans market of the 1990s for predicting default rates in a market that has exploded in size? In the smaller market of the 1990s, some care was taken to ensure that subprime borrowers could pay their debts – and the rate of default was therefore quite low. In the huge market of the years before 2007, no such pains were taken when the money was lent. So the historic record on defaults was irrelevant, although it was viewed by the ratings agencies and investors as gospel. Which shows (and this is a theme to which we we will return) that there are great dangers in relying on experts and historical data, and ignoring common sense.

The belief, based on the published record, that there could never be an extreme nationwide housing slump in the US also turned out to be wrong. The penny dropped when interest rates rose and subprime loans to home owners started to go seriously bad at the end of 2006. The opacity and complexity of the CDOs and the asset-backed bonds suddenly spooked investors. They realised that they had little proper grasp of what they had bought. They feared that the debt pools underlying CDOs could be cesspools. And they wanted out.

Not all investors were losers, of course. After the rate of default on US subprime loans started to increase sharply at the end of 2006, to a rate far higher than was assumed in the financial models that underpinned the original pricing of collateralised debt obligations, some smart investors worked out that the price of these bonds could only go in one direction – down. A number of them, of whom the hedge fund Paulson & Co was the most celebrated, made big bets that the prices of these bonds would fall. To use the jargon, they took out short positions in the bonds, they shorted them (there are a number of ways of doing this: the classic way of shorting is to sell stock you don't already own, with the plan of buying it back at a cheaper price when the price falls; another way of shorting is to take out an insurance contract, a credit default swap, that pays out when the relevant bond defaults). Paulson & Co is said to have made $15bn in 2007 primarily from shorting the subprime bond market. But even after the market started to turn, there were still buyers and holders of these collateralised debt obligations – notably among the world's biggest (and some would say stupidest) banks. What is perhaps extraordinary is that innovation that was supposed to make the banks safer, by spreading the risks of lending to lots of other investors outside of the banking system, actually endangered the banks. They believed their own propaganda that these AAA-rated CDOs and asset-backed bonds were good quality investments. Huge banks like Merrill Lynch and Citigroup of the US and UBS of Switzerland bought tens of billions of dollars of these bonds – on the basis that they got a better interest rate or return from making these investments than from making other AAA investments, such as lending to the US government via US Treasury bonds. They believed that they could always sell the CDOs if they needed the money in a hurry.

Over the course of 2007, it became clear to even the most optimistic of believers in collateralised debt obligations that the financial difficulties and hardship being experienced by the subprime borrowers, the real people with the excessive debts, could not be wished away. The prices of CDOs tumbled.

And then another article of faith about securitisation was revealed to be a dangerous fiction – the idea that there would always be a market for these bonds, that they were the equivalent of cash. Suddenly it became impossible to sell asset-backed securities for any price. Pop went the notion that AAA bonds could always be quickly sold for around 100 cents in the dollar.

What turned the pricking of the CDO bubble into something very serious was that there was contagion to almost all classes of asset-backed securities. Investors decided it was too difficult to distinguish between the really rubbishy CDOs and the better-quality mortgage backed bonds – and opted to boycott all asset-backed securities. This was a double problem for the banks. If, like UBS, Citigroup and Merrill Lynch, they had big investments in CDOs, they incurred crippling losses. But most banks also needed securitisation to raise money: they were hooked on raising money by parcelling up their loans and selling them to investors as asset-backed bonds and asset-backed commercial paper. For a bank such as Northern Rock, selling asset-backed bonds was its primary source of financial fuel. But even a much bigger bank like HBOS had become dependent on selling to investors the mortgages made by its Halifax high street branches.

There were also headaches for more diversified banks like Barclays. Many big banks like Barclays provided contingent finance – guarantees – to financial institutions, called structured investment vehicles (SIVs) and conduits. These were organisations that seemed to be at arm's length from the banks. Collectively known as shadow banks, because they behave like banks but operate outside of the main regulatory net, these SIVs and conduits funded themselves in the asset-backed commercial paper markets – they raised money by selling short-term bonds. But when in 2007 the shadow banks could no longer raise money from selling asset-backed commercial paper, because the market had closed down, they were forced to call in the guarantees provided by the real banks and borrow from those banks. All of a sudden the real banks found that financial exposure to mortgages and other loans that had been removed from the banking system and put into these SIVs and conduits came back into the banking system. It meant that the banks' capital resources were supporting many more loans than was supposed to be the case. The risks being directly supported by banks' capital went up massively overnight. The banks' creditors noticed that there was much less protection for them against the danger of losses. The implosion of the shadow banks, which had originally been set up to make the banks look stronger, crippled the banks themselves.

All of which explains why 9 August, when these asset-backed bond and commercial paper markets seized up, was probably the most important day in postwar economic and financial history. It wasn't the fundamental cause of our current financial and economic malaise. But it was the beginning of that malaise. Think of it, perhaps, as the equivalent of the relationship between the assassination of Archduke Ferdinand and the First World War. And what may shock you is how little notice of what had happened was taken at the time. It was big news in the financial press, such as the *FT*. But mainstream media barely reported what had happened. Politicians didn't interrupt their holidays. We all continued as normal. And the reason is that most of us were living in profound ignorance that our prosperity was dependent on a vast part of the financial system that we had never heard of, that involved the transfer of trillions of dollars around the world in virtual secrecy. If we didn't know of the existence of this system, how could we hold it to account? And when it all went wrong, we were off guard and vulnerable as the big banks that had recklessly gambled in this system held us to ransom.

Central banks and regulators did of course notice that there had been something of a breakdown in the plumbing of the global economy. As I have already mentioned, the European Central Bank lent an unprecedented €95bn of overnight money to European banks, to ensure they had sufficient funds to lend to the shadow banks that had suddenly found themselves unable to borrow on markets. Jean-Claude Trichet, the then President of the European Central Bank, provided this eyewitness account to me:

> We noticed that our own money market was upside down and we understood that it was because of very important information that came in New York the previous day – namely that two or three important institutions had made public that they were incapable of re-financing their asset-backed commercial paper, that the market was not functioning any more. So that created a tension at the end of the day in New York, which was not dramatic but it became more and more important in Asia and then back in Europe. In a way, you had a wave that had been transformed into a tsunami in going through the Pacific and then back to Europe.
>
> (Interview with the author for the BBC, 15 May 2008)

The collapse of the shadow banking system foisted direct exposure to toxic, loss-making securities on to some banks, as those banks were forced to take over these shadow banks. At the same time, those banks that already had large holdings of these asset-backed securities suddenly found they were either unsellable or only sellable at a vastly discounted and loss-making price. Banks were damaged on both sides of their balance sheets: they could not borrow; and the value of their loans and investments, their assets, had fallen dramatically. A number of banks were suffering both a liquidity and a solvency crisis. For banks, this was about as bad as it gets – although it was to take just over a year for the full scale of the financial disaster to be manifested.

Credit crunch

9 August was the start of the credit crunch. Banks around the world – but especially in the US and Europe – found it harder and harder to borrow. And when banks can't borrow, they can't lend. And when banks can't lend, businesses find it harder to raise money for investment, and individuals find it harder to borrow to buy a house or even to shop. So as BBC Business Editor, I spent the autumn highlighting how the housing market was weakening as a result of the credit crunch and how there were signs that it was beginning to have an impact on consumer spending and business investment. I was accused of scaremongering, of talking our economy down. Mainstream economists were forecasting that there would not be a recession; that the British economy would sail through this, with perhaps a modest slowdown in GDP growth. I was trying to show that the squeeze on banks' ability to borrow was a big deal, even though economic forecasts were saying the opposite. Why was my view so different from that of most economic experts? Well, on this occasion there were advantages to being a journalist, rather than a technocrat. From years of observation, which started back at the *Investors Chronicle* in 1983, I

knew how banks and the financial system work. I knew that there had to be a serious negative economic impact if banks were struggling to borrow – because this would ultimately lead to withdrawal of credit from businesses and households, which would lead to an economic slowdown or even recession. And because this was common sense, I was not cowed into the quasi-official view that this was a markets phenomenon of little significance for the real world – although, at the time, I received a good deal of hate mail and public opprobrium for my pains. I turned out to be right. And the reason so many of the professional economists – at the Bank of England, the Treasury, even at the banks themselves – got it wrong and were too sanguine is that nothing like this markets shutdown had ever happened in anyone's memory. They were not feeding into their forecasting models the only financial information that mattered at the time – namely that banks could not borrow. Their models took as a given that banks would always be able to borrow to finance the needs of the economy. Inevitably if you use incomplete or irrelevant data when making a prediction, as economists were doing, you will make a poor prediction.

This is an illustration of an important lesson, which is that as a society we may have become too respectful of experts and certainly too in awe of the claims to scientific certainty of economists. Which is not to say that genuine experts and social scientists should be ignored. But when their views seem to be at odds with observations of what is actually happening in the world, we should trust our observations and experience. Arguably central banks and finance ministers could and should have taken evasive action to mitigate the impact of the banking crisis much earlier, if they had ignored what the official economic forecasts were saying and simply extrapolated from the turning off of the funding tap for banks.

I was not just interested in this general impact of the credit crunch. I was also keen to look at the differential effects on banks. And I was particularly interested in one medium-size bank, Northern Rock, because I knew it was more dependent than most banks on borrowing from the markets that had closed. Funnily enough, it wasn't 9 August but the collapse of Northern Rock that would mark the start of the financial crisis in the public mind: for many this was the moment when anxieties began to build that the years of increased prosperity were drawing to a close. The Rock's woes were the early warning of what had gone so badly wrong in our banks.

Rock in a hard place

Formed in 1965 from the merger of the Northern Counties Permanent Building Society and the Rock Building Society, Northern Rock's roots were in the nineteenth-century movement of mutual self-help – what would now be called community banks – in which local people pooled their savings and lent these savings to those wishing to buy a home. Almost from the start it was a pillar of the economy of the North-East of England. And it retained a social purpose even after converting into a bank, giving up mutual status and listing on the London Stock Exchange in October 1997. It was in 1999 that it made the decision that was to change the course of British financial history: the Rock started to raise money by packaging its mortgages into asset-backed bonds and selling them to international investors. It was a big moment, because securitisation (the sale of mortgages to investors) allowed the Rock to grow much faster than would have been possible if it had continued to lend only what it took in from customers in the form of savings and deposits. The Rock wasn't the only bank to raise money by selling mortgages packaged as bonds.

But the Rock exploited this method of funding more ruthlessly and aggressively than most. And it was encouraged to
do so by City analysts, who applauded the way that the Rock
was now able to grow faster and lend more than competitors.
Investment bankers also loved the Rock, because they earned
big fees from selling the bonds.

I didn't really take much of an interest in Northern Rock till
around 2001. I had left the *FT* to become editorial director of
an on-line service for investors, called CSQuest.com. What
struck me was that this former building society appeared to
be building up something of a City fan club. This made me
slightly uneasy, because the success of businesses beloved of
stockbrokers rarely seemed to last all that long – perhaps
because those businesses ultimately became a bit too confident and convinced they could do no wrong. I tucked away
my unease about Northern Rock till I became a mainstream
journalist again, as City Editor of the *Sunday Telegraph* in
2002. And I wrote this, on 20 July 2003:

> Northern Rock is that rarest of things: a growth stock in a
> commodity business, the provision of home loans. It proved
> this yet again last week when it disclosed that it took 9 per
> cent of the entire market for new mortgages in the first half
> of its financial year, which is roughly twice its natural share,
> based on the stock of loans it holds on its books.
>
> But the margin it earned on its loans was squeezed (this
> is not exactly an uncompetitive or opaque market). Anyway,
> Northern Rock's executives will view me as a Neanderthal
> for questioning whether it can avoid horrible losses when it
> expands at this rate while returns are falling. And I don't
> doubt they sincerely believe their risk controls are impec-
> cable (its CEO, Adam Applegarth, talks a good talk).

But it looks too good to be true, which is a warning as old
as banking itself. Sooner or later, the Rock will find itself in
a hard place.

(*Sunday Telegraph*, 20 July 2003)

My concern that it would all end in tears led to a lunch with
the chief executive, Adam Applegarth, which is how smart
companies respond to criticism from journalists. And for the
best part of four years, I looked like a plonker as the Rock and
the City seemed to be proving me wrong: the Rock's share
price went up and up, as it grew bigger and bigger and became
more and more dependent on the sale of asset-backed securities. In the first half of 2007, the Rock provided 18.9 per cent
of all the new mortgages in the UK, around four or five times
the market share it would have had if it was lending only the
money of its savers. The Rock had found a new – and, it
argued, better – way of running a bank.

The Rock had enormous confidence in its ability to limit
the risks of its loans, even though it was prepared to lend
considerably more than the value of an individual's house. It
offered borrowers both a mortgage and a personal loan,
through what it called its 'Together' product that allowed
customers to raise up to 125% of the value of a property. At
the peak of the housing market in the autumn of 2007, those
who had taken out these Together loans had borrowed 105%
of the value of their respective properties, on average. If house
prices started to fall, a big gap would open up between what
Northern Rock was owed by its borrowers and the value of
borrowers' assets: the so-called 'negative equity' in the homes
of Rock clients would be substantial.

By the end of June 2007, the Rock had borrowed £105bn,
but less than 25 per cent of this came from retail savers and

depositors. The rest of its debts were £54bn from mortgage-backed bonds sold to investors and £27bn that came from other wholesale providers of funds, such as banks and financial institutions. Also, more than £4bn of the Rock's retail funding was held in on-line accounts by savers chasing the best savings rates. Or to put it another way, the Rock was raising most of its money from lenders who were most likely to take their money out or go on a lending strike at the first hint of trouble. So there were risks attached to the way the Rock borrowed – as well as big risks in the mortgages and loans the Rock was providing to home buyers. The Rock was borrowing recklessly and lending recklessly.

I was aware of its addiction to raising big sums on bond markets. When these markets closed on 9 August, I set myself the task of keeping an eye not just on banks in general but on the Rock in particular. It was clear that if these markets did not reopen, the Rock would no longer be viable. This was an open secret in the City, as an analyst at an investment bank conceded to me a few months later:

I think it was really a question of how long will this credit crunch go on for ... My view of that is ... that the credit crunch will end but the key question is, will it end in time to save Northern Rock?

At that point we had no idea, so suspended our target price and recommendation on that day ... At that point it became impossible to know what the true value of the company was. And if we don't have a view as to what a company's worth, you can't have a recommendation and a target price.

The problem with a situation where a bank is unable to finance itself is it [Northern Rock] could very easily be worth zero if this situation continued in perpetuity or it could very easily be worth pretty much what it was before the markets erupted if the markets returned to their former state more or less straight away.

(Banks analyst, interviewed by the author, 2007)

Asset-backed bond markets failed to reopen. And by the weekend of 8–9 September, I was aware that the bank was facing a serious crisis. It was close to running out of cash to repay its creditors. No one would lend to it. There was only one place to go for help, the only British institution able to create money and credit – the Bank of England. It was clear to me that there would be nowhere else for the Rock to look for support, and I got wind that a rescue was imminent – although it then took me a couple of days to stand the story up. On the evening of Thursday 13 September, the Court of the Bank of England (the Bank's board) met and confirmed the provision of the rescue loans. I reported this shortly after 8 p.m. on *BBC News*, when the Court was still meeting, and followed it up with a blog, a radio report and a short film on BBC1's *Ten O'Clock News*. The story felt momentous to me, although the extent of the subsequent public reaction took me by surprise.

For the Bank of England, providing Emergency Liquidity Assistance meant that by definition the Rock had failed. As it needed to be propped up by the central bank, it was no longer viable in its existing form, which was very bad news for the owners and management of the business. But that didn't mean depositors would necessarily lose money. Indeed, on that evening the Bank of England and the Financial Services Authority believed the bank would ultimately be able to repay all it owed to customers, which is what I said in broadcasts. So I was shocked that the morning after I broke the story queues started to form at Rock branches; a run on the bank began. Extraordinary pictures of long lines of people outside Rock branches waiting to take their money out were broadcast all over the world. This was not the sort of thing that was supposed to happen in a stable, mature economy such as the UK. As the then head of the CBI, Richard Lambert, said at the time, it was more redolent of what he scathingly called a 'banana republic'. It was humiliating for Britain and for the British banking industry. The film and stills of the Rock queues have become – for most people – the symbol of the end of the boom years and the beginning of the painful credit crunch.

The Rock was particularly susceptible to a run for a series of structural reasons, notably the relatively large number of its customers per branch and the unusual degree to which many of its savers managed their Rock savings through the bank's on-line service. After my broadcast, customers wanted more information and inevitably turned to the bank's website. This contained no information about what was going on. And because of the unexpectedly huge numbers trying to access their accounts on-line, the website kept crashing. All through the evening, Rock customers emailed and rang me to say how worried they were that they were unable to gain access to their on-line bank accounts or to learn anything useful from the bank. Inevitably therefore on the following morning, 14 September, many Northern Rock customers headed for the Rock's branches. Now precisely because the Rock had been so successful recruiting on-line clients, it had a lot of customers for a relatively small number of branches. At the time, the bank's spokesman said that it had 1.4m savers and just 72 branches – or over 19,000 customers per branch. If only a small proportion of customers decided to visit a branch, long queues would form. Which is precisely what happened.

When bank customers turned up and saw quite how many people were queuing, the sense of unease increased. Inevitably, many customers decided to put safety first and demanded their money. According to the National Audit Office, £4.6bn was withdrawn by savers – equivalent to a fifth of all the Rock's retail deposits – from Friday 14 September 2007 to the close of business on Monday 17 September. There had been no equivalent panic by retail bank customers in living memory. In fact, there had arguably never been anything like a run of this scale in British banking history. Some have drawn analogies with the collapses of Overend & Gurney in 1866 and of the City of Glasgow Bank in 1877. But neither involved mobs of people all over the country demanding their money back. Nor were the assorted British bank failures of the twentieth century examples of mass hysteria in this way. The Rock run, in a British context, was probably unique.

All that said, it was a very different run at Northern Rock – an invisible run by professional lenders such as other banks and big financial institutions – that did the real damage. They did not have to queue to get their money out. They could do it electronically or by phone. And it was their withdrawal of more than £25bn of credit to the Rock which ultimately led the government to provide £31.5bn of rescue loans and other financial aid to plug the gap. What happened at the Rock was the first demonstration of how dangerous it was that banks had become so dependent on borrowing from these professional lenders. In the ensuing months, there were invisible wholesale runs at other much bigger banks. HBOS – owner of Bank of Scotland and the Halifax – financed itself in a similar way to the Rock, though it had proportionately more reliable deposits than the Rock. And Royal Bank of Scotland became dangerously dependent on borrowing for shorter and shorter periods from other banks and big investors, after its reckless takeover of the rump of the huge Dutch bank ABN AMRO, in the autumn of 2007. After Lehman Bros filed for bankruptcy on 15 September 2008, both RBS and HBOS found it increasingly hard to borrow. They suffered a wholesale run, and would have collapsed had they not received secret emergency loans from the Bank of England (which the Bank of England did not reveal until November 2009). From October 2008 to January 2009, RBS borrowed £36.6bn from the Bank of England, while HBOS borrowed £25.4bn from the Bank. More recently, in the autumn of 2011, huge US money-market funds – which look after the savings of millions of Americans – more or less stopped lending to banks in the eurozone, and that escalated into a more general problem of professional lenders withdrawing credit from European banks. That prompted a massive bailout operation by the European Central Bank.

When banks are forced to borrow from central banks such as the Bank of England on this kind of scale, it is the equivalent of being put on a life-support machine. It means the bank is very sick. And the Bank of England – along with most central banks – takes the view that it cannot and will not provide this kind of emergency support for more than a relatively short time. Typically, central banks will provide bridging loans, while the wounded bank raises enough new capital to reassure depositors and creditors that their money will be safe – which should allow the battered bank to start taking deposits and to borrow in the normal way again. Sometimes, as in the case of Northern Rock and Royal Bank of Scotland in 2008, that new capital can only come from the state, through total or partial nationalisation.

What is wrong with central banks, with their ability to create unlimited amounts of money, financing commercial banks on a permanent basis? Well central banks worry that if commercial banks become too addicted to borrowing from them, losses made by those commercial banks may ultimately fall on the central banks – which could undermine confidence in the central banks themselves and therefore in the ability of the central banks to maintain the integrity of their respective currencies. That said, the judgement of how long it is appropriate for a central bank to keep banks alive has been evolving in the past few years and is more art than science. For example, the European Central Bank provided more than a trillion euros of emergency three-year loans to the eurozone's banks at the end of 2011 and the beginning of 2012 – which represents a significantly more generous and longer term commitment than most central banks would have contemplated a few years ago. Some would argue that the ECB has in effect nationalised the eurozone's banking system. But the ECB felt unable to do otherwise, because the alternative was to risk a chain reaction of banks going bust across Europe, which could have catapulted the eurozone into an economic depression as deep and dark as that of the 1930s.

The sovereign wealth funds, US money market funds and other huge professional lenders to banks are supposed to be rational and sophisticated – although in practice they are probably as prone to prejudice and hysteria as the rest of us. Which is why it is very dangerous for banks to be dependent on borrowing from them, because if they decide to boycott a bank, they can withdraw so much cash so quickly that the bank would face almost instant wipeout. In the case of the Rock, the providers of funds who panicked and demanded their money back were not being as unreasonable as all that, because we later learned, after the nationalisation of the Rock in 2008, that the bank had inadequate capital resources. The losses on its mortgages and personal loans, particularly its Together loans, undermined its solvency. In other words, it was bust.

Even in the autumn of 2007, the Governor of the Bank of England, Mervyn King, told me he believed the Rock's retail customers were being rational in asking for their money back – because their savings were only protected by an industry insurance scheme to a limited extent, and the government had not done what it would very soon do, which was to guarantee that no Rock saver would lose a penny:

> At that point, in the absence of a government guarantee, it was actually rational to queue up and take your money out. And it would have been dishonest for us to have pretended otherwise. I thought the Chancellor was extraordinarily successful in giving what reassurance he could, given that at that point he didn't know how far he could go in giving a government guarantee . . . I think it would not have been possible to say to them [the Rock's savers]: 'You have complete reassurance, don't worry, you can go home.' It would have been dishonest to have said that.'
>
> (Mervyn King, interviewed by the author,
> 30 October 2007)

In February 2008, Northern Rock was taken into public ownership. The so-called 'good bit' of the Rock, its branches and deposits, were sold to Sir Richard Branson's Virgin Money four years later, but the vast bulk of its loans remain in public ownership.

The Bank and the bubble

The collapse of Northern Rock is illustrative of one of the big themes of this book. Banks – especially British banks – lent more and more, not only in absolute terms, but relative to their capital, their protective resources, and relative to the British economy. This represented something of a revolution. For a hundred years or so, there was a steady relationship between the size of banks and British GDP. According to figures from the Bank of England, the loans and investments of British banks were equivalent to less than 100% of GDP until the late 1970s. This relatively stable ratio between lending and GDP is what you would expect: a banking system – if it is functioning properly – is there to provide the essential fuel for wealth creation, in the form of credit to households and businesses. As the economy grows, you would expect the demand for credit to increase, but not disproportionately to the size of the economy. Think of credit as oil in the economy's engine – without it, the engine splutters to a halt.

Then about forty years ago, there was a significant boost to the supply of loans. For years, the supply of credit was rationed both by tight regulation and the inability of banks to lend more than they could take in from deposits. But in the 1980s there was a combination of the removal of governments' formal controls on how much banks could lend, the creation of a vast pool of new money for banks to borrow in international or 'eurodollar' markets and securitisation, which made it easy for banks to raise money by selling loans to investors. One consequence was that banks were able to offer more and bigger loans, at a cheaper price, to individuals and companies. It was the equivalent for the banks of a vast energy find for oil companies. Suddenly the problem was not finding the money to lend but finding the customers to borrow it. The ratio of

UK banks' loans and investments to GDP started to rise. By the late 1990s, it had reached 300 per cent of GDP. And by 2008, the ratio of loans to GDP exceeded by a comfortable margin 500 per cent of everything the UK produces every year. The collective balance sheets of Britain's banks were significantly bigger than the value of five years of Britain's economic output. (Yes, I know I am comparing apples with pears – or, to use the jargon, a 'stock' of loans and investments with a 'flow' of output – but it remains a useful comparison, because British GDP gives an indication of the ability of the taxpayers and the public sector to absorb losses on bank loans, if the worst comes to the worst.)

Quite a lot of the lending was surplus to the real underlying needs of people and businesses. Naïve individuals were seduced into spending on credit beyond what they could afford. That is clear from data showing quite how many people today feel trapped by their debts rather than liberated by them. According to research by NMG Consulting and the Bank of England, vulnerable households (or households with little equity in their homes and struggling to keep up the payments in some way) owe more than 15% of British mortgage debt and more than 35% of unsecured personal loans – which are record amounts (although the data only goes back about twenty years). Also the combination of an over-supply of mortgages and interest rates that were kept low by competition and by the Bank of England's interest-rate policy led to inflationary increases in property prices. This increase in prices was unsustainable: between August 2007, the high point for house prices in the recent boom, and their low point in April 2009, house prices fell 23% (according to the Halifax); and as prices fell, and home owners felt poorer, there was a sharp reduction in consumer spending, which helped tip the UK into recession. But when it came to house prices, in a way the UK had the worst of both worlds. During the boom prices rose so much – trebling in the ten years prior to 2007 – that it became almost impossible for young people, starting out in their careers, to buy a home. First-time buyers became few and far between. And some would therefore say that the big disappointment with the house-price crash when it came was that it was not enough of a crash – because a fall of a fifth in prices, after a trebling, still left a chronic shortage of cheap affordable housing for those on low incomes.

Arguably the magnitude of the boom was increased – in a dangerous way – by the failure of the Bank of England to put up interest rates when house prices were surging out of control. The Bank of England sets the benchmark interest rate for the economy, or Bank Rate – which is what commercial banks have to pay when borrowing from the Bank of England. Bank Rate, with the Bank of England as a central bank in the centre of the financial system and able to create money, is probably the most influential determinant of the interest rates that banks charge their customers. When Bank Rate comes down, mortgage rates typically fall; and mortgage rates normally rise when Bank Rate goes up. So to take some of the momentum out of house-price rises, the Bank of England could have set Bank Rate at a higher level, to make it more expensive for home buyers to take out a mortgage and thus push up the cost of buying a house. It could also have taken the edge off a boom in commercial property that was arguably just as dangerous – because losses on their commercial loans have savaged the balance sheets of HBOS, under the ownership of Lloyds, and Royal Bank of Scotland. Why didn't the Bank of England do this? Well it is partly that the Bank of

England's explicit mandate was to keep inflation under control, but inflation defined in a narrow sense, which took very little account of inflation in assets or property. So it has argued that if the official measure of inflation was on target, or heading towards the target, it would have been inappropriate to raise interest rates. And the Bank has also argued that the rise in the interest rate that would have been necessary to stem the housing boom would have been so great – given the momentum of that boom – as to cause quite serious damage elsewhere in the economy (indebted businesses might have gone bust, for example).

Which may be so. But funnily enough, that is not what a senior and influential director of the Bank of England said to me in 2003 – when I asked him whether there was more that the Bank could do to stem what appeared to be unsustainable and dangerous rises in house prices. Here is an explosive extract from that hitherto unpublished interview:

> My view on asset prices is pretty clear ... The reason we care about these evolutions is that they have implications for inflation and activity further down the road. If you build up a bubble in asset prices now, when it implodes that is normally associated with a sharp fall off in activity, financial distress, all that sort of stuff. You can encompass all those sorts of things into what I think inflation targeting is all about. Some people have a narrow conception of what inflation targeting is all about, which is focusing on the target two years out. Now that is not something I would sign up to. Typically these sort of concerns about asset price bubbles leading to financial imbalances that create problems further down the road may require you looking beyond the two-year horizon. Often you know these things are

going to unwind but you just don't know when. But that would be a reason for us intentionally having a projection for inflation that would be a bit below target. So the reason we are keeping policy a bit tighter is because we are worried about the build-up of imbalances and what that might imply further down the road. And the onus on us is to explain that's why we're doing it.

(Senior Bank of England Executive, interview with the author, 2003)

So back then, the Bank of England – or rather a very influential executive there – was clear that speculative bubbles in asset prices were very much something it should be concerned about. The executive elaborated:

I have not really grappled with the really hard issue, which is how you identify when these bubbles are developing. Take the housing market at the moment. There are actually very good reasons why the equilibrium house-price-to-earnings ratio should actually be higher now than it was in the past [here the executive is explaining why at least some of the rise in house prices is well founded]. So given that, actually diagnosing when you've got an unsustainable imbalance building up, which threatens the economy further down [the road], is very hard. So that's where the difficulties lie, in the practicalities of diagnosing what's going on in the economy rather than something about the design of the regime, because I think the regime can encompass the issues.

Having the financial stability wing of the Bank helps in all this, because this is one of the things they are supposed to worry about. Monetary policy is about worrying about the central projection with a nod in the direction of the risk. Financial stability people spend all their time worrying about the risks and how things might go wrong. And of course we have people from the financial stability side on the committee. They constantly remind us of the dangers. And of course there are the people upstairs, the staff economists, they co-operate across the two wings of the Bank.

(ibid.)

I regard this conversation as significant. Because here we have a director of the Bank conceding that preventing a housing bubble and broader 'imbalances' was very much a Bank of England responsibility, and also saying explicitly that the Bank had the tools to do the job (he says 'the regime can encompass the issues'). Which matters, because after the crash of 2007–8, the Bank of England managed to absolve itself of most of the public blame – by saying that it did not have enough formal responsibility for dealing with financial instability and by arguing that interest rates were a blunt and inappropriate tool for choking off incipient asset-price booms. The Bank of England's Governor, Sir Mervyn King, seemed to feel there was no reason to apologise for the Bank's performance in the years when credit was consistently under-priced and asset prices rose dangerously. Also it is striking that the Bank of England has been rewarded rather than punished by the current government: its formal powers have been massively increased, through its legislated takeover of the banking-supervision wing of the Financial Services Authority, to create a new Prudential Regulation Authority, and with the establishment of a new Financial Policy Committee at the Bank, to reinforce its role in identifying and tackling markets that are overheating. Even if Sir Mervyn King is right that the Bank was institutionally inadequate and needed reform, my interview of 2003 shows that the Bank of England did not believe this when the boom was getting going and was aware of the importance of the issue. So there is at least a question for the Bank of England: why did it not shout from the rooftops that the City was worryingly out of control, or advise the then Labour government that the division of powers between it and the Financial Services Authority was not – to use the cliché – fit for purpose? In a roundabout and academic way, the Deputy Governor of the Bank of England, Paul Tucker, conceded in 2012 – I think for the first time – that when Bank Rate was reduced, that brought down long-term interest rates in a manner that contributed to credit in general being under-priced.* It is an admission that the Bank of England's actions contributed to the financial bubble, though it represents an explanation rather than an apology. My disclosure of how the Bank of England believed in 2003 that it had the power to deal with past bubbles may also increase pressure for a review of how it failed to suppress the huge bubbles that developed. The Bank has commissioned outsiders to assess its performance since the 2008 crisis. But its earlier record – which some would see as more important – is not being scrutinised.

In future, the Bank of England's new Financial Policy Committee will have powers to force banks to hold more capital relative to their loans when the banks appear to be lending huge amounts without due regard for the risks – which should, because of the scarcity and cost of capital, oblige banks to rein in their lending. Perhaps next time the Bank of England will prick a bubble before it becomes devastatingly huge. The cost of not dealing with the last bubble

---

* 'National Balance Sheets and Macro Policy: Lessons from the Past', 28 February 2012.

can be seen in many ways – and not just in the human cost of surging unemployment and squeezed living standards for millions of people. Even by the standards of its own narrow task, to keep CPI inflation at 2%, the transition from credit boom to bust has caused serious problems. For instance, in latter years the Bank of England has had to tolerate inflation being consistently and significantly above target: to raise interest rates when so many households and businesses were struggling under the burden of excessive debts would have risked a return to serious recession or worse. And, in fact, it is so worried that the real threat is not the inflation being reported, but the deflation that could ensue if over-indebted households and businesses were to stop spending and investing, that it has taken unconventional measures to keep credit as cheap as possible, notably the creation of £375bn of new money through the process called quantitative easing. When you create money on this scale, there is a risk that at some point confidence in the value of sterling will be eroded in a damaging way. It may not have happened yet. But memories of hyperinflation in Germany in the 1920s or in Zimbabwe more recently explain why central bankers are exceptionally wary of being seen to be manufacturing money. The fact that the Bank of England is taking this risk is – many would say – a measure of its previous disastrous failure to preserve the stability of the economy in a broad and fundamental sense.

In the apportionment of blame for the mess we are in, the Bank of England may have got off lightly. That would certainly be the view of bankers, whose blood pressure can rise in an alarming way when discussing Sir Mervyn King. I wonder if he is aware of the kind of things they say about him behind closed doors. I have been present at lunches where the lack of respect for him shown by prominent business leaders, very

well known figures in the commercial world, has been genuinely shocking: governors in the past have always been treated
with deference. In particular, bankers hold him personally
responsible for the severity of the credit crunch after they
were unable to raise money from securitisation, from selling
asset-backed bonds. He is to blame, they say, because unlike
Trichet at the European Central Bank, he was deeply reluctant to help the banks through their funding difficulties by
lending to them on an unprecedented scale – or at least not
until it was too late, and a whole string of banks, from Northern
Rock through to Royal Bank of Scotland, had more or less
collapsed. Also those running the Financial Services Authority
in the summer of 2007, such as Hector Sants, were at the time
pressing the Bank of England to pump more liquidity into the
banking system, to lend more to banks. Perhaps more embar-
rassingly for Sir Mervyn, Hector Sants disclosed to me in
June 2012 (in a BBC interview) that he urged a scheme of
financial support for the Rock that he believes would have
prevented the catastrophic run on it, but this was blocked by
Sir Mervyn.

Just before the Rock received its emergency bailout from
the Bank of England and before the Rock's depositors queued
around the block to remove their cash from the bank, Mr
Sants – who had recently become Chief Executive of the FSA
– recommended that Lloyds TSB should be granted the loan
it was requesting from the Bank of England to facilitate a
takeover of the Rock. Mr Sants told me:

> I think things would have been different if the government
> and Bank [of England] had taken my recommendation that
> they should provide liquidity support to Lloyds to purchase
> Northern Rock. I think that would have made a difference;

it would have avoided the queues and it would have changed the general climate in relation to the old building society sector that had moved into the banking sector. So at that early stage if we had avoided the Northern Rock problem, which we could have done through that action, then I think the tone and people's view of the UK banking sector would have been different.

(BBC interview with the author, 13 June 2012)

Here is what you need to know. On the weekend of 8–9 September 2007, there was a conference call of the so-called Tripartite of the Chancellor of the Exchequer, who was Alistair Darling at the time, the then chairman of the FSA, Sir Callum McCarthy, and Sir Mervyn King, who is still Governor of the Bank of England. Mr Sants, who did not normally participate in these meetings, was also in the telephone meeting. He recommended that Lloyds should be given the guarantee it wanted that in the event that lenders to the Rock withdrew their funds in the succeeding months – which was a serious risk in the global credit crunch of the time – Lloyds would be able to fill the gap with loans from the Bank of England. But Sir Mervyn King said the Bank of England would not provide the money. And, I am told, the Chancellor said nothing. The rest is inglorious British banking history: Lloyds dropped the takeover; and Northern Rock was set on its path to nationalisation just a few months later. As it happens, in November 2007, I asked Sir Mervyn why he opposed giving the loan to Lloyds (at the time I did not know he was going against the FSA's advice). He said Lloyds was asking for a potential loan of up to £30bn for a commercial deal and that was not something a central bank could provide – and he also advised the Chancellor not to provide what would have been a massive overdraft facility for Lloyds.

There is a reasonable case therefore that if Sir Mervyn had shown a bit more pragmatism and flexibility in respect of the financial support he was prepared to give to banks in the early stages of the credit crunch, that might have tempered the scale of the ultimate crash and recession. Why was he so reluctant to be seen to be bailing them out? Well he has a deep-seated conviction that it would be wrong to reward the banks' recklessness. Many would sympathise with this view on an emotional level. Sir Mervyn is concerned about what social scientists and philosophers call moral hazard, and would argue that if banks and bankers – like any of us – are not made to pay for their mistakes, they will repeat them. However, the case against Sir Mervyn is nuanced. For instance, he supported the Labour government in forcing the banks to raise massive amounts of new capital to strengthen them (with much of the capital coming from taxpayers). Which is why Britain's banks today look more robust than those of the eurozone.

In a cultural sense, Sir Mervyn King represents a revolutionary break with the past. Previous governors have typically been first among equals within the City of London. Even in the rare instances when they were not former bankers, as was the case for Lord George, Sir Mervyn's predecessor, they thought of themselves as part of the City community. However, Sir Mervyn sees his responsibilities only in a national context. He has no truck with the idea that he is the head of the City's community. Although he may work in the Bank of England's elegant parlours at the geographic centre of the City, he does not identify with the City of London to any significant degree. And he has not shied away from bashing bankers. In an interview with the *Telegraph*, for example, in March 2011, he put banks and bankers in a deeply unfavourable light compared with other businesses. Manufacturers, said Sir Mervyn, 'care deeply about their workforce, about their customers and, above all, are proud of their products.' But what about banks? 'There isn't that sense of longer term relationships. There's a different attitude towards customers. Small and medium firms really notice this: they miss the people they know,' he said. The financial industry, he claimed, is poisoned by the idea that 'if it's possible to make money out of gullible or unsuspecting customers, particularly institutional customers, that is perfectly acceptable.' And he contrasted that attitude with decent businesses which 'keep a clear vision of who their customers are, and are run by people who don't think they should simply maximise profits next week.' No previous governor had ever been critical of the banking industry in this sweeping and trenchant way. For bankers, the governor was supposed to be, in a social and cultural sense, one of their own, not – as Sir Mervyn has been – their apparent enemy. What of course has further upset the bankers is that the government, and in particular the chancellor, George Osborne, has conspicuously sided with Sir Mervyn rather than with them.

But Sir Mervyn has not got everything right. And, in a lecture for the BBC in May of 2012, he almost acknowledged that. He said:

We should have shouted from the rooftops that a system had been built in which banks were too important to fail, that banks had grown too quickly and borrowed too much, and that so called 'light-touch' regulation hadn't prevented any of this.

(BBC *Today* Programme Lecture, 2 May 2012)

It was almost a *mea culpa*. But not quite. It was prefaced by 'with the benefit of hindsight' – and when any of us say 'if I knew then what I know now', we are excusing ourselves, not apologising.

CHAPTER 6

HOW THE BANKERS HID THE RISKS THAT BANKRUPTED US, WITH A LITTLE HELP FROM BASEL'S MYSTERIOUS AND SECRET PRIESTHOOD

Basel seems to the casual visitor to be a very odd place to find the world's oldest international financial organisation, the Bank for International Settlements (BIS). Since 1930 it has been where central bankers have come together to discuss their mutual interests and challenges (which is why the BIS is known as the central bankers' central bank). It is a clean, prosperous bourgeois town, quiet apart from the rattle of trams. Architecturally, it is low rise and unremarkable – except for the anomalous 1970s cylindrical tower in Basel's centre, which houses the BIS. The BIS's head office looks like a watchtower. And that is what it is supposed to be, for the global financial economy. Its main role is to help central banks preserve monetary and financial stability – so it keeps an eye out for brewing storms that could shake that stability. Also, as from the end of 1974, the BIS has played host to a special committee, known as the Basel Committee, with a mandate to make the global banking system safer. Because the Basel Committee was created by the central bank governors of the G10 group of what were then the world's most powerful economies, it has great authority, even if it doesn't have legislative powers. For big banks, it is the most important and powerful regulator in the world, because what the Basel Committee decides about how much capital and cash banks need to hold becomes the global norm. If the committee gets something fundamentally wrong, that's not just a problem for banks – it's a problem for all of us too, because of the central role that banks play in wealth creation. So the Basel Committee may be the most important official decision-making body that you've never heard of.

The Basel Committee was established to fill the gaps in regulation that became bigger and more worrying as banking became more international while the oversight of banks remained national. The requirement for a global perspective arose with the growth in the 1960s of the eurodollar market, which made it much easier for banks to borrow in one country and then lend in another. What particularly focussed central bankers' and regulators' minds was the collapse of two banks, Germany's Herstatt Bank in June 1974, and America's Franklin National Bank in October of the same year. In both cases, their operations went across national borders, but it was unclear whether the regulators in their respective home countries had the responsibility and powers to sort out their overseas businesses.

The initial work of the Basel Committee was to come up with an agreement or concordat that would determine

whether lead regulatory responsibility for banks would be
with the regulator in their home countries, or with the regulators where their subsidiaries and branches were based, the
host-country regulators. The presumption was established
that the home-country regulator should be in charge – which
was sensible if the regulator was able to get access to all the
financial information about a bank's global operations via
that bank's head office. But over the years it has become
clear that relying on the bank's home-country regulator,
especially a regulator in a small country with limited regulatory resources, can be dangerous: Iceland's financial regulator did not prevent the UK operations of Iceland's banks
from wreaking financial and economic havoc in Britain
(although it was the way the European Union implemented
Basel's so-called 'home-country' principle that emasculated
the UK's Financial Services Authority in its relations with
Icelandic banks).

In the early 1980s, the focus of the Basel Committee shifted.
It started to write the rules, which would then be implemented
by national regulators, on how much capital banks should
hold as protection against possible losses. The spur was that in
1982 a number of big banks – especially American ones such
as Citibank and Chase Manhattan, but also Lloyds of the UK
– were facing huge losses on their loans to Argentina, Brazil
and Mexico. It is widely thought that if they had been forced
to account for their losses using today's accounting rules, they
would have been declared bust. But back then regulators gave
banks much more leeway to hide losses till they had raised
additional capital and taken remedial action. Even so, the US
Congress was furious with the banks and demanded that
American regulators should force the banks to hold much
more capital as protection against prospective losses.

Even though the American banks were humiliated, they have fearsome lobbying power. And they complained that with banking becoming vastly more international, they would be put at a significant competitive disadvantage if they were compelled to hold more capital than their overseas competitors. They were particularly worried by the threat from Japan's banks, which were becoming the biggest banks in the world on the back of Japan's astonishingly rapid economic growth, and which operated with tiny amounts of capital relative to their loans and investments. You will remember that although depositors in banks and lenders to banks would typically want banks to hold lots of capital, because it means their money would be safer, the managers and owners usually want the banks to hold relatively less capital, in that they see capital as expensive (all else being equal, a bank holding more capital relative to its loans earns less interest and therefore makes smaller profits with which to pay dividends to the owners and bonuses to the executives). So the Americans decided to push for worldwide minimum standards for the amount of capital banks have to hold relative to their assets, to create a more level playing field.

US regulators found that their British colleagues at the Bank of England had similar ideas about what was needed. And although the Basel Committee, under its bluff British chairman Peter Cooke, who had been seconded to Basel by the Bank of England, was working away on writing common standards for capital, its role was temporarily usurped by an Anglo–American entente on new capital rules. Mr Cooke had been a Bank of England lifer, but the Bank of England kept him in the dark about its negotiations with the US Federal Reserve. When they presented their fait accompli, he felt embarrassed and undermined. Even so, with some to-ing and fro-ing, and concessions made to the irked French in particular, the first global compact on capital requirements for banks was formalised in 1988, an agreement that became known as Basel I, the first iteration of the Basel Rules.

At the time, Basel I was of interest to a small circle of regulators, central bankers, bankers, financial analysts and banking correspondents, which included me, as Banking Correspondent of the *Independent* newspaper and then Banking Editor of the *Financial Times*. At the time, I wrote about the new global framework for banks with considerable reluctance: it all seemed so dull. Today I realise I was making a lazy mistake. The way that banks operate should be of interest to all of us, because they have so much power to affect our way of life, for better or worse. I didn't really get that at the time. Like much of the media, and most of our politicians, no alarm bells rang for me that these rules of banking were written by a secret society of banking experts, a financial priesthood. The way it was done, behind closed doors with no serious public debate, was an affront to democracy. But almost no one noticed or cared. Basel I and its successor Basel II mucked things up for all of us. But such is the status of the financial priests that they've only been very slightly constrained by elected governments in writing Basel III.

Gaming culture

It was the cultural impact on banks of the Basel Rules that was particularly pernicious. The rules undermined banks' sense of institutional responsibility for their lending and for the way they managed their balance sheets. Banking moved away from being almost exclusively based on an assessment of the creditworthiness of individual customers and towards the development of strategies to maximise gross lending subject to the

Basel Rules. Or to put it another way, an industry was created to game the rules, to allocate resources in ways that seemed to generate the biggest profits without breaching the rules. The merits of a particular customer or the health of a particular sector or country were often less important than what the Basel Rules stipulated for the capital charge on lending to that category of customer. In specifying the risks inherent in different types of loan to different borrowers – mortgages versus loans to businesses or loans to governments, for example – the regulators distorted flows of credit to those borrowers, often in ways that were both unexpected and dangerous.

As well as making all banks subject to common standards, the Basel Rules introduced two important concepts: risk-weightings for loans and relative loss absorbency for capital (I know we are straying into what seems tediously theological territory, but please don't be put off). Both concepts turned out to be flawed in the execution, and perhaps in theory too. Take the idea of risk-weightings. This grouped together types of loans, according to their riskiness, as determined by the Basel Committee. All direct loans to business, for example, were given a rating of 1, because they were seen as among the riskiest class of credit. This meant that banks had to hold the maximum amount of capital, $8 for every $100 lent, a capital requirement of 8%, on all loans to companies. But residential mortgages were deemed to be less risky. They had a risk weighting of a half, which meant that banks had to hold capital of just $4 for every $100 lent. As for loans to other banks and loans to governments, these had risk weightings of a fifth and nil – which meant that just a tiny amount of capital had to be held against loans to other banks and none at all for holdings of government bonds (which are loans to governments). Now, capital is perceived by banks to be expensive. So these differential weightings gave incentives to banks to keep on their balance sheets those loans and investments where the capital requirement was lowest but the interest returns were highest. There was a powerful motivation for the banks, therefore, to engage in the kind of financial innovation that would create loans and investments that would be classified by the Basel Rules as having low-risk weights but which generated relatively high returns. And hence, for example, there was a great spur from the Basel Rules for the manufacture of those toxic AAA-rated collateralised debt obligations out of subprime loans: if these CDOs were held by the banks for trading, for example, there was almost no capital charge applicable to them.

One disturbing distortion of the supply of credit stemmed from the lack of any differentiation in the original Basel Rules in the risk-weightings attached to loans to big companies and to small companies. It was now equally expensive for banks, in respect of capital requirements, when lending to large, long-established companies and when lending to small, younger businesses. And because big companies did not want to pay banks the relatively high interest rates banks demanded as compensation for the capital charge on these corporate loans, big companies were incentivised to bypass the banking system altogether, by selling bonds to investors. Now maybe it was beneficial for the economy that a new source of credit for big companies was created in this way. But it certainly was not beneficial for banks that they had fewer safer loans to big companies on their books. In this instance, as in many others, the Basel Rules made banks' balance sheets weaker and more fragile – quite the opposite of what the rules were supposed to do.

Also, the lower risk-weightings for mortgages, government bonds and interbank loans (or loans to other banks) provided incentives for banks to channel credit disproportionately to home buyers, to governments and to each other, rather than to any kind of real business. The regulators were in effect encouraging banks to engage in proportionately less lending to real wealth creators and more lending to property speculators, feckless banks (like those of Ireland) and financially reckless governments (such as the Greek government). All of these first order, Basel-induced market distortions were magnified by second order, Basel-spurred financial innovation, with the transformation of subprime mortgages, commercial property loans, credit-card debt and loans to highly indebted or leveraged companies into AAA-rated bonds. The Basel Rules encouraged banks to engage in the re-engineering of loans and investments to make those loans and investments appear to be less risky. So risks became hidden. All this financial innovation made banks' balance sheets much harder to understand and made it almost impossible to see where the fault lines resided in an ever more complex and interconnected financial system.

What did the Basel Committee do when it recognised that national regulators were struggling to keep up with all this innovation and were ill-equipped to assess the risks being taken by individual banks? What they probably should have done was force the banks to simplify their activities and return to the basics of knowing their respective customers and assessing intrinsic credit risk. Instead they made the rules even more complicated, first in an updated Basel I and then in Basel II. What was perhaps more absurd and dangerous, bigger banks were given great discretion to determine their capital needs based on their own in-house risk-management systems, rather than via a crude mechanistic use of the Basel weightings. And the more sophisticated banks with large investment and trading operations were encouraged to use flawed Value at Risk models to determine how much capital they needed to cover the risk of trading losses on their holdings of securities. All that AAA poison made from subprime and private equity debt could be held at precious little capital cost. And there were zero capital requirements on banks for the contingent credit they provided to the shadow banks, the conduits and SIVs, which were among the big customers for all those AAA-rated bonds made out of mortgages and so on.

The Basel Rules helped to turn individual banks into black boxes, institutions whose workings and risks were impossible to see, and they turned the banking system into a dangerous network of interconnected black boxes, where if one went down they all went down. Banks had too many low-quality loans disguised as good loans on their books. And they had lent far too much to each other. If one bank became vulnerable, many banks became vulnerable (which duly happened in 2007–8, and – in the eurozone especially – again in 2011). Banks became more fragile, both individually and collectively: Basel increased the risk that if one bank went bust, all would go bust.

The hideous complexity of the financial system, made more bewildering by the minutiae of the Basel Rules, conferred extraordinary influence on a tiny, largely unaccountable group of analytical firms: the credit-rating agencies. There are three that are prominent: Standard & Poor's, Moody's and Fitch. They became almost the fulcrum of financial globalisation because it was so difficult for even a well-resourced investment firm to calculate the intrinsic riskiness of buying a new-generation financial product, or of lending to one of the sprawling, impenetrable global banks. So they subcontracted these evaluations to the specialist ratings firms – whose

authority became such that they could make or break financial products, banks or even governments. When France lost
its AAA rating in January 2012, it shook markets and was big
news – even though the downgrade by Standard & Poor's had
been expected and was not based on any information or
insight lacked by any moderately intelligent and plugged-in
investor. What is more, although even prime ministers moan
that the ratings agencies have too much clout and are subject
to too little regulation, their power is officially sanctioned, in
that central banks use their ratings when deciding how much
and whether to lend to banks (central banks will typically lend
to a bank only if the bank provides collateral that has a credit-
rating above a certain threshold). But here is what shocks
many: the agencies were a major contributor to the boom in
collateralised debt obligations that wreaked so much havoc,
because they gave AAA ratings to bonds made out of subprime
loans. They made it respectable for historically conservative
banks to load up on AAA-rated CDOs that were almost all
liberally laced with poison. Also, they caused huge borrowing
difficulties for eurozone banks and governments, when there
were rumours that banks and governments were on the cusp
of seeing their credit-ratings downgraded. Which is why, in
Europe in particular, there is an attempt to regulate them
more stringently and shatter their near-monopoly in the
assessment of the credit-worthiness of the world's biggest and
most important borrowers. That said, the financial world
remains so complex and opaque that it defies analysis by mere
mortal investors. The troika of ratings agencies are likely to
wield vast – and some would say pernicious – influence for
many more years.

Basel did something else that looks counter to what any
sane regulator would want: it helped banks exaggerate the

absolute quantity of capital they possessed to absorb whatever losses might arise. Banks were required by the Basel Rules to hold capital equivalent to 8% of risk-weighted assets. But this was divided into two classes of capital: Tier 1 capital and Tier 2 capital, categorised according to the loss-absorbing properties of the capital. And even within the tiers there was a differentiation by quality, between 'core' capital and 'hybrid' capital, and so on. Now the best quality capital is what is known as equity. This is the money that the owners or shareholders put into the bank and it confers ownership of the bank. The benefit of ownership is that the shareholders are entitled to all the profits of the bank – some of which is paid to them in the form of a dividend; some of which stays in the bank to increase the value of the equity. The best way to think of the equity is as what would be left over after a bank has repaid all its debts. Now the price of ownership is that in the bad years, when the bank makes losses on loans and investments, these losses eat into the equity. And as we have already seen, when all the equity is gone, the bank is bust. Which is why the whole point of bank regulation is to make sure banks always have enough capital to stay in business.

How much capital is enough capital? Well, deciding that is more of an art than a science. I asked Peter Cooke in late 2010 how it was that his committee had hit upon the idea that 8% was the correct ratio of capital to risk-weighted assets. He said:

We had these observation ratios; we were monitoring the actual levels of capital in different countries and the constituents and the answer came up round about 7% as an average. So I said: 'It looks to me as though, you know, we need to perhaps be a little more prudent than the average, so let's say 8%.' It just came out of my head, I'm afraid. Nothing more scientific than that.

(Interview with the author for *Britain's Banks,*
Too Big to Save?)

But although the Basel Rules say banks have to hold total capital equal to at least 8% of risk-weighted assets, only 2% of this needs to be in the form of pure or 'core' equity capital. The rest of it could be in other forms, which in theory were also capable of absorbing losses and of thus protecting depositors from losses. So 4% was called Tier 2 capital, and was long-term 'subordinated' debt – which is debt that does not need to be repaid for many years, and whose holders would be paid back after other creditors in the event that the bank is wound up (or closed down). Another 2% could be lower quality or hybrid Tier 1 capital, which is debt where there were mechanisms for converting it into equity (what is known as convertible debt) or debt that never has to be repaid ('perpetual' debt).

In theory, all capital should be capable of absorbing losses, and thus of sheltering depositors and other creditors from the risk of those losses. Those providing the hybrid Tier 1 capital or the Tier 2 capital to the banks were supposed to be well-heeled, sophisticated investors, well aware that they were taking risks in lending to banks in this way. So when banks ran into difficulties in 2007 and 2008, it should have been straightforward for the losses the banks were making to be imposed on the holders of this form of capital. But that is not how it turned out. In practice, banks and regulators were too frightened of the potential consequences of forcing investors and financial institutions to write down what they were owed by troubled banks to whom they had lent in this 'subordinated' fashion. They were worried that it would cause these investors and institutions to pull their money out of weaker banks, thus potentially bankrupting them. Then in early 2009 another complication arose. Regulators noticed that much of this Tier 2 capital was held by insurance companies. And they became concerned that if these insurers were forced to take big losses on their holdings of this debt, the solvency of some of them could have been jeopardised; in other words, they would have gone bust. The banking crisis could have sparked an insurance industry crisis. Unsurprisingly, the view of regulators was that trying to solve arguably the worst banking crisis ever was enough of a challenge; they could do without trying to rescue big insurance companies at the same time (although in the US, the insurance giant AIG did have to be rescued by the government, because it underwrote a vast quantity of credit default swaps, and had to pay out more than it could afford when there were defaults on staggering quantities of the insured debt). When the government launched rescues of big banks like Royal Bank of Scotland, Lloyds and HBOS, there was no attempt to force holders of these banks' subordinated debts to contribute to the rescues by formally writing off what they were owed. In that sense, Tier 2 and around half of the Tier 1 capital turned out to be completely useless in respect of its central function, that of absorbing losses.

RBS and Northern Rock

One terrible consequence of the Basel Rules on risk-weightings and tiered capital, combined with banks' instinctive propensity to 'game' the rules, is that banks ended up lending terrifyingly large amounts relative to the good quality equity capital that was a proper shock absorber, and not just a cosmetic one. Take Royal Bank of Scotland. On 8 August

2008, it claimed to have a ratio of total capital to risk-weighted assets of 13.2% and a ratio of core Tier 1 capital to assets of 6.7% – both of which looked extremely healthy, on paper. But remember that this calculation was done on the basis that many of its loans and investments, its assets, were weighted for the purpose of this capital calculation at zero or close to zero. They simply didn't figure in the denominator when doing the capital ratio calculation, even though they were real loans and investments that could go bad. And of course, RBS was counting as part of its capital all that subordinated debt which turned out to be capital in name only and was no protection against the losses that materialised. If you took out all the fancy-schmancy capital, it had £43bn of ordinary shareholders' equity supporting £1.95 trillion of gross loans and investments (the loans and investments actually made by RBS, as opposed to the much smaller risk-weighted number). Or to put it another way, it had lent forty-five times the value of its capital – which means it only required a fall of 2.2% in the value of Royal Bank of Scotland's loans and investments for all its equity capital to be wiped out, for the bank therefore to be bust. These losses were visited on RBS, and taxpayers had to inject £45.8bn of new capital into the bank at the end of 2008 and in 2009 to keep the bank alive – and that was after it raised £12bn of capital in the spring of 2008 (which at the time was a record amount of capital to be raised by a British company in one lump). Now anyone who has ever lent £10 or made any kind of investment knows that a fall of 2.2% in the value of loans or investments is not a rare event. And yet Royal Bank of Scotland was permitted – by its board, by shareholders, by regulators, by the government – to grow to a size that not only risked bankrupting shareholders but risked bankrupting the British state. RBS had lent and invested substantially more – 40% more – than the annual output of the British economy. If losses on those loans had been much greater, the government's own creditors would have started to question whether British taxpayers had pockets deep enough to prop up RBS. The irresponsibility of RBS's directors, owners and regulators in allowing such recklessness beggars belief, until that is you remember that under the Basel Rules, RBS didn't seem to be taking such big risks at all. Under the Basel measurement, with its capital ratio of 13.2%, RBS appeared to have lent a mere 7.6 times its capital, not the real 45 times. The Basel Rules created the fiction that RBS was managing itself in a conservative way, and was being supported generously by its owners, the private-sector providers of equity and other forms of capital. In other words, for RBS, and for most big banks, the Basel Rules had become a way of disguising their fundamental weakness, rather than doing what they were supposed to do, which was to make them better able to withstand shocks.

If you want an even more shocking example of the inadequacy of the Basel Rules, you only have to look at the balance sheet of Northern Rock shortly before it begged the Bank of England to bail it out. Believe it or not, on 25 July 2007 – or less than two months before it had failed as a bank – the Rock announced it would be reducing the amount of capital it would be holding. It intended to do this by increasing its dividend and returning between £300m and £400m of capital to shareholders. What is quite horrifying is that it was doing this with the encouragement of its benighted owners and with the approval – given on 29 June 2007 – of the City watchdog, the Financial Services Authority. How could this happen? Well it was all due to the new approach to weighting the risks inherent in loans and investment of the revised Basel Rules, what were called Basel II. Here are the terrifying statistics on what Basel II meant for Northern Rock. It had gross assets on its balance sheet of £113.5bn. Under Basel I, these had a risk-weighted value of £33.9bn. However, Basel II put an even lower risk-weighted value on these mortgages and other loans of just £18.9bn. Northern Rock, whose mortgages and other assets totalled £113.5bn, only had to hold capital equivalent to 8% of £18.9bn. Northern Rock in 2007 was being permitted by the FSA, under international rules, to lend seventy-five times its Tier 1 and Tier 2 capital. But if, like me, you think the only capital that matters is ordinary shareholders' equity – which was not supposed to drop below 2% of assets – then Northern Rock was being permitted by the FSA to lend something like 300 times this core capital. Little surprise therefore that the FSA has had to admit that its regulation and supervision of Northern Rock was unsatisfactory. I am not sure if it is comforting or alarming that the Rock collapsed as a bank long before it was able to take advantage of its permission to give capital back to shareholders. Had it done so, the cost for taxpayers of bailing out the bank would have increased by a further few hundred million pounds.

Solvency vs. liquidity

The other great failure of the Basel Rules, and of regulation in general, is that it emphasised solvency – even if in an inadequate, dysfunctional way – but almost completely ignored the importance for banks of liquidity, or how much cash the banks can lay their hands on in a hurry. In a practical sense, liquidity is probably more important for a bank than solvency. A bank that is solvent but has too little cash at a time when its depositors and creditors want their money back is dead. By contrast, a bank that is insolvent but manages to hide its losses can stay afloat for a long time – and can possibly rebuild its capital and thus become solvent again – so long as its creditors and depositors don't all ask for their money back at the same time. Arguably Lloyds and a number of big American banks were insolvent or close to insolvent in the 1980s, after a number of Latin American countries struggled to repay their international debts. But they stayed alive because they were able, under the accounting rules of the time, to hide the full extent of loan write-offs. To paraphrase the great nineteenth-century pioneer of banking theory, Walter Bagehot, a well-run bank (or at least a bank perceived to be well run) can operate with no capital – and pretty much all the capital in the world won't keep a bank alive if it loses the confidence of its depositors and creditors. So it is remarkable and perhaps appalling that regulators paid almost no attention to the liquidity of banks, until after the credit crunch had begun and it was far too late.

How on earth did yet another of these grotesque regulatory lacunae develop? It was because of a belief, which became pervasive after all those innovations that helped banks buy and sell debt, that in a worst case banks could always find a buyer for their loans and investments: so they did not have to sacrifice interest income by holding significant reserves of cash. Or to put it another way, the rise and rise of securitisation, the growth and triumph of bond markets, persuaded banks that there was a vast ocean of cash in the world that they could draw on at a millisecond's notice whenever they needed. This created a general presumption that banks would never again be troubled by a run, because if they ever needed ready money in a hurry, they could always sell their loans and investments on these markets. The consequence was that – under the noses of regulators such as the Financial Services Authority in the UK – banks squirrelled away less and less cash. And that is why the closure of asset-backed debt markets on 9 August 2007 was such a profoundly damaging event. One insight into the calamitous failure of banks to hold enough cash was given by the sadder but wiser FSA in late 2011: it estimated that if RBS in August 2008 had truly wanted to protect itself against the risk of collapse stemming from a run, it needed an additional £166bn in cash and genuinely liquid assets. That shows quite how weak RBS was at the time – and it is yet another indictment of the bank's board, as well as showing the ineptitude of the FSA, in allowing this huge and important organisation to become so vulnerable. There are not many banks in the world with total balance sheets as big as £166bn, let alone £166bn in cash or proxies for cash. The FSA has admitted that the Royal Bank of Scotland needed to hold that much extra in cash just to be confident that it would not be put out of business by the decision of capricious big lenders that they no longer wanted to finance it.

Faith in free-market capitalism

The global banking crisis represented the most catastrophic global regulatory failure in history – and I mean regulatory failure of any kind, not just financial regulatory failure. The rules and regulations for banks incentivised them to maximise and hide the risks they were taking, which was precisely the opposite of what was intended. It was stunningly lousy regulation. But something else went wrong too: there was not enough supervision of banks by regulators, too little interference by watchdogs in how they were practising their trade. Banks were too trusted by regulators to do the right and rational thing. Why? Well there was an ideological conviction that markets work best when relatively unfettered and that interference by regulators and politicians is a necessary evil best kept to an absolute minimum. There was a widespread conviction that we would all be richer – the economy would grow faster, wealth creation would be spurred – if banks and investors were left alone to determine the supply of credit and its price for different customers, subject to the official rates set by central banks. The corollary of the collapse of communism and the triumph of Western-style capitalism and democracy was the pervasive view – whose most public champion was perhaps Alan Greenspan – that free-market capitalism was best of all. There was an almost religious faith in the notion that investors and creditors are always rational and endowed with relevant information when extending credit or buying and selling assets such as shares and bonds.

The idea that markets are efficient and rational might be a useful theoretical construct; an ideal or benchmark for assessing quite how far markets are from a state of perfection. But as almost anyone who has ever worked in financial market will tell you, it does not describe the world as it is. It is a very dangerous precept for regulators and for those in banks overseeing the monitoring and control of risk. And yet it was a precept adopted by these regulators and risk-controllers. Participants in markets are often emotional, excitable and ignorant – never all-seeing and all-knowing. And the idea that aggregating all their many millions of prejudices and instincts through the mechanism of the market will wash out the imperfections and produce a perfect outcome simply isn't borne out by the facts. Market prices can and do diverge from where they ought to be, on a rational assessment, for many months and years. In our story, what matters is that for several years before the crash of 2007–8, massively too much cheap credit was supplied in the UK, US, Ireland, Spain, Greece and so on by bankers and investors allegedly endowed with superior intelligence. What is now clear is that regulators did not believe the evidence of their eyes. As Alan Greenspan has to an extent conceded, they were so in thrall to the ideology that unfettered markets will produce the best economic outcomes that they could not see quite how far from the truth this was turning out to be. In October 2008, Mr Greenspan made this confession to the US House of Representatives' Committee on Oversight and Government Reform: 'Those of us who have looked to the self-interest of lending institutions to protect shareholders' equity, myself especially, are in a state of shocked disbelief.' Mr Greenspan did not believe that banks collectively and systematically could lend colossal sums without due regard for the risks.

The wealthiest people in markets, like the hedge-fund superstars John Paulson and George Soros, build their careers and make their fortunes from exploiting the way that markets constantly misprice assets and behave inefficiently and irrationally. In a sense their newly created wealth is conspicuous proof of how naïve it was of regulators to assume that big financial institutions would instinctively run their affairs in a prudent way. Paulson became rich beyond anyone's wildest dreams in 2007 precisely because he saw that collateralised debt obligations made out of subprime loans were chronically overvalued and that their price would eventually tumble. If these CDOs had been traded in a genuinely efficient market, he would never have been able to place his enormous bets that they would collapse in value, because the price of CDOs would have corrected too quickly for him to put all his money on the table.

There are many reasons why it is foolish and dangerous to assume that the market price is always in some sense the 'right' price. One is the sheer complexity of modern financial products, such as the collateralised debt obligation. And, to be clear, it is not bad luck that there is often a divergence between the actual price of such complex products and their inherent value. The smart investment banker will usually make a high-falutin claim that financial innovation of this sort is aimed at better aligning a product with the risk and reward preferences of the investor. But what in practice is often happening is that the risks are deliberately hidden from the investor in the sheer complexity of the product – which makes it all the easier to persuade the investor to pay too high a price for the product (to extract rent, in the economist's jargon; more bluntly, to gull him or her). Arguably, the veil was drawn back on all this by Fabrice Tourre, the Goldman Sachs executive director accused of fraud (which he denies) in the sale of a collateralised debt obligation with the snappy name of Abacus 2007-AC1. In an email sent to a friend in late January 2007, he said of these complex bonds that:

> When I think that I had some input into the creation of this product (which by the way is a product of pure intellectual masturbation, the type of thing which you invent telling yourself, 'Well, what if we created a "thing", which has no purpose, which is absolutely conceptual and highly theoretical and whose price nobody knows?') it makes me sick at heart to see it blow up in flight ... It is a bit like Frankenstein turning against his inventor.
>
> (translation of email from Fabrice Tourre,
> GS trader, to Fatiha Bukhtouche, 29 January 2007)

Now some of the market fundamentalists, the believers that the private sector can never be wrong, argue that the problem is not in markets, but that regulators are still meddling too much. It is regulation that is imperfect, not markets, they would say. And we've certainly seen that the extant regulation was a long way from satisfactory. If it hadn't been for the Basel Rules, for example, there would have been less of an incentive to create all those complex mortgage-backed securities to get round banks' capital constraints. The Basel Rules contributed to a trend of banks spending less time on assessing the credit-worthiness of borrowers and instead directing credit to customers deemed less risky by those regulator-imposed rules. There was, for example, far too much bank lending for property development in Ireland, Spain, the UK and the US – in part driven by capital adequacy rules, which, in effect, made it much cheaper for a bank to make a property-backed loan than to invest in a new plant for making silicon chips. In the UK, the bias towards commercial property development was particularly pernicious, as research by the Financial Services Authority has demonstrated. This showed that between 1990 and 2008 all of the increase in lending by banks to businesses, as a percentage of GDP, was in the form of commercial-property loans, and that the total borrowing of other non-financial companies such as manufacturers fell (again as measured as a share of GDP). In other words, the British banking system failed in what was perhaps its most important economic function, which was to direct credit to where it could be most productively used in a sustainable sense. Britain's banks – incentivised by the Basel Rules – encouraged economic growth that was based too much on unsustainable property speculation rather than the output of businesses that make things.

But here is where you can see the basic flaw in the argument that the problem in the West is that there is too little freedom for markets rather than too much. In placing absolute trust in financial markets to determine where credit should be allocated and at what price, we ignore our herd instincts and our relatively short-term memories. We have irresistible urges to invest the way that other people are investing. When the price of property is rising fast, for example, we all encounter terrible desires to invest more and more in property, to climb on the bandwagon. As the psychologist Daniel Kahneman and others have shown, our herd-like mentality is fundamental to our nature. This is not a new insight, although we often forgot it. The overwhelming power of the herd to determine market prices in the short term was identified in the mid 1930s by JM Keynes:

> The energies and skills of the professional investor and speculator are mainly occupied . . . with foreseeing changes in the conventional basis of valuation a short time ahead of the general public. They are concerned not with what an investment is really worth to a man who buys it 'for keeps' but with what the market will value it at, under the influence of mass psychology, three months or a year hence . . . The professional investor is forced to concern himself with the anticipation of impending changes, in the news or in the atmosphere, of the kind by which experience shows that the mass psychology of the market is most influenced.
>
> Investment based on genuine long-term expectation is so difficult today as to be scarcely practicable. He who attempts it must surely lead much more laborious days and run greater risks than he who tries to guess better than the crowd how the crowd will behave; and, given equal intelligence, he may make more disastrous mistakes. There is no clear evidence from experience that the investment policy

which is most socially advantageous coincides with what is
most profitable.

(JM Keynes, *General Theory of Employment,*
Interest and Money, 1936)

So it is rational for any investor to try to pre-empt the behaviour of the herd – which of course ensures the primacy of the
herd in determining market movements.

Rose-tinted glasses

When economic conditions are benign for an extended period,
it is human nature to assume that the risks of borrowing and
lending are diminishing. The longer we enjoy rising living
standards, the more we assume that is the norm, and the more
faint and unreal our memories of previous recessions and
hardship become. And so in years of steadily improving prosperity, we become more and more indebted, until we've
borrowed more than we can afford. Few can doubt that
describes what happened in so much of the rich West from
the mid 1990s onwards. The increased myopia towards risk,
the product of an extended boom, afflicted most of us, including the regulators. It would be funny, if it weren't tragic, that
between January 2006 and July 2007, when credit was being
provided by banks in a more reckless way than at any time
perhaps since the nineteenth century, the sixty-one major
topics discussed by the board of the Financial Services
Authority included just one related in some way to the prudential risks taken by banks (or whether banks were lending and
investing cautiously or recklessly). And in the 101 submissions to the board by the FSA's chief executive, again just one
related to so-called prudential issues. As the FSA itself admits:
'until the summer of 2007, therefore, FSA board agendas

reflected the judgement that bank prudential issues were, at that time, a low priority since market conditions were benign.'★ (FSA, 'The Failure of the Royal Bank of Scotland', December 2011). The experts paid to preserve the stability of the banking system were as deluded as the rest of us that the good times would never end.

All of modern history demonstrates this very propensity, rooted in human nature, for markets to swing from boom to bust. And often we should not be too worried about that. The descent from dot-com boom to bust at the turn of the millennium – from absurdly high valuations of technology businesses to the collapse of many of them – did surprisingly little fundamental harm to our living standards. And the boom, irrational as it was, might have done some good – in allowing companies such as Google with brilliant ideas and technology to raise incredibly cheap capital. As for the bust, the thing about falls in share prices is that the losses tend to fall on people and institutions who can take the hit. Of course, it is always very painful to lose money. But pension funds, insurance companies and many individuals invest in shares for the long term. They can usually absorb even a sharp fall in the value of shares by belt tightening of various sorts. The exception of course is when shares have been bought with borrowed money – when the investment is leveraged. Because then a drop in the value of the shares makes it very hard for the investor to repay the debts. At that point the investor is bust.

Here is why it was so unfortunate that banking regulators such as the Financial Services Authority – urged on by the Labour government, but responding to a zeitgeist infecting all mainstream parties – adopted a policy of imposing the

---

★ FSA, 'The Failure of the Royal Bank of Scotland', December 2011.

minimum necessary regulation (often described as 'light touch' regulation). The point is that when there is a boom and bust in credit markets, the losses cannot easily be absorbed. It is no anomaly that the dot-com stock-market bust did relatively little harm to the growth of the British and American economies, whereas by contrast the banking and credit crisis of 2007–8 led to a contraction in UK GDP of 6.3%, years of economic stagnation and the sharpest squeeze of living standards in recorded memory. When share prices fall, pension funds and insurance companies may have to ask savers to contribute more or they may have to reduce the benefits they give to pensioners and savers – which is painful, but not catastrophic, for the savers and the economy. But when investments held by banks collapse in value, or creditors can't pay their debts, banks incur losses that erode their capital. In the worst case, banks go bust and cannot lend at all. In the best case, the squeeze on their capital resources forces them to rein in lending. In either case, the impact on our prosperity tends to be significant and for the worst. When banks can't lend to businesses and households, economic activity grinds to a halt: we all become much poorer. Precisely because regulators sought not to tame markets but to hasten their evolution to a state of perfection, we are all a good deal poorer. In a way we are the victims of the conversion of the governing and regulating class to the financial religion of market perfectibility.

CHAPTER 7

IF EUROPE SUFFERS ONLY A LOST DECADE, IT MAY HAVE GOT OFF LIGHTLY

The greatest immediate threat to the prosperity and financial stability of the world is the weakness of Europe's giant, interconnected banks. Many of them – in Spain, Greece, Italy and elsewhere – are perceived to have too little capital to absorb losses. And in countries where the public-sector finances are perceived to be weak, such as Spain, many of the banks are struggling to hang on to deposits and are finding it almost impossible to borrow from other banks and financial institutions. They have therefore become increasingly dependent on rescue loans from the European Central Bank and the central banks of their respective countries. They have been put on life support, and it is not remotely clear how and whether they will again become healthy, viable and independent. These weak banks cannot stay on the central banks' drip forever. In return for the money they receive from the central bank, they have to pledge their assets, their loans and investments. The limit on how much they can borrow from central banks is the value of assets they have not already pledged to lenders. What happens as and when a big bank runs out of what are known as 'unencumbered' and 'eligible' assets is wrapped in mystery. Would the European Central Bank allow it to go bust, and risk triggering a devastating run on other weak banks and a credit crunch on a truly calamitous scale? Or would the ECB provide the kind of bailout that, in practice, would represent a massive transfer of wealth from the richer, stronger countries, like Germany, to the weaker ones. When I ask senior officials and ministers about this, they shrug and have nothing helpful to say. In the UK and US, we are bystanders in all this – but bystanders at risk of being very badly injured if the eurozone does not restore confidence to its banks.

There is a long version of how this potential disaster was allowed to take its hideous form, and a short version. The truncated narrative begins in the aftermath of the collapse of Lehman Brothers in the autumn of 2008 and – some would say – is a tale of the hubris of the eurozone's leaders. Here is Peer Steinbrück, who at the time was the Finance Minister of Germany, making the legitimate point that much of the crisis of the time was down to the recklessness of US and UK banks – but perhaps enjoying the woes of the City and Wall Street a little too much:

> The way of thinking on Wall Street was quite clear: Money makes the world go round! The logic went like this: The government should stay out of our business! And when we Germans began – and perhaps it was even too late by then – to ask for controls, for more transparency and equity guidelines, they laughed at us at first.
>
> There will be shifts in terms of the importance and status of New York and London as the two main financial centres. State-owned banks and funds, as well as commercial banks

from Europe, China, Russia and the Arab world will close the gaps, creating new centres of power in the financial world.

(*Der Spiegel*, September 2008)

Later that year, in December, the German Chancellor Angela Merkel lauded the putative values of thrift and prudence of the archetypal Swabian housewife in discussing how to clean up global financial capitalism. 'She would give us some short and correct advice,' Mrs Merkel said. 'You cannot live beyond your means in the long run.' And in France, the president at the time, Nicolas Sarkozy, felt France should now instruct Britain and America about how to sanitise the financial system. In November 2009, he told the *Le Monde* newspaper: 'it's the first time in fifty years that France has had this role. The English are the big losers in this business.' Later that month, Mr Sarkozy's candidate, fellow Frenchman Michel Barnier, was appointed the new European Commissioner with responsibility to overhaul the regulation of finance, to the considerable annoyance and discomfort of the City of London. Earlier, in April of that year, Sarkozy had threatened to walk out of the G20 summit in London unless the US and UK were willing to sign up to his vision of stricter financial regulation. 'If things don't go forward in London, there will be an empty chair,' he claimed. 'I'll get up and walk out!'

But Mrs Merkel, Mr Sarkozy and their *confrères* conflated two different things. It may well have been reasonable to heap more blame on Royal Bank of Scotland, Citigroup, Lehman, Bank of America, HBOS, Merrill Lynch and AIG, inter alia, for the banking crisis of 2008 than on banks in Spain, Italy, France, Germany and Greece. But the eurozone's leaders seemed to believe that also meant their banks were significantly stronger than British and American banks. And when hundreds of billions of pounds of taxpayers' money were injected into the likes of Citi, RBS, AIG, Lloyds, Goldman Sachs, Morgan Stanley, Bank of America and so on, banks in the eurozone were forced to raise capital as a protection against future losses, but significantly less than their US and UK counterparts and much less than they needed. Although banks on Wall Street and in London may have been more conspicuously vulnerable, Europe's two most influential governments, France and Germany, were blind – perhaps wilfully so – to the fragility of eurozone institutions. What has shocked the Governor of the Bank of England, Sir Mervyn King, in international negotiations at the Basel Committee and the Financial Stability Board on the necessary measures for strengthening banks, is how French and German representatives blocked proposals to rapidly introduce new and lower limits on the gross lending of banks relative to their capital (the so-called gross leverage ratio) – which is another way of saying that they blocked reforms that would have forced their banks to strengthen themselves. This, according to the British representatives on the Basel Committee and the FSB, was short-sighted pursuit of their perceived national economic self-interest by France and Germany, which has since backfired on them.

Eurozone leaders seemed blind to how their own banks had been massively and dangerously increasing how much they lent relative to their shock-absorbing capital and relative to GDP throughout the boom years. The eurozone economy is almost totally dependent on finance provided by banks: about 80% of loans to households and businesses in Europe are provided by banks, compared with just 20% in the US (where securitisation, or the parcelling up of loans into bonds sold to investors is much more important). Also, eurozone banks were vital sources of loans to governments, whose financing needs were becoming greater and greater. Analysis by the Bank of England demonstrates that by 2010 the eurozone's banks were taking much bigger risks than British and American banks, and as of the end of 2011 they were lending 35% more on average relative to their capital than UK banks, and 65% more than US banks. Moreover, they lent too much to governments – Greece, Spain, Italy and so on – whose ability to repay was increasingly in doubt. To put it another way, eurozone banks had relatively little capital to absorb losses, but had succeeded in exposing themselves to enormous potential losses. They had become the global economy's most dangerous fault line.

The eurozone crisis is both a symptom of the wider crisis of capitalism in the West and a special malaise of its own. Like the woes of the UK and US, rich consuming economies like Spain and Greece are in trouble because they borrowed too much from the producing economies, especially – in their case – from Germany. And, as we have seen, many eurozone banks lent and borrowed far too much in relation to their slender capital resources, their buffer against shocks and losses – and were much slower than their UK and US counterparts to own up to their recklessness. These are the debilitating and dangerous symptoms, triggered by the global crash of 2007–8, of flaws in the fundamental design of this economic and monetary union. Arguably what was always needed for the long-term stability and sustainability of this currency union was a political union between the member states, to permit more rational and speedier responses when confronting Europe-wide challenges such as the weakness of banks.

And although many of Europe's leaders now recognise that the salvation of the euro requires the centralisation of important powers to spend, tax, borrow and to supervise banks – in other words, the creation of something that looks a lot more like a United States of Europe – progress is desperately slow, perhaps because the people of Europe do not seem to be clamouring for the dismantling of the nation state.

A union of currencies without a corresponding union of governments and the centralisation of economic decision-making was always a gamble. The designers of the euro, to whom I have spoken, accept that progress towards political integration of member states was the sine qua non of a stable and permanent currency union. Their excuse for merging currencies in the absence of this merger of governments is that they expected the unification of currencies and economies to bring about, in a steady and evolutionary way, the convergence of governments and governance. They paternalistically decided a single currency was in the best interests of the people of Europe, even if that was not overwhelmingly obvious to those citizens. And they assumed that once the people of Europe had experienced all the advantages and putative economic benefits of a single currency, they would be thrilled to replace the cranking and obsolete institutions of the nation state and national governments with gleaming new federal machinery in Brussels. But, as it turned out, quite the reverse happened. In the early phase of monetary union, the few trappings of federalism associated with monetary union were undermined – namely limits on how much eurozone members could borrow in any year, a ceiling on their deficits. And the perceived high-handedness of the European elite seemed to alienate many Europeans, who became more wary of the accretion of power by Brussels. Or to put it another way, the preferences of citizens and the constitutional changes needed to save the euro have not become aligned. Perhaps they will, as the gravity of the impact on living standards of a eurozone break-up becomes more apparent. But right now, the collapse of the euro, with its power to wreak renewed havoc throughout the global economy, remains a clear and present danger.

One coin to rule them all

The creation of the euro was the last gasp of the generation of European politicians scarred by the endemic conflict between Germany and France for much of the nineteenth and twentieth centuries. The euro was seen by them as the logical final stage in the project to integrate European countries, politically and economically, to eliminate the risk of there ever again being a European war. The prominent government figures who were teenagers or young adults in the early 1940s always say that the great achievement of the European Union (and its earlier incarnations) is that there has been no war for more than sixty years in Western Europe, and that the idea of 'ever closer union', encapsulated in the EU's founding Treaty of Rome, remains a noble one. Today's EU may not be perfect. Since the end of the Second World War, France and Germany have evolved from implacable enemies to fractious siblings that boss around the rest of Europe. But although frequently resented by smaller EU countries for their habit of privately deciding how Europe should develop, even their sternest critics would give thanks that there no longer seems the faintest chance that the fields of Europe will be stained red again by the blood of German and French soldiers.

As for the UK, it has a long history of nudging Europe towards unification, while being wary of joining in that

unification. It all started with Winston Churchill, on 19
September 1946, whose speech at Zurich University is still
cited by the supposedly great men of Europe as an
inspiration:

> I wish to speak to you today about the tragedy of Europe . . .
> Yet all the while there is a remedy which, if it were generally
> and spontaneously adopted by the great majority of people
> in many lands, would as if by a miracle transform the whole
> scene, and would in a few years make all Europe, or the
> greater part of it, as free and as happy as Switzerland is
> today. What is this sovereign remedy? It is to recreate the
> European Family, or as much of it as we can, and to provide
> it with a structure under which it can dwell in peace, in
> safety and in freedom. We must build a kind of United
> States of Europe [. . .] The first step in the recreation of the
> European Family must be a partnership between France
> and Germany.
>
> 　　　　　　　(Winston Churchill, speech at Zurich University,
> 　　　　　　　　　　　　　　　　　　　19 September 1946)

This speech remains apposite. Jean-Claude Trichet – probably the most influential French bureaucrat of the past thirty
years, with a lifetime of public service in the French Tresór,
the Banque de France and at the European Central Bank –
told me about his own vision of a federal Europe, and defined
it as a counterpoint to Churchill's:

> It would not necessarily be the United States of Europe as
> Churchill has recommended in his historic, remarkable
> speech. But it might be something where you would have
> a [central] government and clearly the [European]

Commission is the anticipation of the government of Europe.

(Interview with the author for
The Great Euro Crash, BBC2)

The first important phase in this union of France and Germany was the creation in 1951 of the European Coal and Steel Community. It was a practical and symbolic industrial agreement, establishing joint political control of the basic industries viewed at the time as of greatest economic importance. The logic behind the ECSC was the same as has propelled the European project ever since – including the creation of the euro. France and Germany, and any other country that cared to be involved, would begin to interlock their economies. The ensuing mutual dependence would ward off the kind of conflict that could escalate into war. Then in 1957 came the Treaty of Rome, establishing what at the time was called the European Economic Community. Signed by Germany, France, Italy, Belgium, Luxembourg and the Netherlands, its aim was to reinforce peace and prosperity by 'strengthening the unity' of economies.

With a single European economy as the destination, from the start it was logical to merge the currencies of Europe to create a single currency. Plans for monetary union were first drawn up at the end of the 1960s, when the Prime Minister of Luxembourg, Pierre Werner, was commissioned by European governments to write a proposal for how the six members of the EEC could combine their currencies. In 1970, Mr Werner presented his plan for how a single currency could be launched ten years later. At the time, Mr Werner said he and his fellow European government heads had 'reaffirmed the irreversibility of a process that would lead to economic and monetary union'. But although he was right about the direction of travel, the deadline was too soon.

In the 1960s, the world's financial markets worked very differently from today. Currencies did not rise or fall at the whim of speculators in London and New York. Instead, governments fixed the exchange rates of their currencies relative to the US dollar, which in turn was tied to the price of gold. This was known as the Bretton Woods system, named after the 1944 conference at a New Hampshire ski resort where US and European leaders laid the foundations of the postwar world economic system. Bretton Woods provided a degree of financial stability for the reconstruction of Europe's economies, so devastated by the War. But by the late 1960s, the system was creaking. Some countries – notably the UK and France – found themselves unable to compete in international trade. Wage rises demanded by trade unions meant their exports were uncompetitive. They found themselves importing more and more cheap foreign goods, especially from resurgent Germany and Japan, and having to borrow from the rest of the world to pay for them. The borrowing was unsustainable. The UK was the first to crack. In 1967 the government was forced to devalue sterling – prompting the British Prime Minister Harold Wilson to utter the immortal solecism that he had not 'devalued the pound in your pocket'. Then France followed with a devaluation of the franc in 1969. France's devaluation was not a happy experience. Left-wing students had staged violent protests in Paris the previous year, prompting the unions to hold a general strike. The French authorities bought off the unions with big wage rises, and those wage rises sank the franc. Without the devaluation, French workers would have been too expensive to employ, compared with their counterparts in Germany. If all this sounds familiar, well, it should, because sharp divergences between the costs of employing people in different parts of

Europe blew up a subsequent attempt to link currencies in Europe and are threatening to tear apart the eurozone today.

The Werner plan to create a European monetary system with its own currency was blown up by the instability and volatility of the European economy. In 1973–4, and again in 1979, war and revolution in the Middle East led to a surge in the price of oil. In Germany, the hard-nosed central bankers of the Bundesbank refused to take the risk that the rising oil price would fuel inflation. Their priority was to keep price rises under control. They raised interest rates and kept a tight control over the money printing presses. They made clear to the country's trade unions that they would have to take the higher cost of petrol and energy on the chin by agreeing to only modest wage rises. But in France, it was 1968 all over again. Its government was keen to maintain political stability, and again conceded when unions demanded steeper wage rises to compensate for the higher cost of living. Those increased wages engendered higher prices for the things that French workers produced. Between 1974 and 1987, consumer prices in France tripled, compared with an increase of just 62% in Germany. So, again, the French government tried to maintain the competitiveness of French goods in world markets by devaluing the franc. Between 1971 and 1987, the franc lost 55% of its value against the Deutschmark. These devaluations wiped out the price advantage that would other-wise have been enjoyed by cheaper German workers and cheaper German goods. But stop and think about it for a moment. What if France and Germany had already been shar-ing a common currency during these years? No devaluation would have been possible, and the wage rises demanded by French unions would have quickly made French goods far too expensive on world markets. The French economy would have contracted; unemployment would have surged. France might well have had a crisis similar to the disaster that has befallen Greece since 2008 and is undermining prosperity in other less competitive eurozone economies today.

What is odd, perhaps, is that the fundamental differences between the French and German economies revealed in the 1970s did little to diminish the appetite of Europe's leaders for a currency union. On the contrary, France became even more determined to press ahead. That's because the French government noticed that devaluing the franc had boosted the cost of living in France, leading to even bigger wage demands from the unions. France's President Giscard d'Estaing took the view that the real problem was the pigheadedness of the unions. He calculated that if the franc maintained a rigid exchange rate with Germany, then the disciplining effect of German competition would put a stop to what had become a self-reinforcing cycle of rising wages, rising prices and a falling franc.

In 1979 France and Germany launched what looked like a Bretton Woods for Europe, called the 'Exchange Rate Mechanism'. Under the ERM, currencies were prevented from rising or falling more than a set amount relative to a basket of European currencies, called the European Currency Unit, or ECU. In practice, with the Deutschmark as Europe's strongest currency, it was the monetary policy of Germany's central bank, the Bundesbank, which determined the monetary policy of all ERM members. Or to translate, the interest rates set by the Bundesbank had a huge influence on interest rates in other countries, because, for example, if German interest rates rose sharply and those in France did not, there would be a flood of money out of France, and there would be a risk that the franc would fall below its ERM floor. But this was a sacrifice of economic autonomy that France was prepared to make, because by abandoning the easy fix of devaluation, and following the lead of Germany in the setting of interest rates, it was hoped that the ERM would tame rises in wages and prices in France. It worked; so the idea that the institutions of Europe were making France richer and stronger became more entrenched.

Then came the event that was to transform the debate about Europe's future: in 1989 the Communist Bloc in Eastern Europe disintegrated. Few saw it coming, but one European leader immediately and instinctively recognised a historic opportunity: for Germany's Chancellor, Helmut Kohl, this was his moment to mend his country, by reunifying West and East Germany. However, a united Germany would be a much more powerful Germany, in every way. At a stroke, France would become an inferior nation. This was not an attractive prospect for the French president, Francois Mitterrand. If Germany was again to become Europe's dominant economic and political force, somehow it had to be shackled. For Mitterrand, the shackles would be new European institutions and an accelerated interlocking of economies. He and Kohl – like Britain's Thatcher and America's Reagan – had a boldness of vision, for better or worse, now absent from the governments of the West. In 1984 they met on the former battlefield of Verdun, where they paid their respects to the French and German soldiers whose lives had been taken in two World Wars. The Verdun encounter was a re-pledging of the two countries' determination never again to pit their citizens against each other in armed conflict; it was an implied commitment to build a more united Europe. However Kohl and Mitterrand were in many ways the most unlikely and perhaps unfortunate architects of a single European economy: they conversed through interpreters, they had little

knowledge or interest of economics and they despised economists, whom they viewed as the public-policy equivalent of
plumbers. A degree of wariness of economists is almost
certainly healthy (as I think this book would tend to show) but
there were risks in constructing a single European economy
in defiance of what many would see as the more common-
sense elements of economic theory.

When the Berlin Wall came down, Mitterrand rapidly calculated that it would be impossible to stop the merger of the two
Germanys. So how to stop Germany dominating the
Continent? The answer, for Mitterrand, was that a greater
Europe would trump a greater Germany. And the way to
accelerate the centralisation of decision-making in Europe
that would fetter Germany was to accelerate the unification of
economies through the creation of a single European currency.
That was the theory. Monetary union was a political project
in economic clothing: it would be a precursor to political
union, or the creation of something that looked like a European
federation, a super-state. The problem is that this transition,
from monetary union to political union, was never mapped
out in a formal sense. The hope was that it would just happen.
And as hopes go, this was akin to gambling the prosperity of
an entire continent. What subsequent events appear to have
demonstrated is that a single currency can survive only if
taxing, spending and borrowing for all member countries is
determined centrally, by the equivalent of a single finance
minister for the currency area. However, in creating the euro,
the member governments retained enormous discretion over
the management of their finances. What would happen if the
currency union never led to the desired political union? Not
only would there be no lessening of the political and economic
power of Germany, but the currency union might

disintegrate, with devastating consequences for the prosperity of Europe. But Mitterrand and Kohl ignored the frightening contradiction at the heart of European monetary union. German reunification went ahead in 1990 and plans for monetary union were set in stone in the Maastricht Treaty of 1992.

At the time, plenty of economists – especially in the UK and in the US – warned of the risks of monetary union without a political and fiscal (tax) union. Here is the British economist, the late Wynne Godley, writing in 1992:

> The incredible lacuna in the Maastricht programme is that, while it contains a blueprint for the establishment and modus operandi of an independent central bank, there is no analogue, in Community terms, of a central government. Yet there would simply have to be a system of institutions which fulfils all those functions at a Community level which are at present exercised by the central governments of individual member countries.
>
> ('Maastricht and all that', Wynne Godley,
> *London Review of Books*, 1992)

On this occasion, the economists were right (don't snort, please). The fear was that there would be some kind of economic shock that would hurt one part of the eurozone worse than the rest – and that since the affected area would no longer be able to devalue in order to cope with the shock, the ensuing recession and unemployment would be magnified. As it happened, the fate of Britain in the ERM showed the danger of linking currencies when economies and governments are not unified. As I mentioned, the main direct consequence of being a member of the ERM was that interest rates in other member countries were in effect set by the German Bundesbank. If the Bank of England, for example, moved interest rates in a very different direction from what the Bundesbank was doing with German rates, sterling would either fall through its minimum allowed price versus the Deutschmark or rise above its maximum. But that set up all sorts of tensions when inflationary and economic conditions in Germany and the UK were very different – which happened in the early 1990s. The thing is, that in order to facilitate the combination of the two Germanys, Helmut Kohl offered very generous terms to the East Germans for giving up their currency. They would be able to exchange each of their Ostmarks for a West German Deutschmark. This massively increased the value of East Germans' savings, and encouraged them to spend more. And at the same time, Kohl's government agreed to spend vast amounts of West German taxpayers' money on building new infrastructure in the East. There was a great boost to the German economy, which led to rising prices in Germany, which in turn led the Bundesbank to raise interest rates. In 1992, German interest rates were being kept high by the German central bank, but such high rates were ruinous for a British economy that was weak at the time. The UK had no option but to devalue and leave the ERM in humiliating circumstances, because the alternative would have been a recession even darker and deeper than the one that the UK actually suffered.

In spite of the ERM debacle – which also saw Italy forced out, and should perhaps have served as a warning about the dangers of linking currencies in a Europe of very different economies and with nations proud of their political independence – preparations continued for the launch of a single currency that would become known as the euro. What was

worrying was the widening gap between the views and ambitions of European leaders and those of their citizens: all over
Europe, it was only with the greatest of difficulty that the
Maastricht Treaty passed into law. The parliamentary vote on
Maastricht split the ruling Tory party in Britain. Danish voters
rejected it in a first referendum and a French plebiscite only
narrowly squeaked through. If a successful monetary union
would require political union, Europeans' lack of enthusiasm
even for monetary union should perhaps have sounded an
alarm.

Germany seemed to take a blinkered view of the very biggest
risks. It was fixated on designing the interest-rate-setting
mechanisms of monetary union along the lines of its own
financial system. It wanted the new European Central Bank to
be modelled on its own Bundesbank. The success of the
Bundesbank in curbing inflation over the fifty years since the
War was more than just a matter of good economic policy for
the Germans. In their minds, it was also about the bulwark of
democracy: they viewed the hyperinflation of 1921 to 1924 as
having spurred the popularity of Hitler and the Nazi party. So
for Germany, preserving the value and integrity of the
currency was a priority that it would be fair to describe as an
obsession. That meant the European Central Bank was to be
given a clear and unambiguous mandate to pursue price
stability and nothing else.

Now it is important to appreciate that in the world of central
banking this is not quite the norm. In the US, for example, the
Federal Reserve has a dual mandate to deliver price stability
and full employment. Meanwhile in the UK, the Bank of
England's Monetary Policy Committee has what is known as
a symmetrical inflation target, which means that it is failing if
inflation is below target as well as if inflation is above target.

That means the Bank of England has an incentive not to be so zealous in combating inflation that it pushes the economy into recession. By contrast, the European Central Bank (ECB) has an asymmetrical target, which means it is only at fault if inflation is above the 2% target, not if it is below target. So there is always a temptation for the ECB to keep interest rates just a little bit too high, in order to keep up the downward pressure on inflation – and some economists would say that means growth in the eurozone is always a bit lower than necessary and unemployment a bit greater. Also – and this has turned out to be hugely important – the European Central Bank is prohibited from buying government debt, which is not a prohibition that applies to the Federal Reserve or the Bank of England. The ECB was banned from creating money to lend to indebted governments, because of Germans' memory of the rampant uncontrolled printing of new money in the early 1920s, which destroyed confidence in Germany's currency and meant that a pound of meat cost 900bn marks in Berlin in 1923. The ECB was to focus on the preservation of confidence in the value of the euro, to the exclusion of more or less everything else. And to make sure it could not waiver from the path of monetary rigour, European governments had no power to influence its day-to-day operations. The European Central Bank's mandate can be changed only by a treaty amendment that would have to be ratified by all European Union members: Germany always has the ability to veto such a reform.

Germany's other terms for monetary union included something that was redolent of the very first stages of the erosion of national sovereignty or of political union: there were to be limits on how much a government could borrow relative to its GDP and to the size of its national debt. But another of

Germany's conditions was antithetical to what many would see as the necessary political union, which is that it was to be illegal for eurozone members to rescue or bail out any government that ran into financial difficulties. In retrospect, this looks like the worst kind of compromise. There would be weak constraints on reckless spending and borrowing by the likes of Greece, Portugal, Ireland, Spain and Italy. But if the governments of these countries could not resist the urge to splurge, they were on their own. That at least was the theory: it did not turn out quite like that.

What Germany seems to have underestimated was quite how far interest rates would fall for some countries after joining the euro, and what an incentive this would give them to borrow as if there were no tomorrow. For example, in 1995, the Italian government had to pay an interest rate of 13% to borrow for ten years, much higher than the 7% interest rate paid by Germany at the time. That's because Italy's economy was viewed as much weaker than Germany's, with less capacity to generate tax revenues to service debt. Also its currency, the lira, had a history of being much weaker and more prone to falls than the German mark, so lenders demanded a higher interest rate from the Italian government to compensate them for the risk that the lira would fall relative to the mark and that Italian inflation would be higher than German inflation. However, by 1999 – when the euro was launched – the Italian government's ten-year cost of borrowing had fallen to a mere 4%, just a smidgeon above the interest rate paid by Germany. With the lira now gone, investors assumed that lending to Italy was only a bit more risky than lending to Germany. They ignored the prohibition in the Maastricht treaty on any member assuming liability for the debts or commitments of another member, which was reinforced in Article 125 of the 2007 Lisbon Treaty.

They just took it for granted, in what now looks a desperately naïve way, that Italian debts were now German debts – or rather that all eurozone members stood behind each others' liabilities in a joint and several manner. They could not believe that, in practice, if Italy got into difficulties, the rest of the eurozone would not rally round. With Italy being able to borrow so cheaply and easily in the early years of the eurozone, it had no incentive to reduce its debts – which were already well above what economists would have said were safe or sustainable, at more than 100% of GDP or economic output.

Requirements – and how to dodge them

It is not surprising that investors assumed that eurozone members would do everything necessary to maintain confidence in each others' ability to repay their debts, given that pressure on individual countries to take steps to fix their own finances was repeatedly lessened. Initially, for example, Germany insisted that there were fairly tough economic and financial tests for joining the euro. These included that a country's deficit – the annual gap between what it spends and what it raises in tax revenues – should be no more than 3% of GDP and its national debt should be no more than 60% of GDP. On that basis, Italy, with public-sector debt approaching 120% of GDP, should never have been allowed to participate in monetary union. But the view was taken that Italy, as a founder member of the EEC, could not be excluded from this latest great European adventure. This is how Gerhard Schröder – who was the German chancellor at the time of the launch of the single currency in 1999 – put it:

> You cannot have a common currency in Europe, in the EU, without Italy. Regarding the government debt, as measured

against the gross domestic product, Italy has always broken the criterion. But Italy as a founding member state of the EU was too important to be excluded.

(Interview for *The Great Euro Crash*, BBC2)

The entry test was amended and weakened to allow Italy in. Any applicant to join simply had to show that its debt was reducing towards 60% of GDP, which at the time Italy was able to do. As it happens, this was also convenient for Germany, whose debts had breached the 60% ceiling. But a very dangerous precedent was set: rules established to guarantee the strength and integrity of the eurozone would always be tweaked and fudged if it looked as though they would be broken. Here is one of the many magnificent paradoxes of this story: when it came to the launch of the euro, of the major European economies, only the UK met the entry criteria in a fairly rigorous way; and the UK chose to stay outside the currency union.

Having let Italy in, there was another attempt by Germany to force fiscal rectitude on all eurozone members. The German Finance Minister, Theo Waigel, proposed what would be adopted in 1997 as the Stability and Growth Pact, which translated the entry criteria for the euro into permanent commitments for its members. So in theory, all governments had to keep their deficits below 3% of GDP and debts had to continue decreasing towards 60% of GDP. If any member broke the deficit rule for three years running, they would suffer a fine of up to 0.5% of GDP. At last, perhaps, the eurozone was on the road to political union – although, not for long. Within a few short years it was Germany and France which together tore up the Stability and Growth Pact, and therefore undermined any kind of effective constraints on the borrowing of member countries. In 2003, Germany and France breached the deficit rule themselves. In fact, Germany had broken the rule for three successive years. But there would be no sanctions, no punishment. The Pact itself was described as 'stupid' and too rigid by no less an authority than Romano Prodi, President of the European Commission. In 2005, the pact was formally amended to make it more flexible. To all intents and purposes it was dead.

Years later, I asked Jean-Claude Trichet what he felt – as President of the European Central Bank – about the abandonment of this defence against the profligacy of euro members:

> We were of course shocked ... We had expressed major major concerns, very grave concerns ... Major countries in the Euro area had decided it was not for them and that this pact should be destroyed ... I myself explained tirelessly in my own country [France] that you need a framework, you need rules to be respected and you need surveillance to be sure that the rules are respected.
>
> (Interview with the author for
> *The Great Euro Crash*, BBC2)

What is perhaps most shocking is that not only were the rules imposing budgetary discipline on members or aspiring members weak, but some countries used creative accounting and complex financial transactions to cheat even these feeble constraints. An Italian economics professor, Gustavo Piga, demonstrated for example that Italy in the mid 1990s had used derivative deals to make it look as though its deficit was smaller than it actually was. But it was Greece, a late joiner to the eurozone in January 2001, which was most adept at disguising its true debt and deficit position. At the time of Greece's accession into the currency union, the then President of the European Central Bank, Wim Duisenberg, said of Greece that it still had a good deal of work to do to strengthen its economy. Little did he know how true that was. The Greek government hid a load of military and health spending to make it appear that it qualified for the euro – because getting in had been a matter of national pride for the country that saw itself as the cradle of European civilisation. But then there was the tricky problem of staying within the borrowing limits, especially with the bills for the Athens Olympics to meet. The Greeks learned what many would say was the wrong lesson from their Mediterranean neighbours Italy about how helpful bankers can be in making it look as though borrowing limits are not being exceeded. According to the *New York Times*, the world's most powerful investment bank, Goldman Sachs, was on hand to lend a hand:

> In 2001, just after Greece was admitted to Europe's mone-
> tary union, Goldman helped the government quietly borrow
> billions, people familiar with the transaction said. That deal,
> hidden from public view because it was treated as a currency
> trade rather than a loan, helped Athens to meet Europe's
> deficit rules while continuing to spend beyond its means.
> ('Wall St. Helped to Mask Debt Fueling Europe's
> Crisis', *New York Times*, 13 February 2010)

Greece's government borrowing for 2002 was originally recorded at 1.2% of its GDP. After many revisions, the true figure is now known to have been 4.8%, well above the puta-tive 3% ceiling. But that's nothing. By 2004 – the year of the

Olympics – the Greek government's now-corrected borrowing level had risen to 7.5% of GDP.

For all that eurozone governments fudged and bent and exceeded the borrowing limits, government profligacy is only part of the explanation of what has gone horribly wrong for the eurozone. If the crisis in the eurozone were all about public spending rising beyond what countries were raising from tax revenues, it would be impossible to explain why Ireland and Spain, for example, are now in such dire straits, because neither of them broke that deficit rule – at least not till the 2008 global financial crisis led to a collapse in their tax revenues and a rise in their expenditure (as happened to the governments of most other developed economies on the planet). Spain and Ireland were in many ways paragons of fiscal virtue: for years their governments lived within their means and were repaying their relatively modest borrowings. The Spanish government had cut public-sector debt to just 36% of GDP by 2007, while Ireland shrank its debt to 25%, well below the 60% limit. The German government's debts by contrast were on the rise, and were pushing 65% of GDP by 2007.

But all that putative Spanish and Irish prudence was seemingly for nought. Once the crisis hit, Spain and Ireland were tossed into the same financial inferno as the more conventional sinners, such as the Greek, Portuguese and Italian governments. They were all shunned by investors. They all found it harder and more expensive to borrow. And the reason is that investors look at the liabilities of a government in the broadest possible sense, not just the eurozone's artificial definition of public-sector debts, and they try to assess whether those liabilities are affordable. In the case of Ireland and Spain, what really did for them was the explosive and reckless growth of borrowing and lending by their banks. After boom turned to bust, the banks had to be rescued, and it fast became apparent that the costs of those rescues were more than the Irish or Spanish governments could bear. But it is not just the total value of liabilities heaped on the state, directly or indirectly, that matters. There is also the question of whether the private sector is strong enough and large enough to generate sufficient tax revenues to service the relevant government's debts. And here, again, all these governments had a problem. In the case of Portugal and Greece, their respective private sectors were thought to be simply too small to finance public spending and the debts of the state. And in the case of all these countries, the productivity of their private-sector companies were regarded as too low to provide effective competition to their mighty German competitors. Or to put it another way, the wages and salaries of Greek, Irish, Portuguese, Spanish and Italian workers had risen far too much in the boom years, and were now hobbling their economies.

Boom and binge

How and why did monetary union saddle the likes of Greece, Ireland and Spain with huge public-sector and private-sector debts, on the one hand, and a private sector that became flabbier and less productive? Well, as you will recall, when the currency union was formed, the borrowing costs of all members converged towards the borrowing costs of the strongest member, Germany. Just as we saw in the case of Italy, the interest rate paid by the governments of Spain, Portugal, Ireland and Greece also fell sharply. They could all borrow more cheaply than at any time in the modern era – and were able to do so for the best part of a decade. And here is the important point. These low interest rates did not apply just to what their governments borrowed. It was also cheaper and easier for households, businesses and banks to borrow too. They were all regarded as less risky debtors, because of the perception that the euro would be a stronger and less volatile currency than most of the currencies it replaced, and because of the expectation that the European Central Bank would do a better job of constraining inflation than many of the central banks it subsumed. In countries like Spain and Ireland, whereas their governments were relatively restrained in how much they borrowed, individuals, companies and banks all went on a mad borrowing binge. Property developers in Spain and Ireland borrowed massively from the banks to finance ever larger and glitzier housing developments and shopping malls and office blocks. Rising house prices meant families had to take on bigger and bigger mortgages when purchasing a home. So in parts of the eurozone there was a debt-fuelled property bubble similar to what happened in the US and UK. House prices in Spain trebled between 1996 and 2007, just as they did in the UK. In Ireland they more than quadrupled. These two were the outliers. In Greece, France and even the sober-minded Netherlands house prices rose by two and a half times over eleven years, similar to what happened in the US. In Italy the increment was a more modest 75% and in Portugal 50%.

The sum of mortgages and bank loans to property developers was getting bigger and bigger. And there was a bulge in personal loans, credit card debts, corporate bonds, syndicated loans, loans for leveraged corporate buyouts, and so on. Adding together the debts of Spanish companies and individuals, they were a record 222% of GDP at the end of 2008 (according to research by the consultants McKinsey and Company). Spanish people and businesses owed more than twice the value of everything their economy produced in a year. And these debts had risen as a percentage of GDP at an astonishingly fast rate since 2000, when they were 119% of GDP. It is the rate at which Spanish businesses became indebted that is particularly startling. In 1999, Spanish companies were – along with German companies – among the least indebted of any in the rich developed world, with aggregate debts equivalent to around 50% of GDP. But by 2008, the indebtedness of Spanish businesses had soared to roughly 140% of GDP, whereas that of German companies was more or less unchanged. From the inception of the euro to the present day, the indebtedness of Spain – including all forms of debt – doubled to around 360% of GDP, with sharp increases in the debts of households, businesses, banks and government.

Private-sector indebtedness increased rapidly in many other eurozone countries from the inception of the euro to the end of 2007: by 73 percentage points of GDP in Portugal, 65% in Ireland, 62% in Belgium, 45% in Italy and the Netherlands and 39% in France. There was, however, one economy that did not join the party: Germany. In 2007, German house prices were still marginally below the level they had been a decade earlier, in part because Germans tend to rent rather than buy their homes. And the Germans who did buy property had little desire to take on big debts. German household debts as a percentage of GDP were 64% in 2009, down from 71% in 2000. Over the same period, German corporate debts rose modestly.

Why do these ratios matter? Well, the ratio of debt to GDP is an indicator of the debt burden being placed on a country's citizens and companies. The higher the ratio, the more money people and companies have to pay directly in interest or in taxes (if the debt burden is particularly acute for the government). And what is particularly scary about what happened in countries like Spain and Ireland is that their ratios of debt to GDP rose at a time when their economies were growing very fast. They were enjoying debt-fuelled booms. But rather than using the revenues they generated from all that economic growth to repay debts, they doubled and trebled their indebtedness. Home owners and businesses borrowed to buy property. That drove up prices for houses and commercial property alike, encouraging a construction boom. Their economies became dangerously dependent on all this development. At the height of the frenzy, more than one in eight of Irish employees was working in construction. And more houses were being built in Ireland than in England, despite the population being thirteen times smaller. In Spain, a staggering 5 million new homes were put up between 1997 and 2007, while the increase in the number of Spanish households was just 2.5m. In both countries the creation of vast numbers of surplus properties was financed with cheap loans from banks. Ireland and Spain temporarily enjoyed highly dangerous booms, which tied the solvency of banks, construction companies, construction workers and home owners to unsustainably inflated property prices. But of course the governments of these countries turned a blind eye to the dangers, because all this unsustainable growth was swelling the coffers of the taxman.

There is another important aspect of the perilous nature of the booms in Ireland, Spain and Greece. During the good years – when everyone was spending, the economies were growing quickly, and unemployment was falling – wages rose rapidly in much of the eurozone. In fact, the pay of Spanish, Irish and Greek workers increased much more quickly than the amount that they produced. In Ireland, for example, these unit labour costs – the amount companies have to pay employees for a specified quantity of output – rose 50% from the euro's creation in 1999 until the eve of the 2008 crisis. In Spain they rose 35%, while in Portugal, Italy and Greece (and France) they increased by 20% to 30%.

Jean-Claude Trichet argues that there is a connection between these wage rises and the relaxing of disciplines on public-sector borrowing and spending in 2003, which stemmed from the collapse of the Stability and Growth Pact: first the wages of public-sector workers rose and that forced the private sector to pay more. 'When you have benign neglect in your own public finances, you let your economy lose competitiveness' is how he put it. But the cause is probably less important than the effect. The rising wages in Spain, Italy, Greece and so on – in the public sector and private sector – would not have been such a problem if Germany had not simultaneously become more efficient and productive. The important point is that over the same period, unit labour costs in Germany – the cost of employing Germans to make a specified amount of stuff – actually fell by 3%. Or to put it another way, it became cheaper to manufacture in Germany while it became much more expensive to manufacture in most of the rest of Europe. German workers were becoming more competitively priced compared with their peers in the rest of the eurozone. German businesses and the German economy became far stronger compared with the country's neighbours.

This was not by chance. The improved productivity of the German workforce was by design, and involved sacrifice over a number of years. When Germany joined the euro in 1999, the Deutschmark was locked into the new currency at an exchange rate that at the time appeared quite high for German industry. Back then, workers in Southern Europe, on relatively low wages, seemed cheap compared with their German counterparts – which is precisely the opposite of today's prevailing conditions. So in this initial period, companies in Ireland and Spain had a cost advantage in export markets. Their businesses thrived and the Spanish and Irish economies grew quite fast, whereas Germany's stagnated. Germany was described by the influential *Economist* magazine as 'the sick man of the euro'. A German socialist government, that of Gerhard Schröder, took evasive action. The head of human resources at the motor manufacturer Volkswagen, Peter Hartz, was hired to recommend reforms of Germany's rigid labour market. Based on his proposals, it became easier for all but the biggest firms to lay off workers, unemployment benefits were cut for those not willing to work and more support was given to those looking for a job. The effect was to increase the supply of labour relative to demand, so there was less pressure for wage rises. With their members fearful of losing their jobs, the big unions agreed to a prolonged period of moderate pay rises. The German economy was set on a course to regain its price advantage over Southern Europe (in a way this was a throwback to the way that Germany dealt with the inflation of the 1970s). The wages of German workers were held down. Germany's factories started to gain a significant competitive advantage over their rivals in the rest of the eurozone. And by 2006, Germany's economic growth began to exceed the euro-zone average, for the first time in years. The German unemployment rate fell sharply.

Here is the important point. Because the exchange rate vis-à-vis Italy, Spain, Ireland and the rest was now fixed, Germany was able to keep all of that advantage. There was no longer a

Deutschmark that could and would rise against the peseta or the punt and thus push up the relative cost of German workers. In fact, the opposite happened. With all that cheap debt sloshing around in Southern Europe, and the property boom creating the illusion of wealth, the wages of Southern European workers rose and rose relative to German wages – which made Southern European companies even less competitive.

The reversal of fortunes between Germany and the rest has been stark. By 2004, Germany's current account surplus – the positive gap between what it sells to the rest of the world and what it consumes – had risen from zero in 2001 to 5% of its GDP or output. And that surplus has stayed in the range of 5% to 7% of GDP ever since, even during the recent years of global recession. As for Spain, Italy, Ireland, Portugal and Greece, as their workers became more and more overpriced in world markets, they became deficit countries, borrowers from overseas. By 2008, Italy was running a current account deficit of 3% of its GDP, about the same as the UK. Ireland's deficit was 6%, Spain's 10%, Portugal's 13% and Greece's a staggering 15%. In other words, in 2008 the Greek economy as a whole was spending 15% more than it earned. That is how uncompetitive Greek workers had become. This was completely unsustainable. It was redolent of the imbalances that built up under the postwar Bretton Woods system of fixed exchange rates. Except that this time devaluation was not an option to correct the imbalances.

Now when a country is generating persistent deficits, its currency is overvalued. And if that currency cannot fall, it is very hard to bring what the economy imports and what it exports back into balance – irrespective of whether the government and citizens are behaving recklessly and fecklessly or not. Think about your own behaviour. You will typically try to make your wages go as far as you can, by buying the best goods you can at the cheapest prices. If the currency of your country is strong, perhaps overvalued, the cheapest goods available to you will almost certainly be imported goods. So you and all your compatriots will tend to spend relatively more on imports. Meanwhile the companies of your country may export relatively less, because overseas their goods and services will seem relatively expensive. The consequence of all these domestic and overseas spending decisions will be a deficit for the economy: the residents of your country will in total be spending more than the income generated by the businesses of your country. Some of that deficit, the gap between income and expenditure, can be filled by selling assets abroad, as Britain has done on some scale over the past thirty years. The other way of filling that deficit is by borrowing.

Today, the workers of Spain, Italy, Ireland, Portugal and Greece are paid more than their companies and countries can afford. Which in effect means that the currency of those countries is overvalued. But Spain, Italy and the rest no longer have independent currencies. They no longer have a currency that can adjust to their own economic circumstances. And since they lack a currency able to fall, those countries will continue to run up deficits and borrow from the rest of the world, unless and until something very painful has happened to the workers in those countries: their income and living standards have to fall massively relatively to that of German workers, so that the businesses for which they work can compete effectively again. As we have seen, Italian, Spanish, Portuguese, Irish and Greek workers became 30% to 40% more expensive for companies to employ than German workers are for German companies. That suggests the wages of the Italians, Spanish, Irish and so on will have to fall by at least a quarter relative to Germany in order to allow their respective economies to start paying their way in the world again and to end the pernicious, persistent increases in the indebtedness of their economies. Of course, there is an alternative route to salvation for the Spanish, Italians and the rest: German companies could award massive pay rises to German workers. But although wage inflation has been accelerating in Germany, it has not happened at a rate fast enough or large enough to eliminate German companies' huge productivity advantage.

The appalling and inescapable conclusion for Italy, Spain, Ireland, Portugal and Greece is that to escape from the vicious spiral of worsening national finances, the living standards of their people may have to be squeezed by more than at any time since the 1930s. And there is a terrifying internal contradiction in the idea of public-spending cuts, tax increases and wage reductions, or what we have come to know as austerity, as the route back to health for these economies. So long as a country's currency remains overvalued, and imports therefore remain cheap, most of the spending cuts will fall on the relatively expensive goods and services provided by domestic businesses. In other words, spending cuts may brutally cut the income and employment of workers at home but do relatively little to reduce imports and the country's deficit with the rest of the world. The indebtedness of these weak countries may continue to rise.

To put it another way, Italy, Spain, Greece, Ireland and Portugal may have to reconcile themselves not just to the kind of lost decade of economic stagnation faced by the citizens of the UK, but to year after year of gruelling squeezes on living standards, coupled with unemployment that remains intractably high. And even after all that, these economies may be burdened by more debt than is safe, perhaps even more relative to GDP than they have today. That means they would still be at risk of investors taking fright and refusing to lend to them. Even if the worst is avoided in the short term, a relentless decline in personal prosperity for millions of European citizens could turn out merely to be the long prelude to debt default and fracture of the currency union: Armageddon delayed not dispatched.

All that said, you may have spotted what you think of as a solecism. On the one hand, we have seen how the Germans endured a fair degree of belt-tightening after the launch of the euro, so that their businesses and economy could become more competitive. Why should the people of Italy and Spain be spared the same sacrifices to make their own companies better able to compete in the world's markets? What worked for the Germans should surely be prescribed for Italy, Spain and the others? There is something to this. But it is vital to understand that the benign economic backdrop of the early years of the century is a world away from the endemic and pervasive slow growth of today. When Germany went through its crash diet, the impact on living standards was lessened by the continued demand for its goods and services from a global economy that was growing pretty robustly. Putting it slightly contentiously, the debt-fuelled booms of the rest of the eurozone were what made the belt-tightening bearable for the Germans: much of the spending by the Greeks for the Olympics, or by Spanish and Irish property developers, or by consumers feeling more prosperous all over the eurozone went on goods made in Germany. Greek and Spanish profligacy was a pretty good analgesic for the pain that would otherwise have been felt by Germans from their cost-cutting. The German government also spent relatively freely to limit the pain of the labour market reforms – which is why it breached the eurozone 3% ceiling on budget deficits and blew up the Stability and Growth pact. How different from today, when Germany – in alliance with the eurozone's creditors – is forcing all eurozone governments to reduce their deficits. Also much of the developed world is flat-lining, growth even in India has collapsed and there are fears about the outlook for China. Lecturing Spanish and Italian citizens on how good they will feel if they would only work much harder for less is a bit like encouraging a couple of flabby individuals to get fit by dropping them in the middle of a desert: it might work, or they might collapse for lack of water. What we therefore have to conclude, I fear, is that there is no scenario in which the financially stretched countries of the eurozone can avoid considerable and elongated discomfort. In Chapter 9 we will explore the pathology of the immediate crisis confronting the eurozone. We will measure the risk that the discomfort will in fact be agony, for them and – because the thigh bone's connected to the hip bone, and our banks are connected to their banks – for us too.

CHAPTER 8
IS CHINA THE SOLUTION OR THE NEXT BIG PROBLEM?

When the influential Goldman Sachs economist Jim O'Neill wanted to put the eurozone's crisis into a global context, to reassure us that economic life continues in spite of Europe's woes, he said: 'China is creating another Greece every three to four months.'* What he meant is that the Chinese economy is now so big, and still growing so fast, that the increase in its economic output, its GDP, every twelve to sixteen weeks is identical to the entire output of Greece in a year. If the Greek economy were to disappear altogether, China – at its then rate of growth – would have made up that entire loss in a third of a year. Which is why, for Mr O'Neill, 'Greece is not the most important thing in the world.' Or to put it another way, the decline of the rich developed West is relative as well as absolute. As the economies of the US, UK and Europe have buckled under their record and unsustainable debts, China's economy has gone from strength to strength, supplanting Japan's as the world's second biggest, apparently on course

---

* Speech at the Fonds Professionell Kongress, Mannheim, Germany, January 2012.

to overtake that of the US before too long. For O'Neill, the pre-eminent populariser of the idea that the fast-growing developing economies of Brazil, Russia, India and China (O'Neill's BRICs) are changing the balance of economic power in the world in a fundamental and permanent way, we should count our lucky stars for China. Without its momentum, the entire global economy would be stagnating: economic anaemia would not be restricted to the rich developed West. So here is what should concern us: there is evidence that some of China's success has been built on shaky financial foundations, and that its economic growth may slow more sharply than is comfortable for the Chinese or for us.

Even in the years of China's relentless rise and rise, there has been a price for the UK and the US: its trading success and its giant surpluses are the corollary of our rising indebtedness; its hunger for the materials that feed its factories, nourish an enriching population and create the infrastructure of a modern economy pushes up the prices we pay for basics, from oil to iron to wheat. However one of the big and seemingly immutable facts of the modern world is China's economic growth of between 8% and 14% a year. Perhaps no longer. In the spring of 2012, China's growth dipped below 8%; the outlook is uncertain. Is it time to re-learn the lesson of history that super-charged growth is never sustained forever – and is usually followed either by a painful shock or an extended period of stagnation?

It is hard to overstate just how rapid China's rise has been. From 1978 – when the great reforming leader Deng Xiaoping inherited the economic and social catastrophe left behind by three decades of Maoism – up until 2011, China's economic growth averaged 9.9% every year. That meant the Chinese economy more or less doubled in size every seven and a half years. Thanks to the power of compounding, China's economy in 2011 was nineteen times its size three decades earlier. Over the same period, the size of the US economy grew almost two-and-a-half times, while the UK's scarcely more than doubled. And it's not just the West that China is outshining. In the words of the World Bank, 'if mainland China's thirty-one provinces were regarded as independent economies, they would be among the thirty-two fastest-growing economies in the world.'* Only tiny and oil-rich Equatorial Guinea can be included in that exclusive club of turbocharged economies.

China is on a path to a large extent mapped out by Deng Xiaoping, leader of the Chinese Communist Party from 1978 to 1992. And probably the most important thing to know about Deng is that he took over shortly after what was arguably the worst point in China's social and economic development for hundreds of years. China had been devastated by Chairman Mao's Great Leap Forward, the forced industrialisation and collectivisation of agriculture, followed by the hideous political persecution of the Cultural Revolution. More than 30 million Chinese people had starved to death in the 1960s and millions more were left destitute and homeless. For older Chinese, the memory of that disaster defines how they see everything today: when I have asked them about how their lives have changed, they talk of today's relative prosperity as though they can hardly believe it. Deng only had to look at his neighbours to see which way to go. By the late 1970s, centrally planned Russia was mired in economic stagnation under Brezhnev that would ultimately precipitate the Soviet Union's

---

* 'China 2030', the World Bank and the Development Research Centre of the State Council, China.

collapse. But China's great rival Japan was enjoying the kind of prosperity that Mao had promised but had failed to deliver. That said, it was Singapore under its Prime Minister Lee Kuan Yew – with its mixed economy, combining state planning, state ownership and free markets – that was to provide much of the model for how Deng was to transform China.

China's rise and rise is of greater consequence for the world than that of Japan or the South-East Asian 'Tiger' economies for an obvious and simple reason. Its population of 1.35bn is equal to more than six times the sum of all those other nations. The average population of each of its thirty-one provinces is 43 million people – about the size of Spain. So when a country as populous as China grows fast, it inevitably rises to the top of many international league tables of commercial and industrial strength. China became the world's biggest manufacturer in 2010, overtaking the US. And China is by far the world's biggest exporter, with merchandise exports 28% greater than the number two, America (China has merchandise exports of $1.9 trillion according to the World Trade Organisation). Here are some other boys' own facts about the bigness of China:

> Two of the world's top ten banks are now Chinese; sixty-one Chinese companies are on the Global Fortune 500 list; and China is home to the world's second-largest highway network, the world's three longest sea bridges, and six of the world's ten largest container ports.
>
> ('China 2030' op.cit.)

China overtook Japan in 2011 to become the second biggest national economy in the world after the US (although if the EU were viewed as a single economy, which perhaps looks a slightly absurd idea these days, then China would still be in third place). China overtaking the US to bag the top spot is for most economists a matter of *when*, not *if*. Jim O'Neill says by 2027, whereas the IMF until recently thought it could be as soon as 2016.

But absolute size is not everything. If China is viewed on the basis of the income of its individuals, it remains poor. Based on an amalgam of the assorted measures of income per capita, Chinese incomes are less than a quarter of those in the UK and less than a sixth of America's. And when you travel away from the centre of modern cities such as Shanghai, which seem as prosperous as anything in Europe or the US, you still encounter third-world-style poverty fairly quickly. Perhaps the statistic that says everything about how much further China still wants to travel in its economic development is that 40% of its employed people work in agriculture – compared with 2% for many developed countries. And because China has around a fifth of the world's people, or more than the combined populations of the US and Europe, that understandable hunger for more wealth impinges on all of us. The inexorable transfer of more and more of what we think of as our jobs to China is one aspect. The strain on global resources is another. When a billion Chinese and a billion Indians and a billion Africans start to eat meat, work in steel buildings, drive cars, fly, heat their homes, use electrical appliances, and – to put it simply – live our lives, the basics of existence become scarce and the attempt to limit environmental damage becomes daunting. To take just one example, if each Chinese person consumed as much oil as each American, China as a whole would consume every barrel of oil currently being pumped from the ground anywhere in the world. At a time when the Western economies have been in the doldrums, inflation in the UK, US and the eurozone remained relatively elevated, eating into people's living standards, in part because China's massive appetite for energy, raw materials and food still buoys their respective prices.

China's demand for all these things, and its effect on commodity prices, may have been one of the triggers for the great financial bust in the West. Food prices rose an astonishing 67% from the beginning of 2007 to mid 2008, according to the UN. The price of Brent crude, the benchmark for world oil prices, rose six-fold from 2003 until the eve of the crisis. Metals prices also shot up: copper prices rose five-fold from 2003. In the couple of years before the banking crisis, we were all faced with much higher supermarket and energy bills. For many struggling home owners in the US, whose interest bills were pushed up when their low 'teaser' interest rates rose to more normal levels, it was a choice between paying for food and gasoline or keeping up the payments on the house. It was the dream of a home that was abandoned: the keys were handed back to the lender, and the subprime mortgage bubble burst, with spectacular consequences. But here is what really shows the buying power of China. The commodities market crashed during the 2008–09 recession even more spectacularly than it had risen over the previous eighteen months. By February 2009, world food prices had fallen back to where they had been two years earlier, while Brent crude oil fell back to its level of 2005. But, despite the absence of economic recovery in the West, Chinese demand has since pulled food, oil, and metal prices all the way back up to pre-crisis peaks.

So it is almost as important for us as it is for the Chinese whether the next phase in its development avoids great shocks. In part that depends on the stability and sustainability of the one-party state. In this undemocratic and illiberal country, there are growing signs of unrest, in the face of the perceived corruption and privileges of Communist Party officials. Take the village of Wukan in Guangdong (or Canton, the semi-tropical southern province neighbouring Hong Kong) with its population of 12,000 people. In 2011, the villagers held protests at the seizure of land by local government officials, who then sold it on to developers for a tidy profit. Following the death of one protester – allegedly under torture in a police cell – the village rose up and evicted the entire local Communist Party. A siege ensued, which ended only with the intervention of Guangdong's provincial leaders, who saw to it that new village elections were held, and at least some of the corrupt local officials were punished. According to reports, there are thousands – perhaps even tens of thousands – of protests in China every year by villagers complaining about the theft of their land by local Communist Party officials. That's because land is an immensely valuable asset in China, and one over which private individuals have no permanent legal title. Indeed, these land expropriations are by-and-large legal, if often horribly unfair to farmers. Local authorities have the right to requisition land and pay minimal compensation to the tenants. And these seizures have fed the breathtakingly rapid urbanisation of China, not only by providing the space on which blocks of flats, roads, offices and factories can be built, but also by providing local governments with an important source of the revenues needed to provide vital services. According to the World Bank, 1.4 million hectares of agricultural land were legally requisitioned for urban use in 2003–8, with another 450,000 hectares allegedly expropriated illegally. In total, that's equivalent to almost the whole of Wales being taken away from locals over the course of just those five years.

The land seizure in Wukan is in some respects unusual.

Although it started characteristically enough – village nego-
tiators were arrested and beaten up; the police sealed off the
town – in this instance word got out, which meant that
foreign media started to take an interest. And that's when
the authorities softened their stance. That said, publicity
and international disapproval do not always help those who
feel they are being persecuted for demanding the kinds of
rights and freedoms we take for granted. For example, the
activist and journalist Tan Zuoren was imprisoned for five
years in 2010 for 'inciting subversion of state power'. His
apparent mistake was to ask questions about why so many
schools had collapsed so easily – with the deaths of thousands of children – during an earthquake in the mountain-
ous Sichuan province. Another journalist, Qi Chonghuai,
was convicted of 'extortion and blackmail' in 2008 and
sentenced to four years in prison, later extended by a further
eight years. Qi exposed the corruption behind the construction of new government offices in the eastern city of
Tenzhou. And then there is the blind activist Chen
Guangcheng, who was placed under house arrest and then
imprisoned after campaigning against the forced abortions
and sterilisations carried out in Shandong to help meet the
one-child-per-household target laid down by Beijing. In
May 2012, having briefly become one of the most famous
people in the world by demanding sanctuary in the US
embassy in Beijing, Chen and his immediate family were
permitted to fly to New York. The evidence seems to suggest
that when international media coverage of a perceived injustice in China reaches a certain pitch, the government fears
that China's 'brand' is being so damaged that it is better to
capitulate: persecuting a blind campaigner who argued that
forced sterilisation had no place in a civilised society would

not normally be recommended as an international marketing strategy; and since China's prosperity depends on exports, there could be harm to its growth prospect if 'buying Chinese' became indelibly associated with supporting oppression.

China is not a monolithically totalitarian state. It is not North Korea, where it is a crime to think dissenting thoughts, let alone utter them. The senior ministers I've met – Chen Deming, the commerce minister, and Wen Jiabao, the prime minister – exude charm and culture, and have responded to my questions perhaps less mechanically than has been typical of many British ministers in recent years. The Communist Party's national leaders seem to accept that corruption is a serious problem. That became even harder to deny in the spring of 2012, when the municipal boss of the vast conurbation Chongqing, Bo Xilai, was stripped of his Communist Party responsibilities and privileges. His disgrace stemmed from the involvement of his wife, Gu Kailai, in the murder of a British business man, Neil Heywood, and from accusations that the couple had shifted vast wealth offshore. Gu Kailai pleaded guilty to killing Mr Heywood and on 20 August 2012 she was sentenced to death – but the execution was suspended. And although the authorities try to control the flow of information over the Internet, it is impossible these days to insulate China from the rest of the world. In the fourteen years I've been visiting the country, the people I encounter have become increasingly open about their concerns for its future – and hopeful that one day democracy will arrive. Few are yet ready to say this to me on camera, but they are much less nervous in private conversations. They suggest that the one-party state is not forever, although none of them can explain to me how a peaceful, smooth transition to a plural state can take place. The grip on power of China's Communist Party may not be as iron as it has been, but the collapse of Communism would almost certainly be messy and disruptive.

Chinese whispers

That said, when looking for sources of instability in China, a latent yearning for democracy may not be the most important. There is a sprawling but influential network of China sceptics who believe that the country may be on the verge of following the Soviet Union and Japan into years, possibly decades, of stagnation. They argue that Chinese state capitalism contains the seeds of its own destruction: a Japanese-style bubble in the construction industry and elements of the property market, combined with lousy investments engendered by Soviet-style government corruption. The seeds of destruction may lie in the Chinese obsession with growth, which has served it so well hitherto.

Every five years the Beijing leadership sets out a new five-year plan for the economy's development. It lists targets for everything from wheat prices to energy conservation. But the overriding target is GDP growth. Beijing then cedes responsibility for meeting these goals to the thirty-one provincial governments. Political careers can be made or broken depending on whether a regional party boss achieves or misses them: bureaucrats will do whatever's necessary to hit those GDP targets. Now it is not as bad as in the old Soviet Union, where the expression was coined that if you set a target to produce a million tons of concrete, it would get produced, but it would be foolish to try to build anything with it. But even so, China has learned – perhaps painfully – that not all contributions to GDP growth are of the same quality. For example, building a new school in Sichuan will contribute the same amount to GDP – that is, to the total measured activity of the economy

– whether it is done properly or in such a shoddy way that the school collapses in the next earthquake. Building a new road counts the same towards GDP even if nobody needs to drive on it. A factory's output counts the same towards GDP whether or not it is killing the fish in the local rivers, or causing serious injuries to its employees, or helping to make the air in the neighbouring city unbreathable. To put it another way, there is much more activity in China – particularly construction activity – than in the UK or US that pumps up GDP figures today but which may be doing long-term harm. Also, the official GDP statistics and other official data are usually taken with a huge grain of salt by analysts, because officials of all levels have big incentives to manipulate data to meet targets: unofficial surveys and statistics on indicators of economic activity such as electricity usage are often seen as more useful and accurate.

A second and related issue is that Chinese people may get a worse deal out of their productivity and industriousness than is fair, and one day this may make them seriously grumpy. Farmers robbed of their livelihoods for the sake of rapid urbanisation are just one conspicuous example of enforced sacrifice for the perceived general good. China's exchange-rate policy may be another example. As you will recall, the People's Bank of China – China's central bank – has accumulated more than $3 trillion of foreign currency reserves. It has acquired these dollars by holding down the value of China's currency, the yuan, to make it cheaper for China's exporters to sell their stuff abroad. But although this has supercharged Chinese growth, it has held down the real living standards of Chinese workers: their yuan wages have been artificially devalued, so they cannot afford as much in the way of Swiss medicines, Japanese motorbikes or US electronic tablets (even though they are assembled in China) as they would have been able to do, had the yuan been allowed to rise to its natural level. It is a policy that provides jobs, but jobs that deliver an artificially low standard of living.

Here is the point: wages in China have grown rapidly in the last three decades, but not as rapidly as the total output of the Chinese economy. In other words, Chinese workers have had to make do with a steadily dwindling share of the fruits of their own endeavours. Of the burgeoning income generated by the Chinese economy, the amount paid out as wages has fallen steadily in the last decade, dropping to 48% of GDP by 2008, according to the World Bank. That compares with 61% of GDP paid out as salaries and wages in the US, 64% in the EU, and 62% in Japan. There is what some would see as an amazing irony here. In the last great Communist country in the world, the rewards accruing to labour – to the people – are lower than anywhere else. The point isn't simply that Chinese wages are low. It is that they may come to be seen as unfairly low – at a time when there are extraordinary numbers of millionaires and billionaires among the owners of businesses, and when the lifestyles of Communist Party officials seem lavish. The World Bank estimates that there are 'more than a million millionaires' in China, and in excess of 170 million Chinese people who have to try to get by on less than $2 each day, with most of the extreme poor living in interior provinces of China that don't have access to the coast and the international trade it offers.

There is another way in which most Chinese citizens are short-changed by the economic system. In much of the West, big companies are owned by millions of us through our pension schemes. So the profits and dividends of the Vodafones and Unilevers are our profits and dividends. But in China, the equivalent companies are largely owned either by the state or by private individuals, so the vast profits they make employing workers on such poor remuneration are never recycled back to those workers. World Bank statistics, which may be an underestimate, show that state-owned enterprises generate profits equivalent to 11% of their capital, and the much more efficient private-sector businesses generate a 21% return. These substantial surpluses are typically reinvested in new factories, research and development and offices. They are invested in growing the businesses – rather than being used as they are in the West, to partly finance the pensions and welfare needs of the population (either through private-sector pension schemes or via a public-sector, tax-funded, social security system). It is another way in which China's repressed wages are designed to support rapid growth, which benefits an immensely wealthy minority far more than the majority. China is the world's greatest sovereign paradox: a Communist state promoting extreme inequalities.

Why on earth do the Chinese put up with a system that seems so unfair? Well it is probably because all but the youngest generation have memories of grinding poverty and even of the great starvations of the 1960s. As I have mentioned, Chinese people of my age and older tell me they can barely believe the astonishing economic progress of their lifetimes; that they do not have to worry about where the next meal is coming from. Even today, life on the land is gruelling. Which is why a big part of China's story of the last three decades has been about the relentless flow of people migrating from country to town and city in search of work. On a massive and accelerated scale, it is similar to what happened in Europe and the US during the Industrial Revolution a century and a half ago. A farmer's son or daughter in China can typically earn three times as much stitching shoes together in a factory in Shanghai than from scraping a living off their parents' paddy fields back home. Over the twenty years from 1990, the proportion of Chinese living in cities rose from around a quarter to just over a half – but that is still 30 percentage points fewer people in cities than in the UK and the US. So the World Bank forecasts that another 20% of China's population will migrate to cities in the next two decades. Here are the amazing figures that describe Chinese urbanisation: the number of cities in China with over a million inhabitants almost doubled between 1992 and 2011, reaching 102. Some cities have appeared from nowhere. Shenzhen, which now has a population of almost 12 million people (that's 50% bigger than London), barely existed before 1979, which is when Deng Xiaoping designated it as a 'special economic zone' because of its coastal position next to Hong Kong. One fascinating and really important question is at what point those who have lived all their lives in the new Chinese cities, who never knew the famine and hardship of rural life, begin to query whether they are being seriously short-changed for their backbreaking work in factories and public services.

It has traditionally been the abundance of migrant workers that allowed the suppression of wages and living standards. There are about 200 million of them currently, equivalent to the populations of Britain, France and Germany put together. Often they have travelled hundreds of miles to reach the big coastal cities such as Shenzhen, not unlike the hundreds of thousands of Poles and assorted Central Europeans who have flocked to London in the past ten years. And much like immigrant workers in Europe and the US, Chinese migrants often find themselves treated as second-class citizens in their new homes. They face discrimination not just from the cities' indigenous residents, but from the municipal authorities as well. What little social benefits Chinese people can claim – such as housing, education and health care – are provided by local governments in China. But the country's *hukou* system of residency registration enables the local authorities to deny migrant workers many of these benefits. Which is why in the brief period of factories closing after the global crash of the autumn of 2008, there were extraordinary scenes of mobs of migrant workers returning to the land. I witnessed at first-hand vast numbers of families, with babies strapped to their backs and all their possessions tied up in bundles, trying to go back to their rural homes. In early 2009, I saw deserted and silent factories for mile after mile in Guangdong's vast concrete coastal sprawl. The following year, I heard astonishing stories of an economy grinding to a halt when visiting Inner Mongolia on the other side of the country. The wealthy owner of a giant factory making cashmere pullovers and cardigans told me he had turned off the knitting machines. At the time, there were stories of furious workers taking their bosses as hostages in protest for not having been paid for months. The potentially destabilising social consequences of this great homecoming scared the government into a massive stimulus programme of public spending and bank lending, aimed at restarting the economy.

The migrants returned. But it is striking, however, that in China's main industrial centres there is no longer a glut of cheap unemployed people. When I first visited China in the late 1990s, the employment model was to have hundreds or even thousands of workers living in dormitories attached to factories, working with few breaks from dawn to dusk, for the tiniest of wages. However in the past three or four years, conditions in the Shanghai area, Beijing and South China have improved dramatically (for all the adverse publicity that Apple recently attracted because of employment conditions at factories owned by one of its major suppliers in China, Foxconn). These regions have seen considerable wage inflation, of more than 20% a year, encouraged by substantial increases in the minimum wage set by local government. In 2010 and 2011, the average annual rise in the minimum wage – which varies between regions – was 22%. The main complaint I hear these days from owners of Chinese factories is one familiar in the UK: you can't get the staff; or at least not nearly as cheaply as a few years ago. On my last trip to Shanghai, workers in an electrical factory looked at me as though I had taken leave of my senses when I asked if they lived above the factory; they said that was for peasants only recently arrived, or what we in the West would have called 'immigrants straight off the boat'. They had their own homes and were no longer prepared to work for peanuts. So China's economic model is becoming more nuanced. Businesses that wish to compete on the basis of the cheapest labour costs are building new factories in new cities, close to an indigenous peasant population prepared to toil for low wages. Those companies that stay in places like Shanghai are becoming more sophisticated: they are automating more and relying less on manual labour; they are investing in research, to develop more valuable products that command a higher price; they are even trying to nurture their own brands. When will Chinese businesses complete this next stage in their evolution? That is hard to know, although it may not be as far away as all that, if the success of its global telecoms giant Huawei is any guide. And although China's growth is slowing, this attempt by Chinese companies to compete on more than price may ultimately pose yet another challenge to the manufacturers that survive in Britain and America.

There is another respect in which the balance of power between capital and labour in China is gradually shifting a bit more towards labour: China is a rapidly ageing country; its one-child policy means that there are diminishing numbers of young people entering the jobs market. There are some who believe that in years to come there will be a serious constraint on China's ability to grow through an explosion of its retired population relative to a shrinking working population. Even so, the share of China's cake that goes to its workers remains low, and China still has a big cost advantage over the West. I witnessed that at first hand when making a film for the BBC (*The Party's Over: How the West Bust*, December 2011) about why China saves so much and we in the West borrow so much. The film shows the Shanghai and Midlands employees of a Chinese lighting company, NVC. I met Rena Li, a bright and ambitious middle manager in Shanghai, who earns between £15,000 and £20,000 a year, and lives in a spotless but small apartment. In local terms, she is doing well. But her equivalent in the UK earns four times as much, and lives in a charming detached country house in its own land. On the shop floor in Shanghai, a skilled assembly worker told me she makes £250 in a month, if she does 40 hours of overtime. A worker in Longbridge outside Birmingham, who slightly modifies the lights made in China, earns more than four times as much, for a basic working week that is as long as the Chinese workers' overtime – so in practice his hourly pay is eight times greater. When I talked to the Chinese executive responsible for the UK operation about these disparities in pay between Shanghai and Longbridge, he could not explain them in respect of the quality or productivity of the respective workforces. The pay differential is all about local market conditions, supply and demand. What frustrates NVC is that even paying so much more in the UK, it struggles to find the right people here.

Low living standards for Chinese people are about more than wages. Assorted benefits – pensions, health insurance, unemployment benefits – are limited too. It used to be that China provided an 'iron rice bowl' of such benefits as part of a guaranteed job for life at a state-owned company. But those days are gone. Deng Xiaoping's reforms mean a dwindling number of rice bowls. Whereas even as late as 1998 some 60% of workers still had jobs at state-owned companies, now only about 20% of them do. Instead, most urban workers have less secure, no-frills jobs in China's hundreds of thousands of privately owned factories, construction sites and warehouses. It is inevitable that they feel they have to save, so that they can survive unemployment and retirement. Rena Li told me she saves about 40% of her income, on top of paying for her daughter to have extra tuition so that she can go to a good university, perhaps abroad. In the UK, most people on her income save nothing. On average, Chinese families set aside somewhere between a quarter and a third of everything they earn. Younger people save to provide their children with an education that they hope will allow the next generation to earn considerably more than today's. Older people save to pay for the care they will need when their health gives out. And with family ties in China so strong, the policy of restricting the birth-rate to one child per family perhaps leaves many of today's children anxious that they may eventually have to support four grandparents – which is another spur to save. But they face hideously little choice when it comes to investing their money. Most people put their money in the bank, where the interest they can earn – regulated by the central bank, the People's Bank of China – is derisory. In recent years, the interest on savings hasn't been enough to compensate for rising prices, particularly sharply rising food prices. Since 2004 the interest rate on a one-year savings account – which is set by the central bank – has averaged 2.75%, whereas inflation has averaged 3.25%. For most people, what matters most is food inflation, and that has been 7.75%. So the real value of people's savings has been steadily eroded by rising prices. Of course, savers in British bank accounts would make exactly the same complaint. But in the UK, the economy has not been growing at 10% and there is – by Chinese standards – an astonishingly robust and generous social safety net. For Chinese people to have the value of their savings undermined by official control of interest rates, when the place is apparently booming, seems pretty tough. But possibly the more important point is that, in the absence of a welfare state and few alternative places to put their money, the decline in the real value of savings held in banks encourages the Chinese to save yet more.

Interest rates are so low because China's banking system is designed to convert savings into cheap loans to manufacturers, construction companies and infrastructure projects. To put it another way, low interest rates are another manifestation of how most Chinese people have been forced to sacrifice their personal living standards to help stimulate growth and industrialisation. There is a striking consequence of this Chinese version of what economists would call 'financial repression': unlike what would normally happen in the UK or US, cuts in interest rates that promote investment by businesses also encourage Chinese households to spend less and save more. To put it another way, because most Chinese people do not have debts, monetary policy works very differently in China compared with the West. Professor Michael Pettis, an American economist working at the Beijing Business School, points out that when interest rates are reduced, the Chinese feel poorer, so they increase their savings, in order to hit their personal targets for retirement income or for what they want to contribute to the university fees of their offspring. By contrast, capital spending by companies and regional governments is stimulated when interest rates are reduced or money is made cheaper.

But there is growing evidence that there has been too much construction and investment in recent years: the productive potential of the Chinese economy may have been expanded too far and fast; large loans have financed white elephant projects and will have to be written off. Which is why there is a growing risk – not that China will suddenly be demoted from the great new economic superpower to an also-ran, but that its development may start to be disrupted. Professor Pettis is among those who fear that China could start to behave more like Japan in the 1990s, experiencing a sharp and prolonged slowdown in growth, rather than emulating the unstoppable US of the late nineteenth and early twentieth century. And what makes it harder for China in trying to avoid this fate is that it cannot easily use the tool of interest-rate changes to avoid shocks: if the People's Bank of China raises interest rates to encourage consumers to spend more and give some renewed impetus to growth, it risks seeing a collapse in investment and financial difficulties for businesses in property and infrastructure; and if it cuts interest rates, a much-needed increase in consumer spending would be stymied.

The kernel of what makes China's economy unstable is its dependence on producing goods for export, and on investment in things that offer a reward tomorrow, such as education, homes, offices, roads, ports, factories and so on. Quite unlike the UK and US, China could do with a bit more of an emphasis on instant gratification: the Chinese economy would be on a more sustainable footing if Chinese people spent more and saved less. This is recognised by the government. Its twelfth and latest five-year plan, which came into force in 2011, sets as its primary objective a shift in the economy's priorities away from selling stuff to the rest of the world and towards boosting the living standards and meeting the needs of ordinary Chinese people. But, as we have seen, there are structural impediments to pulling that off at all, let alone without a prolonged deceleration of growth.

That said, China does seem to have reduced its dependence on exporting vastly more than it imports. There appears to have been a remarkable diminution in China's current account surplus, or the amount by which the Chinese economy earns more from the rest of the world than it spends in return. In 2007, China's surplus stood at a whopping 10% of GDP: in other words the country was saving and lending back to the rest of the world a tenth of everything it earned, which as you will know from earlier chapters was dangerous for the deficit countries, such as the UK and US, and for China itself. By the end of 2011, that surplus had fallen to 2.75% – still a big number by some countries' standards, but much closer to being sustainable. This looks like a deliberate policy, because over the same period the People's Bank of China allowed the yuan to gain 8.7% in value against the dollar before its economy ran into a spot of bother in 2012. The Chinese authorities allowed their economy to give up some of the supposedly unfair competitive advantage of its cheap currency.

However, the official figures may be misleading. China may still be addicted to selling overseas, and the shrinking of

China's surplus may only be temporary. In the global recession of 2009, the dollar value of Chinese exports plummeted 16%. Imports also dropped sharply, down 11%. Since then, exports and imports have steadily recovered. But, after an initial rebound, export growth slowed to a rate of just 14% in late 2011, far slower than the 25% rate that China typically enjoyed during the boom years up until 2008. It is highly likely that the stagnation of China's main Western export markets, in Europe, the US and UK, is a major cause of the move towards current account balance, rather than a fundamental erosion of China's competitive advantages. But perhaps more importantly, it is also the reaction of the Chinese authorities to the global economic shock that may have disguised what is really going on.

When the worldwide recession hit at the end of 2008, the Chinese government launched a $590bn two-year stimulus package, the equivalent of 5% of GDP per annum. A quarter of the money went on rebuilding Sichuan province after its earthquake. Most of the rest went on new infrastructure, with a decade's worth of projects brought forward into the space of two to three years. Between 2008 and 2011 the government built, among other things, 25,000km of motorways (more than half the circumference of the planet), an entire high-speed rail network, the five longest bridges in the world, thirty new airports (and another eighty on the way), and new subway systems. On top of that, companies – particularly the big state-owned ones – were pressed into investing more. And the banks were ordered to lend to facilitate the investment: the banks provided a remarkable $1.5 trillion in new loans in the twelve months from October 2008, or 30% of China's GDP at the time, and almost triple the $534 billion provided during the previous twelve months. The cost of the loans was slashed as well. Interest rates on one-year loans were cut by the People's Bank of China from 7.5% to 5.3% in late 2008 and were kept at that level until the autumn of 2010. The borrowing spree that this unleashed eventually started to worry the authorities, but it proved hard to contain. In 2010 the central bank imposed a $1.1 trillion cap on new lending. But the rate of new lending continued much as before, with the banks shifting much of their lending into hidden financing arrangements.

Many of these loans financed the government's infrastructure spending splurge. But a good proportion of them seem to have fuelled rampant speculative property construction. The rate of investment in new real estate in China more than doubled between 2008 and 2011, increasing its share of China's economy from 11% to 16%. And it was the sudden construction boom that, more than anything, helped China to restore GDP growth close to its long-term average of 10%, in spite of the reduction in export growth. The Chinese construction boom – both in property and in infrastructure – is all the more extraordinary given that China was already an economy investing both more and more rapidly than any other of any size on the planet. Total investment spending in China was high at 42% of GDP in 2007. By 2010 it had risen to 49%. That is a level that is unprecedented not only in China's history, but probably in world history. As for consumption – or spending on food and clothes and medicines and other things that Chinese people actually need – that remained stuck at around a third of GDP, compared with more than 70% in the US and two-thirds of GDP in the UK. If we in the US and UK have consumer-driven economies, China is an investment-driven economy like nothing the world has ever seen.

Much investment in China is a good thing. Take roads, for example. China is a vast country, almost the same size as the US. Naturally, China needs highways connecting its territories. In 2011 alone, the country built 11,000km of motorways, bringing its total network to 85,000km, slightly more than the 75,000km of dilapidated interstate highways in the US. So what's the problem? Well, for one thing, China's investment splurge since 2009 has helped to conceal the economy's continuing underlying dependence on exports. The point is that much of the narrowing in its trade deficit stems from a surge in imports caused by the construction binge. In the twelve months to March 2010, China's imports of iron and steel jumped 52% versus a year earlier, copper imports rose 74%, aluminium 87% and coal (which is used, among other things, for steelmaking) by 265%. What this implies is that once the investment splurge is over – once China has more than enough new buildings and roads and railways for this and subsequent generations – the country's imports will fall sharply. That means China will almost certainly start to generate vast surpluses again.

Then there is the question of whether all the new transport links, homes and buildings will actually be used. China's new high-speed rail network is impressive. Starting from zero, China opened some 10,000 kilometres of track between 2008 and 2011. That is equivalent to five times the French high-speed network. Another 6,000 kilometres is in the pipeline. But here is the perverse consequence. Many of the country's migrant workers can't afford to travel on the luxurious and fast new trains. And many of the older trains they usually take have been removed from the timetable. So their annual Chinese New Year trek home has become more fraught and cramped than ever. The high-speed trains depart half empty, while workers are left stranded on platforms.

It is in the property market where there is the greatest evidence of excess. From 2009 to April 2012, China built 2.3 billion square metres of new residential buildings, with a further 3.2 billion under construction. Assuming a fairly generous 25 square metres per person, that's enough in total to provide homes for 200 to 250 million people – or sufficient to house every person in Britain four times over. At the current rapid rate at which Chinese workers are moving to the big cities from the countryside, it represents more than a decade's worth of supply. There were reports in the Chinese media in 2010 that 65 million apartments were not actually using any electricity. It is commonplace to walk through impressive modern developments at night and not notice a single light on. They appear to be deserted. Cities have risen in the scrub and desert almost overnight. In November 2010 I visited the remarkable new city of Kangbashi in Ordos, Inner Mongolia, a vast urban landscape that was constructed over the previous five years on an arid, scrub-like plain in the middle of nowhere. The local Communist Party official in charge of attracting investment to the region, Mrs Wang Linxiang, told me it was being built to house one million people within ten years. That was costing in the order of £15bn a year of investment in the Ordos region – or so she said over a lunch of ducks' tongues and jellyfish. And it looked as though Kangbashi would accommodate not far off a million people already, because there was acre after acre of newly completed or soon-to-be finished residential apartments, office blocks and municipal buildings. It was the public spaces that were most impressive and put town planning in the UK to shame. The town centre boasted an opera house, a museum, a library and a stadium, any one of which was as big and ambitious as anything you would see in London or New York. Their designs would not have been to everyone's taste – the opera house looks like a giant traditional Mongolian hat (think fez with Asiatic twist), and the museum is an enormous bronze coffee bean – but there's no lack of boldness in the architecture. There's also a square not conspicuously smaller than Tiananmen or Place de La Concorde, where there are giant statues celebrating the world-conquering feats of that ambitious Mongol, Genghis Khan. Hubris or sensible long-term planning? Mrs Linxiang said at the time that the city had only 20,000 to 30,000 inhabitants. Recent visitors say that it is still 98% unoccupied, which means its wide avenues remain slightly ghostly, especially at night.

Part of what is happening, according to the Beijing-based economist Patrick Chovanec, is that those with spare cash, who don't like the low interest rates on savings accounts in banks and are prohibited from taking their money offshore, are putting their money into property as an investment. Until recently, Chinese property prices have risen pretty strongly: according to America's National Bureau of Economic Research, residential properties in thirty-five major cities more than tripled between 2000 and 2010, which compares with the kind of unsustainable rises seen in the US, UK, Ireland and Spain. Apparently many of the new property investors are not interested in renting the properties out, because they regard a 'used home' as being devalued in much the same way as we in the West regard a 'used car' as being of lesser value. Since there are no annual property taxes, they are happy to keep the property unoccupied and in pristine condition and wait for the capital gain. Perhaps the lack of occupants in some developments is not a precursor of a bust tomorrow, though it is difficult to see how the price of empty properties can rise in a sustained way.

Residential prices look hard to justify. In Beijing, the average cost of an apartment rose to around nineteen times the income of a typical family in 2010. And for those prepared to let out their investment properties, rents are equivalent to a paltry 3% of the putative market price – which only makes economic sense at a time when it is impossible to earn more than that in a savings account. So since late 2009 the Chinese leadership has been trying to take the momentum out of the housing boom, for instance by reintroducing stamp duty, and ordering the banks to be more restrictive in lending to home buyers (even though most do not take out big mortgages) and property developers. It was not till the end of 2011, however, that the market showed signs of retreating. Since then, there have been sharp falls in prices, sales and construction activity. This has enraged investors, but may not bankrupt many of them, since only a minority have invested with borrowed money. That said, there is a bigger risk of serious financial pain for local government and property developers, which took out substantial loans on the land seized from local communities. If ordinary investors stop buying the flats – now that they know prices can fall as well as rise – then the developers will be left with big debts on impossible-to-sell developments and land. They may go bust and local government may also incur embarrassing losses.

Here's the difficult balance that needs to be struck by Beijing. Property development on its own contributes around 16% of GDP and total investment is almost half of GDP. At the time that China decides or finds that it has more than enough tower blocks and flyovers, an awful lot of construction workers, steelmakers and architects would become unemployed. China's twelfth five-year plan implies that as and when that happens, the government would endeavour to engineer a consumer boom, and all those losing their jobs on constructions sites would become shop workers or cinema attendants. But the shopping spree would have to be insanely manic for China to hit the five-year plan's reduced new GDP growth target of 7% a year. Here is how the numbers work. With China's consumer spending at just 34% of GDP in 2010, while investment spending is 49%, if the government merely succeeded in keeping investment activity static – and sharp falls are more common after such a long boom – then consumer spending would need to grow at a consistent rate of at least 15% a year for the best part of a decade. Even for a population starting from a low base of spending, that would be the mother of all sprees.

There is stuff the government could do to encourage the Chinese to spend more. It could let the currency rise further, which would cut the price of desirable foreign imports. A higher interest rate could be paid by banks on savings. The minimum wage could be increased at a faster rate. There could be greater state provision of health care, pensions and unemployment benefits, to reduce the incentives for saving. But much of what the authorities could do to boost the sense of prosperity for Chinese families would risk putting a lot of companies out of business: a currency appreciation could lead to a squeeze in their sales or profit margins or both; further wage rises would be unaffordable for some; and any increase in interest rates on savings could feed through to higher charges for borrowers, which would be fatal for developers with excessive debts.

A great deal of debt, much of it unaffordable, has built up quickly in China, some of it hidden from view till it was too late. For example, in 2011 it emerged that many local governments had been borrowing money, often illegally, through land mortgage schemes. The total amount of these debts, according to the People's Bank of China, stood at perhaps $2.2 trillion at the end of 2010, well over a third of Chinese GDP. Also smaller privately owned businesses, which found themselves unable to access regular bank loans when lending was tightened in 2010, resorted to illegal borrowing. The eastern city of Wenzhou became a hotbed for illicit lending to small businesses: investment schemes were set up to collect money from savers at a relatively high interest rate, for onward lending to companies. Many of these schemes have gone bust, wiping out people's savings. And the reported problems are not the whole story – right now it is impossible to know how big the iceberg of unpayable debts will turn out to be.

The eventual scale of the bad debts is likely to be exacerbated by the shoddiness of some of the construction and development. In 2011 a high-speed train crashed at Wenzhou killing forty people. Despite attempts by Beijing to curtail reporting on the incident, intrepid journalists investigated. Their conclusion – later confirmed in an official government report – was that the accident was caused by management incompetence and contractors rushing the job. The government report laid much of the blame at the door of the former railway minister, Liu Zhijun, who had just been sacked and accused of corruption. It is highly plausible that more examples of reckless corner-cutting in building projects will come to light, simply because of the sheer magnitude and speed of the infrastructure boom. And, as we have explored, much of what has been built could turn out to be unnecessary, uncommercial and incapable of generating the revenues necessary to service the projects' debts. That would lead to a big rise in losses for banks. How bad could it get? Well, in the late 1990s, some 35% of all the new loans that banks had been ordered to make by the government went bad, according to Professor Chovanec. The signs do not look better this time round. In 2010, the Chinese banking regulator said that of the $1.1 trillion in local government infrastructure loans it had identified at that time, 23% could not be repaid, while a further 50% would need additional financial support from the relevant local governments. At the time the state-owned banks had made provisions to cover losses equivalent to just 2.5% of all their loans, which – says Chovanec – was too little.

The banks are among a group of powerful institutions and individuals who have done very well out of the investment boom and have a vast amount to lose if it goes pop. Apart from the property developers and local government officials, there are also the big state-owned companies that dominate all the big industries in China: energy, oil and gas, shipbuilding, shipping, transport, telecoms, mining, steelmaking, chemicals, and, of course, banking. These are the companies with the greatest *guanxi,* or the precious social, political and business connections that oil the wheels of big deals. They have had the easiest access to cheap loans, and their borrowing and investing played a major role in keeping the economy afloat in 2009–10. Their privileged access to cheap credit in recent years has helped many of these companies fend off competition from the private sector, be it domestic or foreign. To take just one example, in 2004 China opened up the airline industry to private sector firms, and ten new companies entered the market. The state-owned companies responded with a price war, and with aggressive tactics such as blocking the private companies' use of the electronic registration system that they operated. When the state-owned airlines got into trouble during the 2008 financial crisis, the government gave them a $1.6 billion bailout. By 2010, only one of the private sector airlines was left.

The big state-owned enterprises control the basic industries and services on which most of the private sector – the manufacturers, exporters, contractors, service companies and retailers – is dependent. The near-monopoly power of the state-owned enterprises allows them to extract huge rewards or rent from private businesses, by charging them very high prices. In other words, the private sector does the hard work of employing millions of Chinese workers to make the stuff desired by the rest of the world, and state-owned enterprises siphon off much of the profits. So the state-owned enterprises are able to furnish attractive lifestyles to the Communist Party apparatchiks who run and staff them. Also, in the absence of a free press, these huge businesses are largely unaccountable and subject to few external controls. It may be worth noting, in this context, that following the collapse of Communism in Eastern Europe, most businesses were found to be worth considerably less than what Western observers had assumed, with many turning out to be massively loss-making. All of which is a long-winded way of saying that large parts of the Chinese (state-owned) economy may be more dysfunctional and less productive than official statistics suggest.

However, because of the political connections of the state-owned enterprises, serious reform of the Chinese economy rubs up against powerful, entrenched vested interest, as the World Bank notes in its report, 'China 2030'. The World Bank calls for huge state-owned companies to be broken up, and to be forced to face much stiffer competition from the private sector and from abroad. As it points out, private-sector firms have proved much more profitable than the state-owned companies, and have played a much bigger role in generating growth in the Chinese economy. There are some who argue that there is an alternative to breaking up the state-owned enterprises, which would be to force them to pay much bigger dividends to the state, perhaps equivalent to 3% of GDP. This would reduce the number of white-elephant investments made by these gargantuan enterprises. And it could help the government to finance a more developed and comprehensive welfare state, which would deliver an immediate boost to people's sense of their financial security. This, in turn, would encourage households to spend more, to their gain and that of the economy. A Communist state sharing the fruits of labour with hundreds of millions of people? There's an intriguing idea. But the odd thing is that these great lumbering businesses continue to be allowed by the government to accumulate and retain for their own use quite colossal amounts of cash.

Securing the active participation of the Communist Party's leadership in a reconstruction of the Chinese economy, away from the state-owned enterprises with which they have a mutually supportive relationship, is not proving easy. That said, the World Bank's report was jointly prepared with the Chinese government's policy research unit, the Development Research Centre. And it has the blessing of China's ostensibly reformist premier, Wen Jiabao (the Party's number three person). Many of the report's recommendations have been repeated in speeches and writings by the soon-to-retire Wen. And he may well have an important ally in Wang Yang, the relatively liberal party boss of Guangdong, the province that has traditionally been at the forefront of reforms. More importantly, the reform agenda is thought to have the backing of Xi Jinping, the man widely expected to replace the outgoing President Hu Jintao in the top spot on the Politburo Standing Committee at the country's decennial leadership transition in 2012–13. If Messrs Wen, Wang and Xi are sincere in their pursuit of reform, they will have their work cut out, because most of the other members of the current Standing Committee (and the likely members of the new one) appear to have a strong personal interest in maintaining the status quo.

Here's a resonant diplomatic cable, leaked by WikiLeaks, relaying a report from the US embassy (which of course is coloured by its own commercial vested interests):

> China's top leadership had carved up China's economic pie, creating an ossified system in which 'vested interests' drove decision-making and impeded reform as leaders manoeuvred to ensure that those interests were not threatened.

Among the nine current Standing Committee members, the cable said that the number four, Jia Qinglin, had major real estate interests in Beijing, while the number nine and security head, Zhou Yongkang, controlled the state oil monopoly.

Many influential figures in the Chinese government are 'princelings' – children of revolutionary leaders under Mao – or less privileged offspring of later Party apparatchiks, whose family ties have helped them accumulate power and wealth. Even the reformist Wen has his business interests: his wife was reported by the leaked US cable to control the Chinese gems business; his son is one of many princelings who have made it big in the home-grown Chinese private equity business, and use their connections to win lucrative contracts to take over and reconstruct government-owned assets.

The reform faction that Mr Wen represents appeared to score a significant victory with the downfall in early 2012 of Bo Xilai, the powerful Communist Party chief in the Chongqing city-province of central China, who was openly nostalgic for the trappings of Maoism, especially its anthems. The purge of Bo and his associates may be influential on China's future economic direction because he was a great supporter both of state-owned businesses and the construction of massive housing developments. His big government 'Chongqing model' was viewed as the main challenger to the more liberal 'Guangdong model'. Bo's main ally was the Politburo Standing Committee member, Zhou Yongkang, who was reported to have been stripped of control of the country's security apparatus. Which is why experts in the nuances of power shifts at the top the Communist Party believe the modernisers have gained a serious advantage.

In the event, painful financial reality may dictate that reform is inescapable. Bad loans and poor investments have already been made, on a gargantuan scale. The immediate question for a new Standing Committee will be how much longer it tolerates the construction boom. All the genuine infrastructure and housing projects are probably complete, so every month that the boom continues may mean more waste and bad debts. The longer the day of reckoning is delayed, the worse the eventual shock to the economy. And the Party's aim to boost consumer spending, in the twelfth five-year plan, is a statement born of necessity: the investment binge is unsustainable; a renewed focus on exports would be unpopular with most Chinese people, whose living standards would continue to be squeezed, and would alienate much of the rest of the world, such as the US and UK, whose struggle to reduce deficit and debts would be made that much harder.

If it is inevitable that China's economic model has to change fundamentally, what is less clear is whether this will happen with bang or a whimper. The bold option for China's new leaders – in the new Standing Committee, to take office in November

2012 – would be to wipe out the sins of the past. This would involve raising interest rates, forcing loss-making investment projects and businesses (including many big state-owned companies) into bankruptcy, breaking up and privatising the viable state-owned companies, and using the proceeds from privatisations to cover the cost of strengthening banks. But although this might be the most rational way to rebuild the foundations of the Chinese economy, it is thought unlikely to happen. The commercial interests of top Party officials and tens of thousands of Party members, who enjoy relatively cushy jobs in state-owned companies, would be threatened. And the social disruption would be significant and potentially danger-ous. Millions of people employed in construction and related industries – including a significant proportion of migrant work-ers in the big cities – would find themselves unemployed. The Communist Party could in those circumstances be accused of having reneged on its side of China's grand compact, to deliver prosperity, as compensation for restrictive freedom.

More likely therefore is that there will be a conspiracy of silence between political leaders, banks and borrowers about the scale of the bad debts. Rather than put poor property and construction projects into bankruptcy, loans would be rolled over. All sorts of corporate creditors would become the living dead. The banks too would be hobbled, as their resources would be excessively deployed on supporting zombie borrow-ers, and would therefore be incapable of providing adequate credit to those who need it. The consequence of avoiding a short sharp shock could be years and years of economic stag-nation; rather like what happened to Japan over the past twenty years. Which is why it is worth a short detour to exam-ine Japan's supposed lost decades, to see what insights they provide on China's future.

Lessons from Japan

The parallels between China and Japan are striking. In the mid 1980s, Japan gave a nod towards accepting that growth generated exclusively from exports could not go on forever. In the 1985 Plaza Accord, Japan accepted that the yen had become too weak against the dollar. But with the yen rising and Japanese exports becoming pricier, Japan's central bank slashed interest rates – to offset a slowdown in the economy. That sparked a lending binge by banks to property developers and to the country's big industrial conglomerates. The result was a massive construction boom and the mother of all property and stock-market bubbles.

When those bubbles burst in 1990, the shock pushed Japan into what Richard Koo, chief economist at the Japanese investment bank Nomura, has dubbed a 'balance-sheet recession' – which is a useful concept for understanding the challenges we currently face in the over-indebted West as well as what could happen in China. Koo's insight is that there are times when businesses or individuals feel so indebted that they will obsessively prioritise repaying debts. In those circumstances, no incentive to borrow in the form of reductions in interest rates will have the slightest impact. To use the economists' cliché, reducing the cost of borrowing is like pushing on a string: businesses won't invest and consumers won't spend if they've decided that their priority is to save. And the challenge for central banks which set interest rates, the challenge of restarting the economy, becomes greater if the reason businesses and individuals became massively indebted in the first place was to finance purchases of assets – property, for example – and then a bubble in those assets is pricked. The individuals and companies still have their debts, but the assets they thought would cover them shrink in value, sometimes for years and years.

It is important to note that balance-sheet recessions can afflict both surplus economies, such as Japan and China, which save more than they borrow at the level of the entire economy, and deficit economies such as the UK and US. The relevant debts could be businesses taking on loans for investment, consumers running up debts on their credit cards, home buyers becoming shackled by huge mortgages, banks borrowing recklessly to lend recklessly, or governments consistently failing to keep a ceiling on the national debt. The simple pathology is that growth is initially generated by debt-fuelled spending, which is then replaced by saving. Now in order for the spenders to be able to spend, someone had to lend them the money. When a whole country is in deficit, like Britain, ultimately the creditors are the surplus countries: China, Japan, Germany and the oil exporters. But there are also big groups of savers within countries. In China today, the savers have been families and big companies. In Japan, households are colossal savers. In the US (and in much of the West), the biggest savers are the super-rich, who earn far more than they could ever remotely use. During the good years, there seems to be a wonderfully symbiotic relationship between borrower and creditor. The savers put their money to work by lending to the borrowers, who feel richer and richer, especially if they are using their loans to buy assets – property, shares and so on – that are rising in value. Then one day, usually long after borrowers and lenders have been lulled into a false sense of security, the bubble bursts. It suddenly becomes clear that the borrowers have run up more debts than they can repay. So the lenders try to get their money back, which often leads them to seize the assets of their debtors. When the seized assets are dumped on the market, their prices collapse. Which makes the debtors look even more bust than they did before. The borrowers feel poorer, they reduce their spending, the economy slows down and asset prices fall even further. It is a vicious, self-feeding cycle, causing slumps in both the price of assets and economic activity. The borrowers – the businesses and people whose spending and investing has been the engine of growth – can no longer borrow and spend, and they don't want to borrow and spend. In Japan, businesses underwent a complete psychological makeover in the 1990s. For years and years their only priority was to pay off their debts, more or less whatever happened in the economy around them. According to Koo, it was their implacable propensity to save which underlay Japan's lost economic years, the decades when its economy simply would not grow.

During Japan's debt-fuelled boom in the 1980s – and this has parallels with what is happening in China today – the borrowers were institutional and corporate: manufacturers, exporters, construction companies, property developers. After Japan's twin bubbles (property and the stock market) burst in 1990, the loans provided by the banks to these borrowers went sour. Loans that had been made by the banks in the 1980s to finance the construction of overvalued buildings, or the acquisition of overvalued companies, could not be repaid. The Japanese banks found that many of their major borrowers were bust in all but name. In fact, the problem was so big that if the banks had actually recognised the losses they were sitting on – which is what banks are normally supposed to do when debts go bad – then they would have been wiped out themselves. Faced with the prospect of mutually assured destruction, both the banks and their borrowers tacitly agreed to live in a state of denial. The banks did not call in the loans and write off that portion that could never be repaid. Instead they kept rolling over loans to insolvent borrowers. However, with the banks poisoned by these hidden bad debts and desperately needing to be purged, they stopped lending to anyone else. They ceased to fulfil their function of supporting the rest of the economy. Meanwhile, the indebted businesses slashed their spending to a minimum – no more big investments for them – and they used whatever cash they could earn to gradually pay off their debts. Like the banks, they became zombies.

Because they did not go bust, the unemployment rate in Japan throughout the 1990s and after the millennium remained relatively low, at between 2% and 6%. Arguably there were social benefits from the country's collective refusal to own up to the excessive indebtedness of companies and the weakness of banks. But the failure to cut out the diseased part of the economy meant that recovery was delayed almost indefinitely. Property prices and share prices fell and fell during the two decades after the crash. House prices would drop for fifteen years in a row, while it was not till 2008 that the Nikkei stock-market index hit its lowest level since the peak of December 1989. Sustained economic growth never returned.

The Japanese central bank continued to do its best to hold down the value of the yen for the next twenty years, so that beleaguered exporters could keep a competitive edge, helping the country to maintain a modest but persistent trade surplus. That is why Japan, until very recently, has continued to be one of the countries that continued to lend to the rest of the world, in spite of the paradox that its own economy had been hobbled by excessive corporate and banking debts. The Japanese authorities collaborated in sustaining a bankrupt system. Japan's central bank provided emergency loans to the banks, and slashed interest rates to zero. That helped all those over-indebted banks and companies and property developers to delay the day when they were forced to recognise that they had borrowed far too much. And for ordinary Japanese people – just like today's Chinese – with savings not debts, low interest rates meant they felt poorer rather than richer. They were earning far less income on their savings, which was not an incentive to go out and spend. It wasn't until 2002 that the government finally audited the banks properly, forcing them to recognise their losses and rebuild their capital, so that they could lend again. There were a lot of losses: between 1992 and 2005 the banks collectively wrote off 96 trillion yen of debts, or about 19% of Japanese annual output or GDP.

One sensible way forward would have been to change the emphasis in its economy – to rebalance it – away from exporting and towards consumption. If only Japanese people could have been persuaded to spend more and save less, they would have felt better off. Businesses serving the domestic economy would have prospered, tax revenues would have been higher, the economy would have gradually regained momentum. And with Japanese people, unlike businesses, sitting on vast savings, the opportunity was enormous. But the Japanese did not want to abandon thrift, perhaps for deep-seated cultural reasons, but probably also because – as the economy stagnated – Japanese workers worried that their employers would go bust and they would lose their jobs. What's more, a disproportionate number of Japanese were coming up for retirement over the subsequent two decades. The properties and shares they owned had collapsed in value, and they were afraid that their savings were still not enough to keep them comfortable in their lengthy old age.

Because domestic spending was so weak, prices and wages stagnated, and even began to fall. Stagnation became endemic. By 2011, the Japanese economy measured in current yen (which includes the effect of falling prices) was the same size as it had been in 1992. In other words, the economy had failed to outgrow its debt burden. But according to Richard Koo, it could have been a lot worse. He believes the economy would have totally collapsed, had the Japanese government not stepped into the breach by massively increasing its own borrowing and spending. Japan's industries, whose investment spending had turbo-charged the economy in the 80s, were burned out. It was obvious that the country might have to wait forever for Japanese consumers to do what they ought to have done, and become the engine of growth. So Japan's government, in fits and starts, made up some of the shortfall with its own spending.

Whether the Japanese government was right to do so is still – twenty years later – hotly debated. The Japanese economy avoided a 1930s-style Great Depression. Unemployment has stayed low. And people's living standards have continued to rise steadily, albeit slowly. But the government was so determined to maintain the stability of the economy that the necessary structural changes to the economy were delayed. Super-low interest rates, which favoured heavily indebted lame-duck businesses at the expense of thrifty Japanese families, were just one way that the economy was put on crutches rather than taught to walk again. And year after year, as the government spent significantly more than it was receiving in taxes, public-sector debt rose to record levels. As the borrowing of companies and banks was gradually reduced, it was replaced by the rising indebtedness of the state. By 2011, the government's debts equated to a whopping 230% of the country's stagnant GDP, up from 66% in 1991. Probably the main reason the Japanese government has not gone bust is that

Japanese households and, latterly, businesses chose to lend to their government on a colossal scale.

But there is a threat to the Japanese government's capacity to borrow as though tomorrow never comes. After the global financial crisis, the yen – seen, perhaps bizarrely, as a financial safe haven – has been rising in value. Its price has gained more than 50% against the dollar since mid 2007. That sustained rise has been bad news for Japan's exporters, who have now begun shifting production to cheaper locations overseas. It could be worse news for the government. Japanese exporters, with their profits squeezed by the stronger yen, have less money to lend to the public sector. Japanese families, on the other hand, have been able to buy imports much more cheaply. That has encouraged them to start spending – 'At last!' you might say. But if that were to become a sustained trend, if there were a permanent drop in how much they save, they would no longer be a source of cheap loans to the government. In 2012, Japan's current account surplus fell sharply, such that it has become realistic to believe that Japan could start to spend more than it earns, for the first time since 1981. And that would mean the government, Japan's biggest borrower, would for the first time have to depend on the willingness of foreigners to lend it money. The fear in Tokyo is that foreign investors would demand a much higher interest rate for the additional credit than what Japan's households were paid for all those years. Like Italy, that could prove unaffordable for a government with such enormous debts and borrowing needs. However, it is worth bearing in mind that Japan's government could continue to borrow from its central bank. And if foreign lenders became more reluctant to lend the Japanese government the money it needed, one consequence would be a fall in the value of the yen – and that would be a boon to Japanese exporters. That said, and although Japan has formidable industrial strengths and substantial net assets held overseas, this is an economy struggling to regain any kind of forward movement and facing a ticking financial time bomb of an ageing population. If investors decided to stop lending to Japan's government, the blow to confidence in the Japanese banking system, investors' wealth and citizens' prosperity would be calamitous.

What does the Tokyo story mean for China? Well, it is striking – and worrying – that the imbalances that Japan faced in 1990 were in many ways less extreme than China's today. Investment in Japan accounted for around a third of its economy before the crash, compared with half in China in 2012. So a collapse in debt-fuelled investment (or even a moderate slowdown) could be more harmful to China's growth than it was for Japan. As for consumer spending in Japan, it was a half of GDP twenty years ago, lower than in the US and UK, but much greater than the third of economic output contributed by Chinese consumers. From such a low base, Chinese consumer spending would have to surge to compensate even for a relatively small fall in investment – which was a feat that Japan, with a more developed economy and a greater propensity to spend, did not pull off. In Japan, families saved 10% of their incomes in 1990. In China the savings rate is around 25%. The Chinese have a serious savings habit to break. Also the Japanese current account surplus – how much the economy was lending to the rest of the world – was about 2% of GDP in 1990 (and remained in the 2% to 3% range throughout the following two decades). In China, the surplus has fallen from a colossal 10.6% of GDP in 2008 to about 3% currently. And, as I mentioned earlier, that surplus is liable to rise again as the country winds down its investment splurge.

In other words, the challenge for China of reconstructing its economic model in a way that doesn't feed the unsustainable debts of the West or lead to an asset and borrowing bubble at home is even harder than it was for Japan. And Japan failed the challenge. If China's dangerous investment binge is to be curtailed, without a damaging shock to the economy that could cause unemployment and serious hardship to millions of Chinese, the government will need to engineer a consumer spending boom on a scale that is difficult to comprehend – especially since if you go to the new shopping developments in the bustling booming cities of Shanghai, Beijing, and elsewhere, you already see Chinese people shopping with a gusto typical of the West. But they need to shop quite literally till they drop.

A senior British official related a telling story about a recent meeting with a senior Chinese government minister. In Britain, the great concern among ministers is that they are having to make people poorer as they cut government spending in an effort to shrink public-sector borrowing. In China, the government knows that it needs to push people to improve their immediate lifestyles by spending more and saving less. But this Chinese minister was talking about that imperative as though it was some hugely painful duty, rather than the kind of policy that in the West would be seen as an election winner.

If Chinese households can't be persuaded to enjoy material things more, it is almost inevitable that the Chinese government's debts will explode, as Japan's did – because the government will have to spend more than it raises in taxes, to stop the economy collapsing. Even now, if all of the debts of government agencies and departments, local and regional governments, state-owned companies and the various infrastructure projects are lumped together then public-sector debts are substantial. The Chinese economist Victor Shih of Northwestern University in the US – who identified the debts being accumulated by China's local governments – estimates the government's true indebtedness is equivalent to more than 100% of China's GDP, far higher than the 43% debt ratio acknowledged by Beijing.

And what if Chinese property were to plunge in value in the way that Japanese assets did? The Chinese government and authorities would face exactly the same dilemma as Japan's did. Should they encourage banks to force over-extended construction and development companies into bankruptcy, seize assets and write off associated debts – which would lead to big job losses and a reduction in the wealth of countless millions of people, but would be the sine qua non of the banks regaining their strength? Or should there be a concerted attempt to hide the losses, with the risk that the financial strength of banks would be chronically undermined, leading to years of mild but pernicious credit crunch? The tougher option of the short sharp shock looks least likely, given that so many Communist Party members have a vested interest in the preservation of a nepotistic system based around the expropriation of property and favoured treatment for the state-owned enterprises. The probability is of the government taking the option that reduces the short-term pain but may condemn China to an extended period of unsatisfactory growth. However, what's really vital, for China and the rest of the world, is whether either a popping of the property and infrastructure bubble or a slow deflation of it would undermine the grand bargain between an autocratic, one-party government and the people – namely that hunger for democracy is bought off with jobs and rising wealth. Perhaps there is a failure of imagination on my part, but having witnessed the most remarkable enrichment of almost an entire people over the past fifteen years, I find it difficult to believe that richer Chinese citizens won't start demanding greater rights to self determination. Seen through Western eyes, China's political system seems as unbalanced and potentially unstable as its economic and financial system.

CHAPTER 9
WILL EUROPE BANKRUPT THE WORLD?

Not all currency unions are devastating flops. America's has worked pretty well in the century and a half since the Constitution of 1789 gave Congress the power to create money. What is it that prevented the state of Michigan, for example, from blaming the dollarzone for its significant hardship in the last recession? Michigan is the home of Detroit, the capital city of the US car industry, and once the unchallenged automotive manufacturing centre of the world. The US car industry has not been doing too well in the last ten years. And neither has Detroit. Employment in the city has fallen since 2000 by 22%. The unemployment rate, which peaked at 18% in the recent recession, remains stuck in double digits, well above the national average. House prices in the city have fallen by half since the US housing bubble burst (across the US as a whole they've fallen by a third) and are now back at levels last seen in the mid 1990s, or even earlier once you take account of inflation.

Think about what would have happened to Michigan if it had its own currency, the Cadillac dollar, in the last decade. The central bank of Michigan could have cut borrowing costs and created new money to encourage more spending. And the Cadillac dollar would have fallen in value relative to other currencies – including those of the big car-exporting nations Japan and Germany – which would have reduced the global price of Detroit-made cars and made the cost of employing car workers in Detroit less expensive. So the recession in Detroit might have been less severe than it was.

Of course, for all this apparent advantage of going for monetary independence in Michigan, the very idea wouldn't enter anyone's head. The dollar is part of the fabric of the US. And the way that it is ingrained in the very idea of America says a good deal about the necessary conditions for a success-ful monetary union. The point is that along with the monetary union, there is a fiscal union in the US and almost no discern-ible barriers to the movement of people around the US. Also, there is great social and cultural solidarity between the states of America – and American citizens have great respect for the Office of the President and for Congress, if not always for the individuals who serve as President or in the Senate and House of Representatives.

What the people of Detroit know is that they are not on their own when the going gets tough. Although all US states have their own budgets, much like eurozone governments, there are substantial transfers from Washington to limit the economic damage and social dislocation of a major shock – whereas in the eurozone it is largely a case of each nation for itself in and after a crisis such as the 2008 banking meltdown. According to figures from the US Bureau of Economic Analysis, in 2010 there was $532bn of transfers from the US federal government to the individual states, of which $101bn was from a post-crash stimulus package designed by President Obama. And on top of all that, Detroit itself – or rather two of its big three motor manufacturers, General Motors and Chrysler – received exceptional support from Washington's Troubled Asset Relief Program, after they were badly hurt by the global recession. General Motors received funds of just under $50bn and Chrysler $12.5bn of US taxpayers' money. And although this was money that the motor manufacturers were supposed to repay, it was money put at risk: the US government took stakes in the two companies; and the US government seems to have recognised, through gritted teeth, that it will incur huge losses on the support for General Motors. The rescue of these two companies has arguably saved many thousands of jobs in Detroit (although some claimed Obama was splinting lame ducks). It has done so because Washington was prepared to be generous both with the amount of financial support it provided and the terms of that support. In that sense, Detroit cannot really complain that its monetary and political union with the rest of the US has seen it hung out to dry by the rest of the US.

And then there is labour mobility. Unemployment in central Detroit would have been much higher had the city's population not shrunk by an incredible 25% between 2000 and 2010. Astonishing numbers of redundant workers and their families packed up and moved out. Many of them have moved no further than the relative prosperity of the city's suburbs and outer towns. But many more have moved hundreds of miles to other parts of the US, such as faster growing Texas, where job prospects have been much better.

Michigan illustrates three of the ingredients that are probably needed to make a common currency work: a central government, in Washington, which the vast majority of Americans in the many disparate states believe they 'own' in a very basic sense; a jobs market in which people are willing and able to relocate to find work; and a centralised system of payments that can transfer taxpayers' money from one region to help out citizens in another.

In all these respects, the eurozone is underdeveloped, as critics have consistently pointed out since well before the euro was launched. To state the bloomin' obvious, neither the President of the European Council, nor the President of the European Commission, nor the President of the European Parliament is a figurehead capable of uniting and exciting the populations of eurozone countries. None would be seen as having much authority, if (for example) they tried to persuade the people of Germany to make a significant financial sacrifice in the cause of bailing out their fellow Europeans in Greece and Italy. And the European Parliament is widely seen as an inferior legislative body next to national parliaments, even though in some ways it is the more powerful institution. As for job mobility, there is no formal barrier on emigrating from one EU country to another. But there are lots of other hurdles to resettlement, such as a lack of equivalence in national skills qualifications, restrictive working practices in some countries, fragmented housing markets with pockets of extreme shortages of homes, and language differences. These hurdles have proved so high that some young unemployed Spaniards have turned up in Spanish-speaking Latin America and then thrown away their passports, rather than trying their luck in prosperous Germany.

When it comes to taxpayers of one nation helping another, Germany and the rest of the eurozone have very conspicuously not been offering free money to the countries that have struggled to borrow in a conventional way and asked to be rescued: Greece, Ireland, Portugal, Cyprus and Spain. Initially Germany – and especially its central bank, the

Bundesbank – didn't want to help Greece at all, citing the 'no bailout' clauses of the Maastricht and Lisbon treaties. As it became clear that the implosion of Greece would damage all eurozone members, including Germany, bailout loans were provided – first to Greece and then to Ireland and Portugal, with Cyprus and Spain negotiating their emergency aid packages at the time of writing. But Germany initially insisted that these loans should not be subsidised in any way: the interest rate charged on them should be relatively high, almost punitive. Again, as the risk intensified that the ailing countries could be forced out of the eurozone if the costs of rescues were deemed to be too great, Germany relented, and the interest rates were reduced.

But the significant point is this: loans are all that the Germans and the rest of the eurozone have offered to Greece, Ireland and Portugal. And loans are all the European Central Bank has offered to Europe's troubled banks. However, if one of the biggest problems for Ireland, Portugal and Greece – and for Spain and Italy – is that their debts are too great, simply substituting new loans from the rest of the eurozone for loans provided by private-sector lenders does not solve anything in a fundamental way. The debts are still there: it is just the creditors which have changed. A loan from the eurozone (and the International Monetary Fund) buys time for an over-extended economy to sort out its creaking finances in a sustainable way. But it is nowhere near as helpful as the support provided to Detroit by Washington. The US federal government gives money to Detroit and its workers – money which does not have to be repaid. Think how much poorer Detroit and its citizens would have become if they had to repay all the money they received from taxpayers outside the state.

Now, in the eurozone it is not just that Germany and the rest have refused to provide gifts to Greece, Ireland, Portugal, Cyprus and Spain (which, if you will indulge me, I will call GIPCS). Germany has also periodically insisted that loans provided by eurozone taxpayers and the European Central Bank should have preferential treatment above all other loans: they should be repaid before all other loans. In other words, Germany's view is that German taxpayers should never provide either the kind of transfer to Greek or Portuguese citizens that is standard practice between the states of America or even take a commercial risk when lending to such countries. After much wrangling, it was ultimately decided that the eurozone's preliminary and temporary bailout fund, the European Financial Stability Facility (EFSF), should not be given preferred creditor status. But that changed with the establishment in 2011 of a successor to the EFSF, the European Stability Mechanism: emergency loans it provides would in theory rank ahead of all loans made by private-sector lenders, though a notch behind loans from the International Monetary Fund. Or to put it another way, the idea was formalised that when German taxpayers are helping out their neighbours, there should not be even a hint that there is any kind of charity or gift involved. And for the second €130bn rescue of Greece, in 2011, this German prohibition on fiscal aid was reinforced: when private-sector lenders to Greece were strong-armed into writing off 75% of what Greece owed them, more than €50bn of Greek government debt held by the European Central Bank and eurozone national central banks was fully protected. Under the deal, the European Central Bank would be repaid in full by Greece. Now this protection of official lending to Greece had the opposite effect on other financially challenged eurozone economies of a transfer: it meant that commercial lenders to Spain and Italy, for example, felt like second-class creditors; they had been shown that in a crisis, their loans would be treated as inferior to the loans made by the European Central Bank; so inevitably they increased the interest rate they demanded that the Spanish and Italian governments should pay. To put it another way, German medicine was classic puritan medicine: it hurt but it was not clear that it worked terribly well. Which is why when it came to negotiations in June and July 2012 over the provision of €100bn of eurozone rescue funds to shore up Spain's fragile banks, one of the vital questions was whether Germany would grit its teeth and drop its insistence that any money provided had to be classified as the senior debt of the Spanish government – which would therefore automatically downgrade the status of €750bn Spain has borrowed from investors and financial institutions, and make it even harder for the Spanish government to borrow in a conventional way. At the time of writing, that uncertainty was still not resolved, though it looks as though Germany has made a concession: a way may well be found for the €100bn to go directly into the banks, in a series of lumps, so it would not be treated as a direct debt of the Spanish central government.

The simple point is this. In the early years after the creation of the euro, the borrowing costs for the likes of Italy, Spain and Greece fell sharply, because of the naïve assumption of investors that their debts were now – in effect – underwritten by the huge and mighty German economy. But when the crisis broke, Germany, together with the other financially sounder nations, such as the Netherlands, Austria and Finland, made it clear that they wanted to punish the investors who had lent so recklessly to their neighbours. And that determination to teach a lesson to the imprudent lenders and borrowers had the effect of pushing up the borrowing costs for Italy and Spain – the interest rate their governments were forced to pay – to record and unaffordable levels. Even France was tainted: its borrowing costs became significantly pricier than Germany's and also the UK's. The fiscal rectitude of Germany and its hard-money allies had the perverse effect of exacerbating the short-term crisis.

The German government was not alone in inadvertently worsening the tensions within the eurozone. The ECB – created in the image of Germany's Bundesbank – has arguably made conditions tougher for GIPCS plus Italy, in pursuit of the laudable cause of price stability. In the spring of 2011 the central bank under Jean-Claude Trichet decided to raise interest rates, in response to the putative inflationary threat posed by rising world energy and food prices. There should have been nothing automatic about this decision. The Bank of England and the US Federal Reserve were faced with exactly the same inflationary pressures, but chose to ignore them – because they saw them as temporary. As for the ECB, within a matter of weeks it executed an abrupt U-turn, and cut the rate: it was the first act of the central bank's new Italian head, Mario Draghi, who took over from Mr Trichet in November 2011. But by then the damage had been done, with growth in the eurozone even weaker than it had been. As he took office, Mr Draghi's home country, along with Spain, had been pushed right to the edge of a precipice. Italy's cost of borrowing had risen to an alarming 7% – a level that is unaffordable for such a heavily indebted country.

An Italian tale

The story of how Italy went from being part of the eurozone's supposedly solid core to being seen as the toxic rot in that core is instructive. It shows how almost any eurozone government – perhaps even that of France – can find itself boycotted by markets, and therefore on the brink of collapse. What is striking about the financial problems of GIPCS and Italy is that they have a big thing in common, which is that in the round they are debtor nations where there are structural impediments to the repayment of their debts, but the pathology of their individual malaises shows important differences. For example, Italy participated less in the debt-fuelled boom than most of the others. Italian citizens and companies are less indebted than those of Spain and Ireland: Italians' attitude to borrowing is almost Germanic in its caution. And even the Italian government resisted the temptation to go on a spending and borrowing binge in the years immediately preceding the crash. Unlike Greece (and Germany) Italy paid for its public services with tax revenues, rather than by increasing public-sector debts, from 1992 up until 2008. What went wrong? How did Italy get into trouble? Well, it had two primary sources of weakness. Its government may have resisted the temptation to go on a borrowing spree, but many would say it deserves no plaudits – because it was already one of the most indebted of the world's developed economies and the most indebted economy in Europe, by a margin. It borrowed far too much in the 1970s and 1980s and never got the debt down to a sustainable level. The great failure of the Italian government was not to reduce that indebtedness enough in the years of prosperity before the crash. And what makes this debt burden doubly troublesome is that its economy has been almost Japanese in its inability to grow. Over the last fifteen years, the country has managed an average annual growth rate of just 0.83%. Arguably, it has been the eurozone's weakest economy, held back by restrictive working practices and an ageing population (although it has a massive black economy, which – by definition – is excluded from the official statistics). And inside the eurozone, Italy had steadily lost competitiveness, just like GIPCS.

The Italian government's immediate source of vulnerability was that it had to borrow a colossal amount every year to repay its older debts as they fell due, plus the interest it owed. The average maturity of its debt is seven years, half the average maturity of UK government debt. In 2012, Italy needs to borrow a sum equivalent to almost 29% of its GDP or output, around €450bn, according to the IMF. And its borrowing needs will only be a bit smaller in 2013, largely – as I say – because so much of its existing debt needs to be refinanced. This is a source of considerable concern, at a time when investors are wary of lending to any highly indebted eurozone government. And because of the interest bill, the overall burden of its debts is getting bigger every year. By the end of 2011, the ratio of its government debt to GDP was 120%, up from 106% in 2008.

Perhaps the best way of seeing Italy is as the sovereign equivalent of an over-indebted company or bank: when the interest rate it pays shoots up, it is in dire straits. When in the autumn of 2011 there were widespread concerns that the eurozone lacked both the will and the tools to help a large economy like Italy repay its debts, the cost for Italy of borrowing for ten years rose from about 5% a year to more than 7%. Every percentage point increase in the interest bill on Italy's €2trn of debt is another €20bn that Italy will eventually have to find. Once the Italian government is paying that kind of interest rate on a consistent basis, the game is up: any pretence that Italy can afford its debts becomes useless; Italy enters a death spiral, in which investors demand ever higher interest rates for loans to replace maturing loans, and that makes the overall burden of debt lethal. Which is why, at various times in late 2011 and in 2012, Italy faced the terrifying prospect of being boycotted by investors, of being locked out of markets.

Here is another way of showing the gravity of the rise in Italy's borrowing costs. Who would you expect to pay a higher rate of interest when borrowing for three years? Me or the Italian Republic? If you said 'Peston', you are right. The markets apparently regard me as a worse credit risk than the government of the world's eighth largest economy – largely because individuals have a sorrier history in general of repaying what they owe than the public sectors of first-rank developed economies. But here's the thing: the risk premium for lending to the slightly shambolic household of Peston, as opposed to the sovereign nation of Italy, is rather less than I expected. Or at least that was so in June 2012. According to the on-line money comparison websites, I could borrow £10,000 for 5.9%, with very few questions asked of me. As for Italy, it borrowed €3bn for three years on June 14 2012 at an interest rate of 5.3%, in one of its regular bond auctions. The gap between the interest paid by the two of us, 0.6% or 60 basis points (in the jargon), seemed to put us in a similar borrowing category. And before you ask, £10,000 is a bigger proportion of my annual earnings than is €3bn euros as a proportion of Italian output or GDP. So why is the Italian government's credit-worthiness perceived to be only marginally better than mine? Well, Italy starts with rather more debt than me, that elephantine €2trn or 120% of its GDP. My debt is a much smaller proportion of my income. And Italian GDP is shrinking, as is mine – in real or inflation-adjusted terms – but maybe not as fast. Perhaps as important is the €450bn that Italy has to borrow in 2012 to refinance maturing debt and its new borrowing needs, whereas I have no debts that mature this year and need to be rolled over or refinanced. What's more, Italy may have to fork out a few tens of billions of euros to recapitalise its banks – which is less than the bill Spain faces for propping up its banks, but rather more than the banking liability I face. There's another thing: if demand for my output were to fall, I could always cut what I charge for my services; but if Italy's exports are perceived to be too expensive, it cannot cut their price because it has no independent currency to devalue. All in all, and now that I think about it, I wonder whether I should be offended that it costs me more than the Italian Republic to borrow.

What the painful experience of Italy shows is that a loss of confidence by investors is much more damaging for a eurozone country than for a country outside the eurozone. Here is why. Imagine for a moment that Italy still has its own currency, the lira. In those circumstances, even when Italy and the Italian economy are regarded as in dire shape and investors are dumping their Italian assets, some of the liras raised by the asset sales will inevitably end up being invested in lira-denominated Italian government bonds – because in theory they are the safest way of holding liras (if you have to hold some, which as an Italian resident it is almost impossible to avoid). But that automatic funnelling of some investment, all the time, into Italian government bonds no longer happens within the eurozone. Because when an investor sells Italian assets now, the freed-up euros can go anywhere in the eurozone – and if the holder of the euros is looking for the safest investment, he or she will probably end up buying German government bonds. In other words, when investors turn their back on Italy, there is no automatic channelling of money into Italian government bonds. So there is a heightened risk that investor wariness of Italy can turn into a complete inability for the Italian government to borrow any money at all.

The point is that when a government has its own currency, it also has its own trapped pool of lenders. Also, anyone who were to sell lira-denominated Italian government debt would probably sell the lira raised from the sale. And selling the lira actually helps the Italian economy, by making the lira weaker and Italy's exports cheaper. Contrast that with Italy as part of the eurozone. When an investor sells Italian government debt, they can move their money directly into the safety of German government debt. There is no lira to sell. So instead, all of the selling pressure falls on Italy's debt market. And that has the unfortunate consequence of making it more and more expensive for the Italian government to continue borrowing.

This fragmentation of the government debt markets has turned out to be as problematic as the old fragmentation of currency markets in the 1990s that the euro was supposed to have solved. In the 1992 crisis of the European Exchange Rate Mechanism (ERM), speculators and panicky investors sold the lira and the pound for the safety of the Deutschmark as they feared imminent devaluations. Ultimately that was almost the undoing of the ERM – as sterling and the lira both withdrew from it. In 2011 and 2012, the difference was that panicky investors were selling Italian and Spanish government debt for the safety of German government debt, fearing looming debt defaults. And, just as in 1992, all that selling pressure risked becoming a self-fulfilling prophecy. Because there was no way that Italy or Spain could repay their debts if nobody was willing to keep lending them money. By contrast exit from the ERM for the UK and Italy, although embarrassing for them, was a remedy for their ills. Their central banks were able to cut interest rates and their respective currencies fell, helping their economies to recover. But an exit from the eurozone and a default on debts would probably make a bad problem worse for GIPCS or Italy: for reasons that we will explore, banks, businesses and households would all go bust, and recession could mutate into an appalling depression.

For this reason, in the summer of 2011 there were loud calls from politicians (outside Germany), economists and investors – including the hedge-fund investor who profited most from the ERM crisis and sterling's devaluation, George Soros – for eurozone governments to borrow jointly, through a single eurozone government bond, rather than through national government bonds. Just as the single currency had eliminated the opportunity for investors to play off one European national currency against another, it was hoped that the euro-bond would prevent them playing off one government debt market against another. The Italians took up the idea with alacrity: if they could borrow with what they owe guaranteed by German taxpayers, who wouldn't lend to them? Problem solved, surely?

Unsurprisingly perhaps, what appealed to Italy was repugnant to the Germans – and the German government killed the idea. Germany refused even to discuss it (even after the European Commission president, José Manuel Barroso, put together a formal proposal). For Berlin, it was a matter of principle that there should be no formal commingling of liabilities for eurozone countries' sovereign debts, or at least not without the creation of something that looked like a United States of Europe. What Italy borrowed had to be the responsibility of Italian taxpayers alone. That said, there were some clever euro-bond plans being mooted, that might have met Germany's objections, had Angela Merkel felt able to be more flexible. But it was not simply a question of designing a euro-bond with a cap on the risks for Germany. Any such solution would have needed the approval of the country's parliament and constitutional court – which would have been unlikely to be forthcoming. Also much of the German electorate would have viewed any further explicit encroachment on Germany's fiscal independence with horror.

But with Germany making it clear it was not prepared to subsidise any of the borrowing costs for the over-indebted countries as they attempted to get their debts under control, the risks for lenders were made more transparent. That might have been a good idea when the eurozone was launched, because it might have prevented GIPCS borrowing too much too cheaply or given an incentive to Italy to repay debts. But it was far from benign when the governments, banks, businesses and households of GIPCS and Italy had taken on far more debt than was prudent. And since the European Central Bank could not be prevailed on to lend to governments that were being shut out of markets, rescue funds had to be found somewhere. The compromise was a succession of bailout funds: first the European Financial Stability Facility and then the European Stability Mechanism. These were financed by eurozone governments. And because Germany is the euro-zone's biggest economy, it inevitably makes the biggest contri-bution – by a margin – to both. The attraction of these funds for Germany is that they are finite: German taxpayers can see what their maximum contribution will be. But their flaw in providing any kind of lasting solution to the eurozone crisis is also that they are finite: their spare capacity, even when running in tandem for a short period, is a maximum of €500bn (and probably less). And with Spain now needing at least €100bn of this for its banks, there would be nothing left at all, if Italy suddenly found that it could not borrow on markets and made a request for emergency loans to meet its annual borrowing needs of more than €400bn a year. Some would argue that an insurance policy that can't insure against catastrophe is no insurance at all.

By the autumn of 2011, Italy's economic credibility with investors and fellow eurozone members was in tatters. There was a bloodless coup, not by generals, but by faceless bankers and creditors, who were more and more reluctant to lend to the Italian public sector. The government of the colourful plutocrat, Silvio Berlusconi, stepped down. And without any elections, the former EU commissioner, Mario Monti – a respected economist and technocrat – became premier and formed a new government of putative experts. His first actions were to reduce the generosity of pensions, impose a property tax and attempt to crack down on tax avoiders. He also declared war on restrictive employment practices, monopolies and constraints on competition. It was an attempt to boost Italy's endemically low growth rate by improving efficiency – but in the short term, which could last months or even years, more or less everyone in Italy would have to work harder for less. When making a film for the BBC on the eurozone crisis, I interviewed a Roman taxi driver, Roberto Masullo, who was being stripped by Mr Monti of his ability to bequeath a valuable taxi licence to his son, as part of reforms to allow new firms and drivers into the cab market. Mr Masullo's fate is a metaphor for his economy. 'It's a job I've always loved, handed down from father to son,' he told me. 'My grandfather was a taxi driver. And I am the son of a taxi driver. It's a job you're born into . . . fifteen years ago I would have been happy for my son to carry forward the family tradition. Today I hope for him the future will be more rosy and that he might find a better job.' Mr Masullo told me he understood the need for Italy to live within its means, but that acknowledgement does not lessen the trauma of adjustment.

And, of course, the medicine imposed by the eurozone on Ireland, Portugal and – especially – Greece, was even stronger and more aggressive in eating away at living standards. The markets organised their putsch too in Greece, where for a few months the unelected former Vice President of the European Central Bank, Lucas Papademos, took over as prime minister. The economists and bankers – who many would hold responsible for the global financial crisis of 2007–8 by their collective failure to see it coming – were taking over. Meanwhile Germany, reeling from the idea that Italy's huge debts could somehow become German debts, acknowledged the mistake it had made in killing the Stability and Growth Pact – which was supposed to shackle borrowing by eurozone governments – six years earlier. In December 2011, Europe's leaders agreed to revive and strengthen those constraints. And on 2 March 2012, twenty-five of the twenty-seven members of the European Union (all except the UK and the Czech Republic, and including several countries outside the eurozone) signed a fiscal compact. In theory, this compact makes it impossible for any signatory to run a serious deficit ever again: each country is supposed to write into its national law a commitment that its budget must be in balance or surplus, which in practice means that even for countries with low debts, the deficit can never exceed 1% of GDP. Also every eurozone member has made an individual commitment to shrink its deficit significantly by 2013 (at the time of writing, most of the deficit reduction targets look unrealistic and are likely to be missed).

Back to the banks

Arguably, however, the major fault line had shifted, from governments to banks. This should not have been the surprise to eurozone leaders that it was – because they should have been aware that the fate of banks and the fate of governments are inextricably linked. There are a couple of reasons why it is hard for banks to prosper if the financial credibility of their governments in their respective home countries is undermined. First, banks are encouraged by regulators to lend to governments, to hold disproportionate quantities of government bonds: under the rules, these bonds are treated as risk-free, liquid assets. So think about the impact on Greek banks or Italian banks when doubts arise about the ability of the Greek or Italian governments to repay their debts. Suddenly there is a huge risk that losses on these putatively risk-free bonds will wipe out the banks' capital, that the banks will be made insolvent. In fact, it is worse than that. When a big bank gets into difficulties, the only guarantor of its survival, or that its depositors and creditors won't lose a fortune, is the government. But when it is the financial weakness of the government itself that is crippling the bank, then the bank is very much on its own. The cause of a bank's woes cannot simultaneously be its redeemer: the eurozone's sovereign debt crisis was always going to become a banking crisis if it went on long enough.

The eurozone's fundamental problem, as you know, was that GIPCS had been running huge deficits. Their people, as well as their governments, had in the broadest sense been spending and living beyond their means. By contrast Germany, the Netherlands and Finland had been doing the opposite. They had been running substantial current account surpluses, earning a lot more than they spent. A good deal of Germany's surplus or excess savings ended up being lent to the economies of GIPCS and Italy, often transmitted by German banks (either directly or via loans to other European banks). French banks also provided substantial loans to GIPCS and Italy. And just like British and American banks, the eurozone's banks lent more and more relative to their capital. They increased their leverage and took bigger and bigger risks. Among the worst culprits were Ireland's banks and Spain's savings banks, or *cajas*, which borrowed colossal sums and then recklessly lent it to property developers and construction companies, financing massive unsustainable property booms. But they weren't alone; German banks bought the same AAA-rated, subprime bonds – which turned out to be poison – that generated such huge losses for UK and US banks. Austrian, Portuguese, Dutch, Belgian, French and Greek banks all engaged in various kinds of imprudent lending and investing.

There were three-and-a-half attempts to remedy the capital shortages of European banks, with Europe-wide assessments of their health. These were three 'stress tests', in 2009, 2010 and 2011, plus a 'capital exercise' in late 2011. The first tests were widely viewed as almost laughable, because they were overseen by national regulators keen to show their own nations' banks in the best possible light, and because – for political reasons – they were carried out on the presumption that eurozone governments could never default. As officials admitted at the time, they were told by government leaders that they were not to give any credibility to the idea that any eurozone member could go bust. Which of course meant that the stress tests themselves would lack credibility – because the banks were not properly tested for their resilience to almost the only relevant potential disaster of the moment: the risk that some governments would not repay their debts. The myth of the usefulness of the 2010 stress test was exploded when almost the entire banking system of Ireland had to be nationalised at the end of 2010, just weeks after the European Banking Authority had given a clean bill of health to Irish banks in general (although in Ireland's case, it was exposure to over-valued property, not over-stretched governments, that did for its banks). It was the unaffordable cost of rescuing these banks that forced the Irish government to go cap in hand to its eurozone partners and the IMF for emergency loans.

The third stress test, conducted under the umbrella of a new pan-European regulator, the European Banking Authority or EBA, was a bit more robust. But it still fudged the issue of whether governments could default – and allowed banks to understate the potential losses on the government bonds they owned. Again, just a few weeks after the results were published in July 2011, a big bank that had passed the test came unstuck: Dexia, a curious Franco–Belgian–Luxembourg lender, had to be broken up and semi-nationalised.

Fearing that it had lost credibility with the markets so early in its existence, the EBA carried out a rapid re-evaluation of how much capital European banks would need to raise. This capital exercise was based on the more prudent assumption that low market prices of the bonds of eurozone governments might translate into actual cash losses for the banks: default by governments was no longer a censored concept. On 26 October 2011, the EBA and EU governments announced that European banks needed to find €106bn of additional capital, which was increased to €115bn in December. However, even this exposure of banks' weakness did not go far enough, according to some analysts – who were gradually proved to be right, as the parlous condition of Spain's savings banks became more conspicuous. In June 2011, the Spanish government had to grit its teeth and request €100bn from the eurozone's bailout funds, to fill the perceived capital deficit just in Spain's banks.

This attempt to strengthen banks had a second defect, in the degree of freedom given to banks over how they made good the gaps in their capital resources. Unlike what happened in the UK and US in the autumn of 2008, European banks were not ordered to raise the money immediately, and be wholly or partly nationalised if they were unable to get the cash from investors. They were given time and latitude over how they strengthened their balance sheets. This created a climate of uncertainty in which some banks cut back on how much they lent (as you will recall, if a bank has to boost the ratio of its capital to assets, it can do this either by increasing capital or by shrinking assets – and when a bank shrinks its assets, it is lending less). When banks lend less, consumers and businesses have less money for spending. It is a credit crunch. And an economic slowdown always ensues. Put simply, the capital exercise may have damaged the health of the eurozone economy by precipitating a return to recession. And when recession looms, there is a growing risk of enhanced losses for banks on their loans and investments. Put simply, the method chosen for strengthening the banks actually undermined confidence in many of them (for what it is worth, the European Banking Authority provided data in July 2012 showing that most of the banks needing extra capital had raised it – though this did not prove there had been no negative impact on the supply of vital credit).

Attempts to strengthen banks were too little and too late. The financial woes of Italy and Spain – which could well force huge losses on some of Europe's banks – combined with the prospect of a renewed eurozone recession, put the fear of God into those institutions that lend vast sums to banks. Many of these really important creditors were US money-market funds, the institutions that look after trillions of dollars for American savers. Almost overnight, they collectively decided to put their money anywhere but Europe. Between April 2011 and August 2011, they withdrew most of their money from Italian and Spanish banks. They also shunned French banks, because French banks had massive exposure to the vulnerable GIPCS and Italian economies, to the tune of about €550bn. From the middle of 2011 to November, American money-market funds reduced their loans to French banks from €200bn to considerably less than €50bn. This was a serious problem for eurozone banks: the US dollar is the world's most widely used and important currency; an international bank cannot operate without access to plentiful supplies of dollars. So the world's major central banks took evasive action. On 30 November 2011, the US Federal Reserve cut the cost of supplying dollars to the European Central Bank, the Bank of England, the Bank of Japan, the Bank of Canada and the Swiss National Bank. And these recipient central banks in turn pledged to lend whatever dollars were needed by their local banks, at this lowered interest rate – and would continue to do so until 1 February 2013. In practice, it was only the European Central Bank that took advantage in any major way of the loans from the Fed. At the end of 2011, the ECB lent well over $80bn to eurozone banks at the exceptionally low interest rate of 0.59%.

But the problem was not just that non-European financial institutions did not wish to take the risk of lending to eurozone banks. European banks increasingly did not wish to lend to each other. And they especially did not wish to lend to Spanish and Italian banks – for the obvious reason that Spanish and Italian banks were most at risk of being damaged by the financial vulnerability of the Spanish and Italian governments. Now, to repeat a mantra you will have heard a few times in this book, when banks cannot borrow, they cannot lend. And when banks cannot lend, the whole economy slows down, as households and businesses are starved of vital finance. Worse than that, banks get trapped into a negative feedback loop – because recession exacerbates the losses they are likely to incur on their loans. In the case of the eurozone, this particular incipient credit crunch was even more dangerous, because European banks had almost €1trn of their own debts maturing in 2012 – and if they were not able to borrow, they would not be able to repay their maturing debts, and (to state the obvious) they would go bust. If you think I am being sensationalist, this is what Benoît Cœuré, the French member of the European Central Bank's executive board, said to me:

> In the autumn of 2011, the conditions were very dangerous. European banks were facing severe difficulties funding themselves, accessing finance. We were very close to having a collapse in the banking system in the euro area – which in itself would have led to a collapse in the economy and to deflation. And this is something that the ECB could not accept.
>
> (Interview with the author for
> *The Great Euro Crash*, BBC2)

Unable to accept a collapse of the banking system and consequential collapse of the economy, the European Central Bank decided to try and do something about it. That something was called a Long Term Refinancing Operation, or LTRO, and was one of the most extraordinary banking rescues the world has seen (and we have seen a few whoppers since 2007). It involved the ECB offering to lend unlimited amounts to banks for three years at its overnight interest rate, which is now just 0.75%. In the first offer of these cheap long-term lending deals, 523 banks borrowed €489bn. And in the second such provision, 800 banks borrowed €530bn. In gross terms, the ECB provided more than €1trn of these low-interest, long-duration loans. Unsurprisingly, the biggest users were Italian and Spanish banks, estimated by Morgan Stanley to have borrowed roughly 60% of the net new ECB money, with the Spanish banks borrowing a bit more than the Italian ones – which some may see as surprising given that the Italian economy is almost 50% bigger than the Spanish economy. By June 2012, Spanish banks had borrowed €365bn from the European Central Bank, up from €106bn over just seven months. As Morgan Stanley pointed, it means that 10% of all lending and investment by Spain's banks is being financed by the eurozone's central bank, and so ultimately by eurozone taxpayers – a ratio that would not normally be regarded as healthy or sustainable. Pragmatic British banks also borrowed €37.4bn (£31bn) between them. One banker said to me: 'If the ECB is giving money away, how can we turn that down – especially when few others want to lend us a penny?'

What is the impact of all this emergency lending by the ECB? Well, it obviously averted the risk that a series of banks would fall over in the subsequent few months for want of being able to borrow to repay their debts as they fell due. Analysts calculated that the eurozone's banks had borrowed enough from the ECB to meet their refinancing needs for a year or so. But it is very important to note what it did not do. It did not solve banks' capital shortages. These were loans that were supposed to be repaid in full, not equity or money at risk which could easily absorb losses on debts going bad. Or to put it another way, the LTRO could not and did not make euro-zone banks any more solvent. Nor, as it turns out, did the deluge of three-year loans encourage the banks to lend much more. Banks still felt an incentive to rein in their lending to the real economy, to businesses and households, because this support was billed as exceptional – which meant that the banks did not want to lend a good deal more and thus make it harder for themselves to repay the ECB when the time came. The ECB's cheap three-year loans may not have worsened the eurozone's shortage of lending, but they certainly did not turn on the lending tap in any substantial way.

The loans did however provide temporary but powerful respite for the governments of Spain and Italy – because both the Spanish and Italian banks did what many will regard as a self-harming thing. Having been bailed out by the ECB, they then proceeded to bail out the very governments whose finan-cial weakness had to an extent got the banks into their mess. The Spanish banks and the Italian banks as groups increased their lending to their respective governments at a rate for each nation of just over €20bn a month (or more than €40bn between them). This bolstered demand for each nation's sovereign debt, and brought down the implicit interest rate paid by their respective governments quite significantly. Arguably the ECB's LTRO did more to solve the immediate financial crisis than the politicians' austerity deals. But it is not at all clear that the long-term impact will be benign. As of the spring of 2012, Italian banks have lent €324bn to the Italian government and Spain's banks have lent €263bn to the Spanish government. Which means that if the worst came to the worst, and those governments were unable to repay their debts, the banks of those countries would become totally insolvent. The ECB's LTRO therefore exacerbated the unhealthy mutual dependence of banking system and state in Italy and Spain. Perhaps, just as bad, the banks and their owners were taught an unhealthy lesson – which is that if they ran into difficulties, the ECB would be there with unlimited amounts of financial morphine. The probability was increased that eurozone banks would become permanently hooked on central bank dope. And the central bank might never have the guts to permanently shut off the supply of dope, because the commercial banks are simply too important to the eurozone's prosperity.

Breaking up?

It is very difficult to see how the eurozone's banks can be weaned off dope unless and until the risk of a break-up of the eurozone is eliminated. Because until that risk becomes *de minimis*, eurozone banks will find it tricky to borrow from other financial institutions or even hang on to deposits from the citizens of their own respective countries. There are two simple and related reasons. The first is that if Spain, for example, were to go back to the peseta, the value of the peseta would plunge, probably by more than half. So if you have any freedom over where you hold your euros, it is far better to keep them in the banks of a country like Germany, where there is little risk of such a devastating devaluation, than in a Spanish bank. For some creditors, it is better still to move the money out of euros altogether and into dollars, sterling or Swiss francs. To prove the point, there have been statements from some big public companies, such as Vodafone, GlaxoSmithKline, WPP and Reckitt Benckiser, that they are moving their surplus cash out of some eurozone countries on a daily basis. And another pronounced trend has been that Germany's banks, which had been reckless lenders to the likes of the Irish banks, for example, took back much of the money they had lent to banks in the weaker economies. The second potentially devastating consequence of a country leaving the euro is that its banks would incur huge losses and would go bust: Spanish banks for example and their customers would see many of their assets and liabilities converted into new pesetas, whose value would fall sharply, but they would continue to have big liabilities and outgoings in hard currencies, such as the dollar, sterling and any euros they had borrowed outside Spain; and the likelihood would be that their income in weak pesetas would be inadequate to pay the hard-currency debts. As and when there is a worry about the survival of a banking system, it becomes rational for any depositor to remove his or her deposits. And what was disturbing in the latter half of 2011 and into 2012 was data showing a steady flow of deposits out of the economies most perceived to be at risk of leaving the euro, notably Greece but also Spain and Ireland. According to an analysis by Bloomberg, deposits in Spanish, Greek and Irish banks fell 6.5% to €1.2 trillion in the year to 30 April 2012, with cash held in Greek banks falling a stark 16%. The corollary was a 4.4% rise in deposits in the banks of the putative safe haven, Germany, to €2.17 trillion (in theory, if the euro were to break up, a new Deutschmark would actually be worth more than the current euro). As a result, the banks of the financially over-stretched countries became increasingly dependent on borrowing from the European Central Bank and their national central banks.

When I talk to bankers, they concede that they have to do precautionary planning for a possible break-up of the euro – although none of them can conceive how it would happen without banks, businesses and households going bust all over Europe, massive disruption to the supply of credit and a recession far more painful even that what transpired in 2008–9. 'A few bank chairmen had a presentation from an expert in payment systems on what would happen if countries returned to their national currencies,' the boss of a major international bank told me in December 2011. 'He was very interesting on the logistics. He said it would probably happen simply by a unilateral announcement one morning, with no warning or preparation. But it was very hard to see how anyone could benefit from a break-up except lawyers, because millions of disputes would rage for years about whether a contract in euros had to be honoured in euros, and what that would mean.'

Greek tragedy

A eurozone break-up became a much more realistic possibility in the course of 2011 because Greece's economy was becoming sicker and sicker, in response to the medicine applied by the eurozone. And it is Greece which perhaps best shows the human tragedy of the eurozone's attempt to muddle through its systemic crisis. Its fall from grace in the financial markets was rapid and brutal. What now seems almost unbelievable is that in September 2008, just before Lehman went bust, the Greek government only had to pay 0.7% more in interest than Germany when borrowing for ten years. When George Papandreou of the socialist PASOK party was elected prime minister in October 2009, the difference was still only around one percentage point. Then, the following February, Papandreou began to reveal the scale of his predecessors' financial deception. In 2009 government borrowing was not the expected 5% of GDP or Greece's annual economic output, but 15.6%. In 2010, investors stopped lending to Greece at remotely affordable interest rates, and the government went to Brussels and the IMF with a begging bowl.

That deficit – the gap between its expenditure and tax revenues – of almost 16% of Greek GDP is a shockingly large figure that makes the UK government's own record 11.5% deficit look quite modest. Understandably, as part of a succession of bailouts, the eurozone and IMF demanded spending cuts and tax rises. Here are some of the measures imposed on Greece:

- The minimum wage is being cut by 22%;
- Wages have been cut by 20% for public-sector workers, with a further 20% cut planned;
- Some 150,000 civil servants are supposed to be laid off by 2015. About 1,000 of Greece's 16,000 schools are being shut down, as are 50 of its 132 health-care facilities;
- The future pensions of under fifty-five-year-olds are being cut by up to 40%;
- Everyone has to pay an extra 'solidarity' tax of up to 5% of their income (though many are refusing to do so).

This belt-tightening is being imposed on an economy which is horrifyingly weak. Unemployment is well over 20%, and half of all young people. Many Greek businesses have suffered a total collapse in demand for their goods and services. Vast numbers of Greek people spend only on the bare essentials and some cannot afford those. Homelessness has soared. It has become normal for those who once thought of themselves as middle class to survive on handouts from neighbours and friends. One in eleven residents of Athens has been getting their meals from a soup kitchen.

What has all this sacrifice been for? Greece's government deficit was still a high 8.5% of GDP in 2011. Even with a massive write-off of loans to the government by banks and private-sector institutions, Greece's public-sector debts are still expected to be a huge 120% of GDP in 2020. And in spite of all the austerity, or perhaps because of it, the Greek economy was still running a current account deficit of €21.1bn in 2011: this was down 8% compared with 2010, but still represented 10% of GDP. So the Greek economy is still borrowing too much from the rest of the world; it is still failing to pay its way. Why? Because in the absence of the ability to devalue, and because of the inefficiency of Greek business, imports remain better value in Greece than home-produced goods. One manifestation is the 'potato movement': Greek farmers have begun delivering their produce by the lorry-load to impromptu markets, offering to sell them directly to consumers at a tiny mark-up. Cutting out the middlemen in this way helps them to compete with cheap imports in the supermarkets. But for all these creative attempts to avoid penury, spending cuts by the Greek government seem to be hurting more than working: the Greek economy entered its fifth consecutive year of serious recession in 2012, having shrunk by a cumulative 13% since 2008.

By the middle of 2011, it became clear that Greece needed another bailout and – most controversially – a write-off of some of what its government had borrowed from the private sector. But there was no guarantee that even if the eurozone, IMF and private-sector lenders provided this second rescue that there would be any let-up in the relentless squeeze of living standards for Greek people. Hence the surge in popularity for minor parties that called for an end to austerity. The most striking example of how the fringe parties become serious players in Greek politics was that the Marxist Syriza Party led by the charismatic Alexis Tsipras was runner-up in the second Greek general election of 2012. But we are getting ahead of ourselves here. Perhaps the big symbolic event of 2011 was that European leaders and officials started to talk about how Greece had to make up its mind whether it wanted to make the requisite sacrifices to stay in the euro or whether it wished to leave. And the reason that really mattered is not because of the size of the Greek economy or the scale of what it owes: Greece is only 2% of the eurozone's GDP, and if, say, three-quarters of the €372bn debts of its government were wiped out, that would be very painful for its creditors but not devastating for the global financial system. Greece matters because its weakness has exposed as a fragile conceit the notion that membership of the euro is forever. Once a country was inside the eurozone, there was supposed to be no exit. As if to reinforce the point, there is no formal procedure or mechanism for leaving. But if Greece can leave the euro, then in theory any country can leave the euro. And once that is an acknowledged possibility, then any business or investor with a choice about where to put its cash would be taking a crazy risk leaving its cash in the bank account of any country where there is even a small risk of departure from the eurozone – which increases the probability of that departure. In that sense Greece's place in global economic history is that of the small, weak economy that undermined the cohesion of the most ambitious currency union ever created.

During the course of 2011, Greece's problem was that, try as its government might, it could not reduce borrowing as much as it had been ordered to do: austerity had the perverse consequence of suppressing economic activity and tax revenues almost as fast as the government was able to cut public spending. More rescue loans were required if Greece was to avoid default and repay its maturing debts. In July 2011 a second rescue package of €130bn – about 60% of Greek GDP – was agreed in principle. But by September, Greece had slipped even further behind the schedule set by Brussels for cutting its borrowing. Greece's lenders responded by duly refusing to release the next tranche of cash desperately needed by the Greek government to pay its bills. There would be no more money until the Greeks put their affairs in order. The German solution was simple and predictable – Greece had to speed up the austerity measures it had already agreed to implement. And if they were not sufficient, more austerity would be required.

Concern was growing in Greece that the cure was worse than the illness. At the end of October, the Greek government caved in: a deal was hammered out for even bigger spending cuts and tax rises, as well as a fire sale of state-owned companies at what were likely to be rock-bottom prices. Or at least eurozone leaders thought they had a deal. But only a week later the Greek Prime Minister, George Papandreou, announced out of the blue that the new economic plan would be put to a referendum. Even Mr Papandreou's own finance minister was caught by surprise. As for France and Germany, they were livid at the idea that their deal was conditional on the approval of the Greek people. The announcement of the plebiscite coincided with a summit of the G20 nations hosted by the then President of France, Nicolas Sarkozy, in Cannes. Mr Papandreou was summoned to the French Riviera for emergency talks which ended up eclipsing the summit. For the first time, European government heads, the French president and German chancellor no less spoke in public about the possible exit from the euro of a member. President Sarkozy made a statement that would change everything: 'The question is whether Greece remains in the eurozone. That is what we want. But it is up to the Greek people to answer that question.' The Greek government dumped the referendum plan. Mr Papandreou also resigned. What could not be put back in the box was the official recognition that monetary union may not be permanent.

This easy-to-grasp notion, that the euro could be replaced by national currencies, caused unease among citizens and businesses in almost all the weaker eurozone economies. If there was a risk that the strong euro could be replaced with the weak lira or the soft peseta, what was the rational thing for Italians, Spaniards, Irish and Portuguese to do with their savings? In Greece there was more than unease: many savers moved their money out of Greek banks and either transferred it to Germany or put it under the mattress. As of May 2012, the value of deposits held by companies and households at the Greek banks had fallen by a third since November 2009, when the country first got into serious financial trouble. And the total volume of banknotes issued by the Greek central bank increased by 91% – or €19bn euros, about €1,700 per Greek citizen – between January 2010 and April 2012. These latest figures for flight out of Greek banks do not capture what happened in May and June 2012, when the country struggled to elect a new government. The first election, on 6 May 2012, saw inconclusive results, with voters punishing the mainstream parties, the socialist PASOK and the centre-right New Democracy, and rewarding smaller, fringe parties, such as the left-wing Syriza. But with the distribution of seats so fragmented, it proved impossible to form a government. The surge in popularity of Syriza was based on its rejection of the austerity measures imposed on Greece by the rest of the eurozone and the IMF. A subsequent election, to be held six weeks later on 17 June, was seen as – in effect – a referendum on whether Greece should stay in the euro or exit (the term 'Grexit' entered the eurozone lexicon). In the event, after fraught campaigning, New Democracy received just under 30% of the vote, to Syriza's 27%. And New Democracy succeeded, after something of a struggle, in forming a coalition government – which says it is committed to keeping Greece in the eurozone.

Whether it will succeed in that ambition is still unclear. When I talk to bankers, regulators and ministers, they all say that they assume Greece will leave the euro at some point, simply because the impoverishment of the Greeks is unlikely to abate unless its debt burden is significantly eased – which would involve the European Central Bank and the eurozone's bailout funds taking the highly unlikely step of writing off much of what they are owed by the Greek government. The numbers on Greece's debt burden are worth reviewing, because they show how both lenders and the borrower are trapped. The ratio of Greece's government debt to GDP was 165% at the end of 2011. Then came the impact of a new bailout package for Greece, which saw its private sector lenders – mostly banks – agree to cut by €100bn what they were owed by Athens. This was a nominal reduction of what they were owed of more than 50%, which triggered losses of more than 70% for banks because of a simultaneous extension of the repayment date on the residual debt and associated changes in other terms. It was the biggest ever write-off of debt by any government in history – bigger even than what happened in Latin America in the turbulent 1980s. But here is what is striking. Because the Greek government is so far from being able to balance its books and its borrowing requirements remain so large, its debt is forecast to fall by not very much at all, to 153% of GDP by the end of 2012. And then Greek debt is projected to bounce back to a completely unsustainable 161% of GDP again in 2013. On current projections, Greece will remain the second most indebted economy of any size, for the foreseeable future. And pretty much all historical precedent would suggest the Greek economy cannot recover under this kind of debt burden.

The only way to ease the debt burden would be to write off €161bn euros owed by Greece to eurozone governments and the €50bn euros owed to the European Central Bank. But that is something the eurozone's leaders are unlikely to contemplate, partly for fear of enraging the voters in their respective countries. There is another important obstacle to forgiving Greece what it owes – namely that it would further weaken the finances of eurozone countries whose credit-worthiness is already in doubt. Germany could probably afford a 50% write-down of what it is owed by Greece, given the strength of its economy and public finances: such a write-off would be equivalent to just over 1% of its GDP. But the same probably can't be said of Spain, Italy or even France, where the write-down costs would also be around 1% of GDP. And there is a fear that debt forgiveness for Greece would be the thin end of a very thick wedge, such that Ireland, for example, might argue that if Greece were getting what would in effect be a large transfer from the rest of the eurozone, it would like a bit of that too, thank you very much.

All of which suggests that the eurozone will continue to expect Greece to honour all its massive debts. But even before the latest worsening in the eurozone's more general crisis, the IMF was projecting that Greece's economy would shrink by 4.7% this year and stagnate in 2013 – and most forecasters now expect Greece's slump to be much worse. Unless there is some kind of miraculous recovery, the question will continue to loom large for Greek people and leaders whether they should try to escape a crushing debt burden by leaving the eurozone. And if Greece did leave the eurozone, there would inevitably be a withdrawal of cash from banks in other vulnerable economies, which would surely create the imperative for yet more emergency ECB lending to banks. And since the European Central Bank and the national central banks insist on lending only in return for collateral, there is a danger that banks would run out of collateral of sufficient quality. Which means the ECB would face the uncomfortable choice of turning off the life support, and see quite a few banks giving up the ghost, or lending on the basis of inadequate security – and thus taking significant credit risks with these loans. Putting this crudely, German taxpayers would end up doing what their leaders say is out of the question – which is that they would be taking on a huge exposure to the debts of weaker eurozone countries. This would happen not through an explicit agreement to pool and commingle the borrowing of all eurozone members, but via the backdoor of central bank support for weak banks in the likes of Spain, Italy, Ireland, Portugal and Cyprus.

To an extent this is already happening. We have already looked at how the European Central Bank was forced to provide huge exceptional loans to eurozone banks when they were unable to borrow from other banks and financial institutions. But there is a related, massive and hidden form of lending from the European Central Bank and, especially, the German central bank, the Bundesbank, to banks in countries such as Greece that see an outflow of deposits. These hidden loans are a result of the ECB's complicated payments system called Target2. What happens under Target2 is that when customers take their money out of the bank accounts of deficit countries, such as Greece, Italy and Spain, central banks in surplus countries end up lending to the central banks of those deficit countries. Here is a slightly simplified account of how this works: when someone takes €100 from a Greek bank and transfers it to the perceived safety of a German bank, that Greek bank gets the €100 from the Greek central bank, which in turn borrows the money from the Bundesbank.

Here is the thing. As of the end of June 2012, under the Target2 system the German central bank had €729bn of claims on other central banks, equivalent to well over a quarter of German GDP, and up a worrying 57% in just six months. These are euros owed to the Bundesbank by the central banks of the economies where there has been the greatest capital flight, namely those of Greece, Italy and Spain. So, if all of a sudden Greece and Italy and Spain decided to revert to their national currencies, it is an interesting question how much (if any) of the €729bn the Bundesbank could get back. Now it is true that under the Target2 rules, the liability for losses on these balances is supposed to be shared between all eurozone central banks in proportion to their respective shareholdings in the European Central Bank (subject to a couple of adjustments). Which would mean that the Bundesbank's loss from non-repayment of what it is owed by the Greek central bank, for example, would be 28% of what the Greek central bank owes to all the eurozone's central banks. But if the entire eurozone fractured completely, it is difficult to see how that distribution of losses could take place. In practice, the Bundesbank would surely have to take the entire hit – and then, I suppose, it could sue Italy, Spain and the rest for compensation. The big point is that German loans to GIPCS and Italy through Target2 are very substantial indeed. What is hard to predict is whether the German people, as and when they grasp the scale of this commitment, will be furious enough to demand some kind of retrenchment – which would be devastating to the cohesion of the eurozone – or whether they will understand that the wealth of their country is inextricably linked to the salvation of GIPCS and Italy.

There is a gradual recognition among the eurozone's leaders that they are all in this together – in a financial sense – whatever now happens, and that there is enormous potential exposure for Germany to the weaker eurozone countries through the banking system. Which is why the current great hope for bringing stability to the currency union would be the creation of what is known as a 'banking union'. This would involve all eurozone banks being supervised and regulated by a powerful new authority attached to the European Central Bank. Over time, it would also involve eurozone governments collectively agreeing to be the guarantors of last resort for deposits in eurozone banks and for the costs and liabilities associated with breaking up or 'resolving' bust banks. If a banking union were established, it would be a massive step towards an explicit merging of the balance sheets of eurozone member states, towards a very serious fiscal union, because European banks are so huge and (many would say) vulnerable. And for that reason, it will be difficult to convert the aspirations into reality, because German politicians and people may not be ready to make that kind of explicit commitment to help their neighbours, and Germany's constitutional court may not allow it.

But as we have seen, there is a sense in which German qualms about lending to weaker eurozone members has been overtaken by events. The total amount of loans provided by the Bundesbank, together with the central banks of the other surplus countries, the Netherlands, Luxembourg and Finland, to the rest of the eurozone had reached an unprecedented €1trillon, or about 30% of their collective GDPs by May 2012. Meanwhile the Spanish central bank's borrowing was approaching €400bn, the Bank of Italy was borrowing €275bn, while the Greek and Irish central banks were in debt under Target2 to the tune of €100bn each. Even the Banque de France owed €50bn. These are substantial numbers. In effect, the central banks of Germany and the other surplus countries in the eurozone are lending the money that the uncompetitive GIPCS and Italian economies have to borrow if they are to avoid a total economic collapse. The problem is that although this financial help is vital to prevent catastrophe – and shows that there is more financial solidarity between Germany and the weaker nations than is commonly supposed – it is subsistence or survival finance. It is not the kind of support that spurs economic recovery.

It also does nothing to address the eurozone's biggest problem, namely that GIPCS and Italy are uncompetitive. They are still overspending and borrowing too much. And getting their economies into shape is going to be a long and painful process. They are looking at many years of economic stagnation or worse, as governments cut spending, banks rein in lending, unemployment rises, wages are frozen and house prices fall. What's more, by the time they regain their competitiveness, GIPCS and Italy will have accumulated even vaster piles of debt than they have now. Are all those mortgages and company loans and government debts repayable? And if they cannot be repaid, will the banks that lent the money go bust?

Is it worth it? If staying in the euro for Greece, Spain, Italy and so on means living standards falling perhaps by at least a quarter over the coming decade, could the impact of leaving the euro be any worse? Well, it might well be. Let's say Greece did leave the euro. What might happen? Well, drawing from the experience of other countries that have been forced out of similar currency arrangements – such as Argentina in 2002 – the newly reintroduced drachma might lose as much as three-quarters of its value against the euro. That would make it impossible for the Greek government – or anyone else in Greece – to repay any debts still denominated in euros. The Greek banks would be bust. Their doors would have to be closed to prevent panicky Greeks withdrawing their remaining deposits. A collapse in the drachma would also suddenly make the cost of imports – including many foods and most medicines – four times higher. In fact, it may be impossible for Greece to obtain any goods or services from abroad. Remember this is an economy still running a deficit and which is currently only functioning thanks to money borrowed from the IMF, the eurozone's central banks and bailout funds. After a default, it would presumably be impossible for Greece to borrow from commercial banks and it would take a while to negotiate new support from the IMF. The Greek economy, already close to depression, could well implode.

The Greek government, unable to pay bills, would probably ask the central bank – newly liberated from the shackles of the ECB – to print the drachmas that it would need to pay wages and unemployment benefits. But that could destroy confidence in the new Greek currency. So the drachma would continue to plummet, and prices would rise quickly. These are the circumstances that can create terrifying hyperinflation and in which a currency can become useless. Indeed, most Greeks would probably avoid using drachmas at all, and would opt for barter or would deploy the euro banknotes they have stashed under their mattresses.

The legal mess would be hideous. The Greek government would try to re-denominate all extant contracts into new drachmas. That would create big losers. Imagine how you would feel if it was your wages, or your savings, converted into near-worthless drachmas. And it's not just individuals. Healthy businesses could go bust overnight if all their income was converted into drachmas when they were still obliged to pay bills to foreigners in euros or dollars. Faced with financial ruin through no fault of their own, the losers would sue. The Greek and international courts could become overwhelmed by thousands of claims and counterclaims.

And it would be painful and messy for the rest of the eurozone. Anyone who had lent money to the Greek government, a Greek bank, a Greek business or a Greek household could expect to lose the vast majority of what they were owed – either because they would now be receiving drachmas of negligible value or because their debtors would have gone bust. And remember that among the biggest creditors are the European Central Bank and the central banks of the rest of the eurozone, led by the German central bank. Their total exposure to Greece is currently well over €300bn and would become even greater, if – in the run-up to a euro exit – yet more money was withdrawn from Greek banks, because the Greek central bank would be obliged to cover this outflow by borrowing more and more from the European Central Bank.

If, as seems likely, the Greek central bank were unable to repay the European Central Bank, the German people – worried about the losses forced on the Bundesbank as the biggest shareholder in the ECB – would probably begin to criticise the basic infrastructure of monetary union, namely the system by which the ECB and Bundesbank provides loans and liquidity to the banks of other weak economies, such as Spain's and Italy's. But without that arrangement of allowing euros to flow everywhere in the eurozone banking system, Spanish and Italian banks would soon collapse. And that would cause devastating mayhem for the entire eurozone economy.

For the avoidance of doubt, the pain would certainly be felt in Germany. The collapse of Spain and Italy would deprive German companies of hugely valuable export markets. Also if, as would seem highly likely, the euro fractured at this juncture and Germany reintroduced the mark or created a hard-currency new euro with the Netherlands, Finland and Austria, the value of the new mark or new euro would soar, to reflect Germany's exporting strength – and all of a sudden Germany's exports would become much more expensive. Germany would be deprived of the biggest advantage it enjoyed under the euro – an under-valued currency. That would force many German companies into loss. German unemployment would rise sharply. Germany would once again have to cut its costs to improve competitiveness.

Can the eurozone survive?

Is there no hope for the eurozone? Are the only alternatives the misery of inexorably declining living standards in Greece, Ireland, Portugal, Cyprus Spain and Italy (if they stay in the eurozone) versus penury for all members (if the eurozone breaks up)? Well, there are ways to break the vicious spiral of escalating impoverishment. However, they may prove to be unachievable. In the immediate future, probably the only way to end the ratcheting up of borrowing costs for the likes of Italy and Spain, which forces ever bigger squeezes on the living standards of their people, is for the rest of the euro-zone's governments – or at least the financially healthy ones – to make it absolutely explicit that they stand behind the debts of the Italian and Spanish governments (and those of Ireland, Portugal, Cyprus and Greece). In practice, of course, this means that Germany, as the biggest and most powerful economy, would be taking on a formal liability for other governments' debts, which would reassure creditors to those countries that the risk of default had become negligible. Thus the interest rate paid by Italy and Spain would fall. Therefore Germany's underwriting of the rest of the eurozone's debts would probably, in practice, never be called on. That is not to say that this would be a cost-free or cheap option for Germany. If German public-sector debt were now the same as Italian and Spanish public-sector debt, the borrowing costs for the German government would rise from their current record lows. So the question for Germany is whether paying more to borrow outweighs the potential damage from the collapse of the eurozone.

Right now, Germany's mainstream politicians regard this so-called mutualisation of debt as constitutionally and politi-cally impossible. They do not believe Germany's citizens would tolerate having any conspicuous and formal liability for what the Italians and Spanish borrow, even if the country's constitutional court would allow it, which is implausible. Even so, the German Chancellor Angela Merkel has said that collec-tive borrowing by eurozone members and a banking union of shared financial responsibility for eurozone banks' liabilities might be possible, if eurozone governments surrendered their sovereign rights to manage their own budgets and to police their own banks. German succour would therefore be condi-tional on the evolution of the eurozone into a proper federation or a United States of Europe, with taxing, spending and borrowing decisions for its members taken centrally, to prevent big deficits emerging both within the eurozone and between the eurozone and the outside world. One of the most influential founders of the eurozone and a towering figure of its early years, Jean-Claude Trichet, puts it like this:

> In a single market, with a single currency . . . it seems to me that Europe could go for a federation. This is the citizen who speaks there, the citizen for Europe. I am not speaking as former governor of the ECB. But as a citizen, it seems to me that it is probably necessary, taking into account the profound transformation of the world.
>
> (Interview with the author for
> *The Great Euro Crash*, BBC2)

But when the solution is seen in those terms, the magnitude of the challenge is laid bare. There are the practical difficulties of working out precisely which powers of national governments would have to be transferred to a new supra-national finance ministry for the whole eurozone. Some of the foundations for that kind of constitutional change were laid in the new European Fiscal Compact signed on 2 March 2012 which restores and toughens limits on individual governments' deficits. But here is the reason to be pessimistic that the Compact is the start of a trend: the Germans do not believe it goes far enough in limiting the autonomy of member governments; but the new French president, François Hollande, has made it clear that he is unhappy with the way it limits his room for manoeuvre in managing the French economy. And even if French determination to defend the independence of the

Republic can be reconciled with the more federalist ambitions of the Germans, which seems unlikely, there is an even bigger question of whether the citizens of Europe would tolerate reforms that would widen an already yawning gap between their votes and voices on the one hand, and the decisions that determine their prosperity. It will not be easy to create a euro-zone federation that is perceived as enhancing rather than undermining the democratic control of the people.

What will happen to the eurozone? In the early spring of 2012, I asked Helmut Schlesinger, one of the grand old men of European finance – who has been in the crucible of previous financial crises and was president of the Bundesbank when sterling was forced out of the European Exchange Rate Mechanism in 1992 – whether he believed the euro would survive:

> I cannot make any long-term predictions in this regard. One should consider that monetary unions, or more precisely, coin unions, have survived for a long time, but never for more than three or four decades. My personal experience with the German currency is that it has undergone changes at three occasions during my lifetime. When I was born, it was changed into the Reichsmark. When I began to work, it became the Deutschmark. And when I became a pensioner, it became the euro. The average lifetime of a currency is, as, as you can see, limited, as a rule, except when it is a great state [like Great Britain] with an endlessly long, beautiful history, from the Kings of the Middle Ages until the Queen nowadays. Then you have got a long monetary history. But here on the Continent in Europe that is different. And I would say that either we get the United States of Europe, that is an actual political union,

and then that political union gets its own currency, but then it is not monetary union any longer, but the currency of that new state. Or let's stay with the current situation which we find ourselves in at the moment, and then it could be that this monetary union will not necessarily dissolve, but change, extend, scale down. I do not know. My horizon, my prognosis, is very limited in time.

(Interview with the author, 2012)

The implication – not a happy one for any of us, since the UK's economic fortunes are inextricably tied to those of our biggest export market, the Continent – is that the eurozone's history for the coming few years may be one of permanent crisis management. The status quo is unstable. Change is inescapable. The question, impossible to answer with certainty now, is whether that change will be managed, such that the inevitable costs will be controlled and limited, or whether it will be forced, chaotic and engendering a catastrophic global financial crisis.

CHAPTER 10
BANKS STILL HOLD US TO RANSOM

Shanghai, Hong Kong and Singapore, with their futuristic city skylines, electronic hum and tumult, may seem to be in a different universe from the rural town of Watton in Norfolk, which doesn't look or feel as though it has undergone much serious change since the Great Fire of Watton in 1674. You can stay in touch with events on the other side of the planet via a 3G mobile signal, but reception here is weaker than in much of rural China. Even in this sleepy parish, globalisation in all its forms, including financial globalisation, is touching lives, for better and worse – as I discovered when I met Paul Adcock, the fourth-generation owner of an electrical retailer that trades under the family name. Adcocks is a pillar of the modest local economy. Mr Adcock is a respected local merchant, with a fan club of retired ladies and gentleman, who gathered in his shop on chairs by the counter to provide moral support when I visited him to hear his story. Much about his shop – its gentleness and values, if not the digital radios and flat-screen TVs – is redolent of Edwardian England, not Facebook and Twitter England (that said, the editor of the local paper, the *Wayland News*, was keen to have his 140-character synopsis of my encounter with Mr Adcock retweeted to a networked world). In a UK where households are struggling to repay their record debts (a familiar theme to you by now) and where the cheapest place to buy the gadgets and goods Paul Adcock sells is on-line, there should be no great surprise that Adcocks is struggling. In Watton, as everywhere, the locals look up the price on the Internet and then come to his shop to negotiate a reduction on what he has written on the label. His giant nationwide competitors, Argos and Curry's, are suffering. Adcocks is feeling the squeeze like the rest. But what really put Adcocks on the brink of collapse was an encounter with a giant global investment bank, Barclays Capital. If you are surprised, I was too. I knew that BarCap, as it is known, had ambitions to be a huge and influential name in the City, on Wall Street, in Tokyo, Singapore and the great metropolises of China. But in Watton? On a sunny day in early spring 2012, I was talking to a vendor of washing machines and fridges in East Anglia about how he had bought a complicated derivatives product from BarCap: I had to pinch myself.

He tried to explain to me the deal he had done with BarCap. But complex financial engineering is not his forte. So he handed over documentation which showed that in 2007 BarCap sold Paul Adcock an 'asymmetric cap and collar'. This is a fairly complicated amalgam of various swap transactions. A bog-standard swap would be a deal in which a borrower agrees to exchange his or her commitment to make variable interest-rate payments for a fixed rate, as one example: it would be a bet by the borrower that interest rates are going to rise, or – as the banks would characterise it (not always unfairly) – it would be protection for the relevant borrower against such a possible rise. In his asymmetric cap and collar, Mr Adcock was making a series of bets on the future direction of interest rates – although he claims that at the time he had no idea he was doing this. In the event he lost all the bets. And his losses are £50,000 a year in additional interest payments, above and beyond what he would be paying on his £900,000 a year commercial mortgage. To put it another way, he has swapped an interest rate of 3.25%, which is what he would be paying if he had not done the deal with BarCap, for a rate of 9%. It is this additional financial burden, he says, which has put in doubt the survival of an enterprise set up by his great-grandfather almost exactly a hundred years ago.

You only have to spend a few minutes with Paul Adcock to work out that placing bets on what will happen to the Bank of England's policy interest rate, what is known as Bank Rate, would not be characteristic of him. Unless he is one of the world's great actors, he is conspicuously unsophisticated about financial matters, the antithesis of an investment banker manqué. If you wanted to construct the living, breathing opposite of Bob Diamond, the ferociously wealthy former boss of Barclays – who more or less created its global invest-ment bank, Barclays Capital – Paul Adcock would be that anti-Diamond. When Barclays cuts the numbers of its employ-ees, there is a corporate expression of regret, which goes through endless iterations and re-draftings by Barclays' army of internal and external media advisers. When I talked to Mr Adcock about the people he had laid off as he struggles to keep his head above water, he cried. How on earth did Mr Adcock find himself gambling the future of his business in the global investment banking casino?

Mr Adcock says he had no idea he had entered the casino. And in order to get a sense of whether that is plausible, it is necessary to look at his transaction with BarCap. The asym-metric cap and collar was presented to Mr Adcock, he says, as 'free' protection for him against the risk that interest rates would rise above 6.75% (that is the 'cap' bit of the product's name). So it is easy to see why it might have had some attraction to him. But what he claims not to have fully appreciated is that there was a huge contingent cost: under the terms of the transaction, if the Bank of England's Bank Rate were to drop below 4.7%, the interest rate would gradually rise for Mr Adcock to a maximum of 6.25%, plus a margin of 2.75%. To put this another way, Adcocks would see none of the benefit of any cuts by the Bank of England designed to help struggling businesses just like his. Worse than that, when the Bank of England cut interest rates, Adcocks' interest bill would actually rise. Paul Adcock – inadvertently, he would say – had made a bet with one of the world's most sophisticated investment banks that the UK would avoid the kind of economic slowdown that could damage his business. And what he was staking on the bet was his entire business, because the deal with BarCap meant that in a recession Adcocks would suffer the double whammy of lower sales and increased interest payments. It is unclear whether this contingent cost was explained to him. If it was, it is highly likely that he did not understand it, because I am not sure he properly understands it now.

What transpired? At the time that the transaction took place, on 15 February 2007, Bank Rate was 5.25%, well below the 6.75% interest rate cap. Back then, it may well have been the consensus view of economists that interest rates were more likely to rise than fall. But the interest rate would have had to rise a good deal for Mr Adcock to benefit from the promised protection. And, as it happens, the Bank Rate had not been as high as 6.75% since December 1998. However, at the time the deal was done, Bank Rate was a fraction above the 4.7% 'floor', below which the penalty interest rates became payable. Even so, it was to be more than a year before Paul Adcock recognised what a colossal mistake he had made. On 6 November 2008, in the midst of the worst banking crisis and recession for at least seventy years, Bank Rate fell to 3%. Since then Adcocks has been paying interest of 6.25% plus 2.75%, or 9% in total. Bank Rate may have been cut to a record low of 0.5% on 5 March 2009, but not for Adcocks. If Paul Adcock had not taken out these swaps with BarCap, he would currently be paying an interest rate on his commercial mortgage some 64% less than he is actually paying.

Perhaps Mr Adcock is an idiot for doing any kind of deal that he did not understand. Possibly it is a miracle that his business has been kept alive for as long as it has, if he is prepared to make that kind of bet without understanding its consequences. But he sees it differently. He says Adcocks has banked with Barclays since the business was created in 1912, and he has banked with Barclays all his working life. Mr Adcock felt grateful to the bank for expanding the size of his commercial mortgage when he refurbished the shop. He therefore felt under pressure to do what he felt the bank wanted him to do. He took it for granted that the bank would not allow him to do a deal that could threaten the viability of his business. And that, in a way, is why I think what happened to him is significant. To be clear, I am making a point about all of the big banks, Barclays, RBS, Lloyds and HSBC, since they all – to varying degrees – sold inappropriately complex products to small businesses. Unsophisticated small busi-nesses all over the country complain that all the biggest British banks engaged in selling them derivative products that they as customers were never properly equipped to understand. Some businesses were even sold swaps that forced them to continue paying interest to the bank after they had repaid the loan: whether they knew it or not, the businesses entered into a naked gamble on the direction of interest rates just like a big swinging speculator, rather than the cautious employers and wealth creators they thought they were. As it happens, a survey by the lobby group Bully Banks indicates Barclays may have sold proportionately more of these swaps than the others. Also – for what it is worth – the businesses that have contacted me directly claiming to be victims of mis-selling or high-pressure selling have most often been customers of Barclays.

After the horse had bolted, some might say, the Financial Services Authority conducted a two-month review and announced – at the end of June 2012 – that it had 'found serious failings in the sale of interest rate hedging products to some small and medium sized businesses' resulting in a 'severe impact' on many of them. It agreed a settlement with Barclays, RBS, Lloyds and HSBC, which involves them ceasing to actively push the most complex swaps – the 'interest rate structured collars' (of the sort sold to Adcocks) – to small businesses. And the banks promised to provide redress where customers could demonstrate there had been mis-selling (with the process of providing restitution to be scrutinised by 'independent reviewers'). Barclays has set aside £450m to cover the costs of providing this redress, but at the time of writing it is unclear whether Paul Adcock will be freed from the shackles of his asymmetric cap and collar.

For me there is a big point here, which is that banks have been frittering away the trust of their customers in the pursuit of short-term profits – and not just by selling unnecessary interest-rate swaps to small businesses. The egregious scale of the mis-selling of PPI credit insurance to millions of individuals, which the banks estimate will cost them well over £8bn in compensation and other expenses, is another example. What happened is that some time in the 1990s banks started to change from being businesses that nurture long-term relationships with customers into sales machines, looking to maximise commission on every deal to generate big bonuses for staff. Whether this is what their clients would have wanted is moot. But what has particularly upset many of their customers is that they don't feel they were informed by their respective banks of this huge cultural shift. As the experience of Adcocks (and others) shows, many customers continued to believe that their high-street bank would never sell them an inappropriate product, let alone one that could ruin them: they are now bitter and angry at having been too trusting. With the wonderful benefit of hindsight, banks' behaviour seems astonishingly reckless, foolish and self-defeating. Without loyal customers, is any business worth anything? When I asked Barclays about the Adcocks deal, this is what it said:

> Interest-rate risk management products were sold by Barclays to customers in accordance with the regulatory framework. Barclays is satisfied it provided sufficient information to enable clients to make an informed, commercial decision about the products it offers. Barclays has an ongoing dialogue with Mr Adcock. We continue to work with the company, utilising the expertise of our Business Support team to respond to the challenging market conditions faced by the retailing sector.

In other words, Barclays relied on its belief that the deal was in accordance with regulations. But perhaps it is not just the formal regulations that matter. That was suggested a few months earlier, in another context, by the then Chief Executive of Barclays, Bob Diamond, who was running BarCap at the time of the Adcocks deal. On 3 November 2011, he made some remarks about the damage to banks' reputation from their mis-selling of PPI insurance on mortgages and personal loans:

> We want to put things right. But we know it's not enough just to apologise. We have to try to make sure that things like that don't happen again. In part that comes down to culture.
>
> It's a very personal thing, but throughout my career – from my time as a teacher, to my time as a banker – I have seen just how important culture is to successful organisations.
>
> Culture is difficult to define, I think it's even more difficult to mandate – but for me the evidence of culture is how people behave when no one is watching. Our culture must be one where the interests of customers and clients are at the very heart of every decision we make; where we all act with trust and integrity.
>
> (BBC *Today* Programme Business Lecture,
> 3 November 2011)

It may be a bit late for bankers to re-learn the lesson that they are nothing without the confidence of their customers. The political pendulum has swung decisively towards far greater official control – regulatory control – of what they sell and to whom. This is bad news for the bankers and for us, because the administrative costs of complying with new, more detailed and more onerous rules are significant, and banks tend to pass those costs on to customers. There is something tragic about an industry capable of so much social and economic good becoming such a pariah. It is worth thinking about the good that banks, even now, can do. As I mentioned earlier, a world without banks would be a world where only the wealthy could buy a house or set up a business; where companies could only invest in expansion or research new products if they were already generating sufficiently big profits to pay for it all. Our economy would be permanently rigid and sluggish, with little social mobility and few new companies to challenge the incumbents. If you think that describes the world we inhabit, that is in part because our banks hobbled themselves in their transition from boom to bust. But economic stagnation forever, with little hope of a more prosperous future for the corporate and social underclasses, would be worse. The ability of banks to convert savings into loans needed by those trying to build a better future – for themselves or for their businesses – is about as socially useful an activity as it is possible to imagine. But because this transformation of deposits into credit is not just useful but is economically essential, and because banks have shown themselves incapable of carrying out this activity in a responsible way, many would argue they have abandoned any right to argue that the world would be better off if they were largely left alone to do their own thing.

Historically, a line has been drawn between the oversight they require when selling to individuals and when selling to putative financial professionals, such as those who run other banks, or who manage the finances of giant companies, or those who manage our pension savings for us. There has been a presumption that the professionals can look after themselves, and that the strictest regulations only need to apply when the customer is a private person. Whether that line has been put in the right place is challenged by the experience of Adcocks and other smaller businesses to whom the banks sold complex swaps and derivatives – because Adcocks is not protected by the rules that would apply to retail customers. A bit more protection for the likes of Adcocks does not seem an absurd notion: Paul Adcock is not the only small businessman baffled by modern finance, and his lack of sophistication doesn't just imperil his own wealth but also the jobs of the ten or so people he employs; multiply him by the 28,000 swaps and similar products sold to small businesses over the past decade and we start to see banks' potential for serious harm, as well as good.

With the modern evolution of banking into an activity obsessed with innovation, devoted to creating financial products so complicated that few senior bankers understand them, let alone their clients, there is an argument that regulators should have the power of veto over the sale of certain kinds of products to anyone, not just to retail customers. This is not because big businesses or pension funds need protecting from their own stupidity. It is that the economy – all of us – needs protecting from the ability of banks to hide the risks they are taking. We saw that in the way that the risks of making subprime loans to no-income, no-job households were hidden when these loans were repackaged into collateralised debt obligations. The message at the time was that this new financial 'technology' had converted risky debts into super-safe investments, good enough to be consumed by cautious investors. Surely everyone was a winner: there were more solid financial products in the world; and for the first time a social underclass could buy their own homes. But it was all a giant illusion. The riskiness of the loans was simply hidden for a bit. In the end, those holding the collateralised debt obligations lost a fortune. And some poor families, who were never going to be able to repay what they owed, were evicted from their homes. What is worse, the obfuscation of where the losses were actually located undermined confidence in the global financial system, and was the trigger for the worst banking crisis in almost eighty years. Which is why there is a case for saying that a certain degree of complexity in financial innovation should be prohibited. Perhaps the test should be that if a moderately intelligent regulator cannot understand a new financial product, after a jargon-free presentation by a banker lasting no more than twenty minutes, then the product should go straight into the incinerator. Another and perhaps better test might be to assess whether the proliferation of a product could ultimately endanger the health of the financial system, although experience tends to indicate that it is impossible to know that a product is systemically toxic until the damage has been done.

This is not to say there should be no innovation in finance. But it is to recognise that much innovation in recent years has resulted in the exploitation of the stupid and greedy by the clever and greedy. Whether they were cynical and exploitative or simply naïve, the designers of the newfangled products have extracted huge profits from their clients through the sheer complexity of those products and the way that risks were disguised. And there are a couple of reasons why customers may feel that *caveat emptor* should not apply. First is that the collateral damage to unconnected households and businesses – the customers of a reckless bank that bankrupts itself, for example – can be very significant when the risks are ultimately crystallised. Second, most banks have been engaged in the same process of obscuring the true costs of their products and services, to a greater or lesser extent. That has been true in their dealings with individuals and with businesses. So the normal disincentive to gulling customers – namely that they will take their business elsewhere – doesn't seem to apply, because if all big banks are at it, where is a disgruntled client to go?

And what if tighter regulation led to shrinkage of the global financial economy? Some of the growth in financial trading over the past couple of decades has delivered widespread benefits. But that 234 times increase in foreign-exchange trading since 1977, which I mentioned earlier in the book, versus a seven times rise in the nominal economic output of the world, tells us that much of the trading was – for most of us – fatuous at best. The vast majority of foreign-exchange trading was supporting market speculation, not genuine wealth-creating activity by businesses. But there are, of course, practical difficulties in trying to eliminate the socially useless and even the socially harmful surplus trading: quite apart from the practical difficulties in distinguishing good products from bad ones and good trading from bad trading, the reality of globalisation blunts the ability of individual countries to act unilaterally. If, for example, a tiny tax were imposed on almost all financial trading by the European Union, the so-called Financial Transactions Tax, some proportion of that trading would probably shift to jurisdictions – Zurich, Singapore, New York – where the tax could be avoided. The world would not necessarily be a more financially stable place, but jobs would have moved outside the European Union. And this would be a particular concern for the UK, since – according to research by the Corporation of London – some 60% of a Financial Transactions Tax would be paid by institutions based in London.

Perhaps it would be a case of good riddance to bad rubbish. Research by the Bank for International Settlements, the central bankers' central bank, indicates that countries with disproportionately large financial sectors, like the UK, have disproportionately small manufacturing sectors. The explanations are that capital and talent tend to gravitate to the ostensibly big returns on offer in banks, hedge funds and so on, and the exchange rate tends to rise to a level well above what's comfortable for exporters. So, arguably, the British economy cannot be rebalanced towards more making and less financial engineering unless and until the City is less dominant. Which possibly means that a government committed to such rebalancing, as this one is, should not be quite so wary of a tax that would squeeze City profits. But it is hard to be relaxed about any jobs leaving the UK – even ones which, in an ideal world, some may wish we didn't have – at a time when unemployment remains intractably high.

There is little doubt that a financial transactions tax would be more effective if implemented globally. If financial globalisation is real – which it is – then correcting its flaws in the most efficient way requires global decision-making, global governance. But that does not mean we should despair that in the absence of a government for the world as a whole, we are powerless to limit the destructive power of unfettered global financial trends. For example, there is arguably a way of designing a financial transactions tax that, even if it were introduced in Europe alone, would deliver benefits for us. Such, at least, is the view of Avinash Persaud, an influential economist who has worked for various banks and is currently chairman of Elara Capital. His argument is based on the long-term impact of the UK's Stamp Duty Reserve Tax, which levies 0.5% on transactions in UK shares. Although the London Stock Exchange has long campaigned against this stamp duty, the levy has been around in its current form for twenty-five years – and for longer in other incarnations – and hasn't been associated with the mass departure of equity trading away from the UK. In fact, the London Stock Exchange would – paradoxically – probably claim to have been the most successful stock market in the world in recent years as measured by how many leading international companies it has persuaded to list their shares in London. Also, stamp duty raises an invaluable £3bn a year for the Exchequer (with the take from the tax expected to rise by around a third in the coming three years, according to the Office for Budget Responsibility). Tax avoidance does not appear to have undermined this very British transaction tax. Now the proposed European tax would be at a rate of 0.1% on shares and bonds, a fifth of Britain's stamp duty levy, and at 0.01% on derivative transactions. So – in theory – it would create less of an incentive to emigrate from London for avoidance purposes than current stamp duty has done.

In Persaud's view, the relative success of stamp duty is in its design. It is levied on any London-listed shares, regardless of the nationality of those trading the shares (the test for liability to stamp duty is not the residence of the trader or investor). And what really matters is that a transfer of shares is not legally enforceable if the tax hasn't been paid and the deal has not been 'stamped'. Even if investors and banks are based in Switzerland or Singapore, they pay the duty: foreign residents pay 40% of British stamp duty. Which means that if an EU transactions tax were constructed along the lines of the UK's stamp duty, such that it applied to trading in the shares or securities of EU companies, then there would be no point in huge banks, investors and traders quitting London – because emigrating would not allow them to escape the tax. There would only be acute damage to the City of London from a new transactions tax if huge companies, such as BP, or Unilever, or Vodafone stopped issuing bonds and shares in Europe or ceased to hedge their financial transactions in Europe. But the likelihood of enormous companies relocating en masse to protect their investors from a tiny transactions tax seems remote – especially since Europe retains advantages for big companies in the clarity and reliability of its legal system and the stability of its governments.

And what if such a tax reduced the volume of transactions, especially in derivatives designed for purely speculative purposes, by increasing their cost? There is evidence the sheer volume of such deals increases irrational exuberance in markets during good times and manic depression during bad times – which distorts the cost of finance for real businesses. So a dampening of these speculative transactions would not necessarily be a bad thing. Also a transaction tax would disproportionately hurt those trading in securities on the slimmest of profit margins. Even the slim cost of the tax could wipe out these profits. As a result, there would be a reduction in so-called high-frequency trading, or massive automatic trading in shares and bonds carried out by computers that run algorithms looking for price discrepancies or trends. This new hegemony of the machines in stock markets seems to have been associated with a sharp increase in the volatility of markets (the extreme case being Wall Street's notorious flash crash of 6 May 2010). So if there were less high-frequency trading, overshoots and undershoots in markets would become less extreme. Or to put it another way, a financial transaction tax would actually increase the efficiency of the allocation of capital: it would improve the functioning of capitalism, rather than undermining it.

Hidden subsidies

There are those who believe that taxation of markets is never benign, that it always distorts their functioning in a way that ultimately harms us. But those who say that interfering with markets leads to sub-optimal decision-making about how and where capital is allocated, which impoverishes us, would also make the same critique of subsidies. And government subsidies to big banks have been huge. These are not explicit subsidies. Actually that is not quite right. There have been plenty of explicit subsidies to banks in recent years – such as the British government's guarantee of £20bn of borrowing by British banks that is converted into cheaper loans to small businesses through a process called credit easing. At the time of writing, the Bank of England is about to provide an estimated £80bn of subsidised loans to banks, in a scheme called Funding for Lending, which is aimed at increasing the flow of affordable credit to businesses and households. But it is the implicit subsidy that is most striking, which stems from governments' commitment to rescue big banks that get into difficulties.

Perhaps the biggest flaw in modern capitalism is that big banks are so intimately woven into the functioning of the economy that they cannot be allowed to fail, because their failure would wreak havoc on the rest of us. This fear of big bank failures haunting all mainstream political parties in all developed economies was reinforced by the mayhem that ensued after the US Treasury allowed Lehman to collapse. There is therefore an unspoken but unambiguous guarantee that substantial banks will always be bailed out by taxpayers when they are on the brink of collapse. That means it is safer to lend to a big bank than to a small bank. And when any entity is deemed to be safer or a better credit risk, then its borrowing costs – the interest rate it has to pay – will be lower.

What this means is that big, systemically important banks can borrow more cheaply than other smaller financial institutions whose demise would not damage us so much. The concept of a bank being 'too big to fail' is another way of saying that taxpayers provide an implicit subsidy to big banks.

How big is that subsidy? Well, it may be very large indeed. Andy Haldane of the Bank of England calculated that the borrowing costs for British banks were £57bn lower per year between 2007 and 2009 as a result of the 'too-big-to-fail' guarantee. In other words, every single penny of bonus paid out by these banks in those years, and a lot more of their income, stemmed from the implicit subsidy provided by taxpayers. Latterly, if government had been able to credibly say that it was not going to bail out any bank, then no banker could have received a penny of bonus – because the banks' losses would have been even bigger than they were. And, according to Haldane, even after the worst of the crisis the subsidy remained big, at £40bn per annum by the end of 2010. Haldane's methodology has been criticised by bankers, who say the implicit subsidy is perhaps a tenth of what he says it is. But the Independent Commission on Banking, set up by the Chancellor of the Exchequer, George Osborne, agrees that the subsidy is big and real: the Commission says it was worth more than £10bn a year, which, again, would be more than the value of all those bonuses paid out by British-based banks. On the Commission's calculation, taxpayers' promise to prevent big banks from falling over paid for bankers' bonuses.

The existence of that subsidy carries a number of implications. The coalition government cited it when justifying its levy on banks' balance sheets – which raises £2.6bn a year. Perhaps more importantly, it reinforces the idea that banks are not normal private-sector organisations. Some would say it shows that they are actually public-sector institutions: just as financial innovation hid the true risks of many banking deals, so the banks themselves are public-sector liabilities disguised as commercial businesses. This leads many of the banks' critics to argue that bankers should be prohibited from receiving big bonuses until their industry is reconstructed such that banks could go bust without imposing egregious and unbearable costs on the rest of us.

There is also an argument that if banks are permanently in receipt of support from taxpayers, they should be compelled to provide desperately needed credit. If, for example, the economic imperative is for more finance to be available to smaller businesses or first-time buyers of homes, then banks should not be able to shirk their responsibility by making the traditional argument that the risks of some of this lending are too great. They should be forced to take that risk, if ultimately that risk is not theirs or their shareholders', but actually resides with taxpayers. Which is not to say that it would be remotely sensible for cheap loans to be made available to anyone demanding credit. That would be a short route to bankrupt banks and a bankrupt state. But there may be some lending risks which, for public-policy reasons, taxpayers would want banks to take, but which the official shareholders in banks would wish to be avoided. And here is the point: if it turns out that taxpayers are standing behind shareholders as the ulti-mate protectors of banks, then it is taxpayers' wishes that should have primacy.

All of which begs the question whether the Labour govern-ment made a terrible error in the autumn of 2008 by provid-ing almost unlimited financial support to the UK's banks, and £66bn directly as investment in Royal Bank of Scotland,

Lloyds and HBOS, without taking direct control of the banks. For what it is worth, I understand that the Governor of the Bank of England, Mervyn King, believes there was a strong case in the autumn of 2008 for fully and formally nationalising the weaker banks, Royal Bank of Scotland and HBOS. If that had happened, they could have been compelled to provide the finance needed by households and businesses, to underpin a sustainable economic recovery. Sir Mervyn is attracted to the approach taken by the Swedish government in 1992: it took control of almost all of Sweden's banks, laid low by the end of a property boom, and directly organised a reconstruction of the country's banking system. However those running the banks' rescue operation in Britain in October 2008 – two Treasury officials, Tom Scholar and John Kingman, together with Shriti Vadera, who was the main adviser on all things financial to the then prime minister, Gordon Brown – were concerned that full nationalisation would have made the banks less efficient and would have muddied and muddled their purpose. 'They were worried the banks would turn into lumbering versions of the appallingly unproductive Royal Mail,' says a government insider of the time.

The shape of the rescue was determined even before the moment of acute crisis, when Brown had ordered Scholar and Vadera to devise a contingency plan for the worst that could happen. In the event, after RBS and HBOS found themselves unable to finance themselves from conventional, commercial sources, the government injected unprecedented amounts of taxpayers' cash into RBS and the merged Lloyds/HBOS in a series of rescue deals. £45.5bn was provided to RBS and £20.5bn to Lloyds, so that taxpayers ended up owning more than 80% of RBS and more than 40% of Lloyds. It was the most substantial and generous bailout of any industry, in absolute and relative terms, in the history of Britain. But here in retrospect is what may seem quite extraordinary. The chancellor Alistair Darling and Mr Brown, on the advice of Scholar, Kingman and Vadera, put in place special institutional arrangements that actually limited the government's direct influence over the banks. The most important of these barriers between ministers and the rescued banks was a newly created company, UK Financial Investments. It was mandated to manage the Treasury's shareholdings in the banks in an explicitly 'commercial' way, in order to 'create and protect value for the taxpayer as shareholder'. It was therefore an explicit aim of government policy that RBS and Lloyds should continue to manage themselves as independent commercial organisations, with their respective boards making decisions on the basis of what they perceived to be in the interests of their shareholders. Or to put it another way, they were to behave as if they had never been rescued and were not semi-nationalised.

It was a conceit that was supposed to expedite the eventual privatisation of taxpayers' vast shareholdings in these banks. Mr Darling and Mr Brown, advised by the Vadera/Kingman/ Scholar trio, hoped and believed that the best prospect of selling taxpayers' stakes in these banks for a profit in the subsequent few years was for them to think and behave as if they were normal commercial banks listed on the stock market. It was feared that if they were directly managed by ministers, they would become loss-making, public-sector monoliths.

To state the bloomin' obvious, it is impossible to test whether more formal and conventional nationalisation of the banks, along the lines of what happened in Sweden, would have been seriously damaging to the big British banks' intrinsic value. The Swedish rescue itself is widely seen to have been a remarkably successful operation that ended up costing Swedish taxpayers more or less nothing, after the banks were privatised again, while maintaining the flow of credit to the economy. However, it has to be pointed out that the global economic backdrop during the rehabilitation of Sweden's banks was vastly more benign than today's stagnation of the eurozone and the US. What worked for Sweden in a period of expansion and recovery in most of the world might not work right now, when most of the UK's trading partners are in trouble. But it is important to point out that the previous government's attempt to create the illusion of business as usual for Lloyds and RBS – which has been maintained by the current administration – has not been a conspicuous success. The share prices of both banks have collapsed since the rescue: and taxpayers are therefore sitting on potential losses on their shareholdings in Lloyds and RBS of tens of billions of pounds.

Perhaps more importantly, the flow of credit from Britain's banks has been very weak – which is inevitable given that for years they lent too much, to the wrong borrowers, at the wrong price. Some contraction of lending, or deleveraging, is inevitable and healthy. Also at a time of economic uncertainty, it is rational for many businesses and households to be cautious about borrowing. A diminution in the provision of credit by banks may be the outcome of rational decisions taken both by lenders and some borrowers. But there is also evidence that loans are not getting to where they are needed, for a sustained and lasting recovery in the economy. In particular, there has now been around three years of shrinking credit provision to small businesses. And for businesses as a whole, recent Bank of England figures (for the three months to February 2012) showed business-lending contracting at an annual rate of

7.9% – a disturbingly fast rate. Unless small businesses are nurtured, it is very difficult for the UK to escape long-term economic decline. What appears to be happening, in part, is that banks are shying away from the risks of financing younger, riskier businesses, which may well be seen as sensible by the banks' managers and owners, if there are safer places for banks to lend for a respectable return. But it is not necessarily in the interests of the rest of us. To put it another way, a contraction in lending can be the appropriate strategy for an individual bank, but when all banks contract their lending at the same time that can be disastrous for the economy as a whole.

Both the last Labour government and the current government set targets for the banks for their lending to businesses, especially small businesses. But although these initiatives may have slowed down the contraction in lending, they did not actually lead to an expansion in credit provision. And the reason is that banks were given discretion to lend based on their own commercial judgements of the credit-worthiness of the borrowers. Banks took the view – which was not crazy – that in a time of economic stagnation, lending to small businesses remains risky, so no great gushing tap of new loans was turned on. Which brings us to the point that matters. Would it have been better, for a limited period only, for the rescued banks to have been forced to take greater risks than they would have chosen to do? Would it be better now for this to happen? Should the Treasury have followed the example of the Chinese authorities and actually forced RBS and Lloyds to get more money into the economy? Supporters of this approach would concede that it could have led to losses for RBS and Lloyds, as some of the loans would not have been repaid, but it might have jolted the economy out of its long period of torpor. And paradoxically, such a revival in the economy would have been good for the perceived prospects of all the banks and their share prices. Here is their point: if, as now seems likely, British taxpayers are set to lose perhaps crippling sums on their shareholdings in Lloyds and Royal Bank of Scotland, why not at least use those shareholdings as tools to engineer some kind of economic revival?

Breaking up the banks?

What some may see as curious is that, to date, the remedies and reforms for the banking industry have been incremental, not revolutionary, even though the recklessness of banks contributed to the worst contraction of the British economy since the 1930s, and an only slightly less severe hobbling of America's economy. There has been an attempt to mend the superstructure of the existing system rather than going down to the foundations to rebuild from the bottom. That said, a parliamentary inquiry announced in July 2012 by the UK government and chaired by the Tory MP, Andrew Tyrie, may address some of the deeper questions – it is investigating whether the scandal of Barclays and other big banks trying to fix the important LIBOR interest rates reveals fundamental flaws in banks' cultures. But hitherto, governments on both sides of the Atlantic set themselves the challenge of making the minimum necessary changes to the banking industry to reduce the severity and frequency of banking crises, while spurring banks to do better in oiling the wheels of the economy. In 2009, President Obama asked the distinguished former chairman of the US Federal Reserve, Paul Volcker, to make recommendations on how to sanitise banks. And in the UK in 2010, the Chancellor of the Exchequer set up an Independent Commission on Banking, chaired by the economist Sir John Vickers, to advise him on how to make the banks work better for all of us. Their respective prescriptions are significant and serious. Vickers urged that banks be forced to hold considerably more capital as a protection against losses and that a so-called 'ring-fence' be put between big banks' retail operations and their respective investment banks. The big idea of the Vickers commission, which is being implemented by the government, is that if the investment banking business of a Royal Bank of Scotland or a Barclays should get into difficulties, none of the losses should be able to taint their retail banks (and, of course, the reverse would also be true). RBS, for example, would continue to own both an investment bank and a retail bank (the bit of the bank that provides services to individuals and smaller businesses). But they would be in legally separate subsidiaries, with their own pools of capital and cash. And that would have two beneficial consequences. If the investment bank made big losses, those losses would have to be absorbed by the investment bank's discrete pool of capital and by its own creditors. In theory, there would be no contagion to the retail bank's capital, or the funds provided by depositors. Whether in practice the fire-wall will be as robust as Vickers suggests it should be, well that is not possible to judge right now. Much will depend on the linked introduction of what are known as 'resolution' procedures. They would be the processes for breaking banks up in a crisis, so that their essential services – moving money around the economy, protecting deposits, making loans – are preserved and kept functioning, while their bad bits are wound down, at maximum cost for shareholders and commercial creditors, and minimum cost for taxpayers.

By the way, if paying big bonuses to bankers is ever to become more tolerated by the general public again, then banking executives have to hope that resolution becomes a practical reality. Because if banks can go bust in the way that every other kind of business can go bust – foisting huge losses on investors and creditors, with bankers losing their jobs, and with taxpayers not shelling out a bean – then there would be no particular reason why bankers should not be paid in the way that others in the financial industry are paid (unless you believe that high pay is a bad thing in itself). In theory, if resolution were to be perceived to work, then banks would not be able to borrow more cheaply than hedge funds, because they would not be seen as more likely to be bailed out than hedge funds. And in those circumstances, taxpayers' implicit subsidy to banks would shrivel. So there would be a lesser public interest in trying to restrict the size of bonuses.

All that said, there are many in the City and elsewhere who believe that it would have been cleaner and better to separate investment banking and retail banking in a formal manner – in other words, to break up the banks. In those circumstances, there would be no possibility of a retail bank being tainted by the woes of an investment bank, except in the circumstances of an extreme general banking panic. And perhaps more importantly, that kind of separation would lead to important cultural changes. The point is that the mentality of retail bankers and of investment bankers is very different. Retail banking is about careful stewardship of savings, efficiency in moving money around, and prudence in the provision of loans to businesses and households. Investment banking is about doing deals – recommending deals to big investors and big companies, advising big companies and investors on deals, doing deals of their own. To put it another way, retail banking is about careful, long-term management of the grass roots of the domestic economy, whereas investment banking is a glamorous power game involving the big players in the global economy. Inevitably, therefore, when you put together an investment bank and a retail bank, there is a culture clash. Arguably, Paul Adcock in sleepy Watton has been a victim of that culture clash: he was a retail-bank customer treated by Barclays as investment-banking punter. What is really striking is that for all the incredible importance of the retail banking parts of HSBC, Barclays, Lloyds and Royal Bank of Scotland, until recently they have all been run by former investment bankers: Stuart Gulliver at HSBC, Bob Diamond at Barclays (till he resigned in July 2012), Antonio Horta-Osorio at Lloyds, and Stephen Hester at Royal Bank of Scotland. At Lloyds, which does very little investment banking, that may not matter so much – and Mr Horta-Osorio has concentrated on retail banking for almost twenty years. But if you want retail banks to provide the best possible financial support to businesses and households, it is almost certainly better for those banks to be run by retail bankers who are not distracted and seduced by the big short-term profits available in investment banking. And probably the best way to avoid those distractions is to forcibly separate investment banking and retail banking. As one City grandee put it to me: 'Would you put a butcher in charge of a bakery? No. So why put an investment banker in charge of a retail bank? The businesses are completely different and should never be combined.'

In the US, there has been no attempt to go for any kind of break-up of banking conglomerates, although Paul Volcker proposed a reform designed to reduce the riskiness of investment banking: a ban on banks using their own capital resources to engage in speculative trading for their own account. His idea, which has been incorporated in the Dodd–Frank Wall Street Reform and Consumer Protection Act, was that investment banks should only take positions in tradable securities and derivatives when facilitating deals for clients, and should limit the risks they take in their mainstream operations: he wanted them banned from attempting to make big profits for themselves by behaving like hedge funds. In practice, this distinction between what is risk-management and what is a big bet has proved tricky to define and implement. That became very clear in May 2012, when JP Morgan disclosed it faced a huge loss, running to billions of dollars, due to the activities of traders at its London-based Chief Investment Office – who were in theory doing complicated derivatives deals to limit the bank's exposure to losses. In July 2012 it quantified the loss at $5.8bn, almost treble its initial estimate, and warned that there could be a further $1.7bn to lose from the unwinding of the complicated deals. 'We are not proud of this moment, but we are proud of our company,' said Jamie Dimon, JP Morgan's Chief Executive, who prior to the debacle was one of the world's more respected and forthright bankers. The mess at Morgan stemmed from the way that a series of opaque and complicated transactions were heaped on top of each other, each one apparently intended to offset or hedge the impact of the previous transaction, but whose cumulative impact appears to have been just short of lethal. These deals seem to have been initiated by JP Morgan's perhaps laudable attempt to protect itself from the impact of a recession in the eurozone: it used derivative contracts, whose value would have risen if there was a rise in defaults on loans, to mitigate the losses from defaults on the vast loans it makes to companies in the normal course of business. Now whether banks really need to insure themselves against possible defaults in that way is moot. The better protections may be the old-fashioned ones: make sure you lend to businesses with a great variety of different characteristics, so that they are very unlikely to all go bust at the same time; and try to know your customers well enough to measure the risks you are taking.

That said, it may make sense for banks to be allowed some degree of financial protection, or insurance, against changing economic conditions. But how much 'protection' can any bank sensibly need? At the beginning of this year JP Morgan seems to have taken out another series of insurance contracts to heap on top of the first lot. These ones, credit default swaps, appear to have had the characteristic of potentially yielding a profit for JP Morgan if the debt of highly rated companies performed significantly better than that of lowly rated companies. So they can be seen as a hedge against the first hedge. And then there seems to have been a third hedge taken out, described in the *Wall Street Journal* as 'protection on investment-grade bonds', which appears to have been protection against the risk that the second hedge went wrong. Also, according to the *Wall Street Journal*, there was 'a related trade . . . allowing the bank to capture the premium between the cost of default protection ending in 2014 and the cost of protection ending in 2017'. If I am honest, I am not sure what that means. I am also pretty sure, having known these people for thirty years, that quite a few of those who sit on bank boards would struggle to understand it. With three or possibly four huge layers of derivative deals heaped on top of JP Morgan's loans of more than $700bn, no one can surely be surprised that the bank was unable to keep track of the risks it was running. Some have obsessed about whether the Chief Investment Office – which reports directly to the bank's chairman and chief executive, Jamie Dimon – was being disingenuous and was not actually hedging or limiting the risks being run by the bank but was in a covert way taking a punt, placing a huge bet, engaging in speculation. Arguably that doesn't really matter. What matters is that Morgan's attempt to be too clever by half landed it with an enormous bill.

Although there is a good deal to be said for the Volcker rule and for curbing the extent to which banks carry out direct speculation for their perceived advantage, building a more robust banking system also requires confidence that the non-executive directors of banks, the owners of banks, creditors to banks and regulators are all able to monitor what is really going on at any bank and prevent it from taking dangerous risks, before it is too late. This points to what may be among the most important of the lacunae in recent reforms: banks remain impossibly complex and opaque. It is beyond the wit of any mortal to fully understand the risks being taken by these massive international organisations: typically they have operations in many different countries; the type and variety of loans and investments they make are manifold; and their use of financial derivatives is another barrier to understanding the dangers they face. The annual report of Royal Bank of Scotland, as one typical example, runs to an impossible-to-fully-digest 490 pages of data and jargon. Reading it does not convey a deep and comprehensive knowledge of the strengths and weaknesses of a bank that is desperately important to the British economy, but a terrible unease that no mortal could keep a grip on all its myriad operations and investments. And as if to prove the heightened risk of catastrophe for vast and sprawling banks, in the summer of 2012 RBS's computer system for updating customer balances and processing transactions failed, after overnight maintenance on 19 June went disastrously wrong. For several days, RBS – which also owns NatWest in Britain and Ulster Bank, in both parts of Ireland – was unable to provide the most basic of services for its 17m customers. When money did not reach destinations requested by clients, companies were unable to pay staff, newlyweds had to cancel honeymoons, prisoners were kept incarcerated because their bail did not turn up, and thousands of other lives were disrupted. And in Northern Ireland and the Republic, the bank failed to serve customers adequately for weeks. Perhaps this debacle could have happened at any bank, big or small. But it was striking that this hiatus occurred at one of the world's most complicated banks. When the breakdown occurred, I was reminded of what the chairman of one huge global bank once confided to me in an unguarded moment – that he could live to be 200 and would still not have visited all his banks' worldwide offices or really obtained an understanding of the vast number of its operations.

Hoping that the processing and analysing power of computers can compensate for human frailties is probably naïve. As just one illustration, after the loss made by Morgan's Chief Investment Office came to light, Mr Dimon announced that he was abandoning a new financial system for monitoring the risks run by the Chief Investment Office and reverting to the old one – because the newer model was chronically understating the potential losses the bank could have generated on any given day. Mr Dimon disclosed that the Chief Investment Office's transactions had the potential to generate losses at any instant of $129m, which is not far off double what the bank had been admitting as the daily 'Value at Risk'. Or to put it another way, JP Morgan's alarm system would only sound when a (metaphorical) fire at the bank was twice as extensive as the bank thought would trigger the warning. Which is profoundly shocking, partly because regulators rely on banks' own assessments of the risks they are running when making their assessments of banks' health. The thing is that banks are trusted to devise their own risk models, because it is a completely impossible task for bank supervisors to inspect and understand every nook and cranny of a big international bank: supervisors check that big banks are not taking lethal risks, on the basis of the banks' own systems for measures of those risks. But if those systems, like JP Morgan's, actually understate the risks, then all the work of the supervisors becomes otiose. A bank is only as strong as its own early-warning system – and the job of the regulator is to verify that the early-warning system actually works. But the problem is that the only time there is a definitive answer about the effectiveness of that early-warning system is when it fails: in the meantime, the rest of us simply have to trust that the banks and regulators have got it right.

Perhaps the biggest missed opportunity to sanitise the banking system over the past five years is that little attempt had been made to compel banks to become simpler organisations. As we still count the cost of the 2007–8 banking crisis, it remains an open question whether governments and regulators have made a fundamental error in the way they reacted to that crisis. The response of the Basel Committee, the Financial Stability Board, the European Commission and the G20 has been to devise ever more complicated and more detailed rules to limit the risks to banks and the wider economy of the Byzantine complexity of the way banks manage themselves and the astonishing counter-intuitive complexity of products created by financial innovation. But if the financial system that evolved over the past twenty years is now so huge, labyrinthine and opaque as to defy comprehension or reliable risk assessment, maybe a better way would have been to start prohibiting certain activities. Would it have been naïve and futile to attempt to contain the risks of banking by forcing banks to become smaller, more transparent, easier-to-under-stand institutions?

Throwing out the rulebook

As you will recall from earlier chapters, banks hid the risks they were running by gaming the rules, the Basel Rules, that were supposed to make them safer. In practice, banks ended up holding too many investments that had been artificially engineered to appear safe; and they lent too much to govern-ments, too much to home buyers, too much to property companies, too much to other banks, backed up by too little capital. To remind you of one grotesque example: shortly before Royal Bank of Scotland had to be rescued by taxpay-ers, it had made loans and investments forty-five times the value of its capital; which meant that a 2.2% fall in the value of those loans and investments wiped it out. A bank whose balance sheet was substantially bigger than the annual output of the British economy, whose continued existence was vital to the functioning of the British economy, was vulnerable to being blown over by the financial equivalent of a puff of wind. In the end, there was a gale, and RBS had to be propped up by loans, insurance and capital all provided by taxpayers – in a rescue with a gross value of £451.7bn.

You might think, in those circumstances, that the sensible thing to do would be to dispense with the Basel Rules, which had proved themselves to be part of the problem, rather than part of the solution. Arguably a better approach would be to eliminate the banks' incentives to game and dodge the rules, by introducing much simpler restrictions on how much they can lend and invest. The experience of history, for example, suggests that if banks' gross loans and investments could never exceed ten times their loss-absorbing equity capital, if they could never exceed a 'gross leverage ratio' of ten, the banks would almost always have enough capital to withstand whatever shocks and disasters were to befall them – without recourse to taxpayers' bailouts. This, for example, is one implication of an influential study on 'Optimal Bank Capital' by David Miles, Jing Yang and Gilberto Marcheggiano of the Bank of England. What is more, there could be big benefits to banks' and bankers' sense of their own autonomy in the unlikely event that banks were strengthened in this way. If banks' capital resources were augmented to that extent, there would be less need for banks to be second-guessed and minutely inspected by supervisors. The intrusive hand of the government inspectors could be lifted a bit. Bankers could perhaps be trusted to lend where the returns are best and safest, rather than where the Basel Rules determine that the capital costs are lowest. What an extraordinarily revolutionary idea: that if banks' capital resources were more than ample, bankers might behave like normal business people, investing and lending based on commercial judgements rather than on tactics to outfox the regulators. Why has this low-leverage ratio not been introduced? It is partly because regulators have invested too much over the past thirty years in the Basel system that proved inadequate. Abandoning it would be too humiliating for them – or that is what some of them concede to me. Also some regulators have too cosy a relationship with the banks, especially on the Continent – where leverage ratios remain high by international and historical standards. Those arguing most strongly against a lower leverage ratio are the French and the Germans. Which is worrying, because euro-zone banks are, at the time of writing, perceived to be the weakest of all those in developed economies. And the leverage ratios of French and German banks are typically greater than those of British and American banks. At one meeting of the Basel committee of central bank governors and regulators that set the capital rules, the representative of a very substantial eurozone economy said when arguing against a proposal to set a leverage ratio that 'my banks won't like it' – which others at the meeting, especially the British contingent, thought was rather the point of having such a ratio, rather than a reason not to introduce it.

Perhaps more relevantly, some regulators and finance ministers are terrified that forcing banks to increase their capital resources to that extent right now would bring the global economy to a halt. The point is that if banks are instructed to cut the ratio of their loans to capital, they can do that by raising lots of expensive new capital or by shrinking how much they lend. And if in the weak global economic conditions of today banks were to massively reduce their provision of credit, economic stagnation could turn into a depression. Because here is the frightening statistic: most banks are still lending well over twenty times their capital resources. Halving that leverage ratio, which might well be sensible in the long term, could be hideously painful for them and for us if it was done too quickly. Which is another manifestation of how banks have become so big and powerful that – some would say – they have made it impossible to reshape them to serve us.

Rather than opt for simpler regulations that in the longer term would have given more discretion and freedom to banks, the Basel Rules have become even more detailed, complex and difficult to understand. This means that banks' opportunities and incentives to game these rules have arguably become even greater. That said, there will – for the very first time – be a limit on banks' gross leverage. But that limit does not come in till 2018, and it does not even have to be published by banks till 2015 (although in the UK, the Bank of England wants British banks to publish this important ratio from the beginning of 2013). And the maximum leverage ratio is set at thirty-three times – or more than three times what may well be the safe limit based on the available data. Under Basel III, therefore, a bank would be allowed to keep trading even if its core equity capital was just 3% of its gross loans and investments: it would be deemed safe, even though a 3% fall in the value of those loans and investments would bankrupt it.

As it happens, Britain's Vickers Commission, set up by the chancellor, recommended that there should be a leverage ratio for British banks of just under twenty-five – which is higher than what many would see as safe and optimal, but more conservative than the Basel maximum ratio. Now although George Osborne agreed to implement most of Vickers' many proposals to strengthen banks, on the leverage ratio he decided that the UK cannot go beyond the new international norm. In other words, if the Basel III leverage ratio remains at 3%, then that is the ratio that will apply to British banks. Which was a great relief for big British banks, because – with the exception of HSBC – none of them can raise additional capital cheaply or easily. They were concerned that they would have been significantly constrained in their ability to lend, especially compared to overseas competitors. But critics of the banks' sheer size – and there are a few of those around, including the governor of the Bank of England and the chairman of the FSA – will be concerned that there will be less long-term pressure on British banks to return to a more human scale. It is worth reminding you that the UK has more huge banks, relative to the size of its economy, than any other large developed nation. Which is why part of what the chancellor calls 'the

British dilemma' is how to allow our banks to thrive without being so huge that when they get into difficulties they risk bankrupting the Exchequer and British taxpayers.

There is another way of looking at all of this, which is that banks still remain far too big and important to the economy to be allowed to fail – but because of the weakening of public-sector finances that we have seen, there is now a very real question about whether the banks are too big to save. Can governments still afford to bail out their banks? Since the 2008 banking crisis, we have already seen Ireland (in particular), Portugal and Greece being granted emergency funds from the eurozone's bailout facilities and the International Monetary Fund, in part to help them with the costs of strengthening their banks. Spain and Cyprus are also set to receive official aid to shore up their over-stretched banks. In the US, where admittedly banks are much smaller relative to the size of the economy than in the UK and Europe, the big five banks' balance sheets, their assets and liabilities, have increased to 56% of GDP from 43% of GDP at the time of the credit crunch. Which is why, in the US, regulators, central banks and legislators fear that too-big-to-fail remains a live issue. But if they are anxious, you would think that in the UK there would be near despair at the continued extent to which British banks can hold the state to ransom: Royal Bank of Scotland's loans and investments were £1.5 trillion at the end of 2011, Barclays were a fraction under £1.6 trillion, and HSBC's were a fraction over £1.6 trillion. With a GDP in Britain of £1.5 trillion, each one of these banks has a balance sheet as big or bigger than an entire year's output of the British economy. Which shows that if another massive hole were found in any or all of these banks, there would be a serious question about whether British taxpayers could afford the bailout costs. It is therefore an explicit aim of government policy to put as much distance as possible between the liabilities of the state, and the liabilities of the banks. However, many would argue it should also be a priority to shrink British banks, so that a failure by a single bank would have a lesser potential to bankrupt us all.

CHAPTER 11

WE HAVE HARDLY BEGUN TO FIX THIS MESS

Turning the British economy from one whose momentum is provided by debt-fuelled consumer spending and dangerous growth in financial services into one where the engine of growth is investment and exports cannot be an overnight re-tooling. But, many would say, it is doable, and that we start perhaps from a stronger position than is widely acknowledged. For example, the decline of British manufacturing can be seen as having been relative, rather than absolute. Between 1973 and 2011 – a thirty-eight-year period – the total volume of goods produced by British factories actually increased by 8%. But whereas in the 1970s the production of goods contributed about a third of the country's GDP, by 2011 this had fallen to just 11% or 12%. And the contribution of manufacturing within the UK economy, as a generator of wealth and especially as an employer, has dropped sharply. The numbers employed have fallen from 6.6m (or a quarter of the workforce) in 1978, to 2.5m in 2011 (just 8% of those available to work): a staggering 1.5m jobs have gone just in the last decade. The trend had been set for a while. From 1948 to 1973, the total volume of goods produced by the country's factories had been growing at 3.4% per year, which looks a respectable rate from today's vantage point but was considerably slower than in Japan, Germany or even France. The UK dropped further and further down the international league tables in traditional industries such as shipbuilding, steelmaking and textiles that we had dominated during the heyday of the Empire. Take shipbuilding. The UK had been the world number one up until the end of the Second World War. But thereafter Germany, Scandinavia and Japan caught up and overtook it. The higher cost of Britain's unionised workers played a role. But perhaps more important was the UK's failure to keep up technologically. Japanese shipyards were much quicker to employ the faster prefabrication and welding techniques developed (partly in the UK) during the War. With the rise of container shipping and oil super-tankers, most of the yards on Tyneside and Clydeside were too small to produce the larger and larger ships that were in demand. Production in the UK stagnated from the 1950s until the early 1970s – even as global demand for new ships quadrupled – and then went into almost fatal decline. Out of sixty-two shipyards in 1948, only four remained by 2012.

Other heavy industries have followed the same path. Steel production has fallen by about 60% since 1969. In Sheffield – the city in which stainless steel was invented a century ago – shopping malls and leisure centres now occupy the sites of the old steel forges and furnaces. The city's stainless steel industry was absorbed by a Swedish company in 1992. Seven years later, plate production was moved to Sweden, and seven years after that coils production went to Finland. The common theme among these heavy industries is that they employ low-skilled labour. To succeed, such businesses either have to keep wage costs really low, or else continually invest in new technologies to maintain productivity. Britain was not brilliant at either. After union power was smashed by Margaret Thatcher in the 1980s manufacturing output did increase a bit, but employment continued on its downward path. There was a drop of more than three-quarters in employment in the once-great British industry of textiles between 1988 and 2006.

There are, however, patches of superior performance. Thanks entirely to foreign owners, the UK car industry has recovered from near extinction. After peaking at 1.9m cars in 1972, output halved in the rest of that decade. It has been a volatile subsequent thirty years. With the arrival in the UK of Nissan, Toyota and Honda – and big takeovers by BMW, Volkswagen and Tata Motors of India (which bought Jaguar Land Rover from Ford in 2008 for £1.15bn) – production clawed its way back. The next peak in production came in 1999, with 1.8m cars produced. Then there was a drop to a plateau of around 1.6m cars around a decade ago, before production fell off a cliff in the global recession to less than a million units in 2009. Since then, there has been a recovery, to 1.3m cars last year. What is striking and encouraging is that 1.1m of those British-made cars are exported. In the first three months of 2012, there was an extraordinary event: the British automotive sector recorded its first trade surplus since 1976. The UK sold more cars and components than it bought, which is pretty amazing for an industry that many had written off. The growth has been spearheaded by Japanese Nissan, whose plant in Sunderland produced 480,485 cars in 2011, a rise of 13.5%, and by Indian-controlled Land Rover, whose production increased a third to 238,237. The success of Jaguar Land Rover under its owner, Tata Motors, has been striking. In the year to the end of March 2012, Jaguar Land Rover's profits rose by just over a third to £1.5bn, on the back of a

27% increase in the number of cars sold, to 305,859 units. What is encouraging for Tata and for the UK is that sales to China soared 76% to 50,994, sales to India jumped 153.3% to 2,138, and sales to Brazil rose 62.2% to 9,027. These are the markets that British manufacturers have to crack, if the growth of the British economy is to resume at anything like its previous rate. And although British exports of goods and services to China are growing and were a fraction over £10bn in 2010, they remain small compared with £25bn to the tiny and near-bankrupt economy of Ireland. As the Chinese Commerce Minister, Chen Deming, said to me in 2010, the UK has to get better at producing and marketing what China actually wants. One of his counter-intuitive critiques of British industry – given that so much of Britain's textile capacity relocated to China years ago – was that British tailors and shirt makers make garments with sleeves too long for Chinese men. He told me that when he spoke to a British manufacturer about its failure to customise its clothes to suit the typical Chinese man, this manufacturer allegedly said that it expected Chinese economic progress to be accompanied by a lengthening of Chinese arms. That said, the onus is not just on British companies to reconfigure their production to Chinese needs and tastes: the UK's recovery would be helped if China were to reduce barriers to the sale of services and goods where British firms have a competitive advantage (though this was not an argument that Mr Chen found particularly compelling).

In today's highly competitive world, the best and most enduring route to success is brainpower and quality. But in the short term, a cheap currency can give a very helpful boost. The impact on manufacturing of the value of the pound has been conspicuous. After sterling's ejection from the European Exchange Rate Mechanism in 1992, when the pound fell 17%

in value, manufacturing output surged 12%. But the recovery fizzled out after the pound rebounded by 25% during 1996–7. In the few years before the crash, the strength of the pound meant that many exporters had to be among the world's very best to prosper: if they could not compete on price, they had to compete on quality. If they were not best in class, they went to the wall. After 2000, as a proportion of GDP, manufacturing in Britain shrank by a third to around 11% or 12%. That compares with 20% in Japan, 19% in Germany and Switzerland, 16% in Sweden and 13% in the US. That said, for all we might prefer to make more things, we should not be obsessive about this. Britain is a world leader in many exportable services apart from finance. Business services, excluding the City, are bigger than manufacturing, contributing 14% of everything we produce. Britain can take pride that it has great non-financial services: architectural practices, advertising agencies, lawyers, media firms, management consultants, civil engineers, and all manner of creative companies. Even so, those who argued in the post-Thatcher era that making things was not important at all would probably recant today. Fortunately we do have outstanding manufacturers – of which Rolls-Royce in hi-tech aero-engines, GlaxoSmithKline in pharmaceuticals, Diageo in alcoholic drinks, and JCB in construction equipment are just a few major examples.

When I visit companies around the UK – Dyson in Malmesbury, Wiltshire, ARM in Cambridge, as just two examples – I am immensely impressed by their sense of purpose, their commitment to be the best, their enthusiasm and team spirit, their substantial investment in research and product development. Even so, what is striking about many of these successes is how much of what they do has gone offshore. ARM designs the microchips that other companies then manufacture under licence by the billion to be the pulsing hearts of smartphones, tablets and a growing list of consumer electronics goods. Dyson is arguably the most innovative creator of household electricals in the world, but its vacuum cleaners and fans are made in Malaysia. These are businesses that create very high quality jobs for highly educated people. But their intellectual leadership creates a disproportionate number of jobs for people with lower and intermediate skills outside Britain. As a nation, our relatively relaxed attitude towards these jobs going abroad may not have done us any favours. We looked at Asia's lower labour costs, shrugged, and decided not to bother to compete any more in making, as opposed to designing. By contrast, Germany's manufacturing sector is almost twice the size of Britain's as a share of GDP and yet its labour costs are more than a third higher than in the UK. How does Germany combine high manufacturing employment and high wages? It is the result of a 10% productivity advantage over Britain – which itself is a consequence of investment in machinery that is twelve times what is spent in Britain in absolute terms, and research spending that is 50% greater in proportionate terms. On a tiny scale, the success of Will Butler-Adams and Brompton Bicycle in designing and making world-class foldable bikes in West London – with turnover going from £2m to £16.5m over a decade – is one of many inspirational examples of the opportunities for Britain in manufacturing if we are to follow Germany's lead and invest for the long-term.

Here, arguably, is one measure of the endemic weakness of manufacturing and also of the potential to be tapped: just 9% of British graduates in Science, Technology, Engineering and Maths subjects entered manufacturing in 2010, according to the Higher Education Statistics Agency. We are churning out one of the best-educated workforces in the world, but, arguably, they are going into the wrong jobs, if they can find work at all. If more of them can be persuaded to enter manufacturing or set up their own manufacturing businesses, the economic future of all of us would be improved. Since the 2008 crisis, and with the pound having lost a quarter of its value, manufacturing has performed better than the rest of the economy. But output is still below where it was three years ago, and that is worrying. Britain is still probably the tenth biggest manufacturer in the world, although Brazil, South Korea and India now produce more than the UK. Whether the UK can climb that league table is doubtful, in a world of unstinting competition from developing economies. But equally there is no reason to be resigned to seeing Britain become an even more divided society, with an elite of hedge fund managers and so-called creatives served by a mob of shop workers and cleaners. There is another way, in which rewarding jobs (where the reward is about more than money) are widely available. We have most of the ingredients for this better way: excellent universities; schools capable of being as good as any in the world; a culture of creativity, tolerance, and openness.

But the sort of structural changes that are needed, to return the UK economy to sustainable growth – what we call rebalancing and re-tooling – are so substantial that it is unsurprising the UK economy has failed to grow in any meaningful way since the end of the Great Recession of 2008–9. Once households have collectively recognised that it is rational to reduce their debts, as they apparently have, even the record low interest rates engineered by the Bank of England cannot persuade them to go back on a spending spree – which may be a good thing for our long-term stability, but means that

right now what was the great engine of growth is barely ticking over. As for the reconstruction of the economy into one
based more on saving, investment and exports, that was never
going to happen overnight, even at a time of general economic
prosperity. But the process is harder and takes longer when
our most important export markets, in the eurozone, are so
weak and may yet weaken further. At the time of writing,
Britain is back in a prolonged but shallow recession. That
return to economic contraction can be laid at the door of the
uncertainties over the future of the euro. Manufacturers are
experiencing less overseas demand than they had hoped to
find for what they make and companies in general are delay-
ing investments because of the risk of implosion of the
currency union – which would force the UK's biggest foreign
market, the European Union, into severe recession. But even
before the threat of an uncontrolled fragmentation of the
eurozone, the British economy remained in a vulnerable state
of recovery. Ever since the credit crunch of 2007–8, I have
consistently believed that if an explosion of debt had maintained the UK's average growth rate at around 3% a year
from 1992 to 2008, the subsequent repaying of debt – the
period of deleveraging – would see us grow at 1% or so on
average for the subsequent decade after we had hit bottom
(which we did in 2009). It was a hunch, albeit one informed
by pouring over pages of data and charts. But nothing that
has happened since has changed my judgement that 1%
growth may be the best we can expect, on average, for many
more years yet. After that, of course, our fate is down to us.
If, like Germany, we can work harder and smarter, and can
produce the goods and services the rest of the world wants,
we can certainly grow at the rates we enjoyed before the
crash. But this time we will have earned our prosperity, rather

than borrowing it from China and the producing countries in an unsustainable way.

As you are probably tired of hearing me say, we are a rich country, one of the richest in the world – about twentieth on a per-head basis and fifth if the smallest economies are excluded. Of course, we will drop down all sorts of league tables for the size of economies and per capita income as the developing economies of Asia, Africa and Latin America continue to power ahead. However, the sensible thing for the UK to do is to count its blessings and make the most of them. And here is where the challenge will reside. We are going to have to return to the old-fashioned virtue of deferring gratification, or what Andy Haldane of the Bank of England calls 'patience'. In the years before the crash, we took it for granted that we could have it all now. Investors wanted instant returns, so banks took crazy lending risks, and we saw the explosive growth of hedge funds and private equity looking to maximise short returns. Most of us borrowed more and more to buy houses and apartments, and to purchase the latest gadgets, clothes, interior decor and cars, the essential trappings of the putative good life. Politics was about sharing out an ever-growing cake: we could have more police, more health services, more education, all at the same time. The contest between the parties was a beauty parade based on who was the most competent and efficient in enriching all of us. Voters were not presented with difficult choices about which public services really matter or whether significantly more should be taken from the affluent to help the poor. Labour, Tories and Lib Dems all converged on a crowded political centre ground, in which there were limited ideological and ethical distinctions between what the parties were offering. But endemic low growth surely means the end of the 'have-it-all-now' society. This is how Jeremy

Heywood, the cabinet secretary and Britain's most powerful civil servant, put it, in an address at the Institute of Government in June 2012: 'We are 25% through fiscal adjustment. Spending cuts could last seven, eight, ten years.' That represents a change to the structural foundations of British politics, and it may mean that citizens will want the parties to offer more than proof of competence. They may be required to offer competing visions of the good society that are more differentiated than we have seen since a privatising Margaret Thatcher was prime minister in the 1980s.

I think we all know what years of anaemic growth mean for our individual lifestyles. So I am not going to labour that point. Political parties are stumbling and fumbling towards working out whether a low-growth world of deferred gratification will see the vast majority of British people coalesce around a revised set of values, ones that would be seen perhaps as slightly more leftish than in recent years, or whether the centre will fragment and we will have a return to a starker left–right split. History would suggest that in a time of economic dislocation, where the interests of haves and have-lesses can diverge for an extended period, a sharper delineation between left and right will re-emerge, and greater opportunities for electoral success may be presented to minor and fringe parties. Could the government's reduction of the top rate of income tax from 50p in the pound to 45p – characterised by the government as improving incentives for wealth creators; castigated by Labour as rewarding the rich – mark a return to the closer alignment of Labour and Tories with a particular class? It has not really happened yet. But it may do when David Cameron and Ed Miliband are forced to think seriously about how to allocate the contents of a shrinking public purse in the run-up to the next election. These may well be the conditions in which the Tories would offer lower taxes and a shrinking of the state, while Labour would push up taxes on the wealthy and promise a relatively bigger provision of public services. Both sides will be pondering whether the rebirth of the left in France represents Gallic exceptionalism or the shape of things to come.

Alternative to austerity

Even now, there is a significant divide between the coalition government and Labour about the speed of government retrenchment – with Labour arguing for temporary VAT cuts and a slower deficit-reduction path. It is also an issue that pits economists against each other. At the heart of all this is the question of how much harm has been done to the UK's productive potential by the financial crisis. Bill Martin and Robert Rowthorn, two Cambridge economists, calculate that the output of the British economy is '14% below the level that it would have attained had growth continued at the pace seen before the banking crisis'.* That represents more than £200bn of lost annual income. And, for Rowthorn and Martin, it suggests that there exists plenty of spare capacity to meet higher demand. They accept that the spare capacity is probably not as high as 14%, but they dispute that it is as low as 2.5%, which is what many in government believe it to be. Rowthorn and Martin argue that many bigger companies kept on workers in the downturn rather than making them redundant, and that these workers are still being under-used. 'Output is well below potential because workers, while cheaper to employ, are not working to potential,' they say. 'More output

---

* 'Is the British economy supply constrained II. A renewed critique of productivity pessimism', May 2012.

could be produced, but not sold. There is an effective demand failure, high unemployment, under-utilisation of the employed workforce – a form of "labour hoarding".' On their analysis, if government stimulated demand by cutting tax and spending more, the private sector would respond by producing and selling more, with the consequence that GDP and tax revenues would both recover. What this means, for Rowthorn and Martin, is that the so-called 'cyclical' element in the UK's public-sector deficit could be as high as 6% of GDP, as opposed to the 2% estimated by the Office for Budget Responsibility, the forecasting body that is supposed to provide the empirical or evidential backing for the Chancellor's budget judgements. Or to put this in English, the higher the cyclical element in the deficit, the less that government has to cut public spending or raise taxes in a permanent way to strength the public finance. If the 'cyclical' element in the government's deficit is as high as 6%, then a bit less austerity would not be the road to fiscal ruin, because a greater proportion of the government's huge and unsustainable deficit would be closed by an eventual recovery in the economy. Now it has to be said, Rowthorn and Martin don't represent the consensus view, although their view is shared by credible economists. We will not know whether they are wrong or right for years, by which time a great deal of the UK's productive potential will have been lost forever, and it will be too late to do anything about it.

It is also important to point out that the government's austerity has not been hair-shirt austerity. Current spending by the public sector continues to make a positive contribution to economic growth, albeit a mild one, at a time when manufacturing is flat, business and financial services are contracting and construction is shrinking quite fast. That said, substantial cuts in government investment have been a big drag on growth. Also, for all the government's rhetoric about the imperative of cutting the deficit, it is shrinking slowly and the national debt is rising inexorably. When the coalition took office, in May 2010, the national debt was £760bn. Public-sector indebtedness is now above a trillion pounds and it is difficult to see how it can ever again fall below that totemic level. On the government's projections – those of the Office for Budget Responsibility – the debt will be £1.365 trillion in 2015, which is when it plans to hold the next general election. The austerity that the government's creditors apparently love so much is delivering an 80% rise in the national debt, on the official estimates. But what is striking is that the government is able to borrow at record low interest rates – negative interest rates after account is taken of inflation – so in effect the money is free.

If the government borrowed a bit more in the shorter term, with the prospect of generating incremental growth and extra tax revenues such that borrowing in the longer term might actually fall, would its creditors react with horror? Would the big pension funds and banks go on strike and refuse to lend any more? That, just like the question of whether more public spending would actually generate a lasting increment in growth, is unknowable. That said, in a world where there are greater doubts about the credit-worthiness of a large number of other developed economies – Italy, Spain, Ireland, Portugal, Greece and even France – the UK government may have more latitude to alter the path of deficit reduction than it currently believes. The point is that investors have to put their money somewhere, and in an ugly contest, the UK looks less fiscally hideous than many others. That is the implication of an analysis by the International Monetary Fund, which showed that the UK's public finances are less vulnerable than any other major economy, even Germany's, to a sharp deterioration if interest rates were to rise sharply or if growth were to fall. The UK Exchequer seems to be better at collecting taxes whatever the economic weather than the treasuries of other countries. And, as I have mentioned, the UK Debt Management Office has done a decent job of insulating the public sector from potentially nasty interest-rate shocks by borrowing on behalf of Her Majesty's Government at fixed rates of interest for the long term.

Those who argue that the UK government should be spending more or taxing less often point to the US, where recovery has been a bit stronger – and where President Obama has not embraced austerity, even though America's public finances are in worse shape than Britain's. On the IMF's figures, the ratio of government debt to GDP in the US is 106.6%, compared with 88% in the UK. And the US needs to borrow a sum equivalent to 25.8% of its GDP, to fund its deficit and roll over maturing debt, compared with 14.8% in Britain. That said, the American government can probably take greater liberties with financial orthodoxy than a smaller economy such as the UK, because so much of the world's trade and business is conducted in dollars and that means there is a natural demand for US government debt. So many businesses and investors have to hold dollars, it makes sense for them to park those dollars in US Treasuries where they can earn interest. In other words, the US government can usually take it for granted that it can borrow, in all climates and all seasons. Whether the US can and should continue to take it for granted that it will never face a boycott by investors and creditors is moot. But what matters here is that it is harder for the UK to ignore fiscal conventions than it is for President Obama. Even so, it is not irrelevant that the US has been suffering from milder economic anaemia than Britain – and the tonic may have been a rejection of fiscal retrenchment.

America is however something of a paradox. Its slightly stronger recovery can be cited not only by the left as a reason for countries like the UK to go slightly easier on austerity but also by the right as evidence of why mollycoddling banks and over-stretched borrowers is a mistake. There is a gripping and potentially relevant difference between the post-crash experience of the UK and the US in how banks have treated households that have borrowed too much. As we have seen, in America banks were brutal by European standards in the way they treated customers unable to pay debts. Where home owners could not keep up the payments on home loans, families were evicted, properties were seized, debts were written off. In Britain, there has been a more humane approach – called forbearance, in the jargon – where banks have allowed families to defer some of their payments. But the problem with the supposedly more humane British approach is that the debts are still bearing down on households, preventing them from climbing out from under them and building a life on more solid financial foundations. The banks are also weighed down by these loans: they fear that one day they may have to write off the mortgages, which means that they see themselves as having depleted resources with which to provide credit to households and businesses with legitimate needs. Some would argue that the British economy would have recovered faster if banks had felt able to seize the assets of corporate and personal borrowers crippled by the sheer size of their debts and then write off the losses. But is it too late for UK banks to adopt the American approach of ripping off the Band-aid with one sharp jerk? In a country with the welfare-state tradition of Britain, the sensible approach might be for banks not to behave like de facto social services, but to make a rational decision on the ability of creditors to repay, and then for the state to provide social housing for people forced to leave their properties or training and benefits for employees whose jobs are put at risk by bankruptcy procedures. Of course, right now those additional burdens on the state may be more than it can bear. Which is why ministers are grateful that banks are behaving – in their view – responsibly, by not calling in debts in a precipitate way. Also, the time may have passed where banks can raise the requisite additional capital – from either the private sector or the financially stretched public sector – to absorb the losses from cancelling loans to irredeemably over-stretched borrowers. Muddling through with troubled debtors, otherwise known as forbearance, may be unavoidable. But it is moot whether in the long run the growth potential of the British economy is enhanced or reduced by using limited bank resources to keep the heads of debtors just above water.

We are the owners

One reason why people would be highly sceptical of any bankers' claims that they were being cruel to be kind in closing businesses or seizing homes is the widespread perception that they operated their own organisations largely to generate personal gain, with underwriting provided by all of us, thanks to taxpayers' promise that big banks will never be allowed to go bust. Even the interests of the owners were given short shrift by banks' executives. And since the owners are to a great extent millions of us, through our pension savings, we've paid a treble price for bankers' short-sighted selfishness: through the contraction of the economy that followed the crash;

through the colossal sums we have injected into the banks to bail them out; and through the collapse in value of the banks' shares, held by us either directly or through pension plans and life insurance. This question, therefore, of how we can get banks and indeed all companies to better serve the interests of the owners – all of us – is an important one. At this juncture, it is important to point out that the extent of our ownership should not be overstated. About 40% of the shares in a typical company listed on the London Stock Exchange are held by investors outside the UK, according to the Office for National Statistics. To an extent that reflects the growing trend for overseas businesses – especially those in mining and commodities – to list their shares in London: FTSE 100 members include the Kazakh mining giant ENRC, the Swiss-based commodities trader Glencore, and the Chilean conglomerate Antofagasta; inevitably many of their owners will be offshore. But much of the rest of the shares will be with you and me in various guises: insurance companies with 9%, pension funds with 5%, individuals with just under 12%, charities with 1%, banks with 2.5%, and other financial institutions with 16%. That last category of other financial institutions includes hedge funds. And even those hedge funds may represent you and me, if they take money from pension funds (which many do). The point is not that the disgruntled mob owns every share in every British company; but we probably own 30%, and our voice has rarely been heard.

What is remarkable is that on one issue, and one issue only, those who manage our pension savings have – for the first time – begun to express fairly public criticism of the approach taken by company boards. The issue is executive pay: investors have shown sympathy for the popular view that the rewards of senior executives have become too big in relation to the performance of their respective businesses. Thus in the spring of 2012 there was a series of protest votes at the annual meetings of leading companies. There was a substantial minority of investors who voted against the huge rewards for Barclays' executives, with their discontent mainly about Mr Diamond's remuneration, and also against the remuneration packages at easyJet, the airline, Prudential, the insurer, and Xstrata, the mining group, among more than forty companies where there was significant shareholder dissent on pay. Also, a majority voted against the remuneration policy at another insurer, Aviva, the media giant WPP, the motor distributor, Pendragon, the oil and gas company, Cairn Energy, and the minerals group, Centamin. It's certainly significant that shareholders have become more willing to humiliate individual companies in this way. That said, it is unclear whether shareholders' concerns will lead to executives being paid less, or in some way more fairly. In June 2012, investors were promised more power to influence executive pay, and more relevant information to inform their judgements, by the Business Secretary, Vince Cable: he will change company law to give them a binding vote on companies' pay policies at least every three years (the current annual votes have only an advisory status); and companies may be spurred to simplify their complex schemes for rewarding their top people, by publishing a single number for everything that each top executive has earned in the previous twelve months (on that measure, Bob Diamond was the top earner for 2011, making just under £21m, including rewards from his past incentive schemes).

In my last book (*Who Runs Britain?*, Hodder, 2008), I explored in detail the implications of the widening gap between the pay of those at the top and the rest. I will not rehearse all of that again at great length. That said, the gulf between the pay of those who run our biggest companies and average earnings has widened again. According to an authoritative survey by Manifest/MM&K, average total pay awarded to a FTSE 100 chief executive in 2011 was £4.8m, including bonuses and other longer-term incentives. That is 184 times the typical pay of a British full-time employee, which is just over £26,000. It compares with a ratio of bosses-to-workers pay of 19:1 in 1989, towards the end of Margaret Thatcher's period in office – which is significant in that she was a proponent of increasing incentives for those at the top, but pay differentials remained comparatively modest by today's standards even after she had been at it for a decade. And at the time I wrote *Who Runs Britain?* in 2007, the ratio of top bosses' rewards to those of most British people was 75:1. So, on that measure, inequality has worsened significantly in just a few short years. And here is why even an ardent Thatcherite might argue that rewards for bosses are out of control. Research commissioned by BBC Radio 4's *More or Less* radio programme from the consultants Obermatt shows precisely zero correlation between financial rewards for company bosses over the three years from 2008 to 2010 and the performance of their businesses (their profits growth and what is known as total shareholder return, which is a combination of the share price movement and dividends paid to owners). Or to put it another way, senior executives were receiving enormous pay rises for no good reason at all. Obermatt says it found exactly the same lack of link between top executives' remuneration and corporate performance in Germany, Switzerland and the US. Big companies talk the talk of only giving lavish rewards to executives when the owners of companies are also being handsomely rewarded. But in practice, company boards – often aided by highly paid remuneration consultants – have bamboozled shareholders with complex formulas for determining bonuses and pay-outs from so-called Long-Term Incentive Plans. Belatedly, the owners – or rather the stewards of our savings, the pension fund and other investment managers – appear to be wising up. But although the protest votes at the annual meetings have been sententiously nicknamed a 'Shareholder Spring', it is too early to know whether the days of inflated bonuses are numbered, or whether we'll continue to see massive pay-outs given to executives for the mediocre management of their companies.

The media – both mainstream and social – has taken a strong and emotional interest in the large amounts being pocketed by executives, partly because of the perceived injustice that some of those most responsible for our mess are still being paid handsomely, whereas job insecurity for most people remains high and the pay of the vast majority is being eroded in real terms. The noise has been so great that those who manage our pension savings have been forced to take account of the popular mood, even though some of them are nervous about the implications, in that their pay too remains large by most standards. The very interesting question is whether this is the start of a sustained narrowing of the yawning gap between the perceived interests of the boards of companies and those of the ultimate owners of companies. It might just be, because of the growing influence of campaigns on Twitter and Facebook. I have been struck, for example, by the growing awareness in boardrooms of what is being said on social media about not just executive pay, but companies' impact on the environment and whether big businesses pay their fair share of taxes. And among these, tax is the electric issue of the moment. There is a growing view that companies that benefit from all the advantages of being based in a stable country like Britain – especially the expensive 'infrastructure' that includes an effective legal system, police who enforce the rule of law, education that improves the quality of the workforce, a health service, a transport network and so on – should pay the proper price for those advantages, through the tax system. That said, companies' boards will always say that it is their fiduciary duty – their duty to the owners – to minimise their tax bills. It is the shareholders' money, the directors say, and if there are legal ways to shelter that money from the taxman, then they would be wrong not to exploit them. But the ultimate owners – the providers of savings to pension funds, if not the fund managers who are the guardians of those savings – are shouting on Twitter and via the *Daily Mail* that they do not expect companies to engage in aggressive tax avoidance. There is some sign that boards are listening.

Take Vodafone, the mobile phone giant. It has always been adept at managing its tax bill. City analysts have identified Vodafone as a multinational that succeeds in keeping its worldwide tax well below the UK corporation tax rate. In 2011–12, it paid no UK corporation tax at all. Presumably worried by negative perceptions of this in its home country, Andy Halford, Vodafone's Chief Financial Officer, wrote to journalists to explain that 'as is the case for all businesses, our UK corporation tax liabilities reflect statutory allowances for capital investment and interest costs' – and that Vodafone had invested £575m in Britain during the year. He was also keen to put a new gloss on Vodafone's long-running dispute with Her Majesty's Revenue and Customs about how much it owed under the Controlled Foreign Companies rules, which was eventually settled in 2010 when Vodafone agreed to pay £1.25bn. Some MPs on the Public Accounts Committee questioned whether the taxman had let Vodafone off lightly. So Mr Halford was keen to highlight that the National Audit Office, the watchdog of how the public sector spends and raises money, eventually ruled that the settlement represented 'fair value for the wider taxpaying community'.

Vodafone is one of the businesses that campaigners tend to cite when protesting on social media against companies paying relatively low tax rates. So there was a bit of a frisson when Vodafone announced its intention to buy Cable & Wireless Worldwide (CWW), owner of an extensive fibre-optic cable network in Britain, for £1bn, because the deal seemed to present a great opportunity for it to cut its tax bill. The notes to CWW's accounts show it has a £5.2bn UK 'capital loss', which in theory is permanently available to reduce the tax payable on UK profits. According to CWW, this 'unrecognised deferred tax asset' of more than £5bn can reduce the tax bill of any company 'making profits in the UK telecoms space'. Or to put it another way, it seemed to allow Vodafone the opportunity to slash the tax it pays on its very substantial earnings in the UK – earnings that are a multiple of CWW's – which would have been controversial. But when I talked to senior Vodafone people, they said they understood the explosiveness of this issue. And when it issued its state-ment on 23 April 2012 confirming its plan to buy CWW, it said that 'CWW's tax losses and capital allowances are not key to the rationale underpinning the offer. Vodafone does not believe it can utilise CWW's tax losses and it has not ascribed any value to the possibility of using CWW's capital allow-ances against Vodafone Group's existing UK operations.' Vodafone knows that if it does find a way to use CWW's capital allowances to delay the moment when it starts to pay UK corporation tax again, there may be loud complaints: £5bn would pay for lots of schools and hospitals.

Vodafone is British in a formal sense but it thinks of itself as a global company. And one reason why it feels the need to make the most of its cash is that it is in competition with other global companies that also feel compelled to keep as much money as legally possible away from the taxman. For example, the giants of the on-line and consumer-technology industries, American by origin, have complicated global structures that allow them to pay almost no corporation tax in the UK, in spite of the fact they have massive sales here. The recent accounts of Apple, Amazon, Google, eBay and Facebook appeared to show they collectively paid UK corporation tax of less than £20m, in spite of generating sales here of more than £12bn. These are businesses that have had a massive impact on the UK economy, transforming the media, retail and advertising industries. They are hugely successful. And yet, quite legally, they domicile themselves in countries that have incredibly low tax rates, which allows them to pay very little direct tax in Britain on their British earnings. Their relatively small contributions to the Exchequer have become contentious. But because they are US companies with US owners, their boards are almost certainly less conscious of the furore in Britain about all this than Vodafone's board has been. There is, as you will have noticed, a magnificent paradox here: social media, Facebook and Twitter, can be seen as helping to democratise decision-making in big companies, shortening the gap between owners and directors; but the more that a company feels global rather than national, the wider the gap there is to bridge. Arguably Facebook itself encapsulates the paradox: it pays little tax in Britain, yet it is the medium for protests about multinationals that escape what some would see as a duty to pay corporate taxes wherever they derive significant benefit.

A world of problems

This brings me, in a slightly roundabout way, to perhaps the main reason why the mess or messes identified in this book are a long way from being cleared up – and goodness only knows when they will be cleared up. The thing about globalisation, especially financial globalisation, is that it is global. When globalisation goes wrong, it requires global decisions to fix it. But it will not have escaped your notice, I think, that government remains largely national. So it is very difficult to prevent countries setting wildly different tax rates, which provides the opportunity for multinationals to construct themselves in such a way that for tax purposes they are based where taxes are lowest – Dublin, for example – thus depriving the public sectors of higher-tax countries, such as the UK, of what many would see as the appropriate revenues from those multinationals. There are, of course, all sorts of official bodies that attempt to take a world view and formulate global solutions. But whether it is the World Trade Organisation, trying to remove barriers to trade, or the attempts by the United Nations to formulate a new convention on tackling climate change, failures and delays in reaching decisions are endemic. In the financial and economic sphere too there are institutions that bring together the governments of the leading economies to push through reforms ostensibly in the collective global interest. In banking and finance, there are the Basel Committee on Banking Supervision and the Financial Stability Board. For the economy, there is the G20 group of the world's biggest economies – which supplanted the G8 as the main forum for discussing international economic issues at the time of the 2008 crash. The G20 is a more relevant decision-making body than the G8, because it is more representative of where power resides in today's world: the developing economies, China, India, Saudi Arabia, South Africa, and Brazil, inter alia, are all at the top table for the first time. But although the G20 is more representative, it is no more decisive or effective than what went before. And how can it be, when all decisions have to be unanimous? The process of finding a consensus on the way forward means that agreement is always a compromise, a kind of gloopy soup made out of national interests, whose recipe is intended to prevent any country feeling that it is a loser.

On the Basel Committee, as we have seen, the simplest and boldest reform – limiting how much banks can lend to a relatively low multiple of their capital resources – has been blocked by France and Germany. There has been a compromise: that by 2018 banks would reduce their leverage to thirty-three times their capital. Which does not represent much additional protection for taxpayers, since there would only need to be a 3% fall in the value of a bank's loans and investments, its assets, for a bank to be bust. The structure of banking regulation has been modified but not fundamentally reformed. Banks will be forced to hold more genuinely liquid assets as a protection against runs. And they are under pressure to be less reliant on short-term, flighty finance. But the Basel system of weighting loans and investment according to their supposed riskiness, those poisonous incentives to game and cheat the rules, remains intact. Which means that banks will continue to devote their resources to those loans and investments deemed by the regulators to be least risky, rather than making their own proper commercial judgements about how and where to extend credit. And thus banks will still be able to pull the wool over the eyes of owners, creditors and regulators about how strong or weak they really are. We remain a long way from a world in which the risks being taken by banks are transparent and where we can be confident that if a big bank collapses the costs will be absorbed where they ought to be absorbed – by owners and creditors; not by all of us.

The two other big causes of global instability have also not yet been addressed. In spite of intense pressure from other countries big and small, including the US, there remains an understandable reluctance by Germany to make what would be very significant national sacrifices to preserve the eurozone, to prevent the fragmentation of the currency union. As we have seen, what is pulling the eurozone apart is that German productivity is so much greater than that of Italy, Spain, Portugal and Greece. Unless and until that changes, Germany will sell much more to them than they sell to Germany. So their indebtedness will become bigger and bigger, until they go bust – unless they slash the wages of their people or there is rampant inflation in Germany that undermines its productivity advantage, its competitiveness. Right now, German wages are rising faster than for some time, but not fast enough. Also Germany is the main underwriter of the rescue funds for over-indebted eurozone countries. But what Germany will not do – or at least not at the moment – is merge its balance sheet with those of other eurozone members, which would allow those other eurozone members to borrow at permanently lower interest rates, but would also impair Germany's perceived credit-worthiness. Germany refuses to give what it sees as a blank cheque to neighbours over which it has only limited control. Angela Merkel has said that the creation of 'euro-bonds', which would be the method by which eurozone countries borrowed collectively, or a full-scale banking union, in which eurozone countries combined their resources to support eurozone banks, cannot be contemplated while individual governments can take Germany's money and do what they like with it. What she heralds as the solution to the eurozone's woes (though she does not use this language) is a United States of Europe, a political union in which decisions on how much governments could tax, borrow and spend would be taken centrally, rather than by individual sovereign parliaments. In a way, Germany is saying that if Spain, Italy and the rest want a permanent solution to the eurozone's crisis, they have to stop thinking of themselves as nations in a conventional sense. Yet it is quite difficult to envisage how France, for one, would ever surrender the right to economic self-determination. It is possible that through fudge and muddle, with Germany recognising it has to subsidise its neighbours more than it would wish in order to preserve its export market, a workable eurozone federal system will be established. But that cannot be guaranteed, and in the meantime it is difficult to see any escape from years of stagnating or declining living standards for the people of Southern Europe and Ireland.

Finally there is the biggest flaw in financial globalisation: the global imbalances; the mad recycling of the massive surpluses of the great producing countries (like China, much of Asia, and Germany) into the debts of the consuming countries (including much of Europe, Britain and the US). The extraordinary system where the faster-growing poorer countries, especially China, finance the lifestyles of people in the richer ones, such as America and the UK, has not been dismantled. Since the crash, there has been some narrowing in the surpluses and the deficits. And there have been some fundamental changes, which suggest that at least part of the shrinking in the imbalances will be enduring – namely that Chinese labour costs have risen by more than a fifth in the past couple of years, while those in the US and UK have stagnated, so in theory Chinese consumers should be spending a bit more and Western ones a bit less. But the most recent economic evidence suggests that the fundamental problem remains: China's surplus remains large and intractable. What is cause for concern is that China has not succeeded in persuading its people and businesses to save much less. Chinese people are still living too much for tomorrow, not enough for today – precisely the opposite of what is wrong with the behaviour of most of us in the rich developed world. Until Chinese citizens recognise that they can afford to spend more on themselves, and therefore start to buy more of the stuff that we in the West produce, it is very difficult to see how our excessive debts can be cut in anything but a very painful way.

If there were a proper global government, it would be simpler to put in place policies that would encourage us – most of the households in Britain, America and Europe – to save more and spend less, while Chinese households spent more and saved less. And British businesses could be spurred to invest more as the corollary of Chinese businesses investing less and dispensing more on wages and dividends. But instead what we have are policies in the West – such as abnormally low interest rates – that are designed to encourage consumers to keep on spending, despite their anxieties about their huge debts. Meanwhile in China there is understandable reluctance on the part of the government to abandon a policy of generating growth via cheap exports, by holding down the exchange rate and encouraging massive investment. This policy has been hugely successful in creating hundreds of millions of jobs, but even so there are still vast numbers of people living frugally on the land and struggling to make ends meet. Although the Chinese authorities are signed up to the idea of turning China into more of a consumer-led economy, they are wary of relying too much on this transformation: Chinese households spend so little right now, it is inconceivable that China's growth could be maintained at anything like the rate necessary to sustain desired job creation if the strain were to be taken exclusively by consumer spending. That said, it is a bit odd that the Chinese government is not forcing the giant state-owned enterprises to pay it vastly more dividends, which in turn could finance a more generous welfare state and thus reduce people's propensity to save so much. However, as Chinese ministers have said to me, the Chinese government is adamant that it will manage the reform of its economy at the pace that suits China, not the pace that might suit the US and UK. And a one-party government – whose legitimacy probably depends on there being no serious hiatus in the process of creating more and better-paid employment – feels it cannot take risks that could seriously, if temporarily, undermine growth.

Moving forwards

If the fundamental causes of what got us into our predicament – global imbalances, eurozone imbalances and the hidden risks in banking and finance – are still with us, that is reason to be cautious about the future, but not to despair. Financial globalisation may make us feel small, almost powerless. But we do have the ability to improve our fortunes, at least in the long term. If the eurozone were to go down, that would be damaging for us, because 40% of our exports go to eurozone countries and our banks are connected to their banks and their economies. If their banks were to run out of cash or to suffer life-imperilling losses, ours would be in serious difficulties. If their economy were to go from mild recession to serious recession, it would be almost impossible to see how we could avoid that fate. But in the UK all we can do is protect ourselves from the potential shocks, not paralyse ourselves by obsessing about them.

The priority for us is to rebuild our economy on firmer foundations, so that we are less vulnerable next time. The opportunities are manifold, and we should remember that not everything about financial globalisation is toxic. For example, it was the practice of securitisation – of turning loans made to households and businesses into bonds for sale to investors – that was disastrous, not the theory. It was the lousy evaluation of the risks of the bonds, and the fact that they were bought by banks as well as proper long-term investors, that made them so dangerous. But if securitisation can match the borrowing needs of businesses and households with the investing needs of our pension plans, thus reducing the economy's dependence on banks, that might be a good thing. Economic recovery in the US appears to have been bolstered by the smaller role that banks play there in financing the economy than is the case in the UK and Europe. Securitisation, which became a dirty word in the crash, has been a boon for America, because – with the exception of the serious interruption in 2007–8 – it allows money to flow more smoothly from those who generate it, businesses and households, to those who need it, also businesses and households. That flow does not get interrupted by a crisis of confidence in the creditworthiness of the middlemen, the banks. And during the inevitable and periodic bouts of panic, when those who are stewards of our long-term savings, the pension funds and insurance companies, become anxious about whether households and companies can repay their debts, it would be easier and cheaper for a central bank or government to guarantee those debts for a short period – which is what happened in the US – rather than having to invest in and prop up bust banks. Also, if there has to be a subsidy provided by taxpayers for certain kinds of lending, surely it is better that the subsidy applies directly to the loans – as happens in the US – where it can be passed on to borrowers, rather than going to the banks, where much of the subsidy will be taken by bankers in their bonuses. It is no coincidence that in the US, where the economy is less dependent on banks and more on securitisation, the government has sold the stakes it took in the big banks, and mostly at a profit. By contrast in the UK it looks as though taxpayers will own huge slugs of Lloyds and Royal Bank of Scotland for many years, and may ultimately incur huge losses. Even now, the British government feels obliged to subsidise the borrowing costs of banks, with its new Funding for Lending Scheme, rather than providing a direct subvention to those who need the money – businesses and households.

Information technology provides a second way to marginalise the banks. For example on-line peer-to-peer or person-to-person lenders are springing up – Zopa and Funding Circle are just two examples – which directly match people and companies who have surplus cash with people and companies looking to borrow. If you place your money with a peer-to-peer lender like Zopa, you are not lending to Zopa, in the way that you are lending to Barclays if you put your money on deposit with Barclays. You are actually lending to the individuals who have registered with Zopa. When those borrowers can't pay up, it is you as the lender who takes the loss, not Zopa. And what's more, you commit to lend for a certain length of time – and you can only get your money back quickly if someone else is prepared to buy your loans from you. The important point is that businesses like Zopa and Funding Circle do everything that banks do, except that all the credit risk (the risk that the borrower can't repay) and all the liquidity risk (the risk that you as lender won't be able to get your cash when you need it) is with the lender – not with Zopa or Funding Circle. Now you may think that you would be out of your mind to take on all those risks. You may say hooray for banks that are happy to insure you against credit and liquidity risk. But there is quite a big cost of being insured by the banks against those risks. If you are prepared to take those risks, you in effect extract the hidden insurance premium you pay to the banks. Or to put it another way, you get a much higher interest rate. Also, although those risks are real, Zopa and Funding Circle are not lending your money to just anyone. They're not throwing your money away. They have access to all the credit assessment data used by the banks, and make credit checks on your behalf on all those requesting loans from them. Which means that in normal economic conditions, the losses you should face on loans made through them would be pretty small. And if you need your money back faster than you expected, you can normally sell the loan to another lender. Now from a public-policy point of view, what the Zopas and Funding Circles do seems pretty attractive. They provide new sources of finance for businesses and households. But perhaps more importantly, they make the risks of lending much more transparent to the providers of credit, which (just to remind you) would be you and me in a very direct sense – rather than you and me via our need to bail out banks as and when they behave recklessly. If these person-to-person lenders were to really take off, they would not end the extremes of boom and bust in the credit cycle. In benign economic conditions we would probably be as prone to lend too much too cheaply as banks have proved to be. But in the bust, we would probably grin and bear our losses, as individuals, rather than having the losses socialised, borne by everyone, as happens in our bank-dominated financial system. That, surely, would be a good thing.

Apocalypse later?

Right now, we remain horribly dependent on banks, for about four-fifths of our funding needs. So it is naïve to believe that just because we avoided the absolute worst that could have happened in 2008 – the complete collapse of the banking system – we have therefore kept catastrophe at bay forever. There are reasons to be fearful that conditions that could provoke a second banking meltdown are being created. To understand why, I have to resort to two ugly pieces of banking jargon, 'forbearance' and 'encumbrance'. They help to explain the pernicious trends in finance of our new age of economic stagnation and – in part – why the banking system remains in a dire condition.

As I have mentioned, forbearance is when creditors relax their normal lending criteria and conditions, so that their debtors don't go bust. We have already seen that up to 8% of all those with mortgages in Britain are enjoying a holiday on payments, or have changed to paying interest only, or are enjoying some other relaxation of normal lending conditions, according to an analysis by the Financial Services Authority for the Bank of England. And in the commercial property market, the lending terms on some £50bn of troubled loans have been waived. The idea behind forbearance is a laudable one: if the mortgage borrowers in financial distress had been thrown out of their homes, the social and economic impact would have been nasty. There would have been tens of thousands of people with nowhere to live, house prices would have plunged, losses for banks would have been exacerbated. And if the banks had foreclosed on all the commercial property loans in breach of covenants, there would again have been an acceleration of losses for borrowers and lenders. But there is a problem with forbearance: it undermines the confidence of those who lend to banks. They fear – rightly – that the banks are not as strong as their accounts would indicate. The point is that forbearance may only defer the pain for the borrower and the losses for the bank, rather than avoid it altogether. So if you are a creditor of a bank, you are legitimately concerned that forbearance is a way for banks to avoid raising the amount of capital the banks need to absorb potential losses.

If you want a bang up-to-date lesson on forbearance as an accident waiting to happen, you only have to look at the £60bn plus capital shortfall at Spain's banks, identified only after independent consultants took a look at the quality of their loans. And that hole in Spain's banks may yet be seen to be even bigger and deeper than first thought. Or to put it another way, forbearance is another contributor to the undermining of trust in the integrity and strength of the financial system. Which brings us on to so-called 'asset encumbrance', which has become the funding trend of this moment precisely because trust in the integrity and strength of the financial system has been wiped out.

Asset encumbrance is when a bank has to pledge its assets – the loans and investments it has made – to a creditor when borrowing from that creditor. It is the security or collateral that banks provide to those from whom they borrow. Now before the great crash of 2007–8, most banks were able to borrow as much as they liked in an unsecured way. To employ the appropriate lingo, liquidity seemed to be unlimited and cheap. Banks could borrow as much as they needed purely on the strength of their names and reputations from other banks and financial institutions without providing any collateral or security. But that unsecured interbank market more or less closed down in 2007 and 2008, and has never properly recovered. And part of the reason it has never properly recovered is that those who control vast pots of money in Boston, Singapore, Geneva and so on are concerned that big Western banks are weaker then they seem (so a big hello again to 'forbearance').

Banks have become increasingly dependent on various forms of secured borrowing, especially in what's known as the repo market, which is where banks swap bonds and other assets for loans from hedge funds and specialist parts of banks. Now you may have worked out there is a fundamental problem when – as is happening – the banking industry moves from a system of unsecured borrowing to one of secured borrowing: we move from a world where there is unlimited money for banks to one in which banks can only borrow up to the value of their unencumbered assets. What is more, the increasing use of secured borrowing by banks becomes self-reinforcing: as any bank pledges more and more of its assets to creditors, so it has fewer free assets, which means it looks weaker, which in turn means that anyone thinking of providing an unsecured loan to that bank will charge a penal rate; so, in effect, the growth of the secured lending market militates against any recovery in the unsecured lending market.

Here is the important number, from the latest annual report of the central bank's central bank, the Bank for International

Settlements: a fifth of all European banks' assets were encumbered, or pledged to borrowers, in 2011.

Please don't take any great comfort from the fact that 'only' a fifth of European bank's assets are pledged to borrowers. First, that understates the true position, because the statistic is months out of date. Second, some assets can't be converted into a form suitable for secured borrowing. Third, and most important, it would be a disaster if banks pledged massively more than that, because there would be nothing left over to underpin the savings of European citizens. Here is the thing: we haven't talked about the ginormous elephant in the room, which is that banks borrow most of their money in the form of deposits provided by you and me. And if the banks pledge all their assets to institutional lenders of various sorts, we might worry whether there is anything left to pay us back with. As you would expect, in stressed parts of the eurozone the growth in secured borrowing has been exceptionally rapid: between 2005 and 2011, the ratio of encumbered assets to total assets increased ten-fold for Greek banks, to one third of the total. That implies Greek banks have almost no spare assets to pledge for secured loans, if they are to keep anything back to cover the money they have borrowed in the form of deposits from ordinary Greek citizens. The pledging of all these assets by Greek banks is a tragedy waiting to happen for Greek savers.

Now this vicious contraction of banks' capacity to borrow or fund themselves is exacerbated by the downgrading of their credit-worthiness by ratings agencies. These downgrades are a treble whammy:

1) When banks' credit-ratings fall below a certain threshold, it becomes impossible for them to borrow from

certain non-financial lenders, such as some local authorities, sovereign wealth funds, companies and so on
(Royal Bank of Scotland, for example, has already fallen
through this threshold);

2) After a downgrade, lenders demand that banks pledge
   even more of their assets for a specified value of loan, so
   downgrades accelerate the rate at which assets become
   encumbered;

3) Banks that engage in what are known as over-the-counter derivatives transactions have to put up more of their
   assets as margin or security in these deals.

Here are two indications of the damaging impact of downgrades. First, Royal Bank of Scotland disclosed in June 2012
that it will have to pledge an additional £9bn of assets as
collateral following a downgrade of its credit-rating by
Moody's. That is £9bn of assets that are no longer available to
support lending to the real economy. Second, in advance of
downgrades of Spain's banks, also by Moody's, the European
Central Bank announced it would be less fastidious about the
official quality of collateral it and Spain's central bank would
demand when lending to Spanish banks. Or to put it another
way, the ECB exercised forbearance on Spanish banks:
Moody's downgraded large numbers of Spanish banks to
junk; so the response of the central bank was to relax the terms
on the loans it makes to Spain's banks. The eurozone's taxpayers, the ultimate owners of the European Central Bank, are
therefore taking greater risks.

   You will have gathered by now that there is a final chapter
in this encumbrance story, which is that when banks can no

longer raise money by pledging assets to commercial lenders they are forced to raise what they need by pledging assets to central banks in return for loans.

This is when banks go on life support, and it accurately describes the parlous condition of a large number of banks in Spain and others scattered throughout the eurozone. So long as these banks retain assets of sufficient quality, they can continue to claim to be viable, or at least potentially viable – even if they are only alive because of credit they've received from the European Central Bank, for example, or from their national central banks. But the assessment of the requisite quality is tricky. As we have seen in the case of Spain, after Moody's came to a verdict that the quality of Spanish banks' collateral had deteriorated, the response of the ECB was to lower the quality threshold for lending to those banks – which, in theory, significantly increases the risks for all eurozone taxpayers from the finance provided by the ECB and the Bank of Spain to Spanish banks. Here is the big imponderable: what will the ECB do at the moment that a big bank runs out of unencumbered assets or of unencumbered assets of appropriate quality? This is a very real possibility, according to regulators and bankers. Would the ECB do something that central banks are never supposed to do, which is provide unsecured loans, and in the process put itself and eurozone taxpayers at risk of very serious losses? Once this Rubicon had been crossed, there would be a danger of bank liabilities and government liabilities being commingled in a lethal way, which might destroy the conceit that the indebtedness of much of the eurozone could be reduced to a sustainable level without a devastating default. Or would the ECB allow the asset-strapped bank to fall over, and risk a chain reaction of collapsing banks?

All of this is a long-winded explanation of why Europe's dependence on banks – including banks that are currently perceived to be too close to insolvency for comfort – is extremely unhealthy, especially given the fact that the UK and US banking systems are so perilously connected to the eurozone banking system. Globalisation, especially the financial form of globalisation, requires us to be constantly vigilant about the location of the big concentrations of risks, wherever they might be in the world. In the past, we have been sloppy and naïve about the financial system in so many ways: about the vulnerability of our banks and economies to events on the other side of the world; about how we divide responsibility and accountability between the state and private companies; about which costs should fall on individuals and which should be borne by society. Banking and finance became so complex that we could neither identify which banks were behaving most recklessly nor assess the sheer size of their enormous bets. Nor did we realise that when the bets went wrong, the losses would fall on the state – on taxpayers. Reforming all that has so far been a very imperfect work in progress. And if we are to salvage our economic future, without abandoning globalisation, we need to come out of denial in other ways too. We need to admit that we have been living beyond our means for fifteen years or longer: the increases in our prosperity have been borrowed not earned; we used too much credit to have it all now, to buy the lifestyles we thought we deserved. But if we can no longer borrow as if tomorrow never comes, that means years of stagnating living standards. And if we are now to pay our way in the world, that means working harder and smarter. If there is a genuine tragedy here it is that the price of our greed and

mismanagement of the economy is highest for the blameless generation: our children. They enter an employment
market offering too few fulfilling opportunities, and
although asset prices have fallen since the crash, the price
of residential property remains way above what most young
people can afford, especially at a time of tight credit for
those potential borrowers regarded as higher risk.

Unlocking our potential

We can fix this mess and build a better life. We have to fight
the natural temptation to feel trapped by the sheer size of the
challenges. In that context, the government's rhetoric of
battening down hatches ahead of a possible eurozone disaster
may not boost confidence – even if it is important to make
contingency plans to repatriate British citizens who might
become stranded on the Continent in the absolute worst case
of a total malfunction of payment systems, or to prevent
uncontrolled immigration to Britain were certain economies
to melt down. The first step is the hardest, which is to own up
that we are on a path to impoverishment unless we fix two
very big things. Firstly, we in Britain need to see that in the
long term we can only win with our brains, which means there
is no greater priority than investing in our schools and universities, and encouraging students to aim as high as they possibly can. The lack of social mobility in the UK may be an
impediment to improved prosperity, because so much talent
is being wasted. A survey by the Sutton Trust showed how
those educated in fee-paying schools represent far more than
their 7% natural share of top jobs: in fact these schools, which
offer relatively few free places, supply more than 50% of
FTSE 100 chief executives, judges, top doctors and cabinet
ministers. The imperative of creating the conditions in which

all young people can make the most of themselves is one reason why I have created a charitable project called Speakers for Schools. It is a network of 850 (and rising) brilliant and inspirational people – writers, scientists, business leaders, engineers, generals, comedians and so on – who have committed to give talks for free in state schools on the big subjects that are not necessarily on the curriculum. The idea behind creating a culture of prominent people going into state schools as a matter of course is to show the students, especially those from seriously underprivileged backgrounds, that they matter, that they are valued, that they have what it takes to succeed, and they should be as ambitious for themselves as they can be. The more they make of themselves, the better off we will be as a nation.

The other big thing we need to fix is global finance. Unless and until banks and bankers start to work for people again, much of the world – notably the rich West – will struggle to raise living standards, and won't be able to abolish the fear that risks taken to generate rewards for bankers could propel us into another crisis. But in managing the transition from a society built on debt-fuelled shopping into one powered by saving, investment and exports, we need to tread carefully. If we curtail domestic household and government spending too fast, in the absence of global co-ordination that would see stronger economies expanding rapidly and buying vastly more of our goods and services, we will be back in the grips of extreme recession. And this time, if unemployment were to soar and government deficits were to widen again, or if taxpayers were forced to bail out ailing banks a second time and there was a further explosion in the size of public-sector liabilities, the consequences for Britain or even the US could be devastating. We should not be lulled into a false sense of security by the fact that it has never been cheaper for the British and American governments to borrow. One reason loans are almost free for the UK and US is that they have central banks creating record amounts of money which has been used to buy government debt. Another is that investors have to put their money somewhere, and the UK and US look somewhat more attractive then much of the eurozone, where the risk of devaluation and default is not negligible. But to describe the attraction of lending to the US and UK governments in those terms – as based on their ability to magic into existence new money and the fact that they have fewer warts than the others in this ugly contest – is to recognise the fragility of their credit-worthiness. We are living in an age of scantily clad emperors. But we dare not admit how few clothes any of them have, till some at least are respectably dressed again.

CHAPTER 12

IN THE HUMILIATION OF BARCLAYS, IS THERE HOPE?

If 9 August 2007 represented the start of the credit crunch, the official beginning to years of market mayhem and economic stagnation, 7.30 a.m. on 3 July 2012 felt almost as important. This was the moment that Barclays announced the resignation of its American chief executive, Bob Diamond. One reason it mattered is that Mr Diamond had become the potent symbol of the boom years at the big banks and in the City of London, the living embodiment of a particular modern version of the global bank. Diamond-style banking involved the combination of a huge position in retail banking in Britain with a massive global investment bank: Barclays was and is huge in London and on Wall Street; its forte was in the creation of complicated financial products, especially those that helped well-heeled clients avoid tax, and it delivered enormous bonuses and other rewards for investment bankers, especially Diamond himself. Diamond was one of the most plausible and persuasive salesmen the City has ever seen. This is a man who, long after Barclays started to face allegations that it was too aggressive in avoiding tax and in using ruses to exaggerate its strength, was reported to have been in the cockpit to help land Prime Minister David Cameron's chartered plane, an Airbus A340-300, on their return from a trade mission to Africa. Mr Diamond was widely seen as the banker who got what he wanted, including a minimum of £120m in pay, bonuses and other rewards since he joined Barclays' board in 2005, nine years after arriving at the bank.

Mr Diamond's departure does not mean that there will suddenly be a formal separation of retail banking and investment banking, which many would like to see, or a slashing in top bankers' gargantuan rewards, or an end to the brashness and fiendish complexity of global investment banking, or a rapid reduction to human-scale in the size of banks. But the circumstances of his departure make it much more likely that there will be a structural and cultural overhaul. The revelation that Barclays and possibly another seventeen or eighteen global banks were for years trying to rig important interest rates in the pursuit of big profits and bonuses, and at the potential expense of clients, prompted a collective outpouring of disgust, despair and exasperation, even among the ministers and politicians who had been trying to give them the benefit of the doubt. There was a general sense that the heart of the banking system had become rotten and corrupted, and that incremental reform would not provide the needed cleansing.

Mr Diamond's farewell was theatrical and emotional. The day after he announced he would be quitting, he appeared before MPs on the Treasury Select Committee, and performed his own version of a country music tearjerker:

I love Barclays. That's where it starts. I love Barclays because of the people. It is sixteen years ago today, on 4 July 1996, that I began at Barclays, and it has been sixteen years of tremendous enjoyment; and that enjoyment has been driven

by the incredible 140,000 people in over fifty countries
around the world.

(Bob Diamond, evidence to
Treasury Select Committee, 4 July 2012)

But the best way for him to cherish and protect the bank he
loves so much was for them to go their separate ways. 'History
will judge Barclays as an incredible institution because of its
people,' he told his audience of MPs. 'We need to get through
this period and the best way to do that was for me to step
down.' It sounded like the heroic end to a titanic struggle. In
fact, the previous few days had been a soap opera of revelations of serious wrongdoing by Barclays, followed by something that had never before happened at any big bank – the
resignation not only of Mr Diamond as chief executive, but
also of the chairman, Marcus Agius, and the chief operating
officer, Jerry del Missier. And in the case of Mr Diamond, he
had been forced out by the Governor of the Bank of England,
Sir Mervyn King, and the Chairman of the Financial Services
Authority, Lord Turner, who had told Mr Agius that they
would be happy for Mr Diamond to stand down. No senior
banker can stay in post when the confidence of the Bank of
England and the Financial Services Authority is lacking, as
Mr Diamond conceded to MPs: 'It was clear to me on Monday
that . . . the support from the regulators was not as strong as it
had been and I needed to take this step.' This was history: it
was the first time the current governor of the Bank of England
had used what is known as 'moral suasion' to overhaul the
management of a bank. When I disclosed how this had
happened in my reports for the BBC, I quoted a well-placed
source as saying: 'This is a case of the governor getting his
way by the inflexion of his eyebrows. It is how it used to

happen and it is a good thing that it is happening again.' What I subsequently learned was that the big push had come on the evening of Monday 2 July, when Sir Mervyn King made it clear to Mr Agius, and to Barclays' senior independent director, Sir Mike Rake, that he felt it would be appropriate for Mr Diamond to resign. He told them that he had consulted the Chancellor of the Exchequer, George Osborne, who felt the same. This was a dramatic intervention. No governor of the Bank of England had acted to force out a bank boss for at least fifteen years, or since the Bank was stripped by the Labour government of its powers to supervise and regulate banks. These powers are being restored by the current government in 2013.

The tumult of Mr Diamond's final days at the helm began on 27 June 2012, when at lunchtime in the UK there were a series of shocking announcements by regulators on both sides of the Atlantic, the UK's Financial Services Authority in the UK, and the Commodity Futures Trading Commission (CFTC) and Department of Justice in the US. They announced that Barclays would be paying a record £290m in penalties for attempting to manipulate important interest rates, called LIBOR and Euribor. These interest rates really matter to all of us: they help to determine the prices of deals worth hundreds of trillions of dollars and influence the interest rates that millions of people pay for personal loans and mortgages. Put simply, Barclays owned up that for four years between 2005 and 2009, it repeatedly lied about the interest rate it was paying to borrow. The statement from the CFTC summed up the wrongdoing: 'Barclays ... attempted to manipulate and made false reports concerning . . . benchmark interest rates to benefit the bank's derivatives trading positions by either increasing its profits or minimizing its losses.

The conduct occurred regularly and was pervasive.' It added that after the start of the credit crunch in August 2007, all the way through to early 2009, Barclays made 'artificially low . . . submissions' about the interest rate it was being forced to pay to borrow to 'protect Barclays' reputation from negative market and media perceptions concerning Barclays' financial condition.' This was done, according to the CFTC, 'as a result of instructions from Barclays' senior management'. In other words, Barclays was pretending that it could borrow more cheaply than was actually the case, to reassure its owners and creditors that lenders had more confidence in it than was true.

There were two distinct phases to the rule-breaking at Barclays. In the first phase, at Barclays Capital – the business more or less created by Bob Diamond, which he ran till becoming chief executive of Barclays at the beginning of 2011 – traders tried to rig LIBOR rates to maximise profits or minimise losses on their own deals, so as to enhance their bonuses. These rates are set by a committee of bankers organised by the UK banking trade group, the British Bankers Association. They are supposed to show the average interest rates paid by banks to borrow in a series of different major currencies, such as sterling and dollars, and for different maturities. A typical and important LIBOR rate would be the price for borrowing dollars for three months, for example. The LIBOR rates are important because the price at which banks can borrow is supposed to be the best guide to the price at which the rest of us can borrow from banks. Historically, therefore, they were seen as perhaps the most important indicator of credit costs and availability. Also, some loans to households and businesses are explicitly linked to LIBOR rates. And valuations of derivative transactions worth multiples of the output of the global economy are based on LIBOR. For example, the dollar

LIBOR rate is the basis for the settlement price of three-month eurodollar futures contracts traded on America's Chicago Mercantile Exchange that were worth $564 trillion in 2011. Also the price of swaps deals worth approximately $350 trillion and loans of $10 trillion rise and fall depending on what happens to LIBOR. It is precisely because the LIBOR rates are so central to the operation of such important financial markets that it really matters that the process for setting LIBOR is robust and credible. Any suggestion that the banks setting the LIBOR rates may be trying to fiddle them is not only shocking but undermines confidence in the fairness and efficiency of markets. It is not an exaggeration to say that trust in financial globalisation is put at risk.

What is extraordinary, perhaps, is that such important prices were determined by bankers for bankers, with barely any oversight by regulators. To be clear, the LIBORs are not the only hugely influential benchmark prices that are set by a club of banks and financial institutions according to rules written, implemented and policed by the banks themselves and subject to little outside scrutiny. As derivatives and commodities markets exploded in size over the past two decades, and became much more important to all aspects of the economy, banks retained remarkably unchallenged control over the mechanisms for determining representative prices. That would be all very well in a world of scrupulous probity, but in the light of the LIBOR scandal, this self-regulation no longer looks sustainable. The point is that tiny changes in the LIBOR rate could make the difference between profit and loss on traders' deals, and – by extension – the difference between what they would call a 'fuck-off' bonus or something more modest. What has now become clear is that the temptations for Barclays' traders – and for traders at other banks – to try to move the LIBOR rates to generate those bonuses were simply too great. They therefore put pressure on their colleagues sitting on the LIBOR rate-setting committees to submit false reports of Barclays' borrowing costs, in the hope that this would nudge the LIBOR rate towards a level that would maximise profits on their respective deals, or shrink losses. The CFTC put it like this:

> Barclays' traders located at least in New York, London and Tokyo asked Barclays' submitters [those submitting borrowing costs to the LIBOR committees] to submit particular rates to benefit their derivatives trading positions, such as swaps or futures positions, which were priced on LIBOR and Euribor. Barclays' traders made these unlawful requests routinely.

A picture emerges from emails obtained by the regulators of a culture of endemic dishonesty in a clique of Barclays' traders and managers. The traders would ask for a LIBOR rate to be fiddled and they would receive replies such as 'for you, anything' and 'done . . . for you, big boy'. These traders worked for Mr Diamond. But the regulators said there was no evidence that he knew about their attempts to rig the market. He told MPs: 'When I read the emails from those traders, I got physically ill. It is reprehensible behaviour.'

Some have argued that the failure of Barclays to identify and crack down on the traders' misbehaviour shows serious flaws in management controls, which should be laid at the door of Mr Diamond, since he was the boss of the investment bank, Barclays Capital. Perhaps more embarrassing for him is what the debacle exposes about the flawed culture of Barclays Capital, in that Barclays Capital was the institutional expression of what he wanted to achieve in banking. All that said, and the reason this story will run and run – with far-reaching implications for the entire global banking industry – is that Barclays was not the only bank attempting to manipulate these rates. Regulators around the world are investigating many of the Western world's biggest and best-known banks and financial institutions for trying to fix LIBOR and other benchmark prices. In the judgements against Barclays, there is evidence of its traders colluding with traders at other unnamed banks in attempted market-rigging, especially in so-called euro swaps via Euribor rates. At the time of writing, it is clear that there will be heavy fines levied on Royal Bank of Scotland, for example, for the same offences. Arguably Barclays has been unlucky in being the first to reach a settlement with the regulators. And the regulators to whom I have spoken say that Barclays deserves some credit for having co-operated with their investigation to a greater degree than other banks.

The second and subtly different phase in Barclays' misbehaviour ran from 2007 to 2009, during the credit crunch and banking crisis. In this latter period, Barclays' managers understated the banks' borrowing costs to the City committees setting LIBOR rates, for the purpose of pretending that its creditors had more confidence in the bank than was actually the case. At the time there was an appalling climate of fear, in which no bank felt completely confident of survival. In this climate, Barclays was among the least trusted of the banks. For years, investors feared they didn't properly understand how its complex investment bank earned its profits. Ministers and officials felt it was arrogant and opaque as an institution. I know this because it was one of the big talking points in my milieu. It was this lack of trust which meant that Barclays had to pay more to borrow than other banks. For any creditor, trust in the borrower is probably more important than anything else; any uneasiness about the strength of the debtor translates into the debtor being forced to pay a higher interest rate.

I recall talking about the relatively high rate Barclays was paying to borrow to people in government and Whitehall. It was both intriguing and disturbing to them. The Deputy Governor of the Bank of England, Paul Tucker, also made clear his concerns about Barclays' seemingly steep borrowing costs in a conversation he had with Bob Diamond on 29 October 2008, according to an email sent by Mr Diamond to two of his colleagues the following day. This email was interpreted by one of its recipients, Jerry del Missier – who was Mr Diamond's deputy at Barclays Capital – as an instruction from the Bank of England to pretend in submissions to the LIBOR committees that the bank's borrowing costs were lower than was the case. However, in July 2012, Mr del Missier told MPs on the Treasury Select Committee that his understanding of what had transpired between Mr Tucker and Mr Diamond came primarily from his own phone conversation with Mr Diamond on 29 October. The email merely confirmed for Mr del Missier what he thought he knew already. Mr del Missier then relayed what he viewed as this command from the Bank of England, that Barclays should understate its borrowing costs, to the head of the bank's money-market dealing desk.

Mr Diamond and Mr Tucker both say Mr del Missier got it wrong, that there was no such instruction to lie. This is one of those events where there is a degree of mystery about what transpired, because Mr Diamond and Mr del Missier's recollections are so different. Regulators eventually determined that Mr Tucker had not given such an order to Mr Diamond, and they found neither Mr Diamond, Mr del Missier or Mr Tucker guilty of wrongdoing. As for Mr Tucker, he has explained in his evidence to MPs that he had been trying to tell Mr Diamond that Barclays at the time was too conspicuous and noisy in the way it was paying a higher interest rate to borrow than other banks. He was warning Mr Diamond that if Barclays' money-market and treasury dealing desks did not show a bit more discretion in how they borrowed and how much they were prepared to pay to borrow, they risked spooking investors to such an extent that they might find the market became closed to it. In other words, he thought he was telling Mr Diamond to get the banks' dealing desks to borrow more judiciously, rather than lie about their borrowing costs. He wanted to prevent Barclays becoming the third big bank of the time to endure the kind of funding crisis that would see it being rescued by taxpayers and semi-nationalised. But both before the conversation between Mr Diamond and Mr Tucker and subsequently, Barclays did lie to the LIBOR committees about the interest rates it had to pay to borrow, in a systematic way and on the instructions of management. What is striking is that Barclays was understating its borrowing costs, but these were still higher than others banks – and higher than the borrowing costs of banks such as Royal Bank of Scotland, which we now know to have been in much more serious financial difficulties than Barclays. Which is why Mr Diamond is convinced that most banks were giving misleading information to the LIBOR committees.

Many would say that the proper lesson for Barclays from these funding tensions was that it needed to regain the trust of the market, by perhaps simplifying its operations and making them more transparent. However, that was not something that could be achieved overnight, even if it occurred to the bank. Was

Barclays' lie about what it was paying to borrow justified, especially if the survival of the bank was at stake? As it happens, a number of senior figures in the City who are unconnected to Barclays think this lying was the right thing to do in the circumstances. They think Mr Tucker encouraged Barclays to lie and they applaud him for doing so (although, as I have said, Mr Tucker denies this). Which, depending on your prejudices, is either evidence of a cancerous moral relativism at the heart of the City or common-sense realism. Either way, there is no doubting the momentous consequences of the revelations. In a way, what is bizarre is that the Financial Services Authority and the board of Barclays initially failed to predict quite how shocked and outraged people would be by the disclosures of the banks' lies. The FSA did not initially demand any resignations at Barclays. However, on the afternoon of 29 June 2012 – after forty-eight hours of deafening criticism of Barclays' conduct in the media and by politicians – Lord Turner had a conversation with Mr Agius in which he said Barclays' board should consider whether Mr Diamond was still the right individual to oversee the cultural change perceived by the FSA to be necessary to the bank. Lord Turner later told MPs that the words he used when talking to Mr Agius were: 'You have got to think about whether that is possible with Bob Diamond or whether it is simply impossible.' That said, he also conceded to Mr Agius that he could not direct Barclays to dismiss Mr Diamond, because the FSA had not formed a formal judgement that Mr Diamond was unfit to lead a bank. Even so, Lord Turner believed he was giving a push to Barclays' board to secure Mr Diamond's resignation. Strikingly, Mr Agius and his colleagues read the conversation differently. Barclays sources tell me that they did not believe Lord Turner had made it explicit that the FSA had lost confidence in Mr Diamond. Within hours, Barclays' non-executive directors decided at an emergency board meeting that none of the senior directors needed to quit: the chief executive and chairman could battle on, they felt.

What was therefore perhaps odd is that twenty-four hours later, the chairman, Marcus Agius, took a personal decision to quit, which I disclosed on the BBC the next day and which was announced first thing Monday morning. He felt he was doing the honourable thing. Also some shareholders felt that Barclays needed a new chairman. However, Lord Turner, Sir Mervyn King and the chancellor George Osborne all believed that the wrong banker had resigned – and Sir Mervyn delivered this message to Mr Agius on the evening of 2 July. At 7.30 a.m. on 3 July, Mr Diamond's exit was announced, followed by Mr del Missier's a few hours after. Almost two months later, Barclays appointed a retail banker, Anthony Jenkins, as Mr Diamond's successor (on a pay package worth a maximum of £8.6m a year). But for a period, the impression had been created that one of the world's biggest and most important banks had no control over its destiny.

This is not just a big moment for Barclays. The ramifications are likely to be huge for many of the world's biggest banks. It is not only their reputations that are being blackened. They face enormously expensive civil lawsuits from investors, who allege that they have been gulled out of their rightful profits on huge derivatives and securities deals by banks' attempted rigging of LIBOR and other rates. There could even be claims for restitution from millions of people with LIBOR-linked mortgages and personal loans. Damages, compensation costs and fines payable by banks could run to more than $20bn, say analysts. There are some bankers who believe that the eventual bill for some banks will not be far off what they lost in the banking crisis of 2008–9.

And there is likely to be a second serious consequence for banks. We have seen how they made vast profits in private derivative deals – in the so-called over-the-counter market – well away from the oversight of regulators. The disclosure that they abused the privilege of privacy in transactions dependent on LIBOR interest rates is likely to mean that much more regulation, supervision and transparency will be forced on them. There are two sides to this. First, all sorts of important benchmark interest rates and prices, not just the LIBOR ones, are likely to become subject to formal official oversight, rather than being set by self-selecting and self-policing groups of banks and financial institutions. You would be surprised by how much this may matter to the rest of us, since these benchmarks can affect what we pay for mortgages, personal loans and even energy. Second, I have mentioned that many of these derivative markets are a kind of Wild West, more vulnerable to abuse and manipulation in the pursuit of profit than centralised, visible markets such as the London Stock Exchange. If, as seems likely, the veil is permanently drawn back on these markets – if the disinfectant of sunlight is applied – and regulators decide to keep a constant beady eye on them, this act of cleansing will probably make the relevant transactions much less attractive to banks and investors. It will be a fascinating test of how many of the transactions are a utilitarian response to legitimate investment needs, and how many are seedy attempts to gull clients or profit unfairly from confidential privileged information. These markets, as and when they become more tightly regulated, are likely to shrink – which, many would say, would be no terrible thing. And the associated extraction of rent or excessive fees from bankers' clients, which generates big bonuses, would probably shrivel too.

Can we have the banks we deserve?

Some would say, however, that there is one question of over-riding importance begged by the LIBOR scandal: how do we create the conditions for banks to become the sort of institutions we need and deserve? This is not just about their integrity and honesty. It is also about the very basic services they provide. One of the most revealing analyses I have seen is by the Financial Services Authority, which shows that between 1987 and 2009, the amount of credit provided by banks to British businesses – other than property and financial businesses – fell pretty sharply as a share of GDP, whereas lending to property companies soared. In other words, at a time of massive growth for British banks, UK banks actually provided less support to manufacturers, exporters and service businesses; they shrank the nourishment they provide to the kind of businesses the country needs if our living standards are to resume an upward trend. Between 2000 and 2009, the total volume of loans made to buyers, renters and developers of commercial property increased four-and-a-half-fold. As a share of total lending by UK banks, property loans increased from 5% to 10%. And relative to the total size of the economy, they increased from 5% to 18% of GDP, when lending to the manufacturing sector fell from 6% of GDP to just less than 4%. Bank lending spurred a rampant commercial property boom and a brutal bust in the last ten years. From the beginning of 2002 until the summer of 2007, commercial property prices rose 53%. But then property prices fell 42% over the following two years, to bring them in 2009 to their lowest level since 1997. The bust has left the banks sitting on a huge pile of potentially unrepayable loans. A recent study by De Montfort University showed that lenders to UK commercial property still have 10,000 'distressed' loans on their books and 9,400 in technical default. With a value of £24.3bn, the distressed loans are all in breach of covenant and represent 13% of all property lending. Banks, understandably and predictably, are now trying to shrink their financial exposure to commercial property – which of course keeps the commercial property market in the doldrums and increases losses for banks on their property exposure. That means there is even less credit available for the kind of real businesses whose expansion is essential to the UK's long-term economic future.

The sluggishness of Britain's recovery since 2009 – the absence of recovery, some might argue – has a number of causes, which we have already explored. Perhaps the most important one is that there is a growing realisation that we have to take steps to start living within our means, over the longer term. Which in turn has seen most of us, households, businesses and government, try to reduce debts, or – where this has not been possible, as in the case of government – endeavour to take on new debts at a slower rate. When none of the main actors are borrowing as they were to fuel spending and investment, growth slows. But what is not helpful is that in lending less, the banks are also accused – by the Bank of England and ministers, inter alia – of not lending in the most useful places, when they lend at all. Young companies with bags of potential and young people with bags of potential feel ill-served by the traditional banks. And although the banks recognise that fledgling businesses and newly created households are our future, they are scared of the risks of lending to them, especially in a time of recession.

The innocent pay a price for the national indebtedness that they did not choose or cause. They are the victims of the UK's inability to pay its way in the world for almost thirty years, with a current account deficit that has refused to disappear. Until we become less dependent on credit from abroad in that sense, the indebtedness of the economy cannot fall. And what is worrying is that belt-tightening by households, businesses and governments is hurting British producers as much as overseas ones; our fundamental problem – that we consume more than we earn – has not been eliminated. To state the obvious, we need to invest far more in industries capable of selling what the rest of the world wants. But hang on a moment, don't we have one of those? Is not the City of London that rarity: a British world-class, world-beating industry, with huge global banks like Barclays among its top-drawer constituents. When banks like RBS and HBOS are not bankrupting the UK by losing money at a rate that few businesses from any country can match, aren't the City's insurers, hedge funds, private-equity firms and even the better-run banks, such as HSBC, reasons to be proud and thankful rather than fearful and bitter? There may be something to that, even for those who regret the astonishing sums earned by the small numbers at the summit of the banks and hedge funds – and who argue that the bankers' and hedgies' spoils undermine social cohesion, create wealthy ghettoes where only these superstars can afford to live, and suck talent from other important industries and occupations. But although it may well be little short of self-immolating madness to wish away the City in its entirety, a prime minister such as David Cameron – whose father, grandfather and great grandfather were all stockbrokers – also seems to have recognised that we had far too many of our eggs in the banking and finance basket.

In the decade before the crash, about a third of Britain's growth came from the expansion of financial services, of which a very important element was the reckless growth of our banks'

borrowing and lending. If there has been a sea change in banks'
attitudes, as they are becoming more cautious, and if in a global
sense some of the froth has been blown off markets, part of
that growth may have gone forever. After the boom, with our
banks now retrenching to make themselves stronger, it is not
only their customers who suffer, as credit has become harder
to obtain. When there is less money around in general, the
banks sell fewer financial services and products here and
abroad, which further dampens their economic contribution.
Between 2008 and 2011, some 140,000 jobs were lost from
financial services as a whole, or about 11% of the workforce.
Around a quarter of the contraction of the British economy
since its peak in 2008 can be laid at the door of the contraction
of the City.

But any judgement on the City has to note that it is a net
exporter, in an era when most of the British economy borrows
from the rest of the world (often facilitated by the banks). In
2011, the country ran a surplus on its overseas sales of financial and insurance services of £38bn, or 2.5% of our GDP.
That is not to be sniffed at, given that the UK imports a lot
more goods than our manufacturers and oil companies are
able to sell overseas. In 2011, the trade deficit in goods was
just under £100bn. Or to put it another way, if it were not for
the City's contribution, the UK's deficit on sales of goods and
services would be about 40% greater. On that basis, you might
think that whether or not we like the income inequality that
comes with a large and successful financial sector, we would
be potty to do anything but nurture the success of the City
and cheer if it revives. Because without it, the UK would be in
an even deeper hole.

However, that cheer should probably be nuanced, now that
we know that so much of the City's recent success – most

notably its reliance on short-term borrowing to finance an insane lending binge – was dangerous and unsustainable. Shortly before this book went to press, further evidence emerged of big British banks cutting corners in other ways. In July 2012, the quintessential global bank HSBC faced savage criticism from a US Senate Subcommittee for failing to implement adequate safeguards against money-laundering and movements of cash to and from terrorists and criminals, and also for not properly checking whether billions of dollars it moved from Mexico to the US included the spoils of drug-trafficking. HSBC apologised and said it had imposed rigorous new oversight on where money is being moved. HSBC expects these transgressions will cost it $700m in fines and penalties. The following month, another British-based international bank, Standard Chartered (SCB), was accused of breaching American sanctions on conducting banking business with Iran. The New York State Department of Financial Services said Standard Chartered 'schemed with the Government of Iran and hid from regulators roughly 60,000 secret transactions, involving at least $250 billion, and reaping SCB hundreds of millions of dollars in fees'. Standard Chartered denied the accusations but – after a few days of wrangling – it agreed to pay a penalty of $340m and to a two-year review of its money laundering controls by the New York regulator. As for Barclays, it disclosed that it is being probed by the Serious Fraud Office in relation to fees paid in 2008 to Qatar Holdings, an offshoot of the investment arm of the oil-rich Arab state. The SFO's enquiries follow a related investigation by the Financial Services Authority into whether Barclays properly disclosed the fees it paid when raising money from Qatar.

Also during the City's and British banking industries' gold

or platinum age of supposedly unassailable triumph, the value of sterling rose to levels that harmed other industries, such as manufacturing, thus undermining a steadier source of jobs and tax revenues. And the enormous rewards on offer in the City were a magnet for Britain's brightest and best young talent. Or to put it another way, the success of the City contributed in a direct way to what has been called the hollowing out of manufacturing. In 1970, the UK had a positive manufacturing trade balance equivalent to 4.9% of GDP. In the subsequent forty years, which coincided with the rise and rise of financial services, there was a swing of 10 percentage points, to a deficit of 4.7%. It appears that the City is a selfish industry, one that crowds out other wealth generators rather than doing what we might have expected, which is to nurture them. We can't have our City cake and eat our manufacturing cake. It seems to be a choice between one or the other: a fast-growing financial services industry where the rewards are concentrated on a globetrotting few; or a more broadly based economy, which will be years in the making, and will see us struggling to maintain our standards of living during the years of transition.

Unless, that is, the shock of the scandal at Barclays and other banks, and the departure from the stage of the great champion of banks as traders and sales machines, Bob Diamond, were to lead to a revolution in the way our banks and bankers see themselves. A grand parliamentary committee has been set up by the government to investigate the cultural and – perhaps – ethical side of what has gone wrong at our banks. If bankers could see the virtues of self-deprecation, if they abandoned the idea of themselves as wealth generators in their own right, if they ceased their invention of complex new products and fiendish devices for extracting more fees from the clients, if they acquired the virtue of patience and only took substantial incremental rewards when supporting customers over many years, that would be a pretty good start, their critics would say.

Is it possible that banks and bankers can derive satisfaction from serving the economy's wealth generators, the businesses big and small that create sustainable employment, sell overseas and generate enduring revenues that can be taxed to finance essential public services? Banking is a service industry, but too often in recent years bankers saw themselves as masters, not servants. Can banks and bankers find honour in providing the affordable mortgage to a young family or be exhilarated by trying to properly understand the credit needs of a growing business, rather than chasing the next big bonus-generating deal? If so, then maybe that cancerous mistrust between the providers and receivers of finance, between the bankers and us, can be replaced by a spirit of co-operation that might, in time, rehabilitate our limping anaemic economy and restore our confidence that we will again be able to earn our standard of living and pay our way in the world.

ACKNOWLEDGEMENTS

The best thing about being a journalist is that I speak to insightful and brilliant people every day. And the way I tend to work is to bounce ideas off them and see what comes back. However none of them would thank me for acknowledging them by name, because they might be accused of leaking to me in my day job at the BBC – and that would not help them (or me). But they know who they are, and I hope they know I am grateful that they can be bothered to chat to me.

But two people need singling out, because they read the text and gave me sage advice. They are Howard Davies and Malcolm Balen. Funnily enough, Howard is the first person who ever tried to explain derivatives to me, twenty-five years ago, when I was a junior reporter on the *Independent* newspaper. He was then head of the Audit Commission, a watchdog of public finances which was at the time investigating how the borough of Hammersmith and Fulham had lost a fortune placing big bets on the direction of interest rates (why are there so few really new stories in the world?). All those years ago, Howard set me on the road to understanding why even the most complex and opaque parts of the financial economy matter to all of us, so perhaps you can blame Howard, among others, for my enduring interest in this stuff.

As for Malcolm, he is a senior editor at the BBC who was obliged to read the book, to reassure my bosses there that it would not compromise my or the corporation's impartiality.

Malcolm ended up doing more than that. He spotted errors and gave good counsel, for which I am very grateful.

The BBC is – probably – the finest news organisation in the world. Of all the lucky breaks I have had in a journalism career that will soon run to thirty years, the luckiest may well have been becoming BBC Business Editor on 13 February 2006. There has been no greater privilege than to be the narrator of the end of the great boom, the subsequent years of bust and stagnation, and the accompanying reconstruction of the global financial economy. We are living through history. It is as good as it gets for a hack like me to have the daily opportunity to give the first account of that history to the BBC's huge and demanding audience.

I therefore need to thank my brilliant and supportive BBC colleagues. Those I have worked closest with include Carolyn Rice, Steph McGovern, Emma Ordidge, Harriet Noble, Jon Zilkha, Piers Parry-Crooke, Jeremy Hillman, Helen Boaden, Fran Unsworth, Huw Edwards, Robb Stevenson, Katie Fraser, Katherine Gogarty, Alan Connor, Catherine Wynne, Jane Beresford, John Thynne, Sam Bagnall, David Stenhouse, Simon Hamer, Daniel Dodd, Giles Wilson, Tim Weber and Mark Byford. To all of them, and to many others at the BBC, I want to say ta and – to one or two – sorry for being a pig-headed pain.

INDEX

An invitation from the publisher

Join us at www.hodder.co.uk, or follow us
on Twitter @hodderbooks to be a part of
our community of people who love the very
best in books and reading.

Whether you want to discover more about a book
or an author, watch trailers and interviews, have the
chance to win early limited editions, or simply browse
our expert readers' selection of the very best books,
we think you'll find what you're looking for.

And if you don't, that's the place to tell us what's missing.

We love what we do, and we'd love you to be a part of it.

www.hodder.co.uk

 @hodderbooks

HodderBooks

HodderBooks